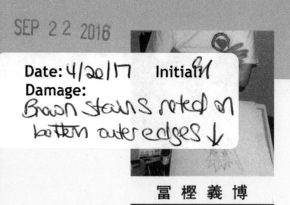

冨樫義博

It's temporary, of course.

Yoshihiro Togashi

Yoshihiro Togashi's manga career began in 1986 at the age of 20, when he won the coveted Osamu Tezuka Award for new manga artists. He debuted in the Japanese **Weekly Shonen Jump** magazine in 1989 with the romantic comedy **Tende Shôwaru Cupid**. From 1990 to 1994 he wrote and drew the hit manga **YuYu Hakusho**, which was followed by the dark comedy science-fiction series **Level E,** and finally this adventure series **Hunter x Hunter**. In 1999 he married the manga artist Naoko Takeuchi.

HUNTER X HUNTER Volume 6
SHONEN JUMP ADVANCED Manga Edition

STORY AND ART BY
YOSHIHIRO TOGASHI

English Adaptation/Gary Leach
Translation/Lillian Olsen
Touch-up Art & Lettering/Mark Griffin
Design/Amy Martin
Editor/Pancha Diaz

Published by VIZ Media, LLC
P.O. Box 77010
San Francisco, CA 94107

10 9 8 7 6 5 4
First printing, December 2005
Fourth printing, May 2016

www.viz.com

SHONEN JUMP ADVANCED
www.shonenjump.com

SHONEN JUMP ADVANCED MANGA

HUNTER × HUNTER

ハンター×ハンター

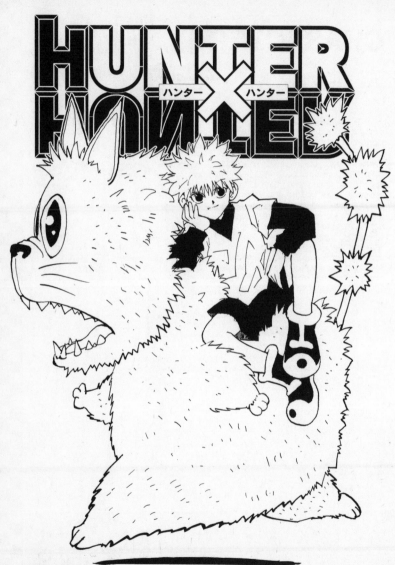

Story & Art by

Yoshihiro Togashi

Volume 6

CHARACTERS

The Story Thus Far

GON DREAMS OF BEING A HUNTER LIKE HIS FATHER, AND APPLIES FOR THE ULTRA-CHALLENGING LICENSING EXAM. THE SO-CALLED FINAL TEST IS OVER, AND GON AND HIS FRIENDS ARE NOW LICENSED HUNTERS AND HAVE HEADED TO KUKUROO MOUNTAIN TO REUNITE WITH KILLUA, WHO DELIBERATELY FAILED THE FINAL TEST. THEY CLEAR THE "TESTING GATE" INTO THE ZOLDYK FAMILY ESTATE, AND THE FOURSOME IS BRIEFLY REUNITED. HOWEVER, KURAPIKA AND LEORIO GO THEIR SEPARATE WAYS TO WORK TOWARDS THEIR OWN GOALS, PROMISING TO MEET UP AGAIN IN SIX MONTHS IN YORKNEW CITY. GON, SEEKING TO PAY HISOKA BACK FOR HIS "FAVOR" IN PHASE FOUR, HAS GONE WITH KILLUA TO TACKLE THE CHALLENGES OF THE HEAVENS ARENA!

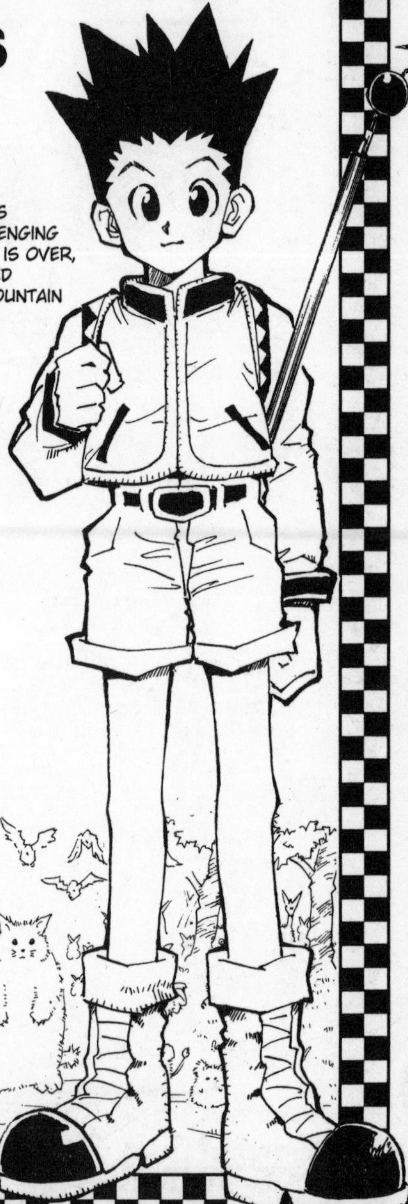

Gon

OUR EAGER HERO.
HAS BECOME A HUNTER IN
HIS ONGOING EFFORT TO BE
REUNITED WITH HIS FATHER!

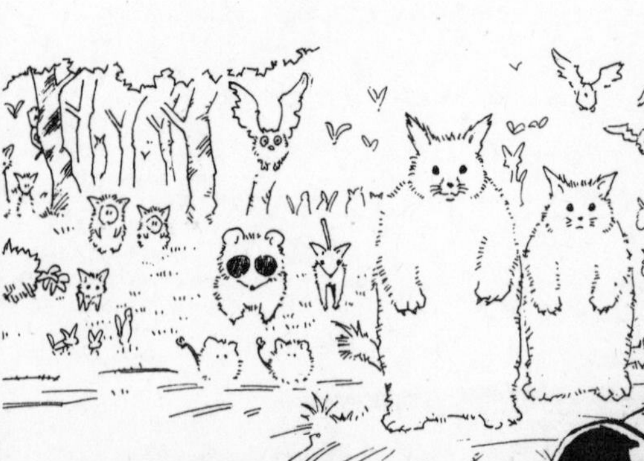

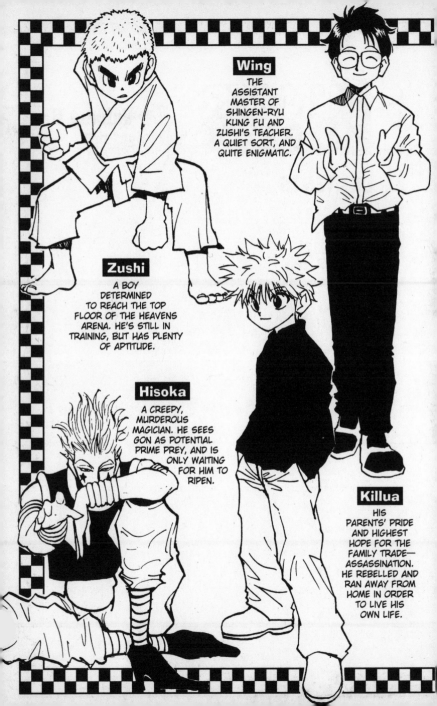

Wing

THE ASSISTANT MASTER OF SHINGEN-RYU KUNG FU AND ZUSHI'S TEACHER. A QUIET SORT, AND QUITE ENIGMATIC.

Zushi

A BOY DETERMINED TO REACH THE TOP FLOOR OF THE HEAVENS ARENA. HE'S STILL IN TRAINING, BUT HAS PLENTY OF APTITUDE.

Hisoka

A CREEPY, MURDEROUS MAGICIAN. HE SEES GON AS POTENTIAL PRIME PREY, AND IS ONLY WAITING FOR HIM TO RIPEN.

Killua

HIS PARENTS' PRIDE AND HIGHEST HOPE FOR THE FAMILY TRADE— ASSASSINATION. HE REBELLED AND RAN AWAY FROM HOME IN ORDER TO LIVE HIS OWN LIFE.

HUNTER × HUNTER

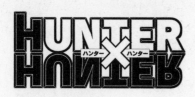

Volume 6

CONTENTS

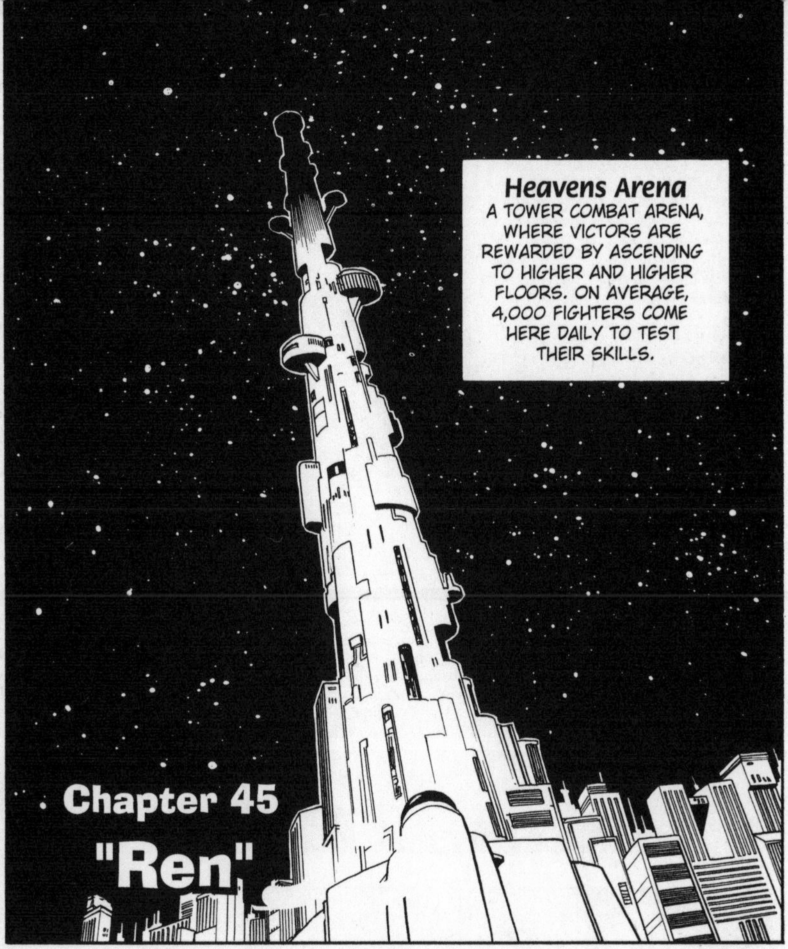
Heavens Arena
A TOWER COMBAT ARENA, WHERE VICTORS ARE REWARDED BY ASCENDING TO HIGHER AND HIGHER FLOORS. ON AVERAGE, 4,000 FIGHTERS COME HERE DAILY TO TEST THEIR SKILLS.
Chapter 45
"Ren"

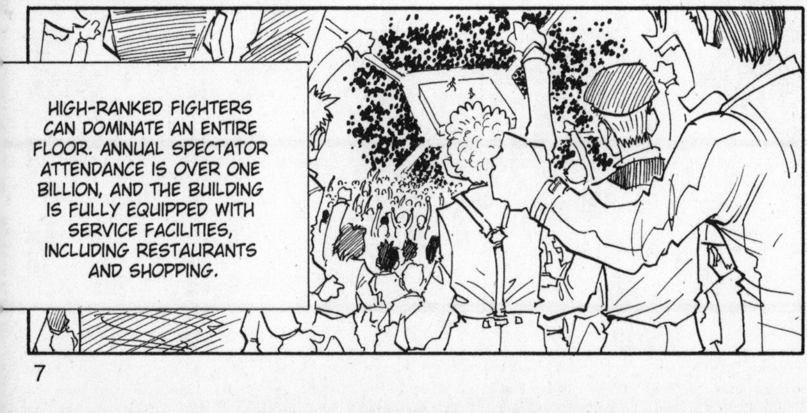
HIGH-RANKED FIGHTERS CAN DOMINATE AN ENTIRE FLOOR. ANNUAL SPECTATOR ATTENDANCE IS OVER ONE BILLION, AND THE BUILDING IS FULLY EQUIPPED WITH SERVICE FACILITIES, INCLUDING RESTAURANTS AND SHOPPING.

THE BUILDING IS DIVIDED INTO 20 10-FLOOR DIVISIONS, UP TO THE 200TH FLOOR.

THIS WAY, PLEASE.

WHICH MEANS THAT A FIGHTER WHO WINS ON THE 50TH FLOOR ADVANCES TO THE 60TH...

...AND ONE WHO LOSES GOES DOWN TO THE 40TH.

WOW...

THEY COMP YOU A ROOM ONCE YOU REACH THE 100TH FLOOR.

YOUR STOP— THE 50TH FLOOR!

8

HI.

OSU!

BOW

I'M GON. NICE TO MEET YOU.

KILLUA.

MY NAME IS ZUSHI! WHAT'S YOURS?

SORRY WE MISSED YOURS—YOU'VE OBVIOUSLY ADVANCED.

I WATCHED YOUR FIGHTS. YOU GUYS ARE *PRETTY AMAZING!*

YOU MUST BE *AT LEAST AS GOOD* AS US.

I STUDY *SHINGEN-RYU KUNG FU* MYSELF!!

WHAT SCHOOL DO YOU TWO BELONG TO?

SNAP!!

THANKS. I'M HERE TO IMPROVE.

9

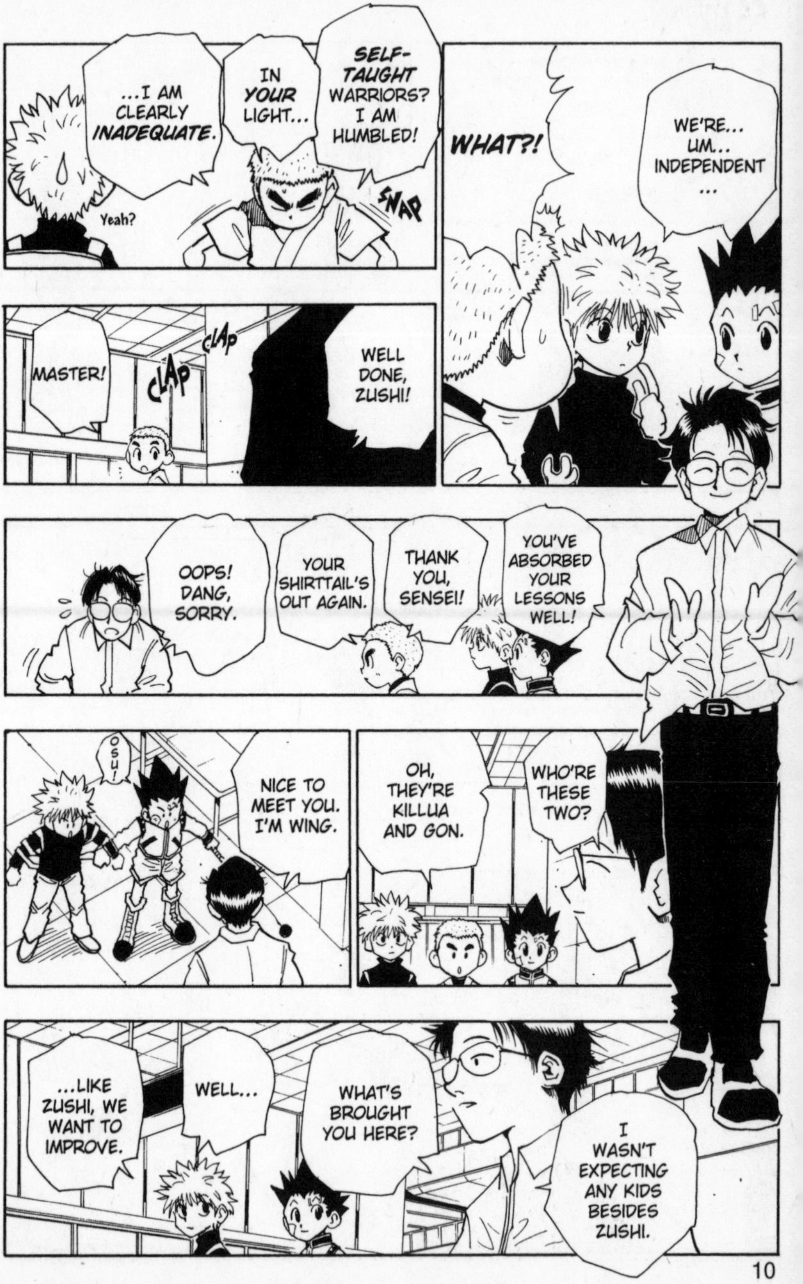
WE'RE... UM... INDEPENDENT ...
WHAT?!
SELF-TAUGHT WARRIORS? I AM HUMBLED!
SNAP
IN YOUR LIGHT...
...I AM CLEARLY INADEQUATE.
Yeah?
WELL DONE, ZUSHI!
CLAP
CLAP
MASTER!
YOU'VE ABSORBED YOUR LESSONS WELL!
THANK YOU, SENSEI!
YOUR SHIRTTAIL'S OUT AGAIN.
OOPS! DANG, SORRY.
WHO'RE THESE TWO?
OH, THEY'RE KILLUA AND GON.
NICE TO MEET YOU. I'M WING.
OSU!
I WASN'T EXPECTING ANY KIDS BESIDES ZUSHI.
WHAT'S BROUGHT YOU HERE?
WELL...
...LIKE ZUSHI, WE WANT TO IMPROVE.

READ THIS WAY

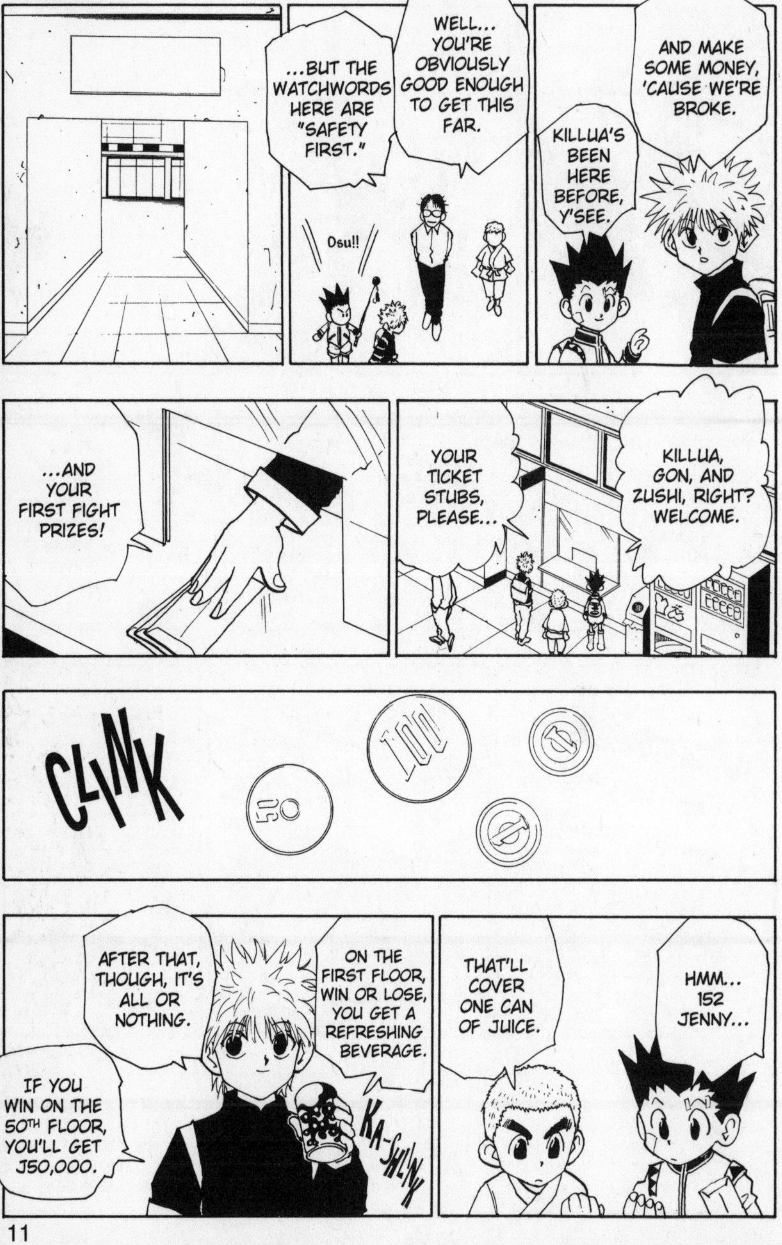
AND MAKE SOME MONEY, 'CAUSE WE'RE BROKE.
KILLUA'S BEEN HERE BEFORE, Y'SEE.
WELL... YOU'RE OBVIOUSLY GOOD ENOUGH TO GET THIS FAR.
...BUT THE WATCHWORDS HERE ARE "SAFETY FIRST."
Osu!!
KILLUA, GON, AND ZUSHI, RIGHT? WELCOME.
YOUR TICKET STUBS, PLEASE...
...AND YOUR FIRST FIGHT PRIZES!
CLINK
HMM... 152 JENNY...
THAT'LL COVER ONE CAN OF JUICE.
ON THE FIRST FLOOR, WIN OR LOSE, YOU GET A REFRESHING BEVERAGE.
AFTER THAT, THOUGH, IT'S ALL OR NOTHING.
KA-SHLINK
IF YOU WIN ON THE 50TH FLOOR, YOU'LL GET J50,000.

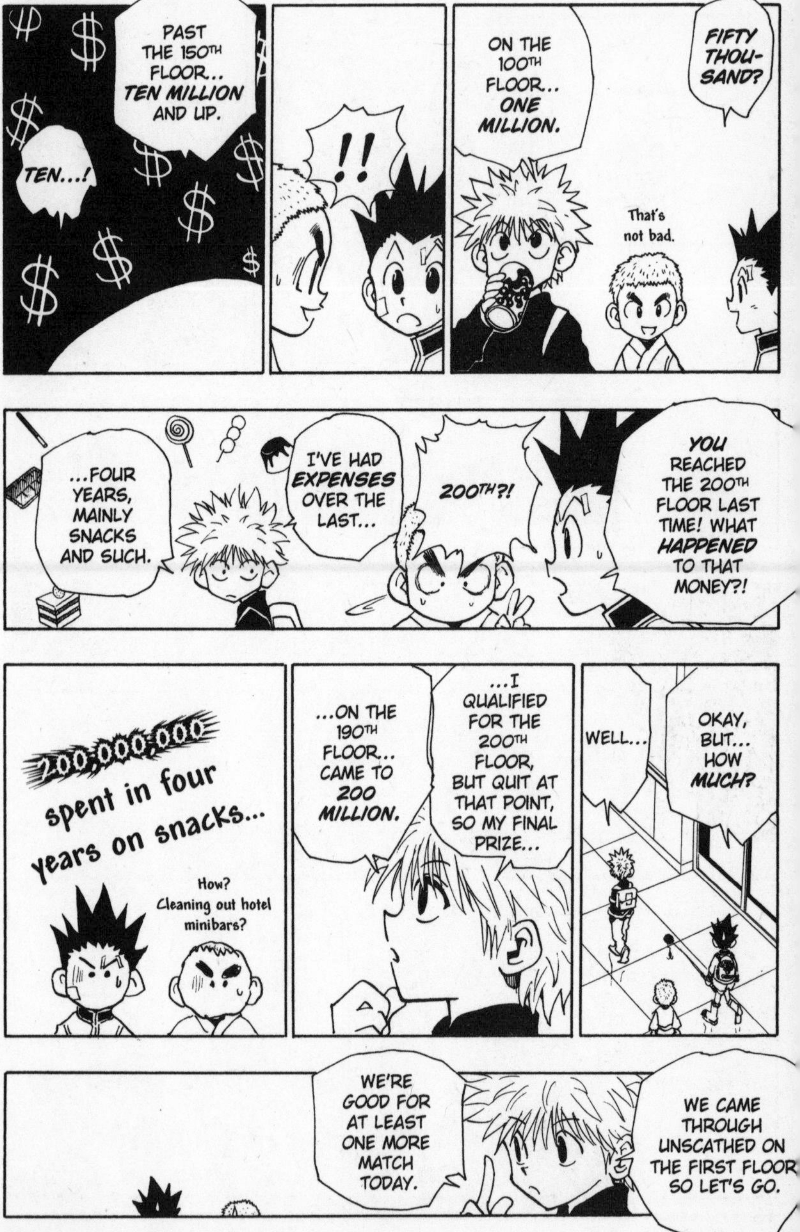
FIFTY THOUSAND?
That's not bad.
ON THE 100TH FLOOR... ONE MILLION.
!!
PAST THE 150TH FLOOR... TEN MILLION AND UP.
TEN...!
YOU REACHED THE 200TH FLOOR LAST TIME! WHAT HAPPENED TO THAT MONEY?!
200TH?!
I'VE HAD EXPENSES OVER THE LAST...
...FOUR YEARS, MAINLY SNACKS AND SUCH.
OKAY, BUT... HOW MUCH?
WELL...
...I QUALIFIED FOR THE 200TH FLOOR, BUT QUIT AT THAT POINT, SO MY FINAL PRIZE...
...ON THE 190TH FLOOR... CAME TO 200 MILLION.
200,000,000
spent in four years on snacks...
How? Cleaning out hotel minibars?
WE CAME THROUGH UNSCATHED ON THE FIRST FLOOR SO LET'S GO.
WE'RE GOOD FOR AT LEAST ONE MORE MATCH TODAY.

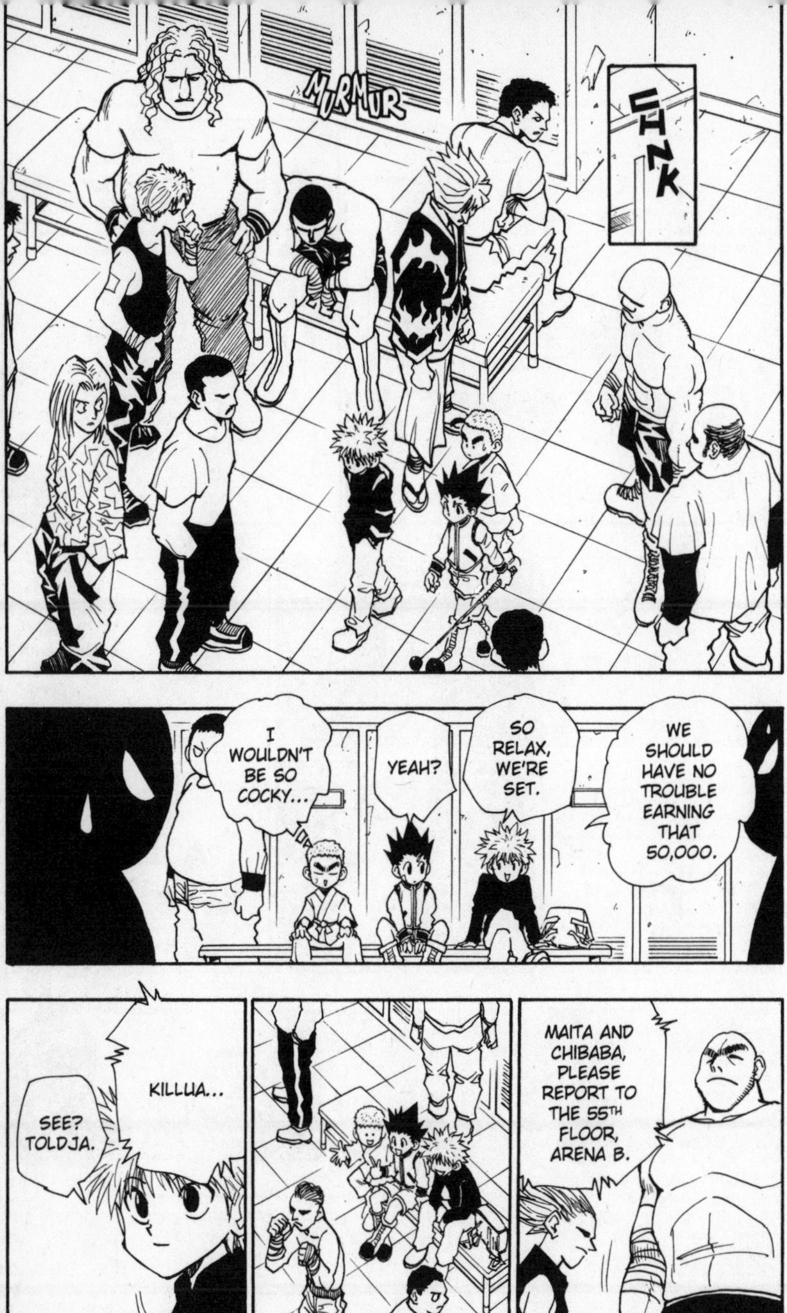
CHNK
MURMUR
WE SHOULD HAVE NO TROUBLE EARNING THAT 50,000.
SO RELAX, WE'RE SET.
YEAH?
I WOULDN'T BE SO COCKY...
MAITA AND CHIBABA, PLEASE REPORT TO THE 55TH FLOOR, ARENA B.
KILLUA...
SEE? TOLDJA.

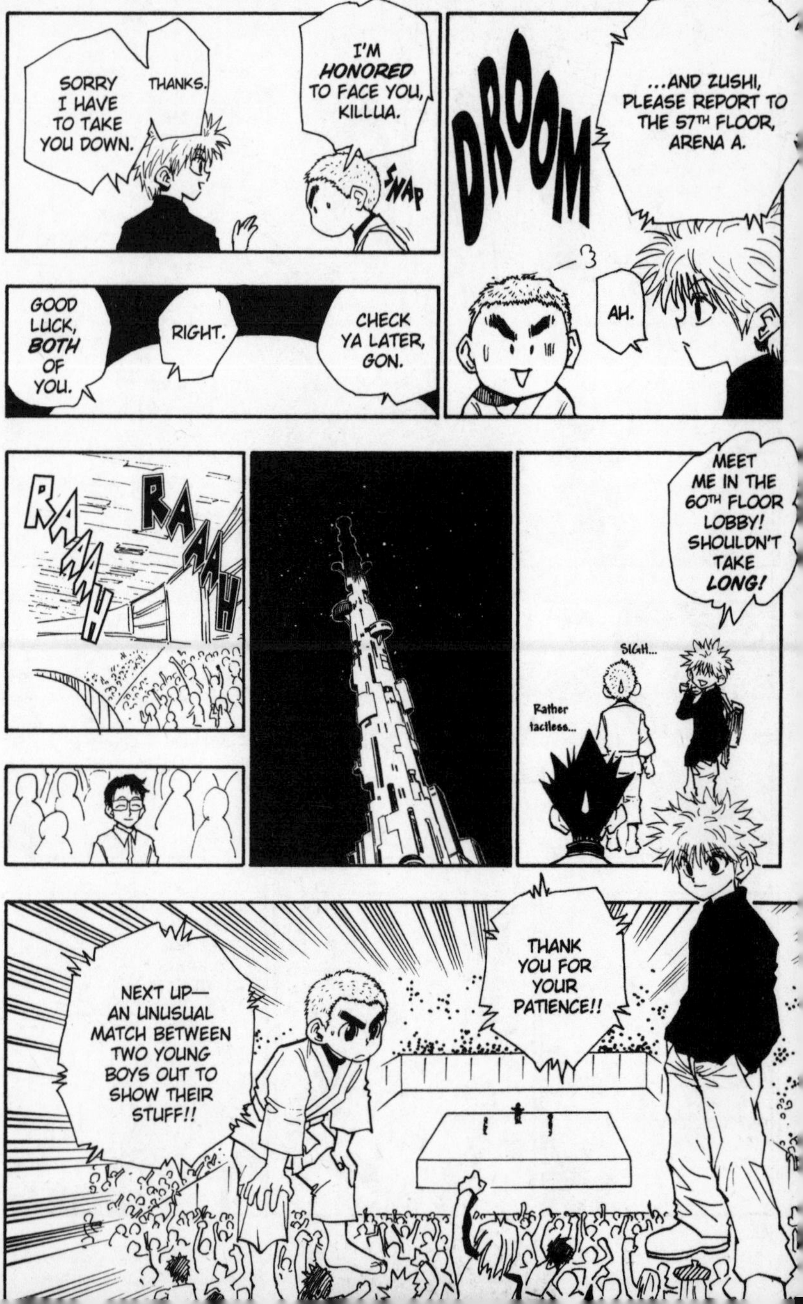
DROOM
...AND ZUSHI, PLEASE REPORT TO THE 57TH FLOOR, ARENA A.
AH.
I'M HONORED TO FACE YOU, KILLUA.
SNAP
THANKS.
SORRY I HAVE TO TAKE YOU DOWN.
CHECK YA LATER, GON.
RIGHT.
GOOD LUCK, BOTH OF YOU.
MEET ME IN THE 60TH FLOOR LOBBY! SHOULDN'T TAKE LONG!
SIGH...
Rather tactless...
RAAAH
RAAAH
THANK YOU FOR YOUR PATIENCE!!
NEXT UP— AN UNUSUAL MATCH BETWEEN TWO YOUNG BOYS OUT TO SHOW THEIR STUFF!!

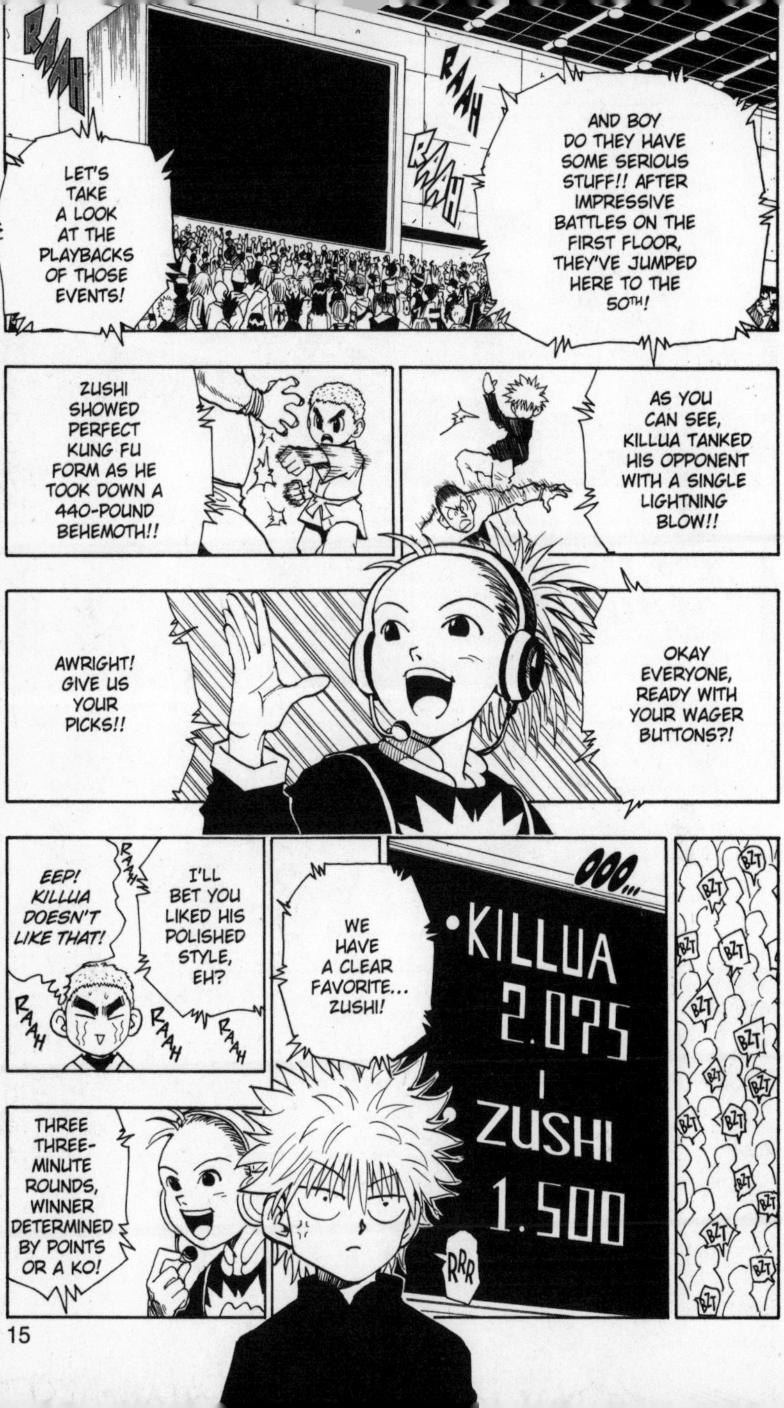
RAAH
AND BOY DO THEY HAVE SOME SERIOUS STUFF!! AFTER IMPRESSIVE BATTLES ON THE FIRST FLOOR, THEY'VE JUMPED HERE TO THE 50TH!
RAAH
RAAH
LET'S TAKE A LOOK AT THE PLAYBACKS OF THOSE EVENTS!
AS YOU CAN SEE, KILLUA TANKED HIS OPPONENT WITH A SINGLE LIGHTNING BLOW!!
ZUSHI SHOWED PERFECT KUNG FU FORM AS HE TOOK DOWN A 440-POUND BEHEMOTH!!
OKAY EVERYONE, READY WITH YOUR WAGER BUTTONS?!
AWRIGHT! GIVE US YOUR PICKS!!
BZT
OOO...
•KILLUA 2.075
•ZUSHI 1.500
WE HAVE A CLEAR FAVORITE... ZUSHI!
RRR
RAAH
I'LL BET YOU LIKED HIS POLISHED STYLE, EH?
EEP! KILLUA DOESN'T LIKE THAT!
RAAH
RAAH
RAAH
THREE THREE-MINUTE ROUNDS, WINNER DETERMINED BY POINTS OR A KO!

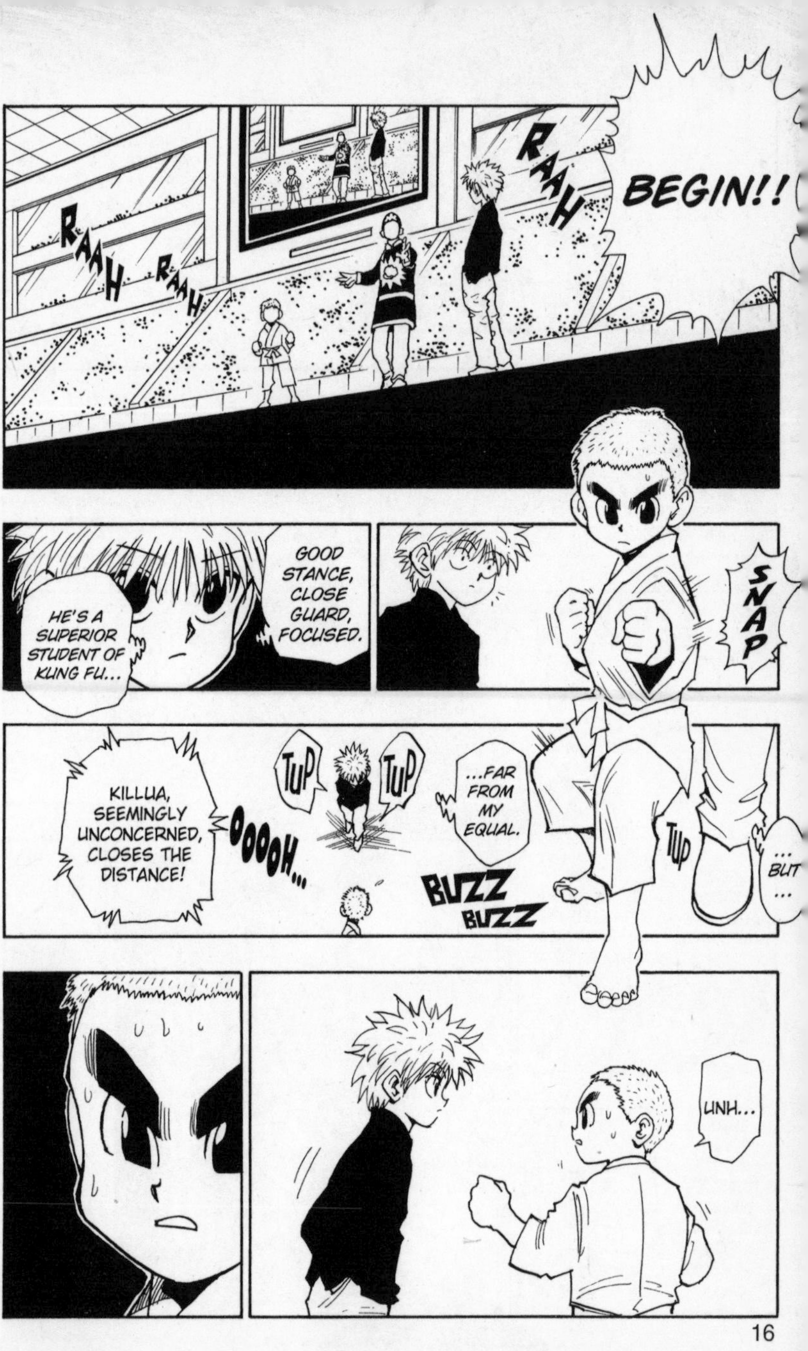
BEGIN!!
RAAH
RAAH
RAAH
SNAP
GOOD STANCE, CLOSE GUARD, FOCUSED.
HE'S A SUPERIOR STUDENT OF KUNG FU...
...BUT...
TUP
...FAR FROM MY EQUAL.
TUP
TUP
BUZZ BUZZ
OOOOH...
KILLUA, SEEMINGLY UNCONCERNED, CLOSES THE DISTANCE!
UNH...

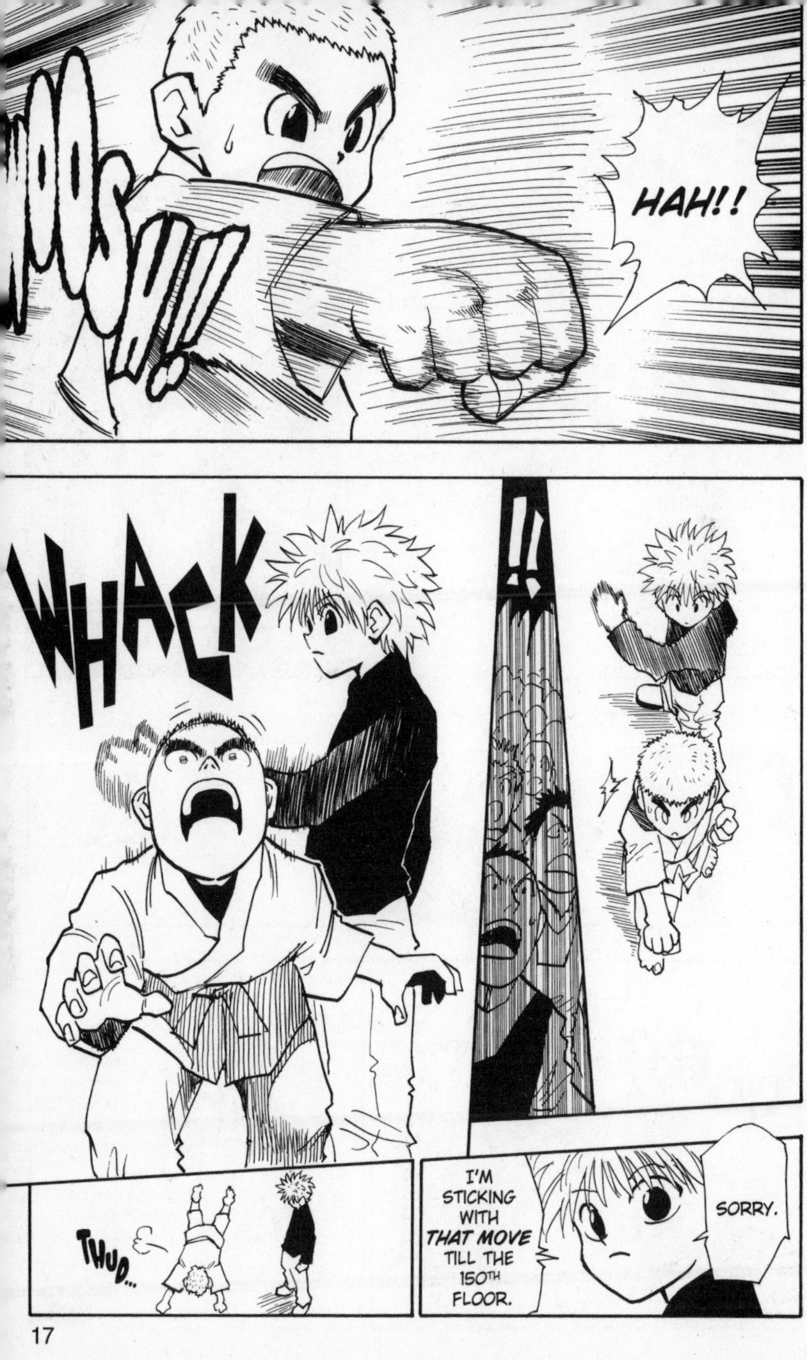
HAH!!
!!
WHACK
SORRY.
I'M STICKING WITH THAT MOVE TILL THE 150TH FLOOR.
THUD...

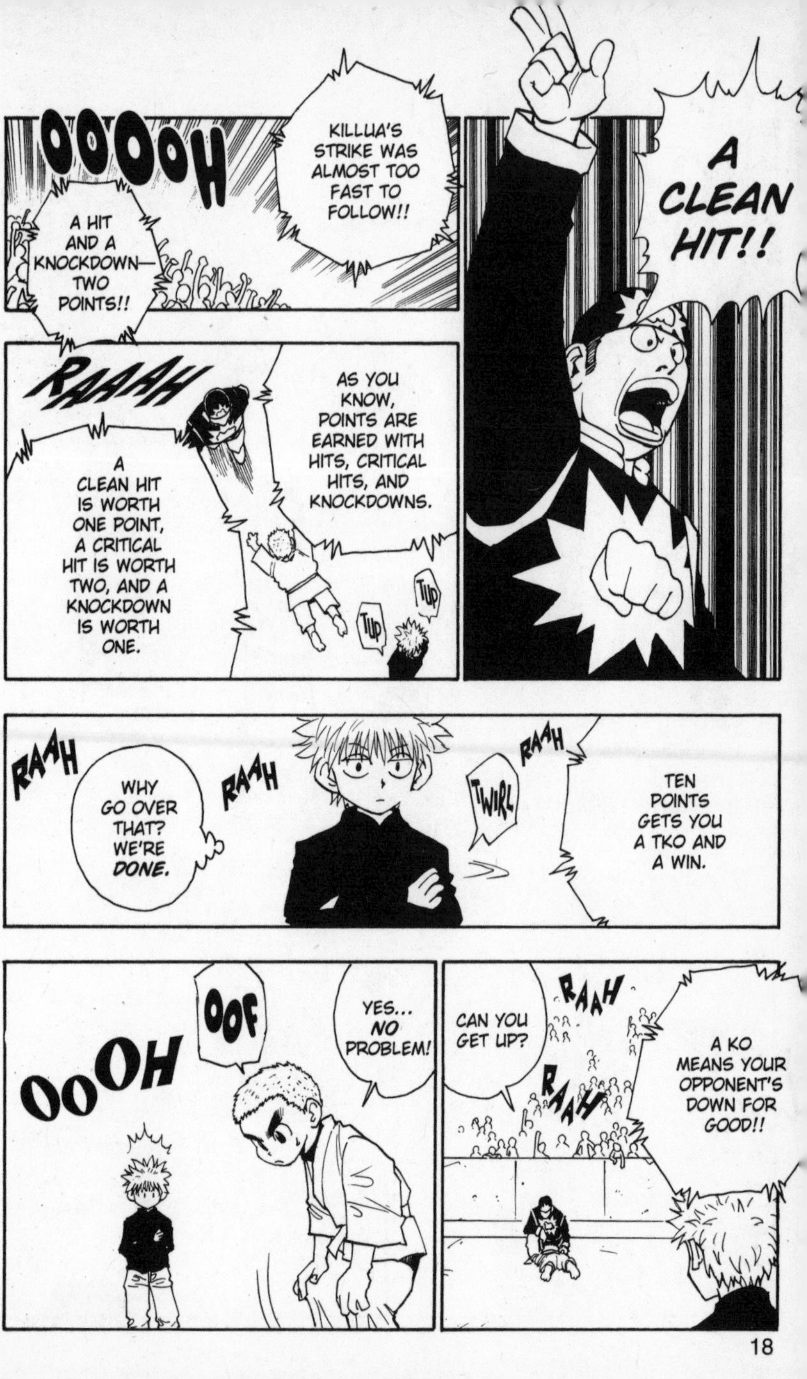
A CLEAN HIT!!
KILLUA'S STRIKE WAS ALMOST TOO FAST TO FOLLOW!!
OOOOH
A HIT AND A KNOCKDOWN—TWO POINTS!!
AS YOU KNOW, POINTS ARE EARNED WITH HITS, CRITICAL HITS, AND KNOCKDOWNS.
RAAAH
A CLEAN HIT IS WORTH ONE POINT, A CRITICAL HIT IS WORTH TWO, AND A KNOCKDOWN IS WORTH ONE.
TUP
TUP
TEN POINTS GETS YOU A TKO AND A WIN.
RAAH
TWIRL
RAAH
WHY GO OVER THAT? WE'RE *DONE.*
RAAH
A KO MEANS YOUR OPPONENT'S DOWN FOR GOOD!!
RAAH
RAAH
CAN YOU GET UP?
YES... *NO* PROBLEM!
OOF
OOOH

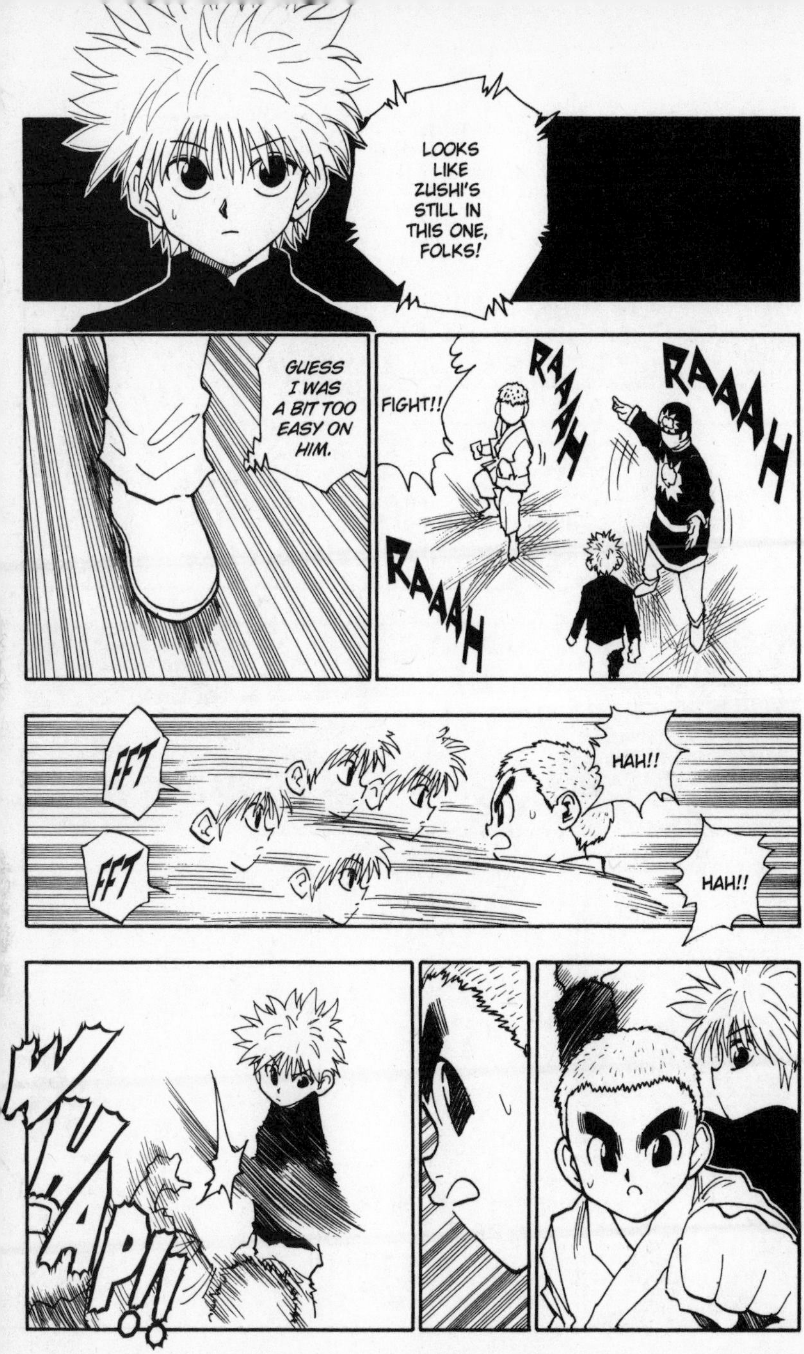
LOOKS LIKE ZUSHI'S STILL IN THIS ONE, FOLKS!
RAAAH
RAAAH
FIGHT!!
RAAAH
GUESS I WAS A BIT TOO EASY ON HIM.
HAH!!
HAH!!
FFT
FFT
WHAP!!

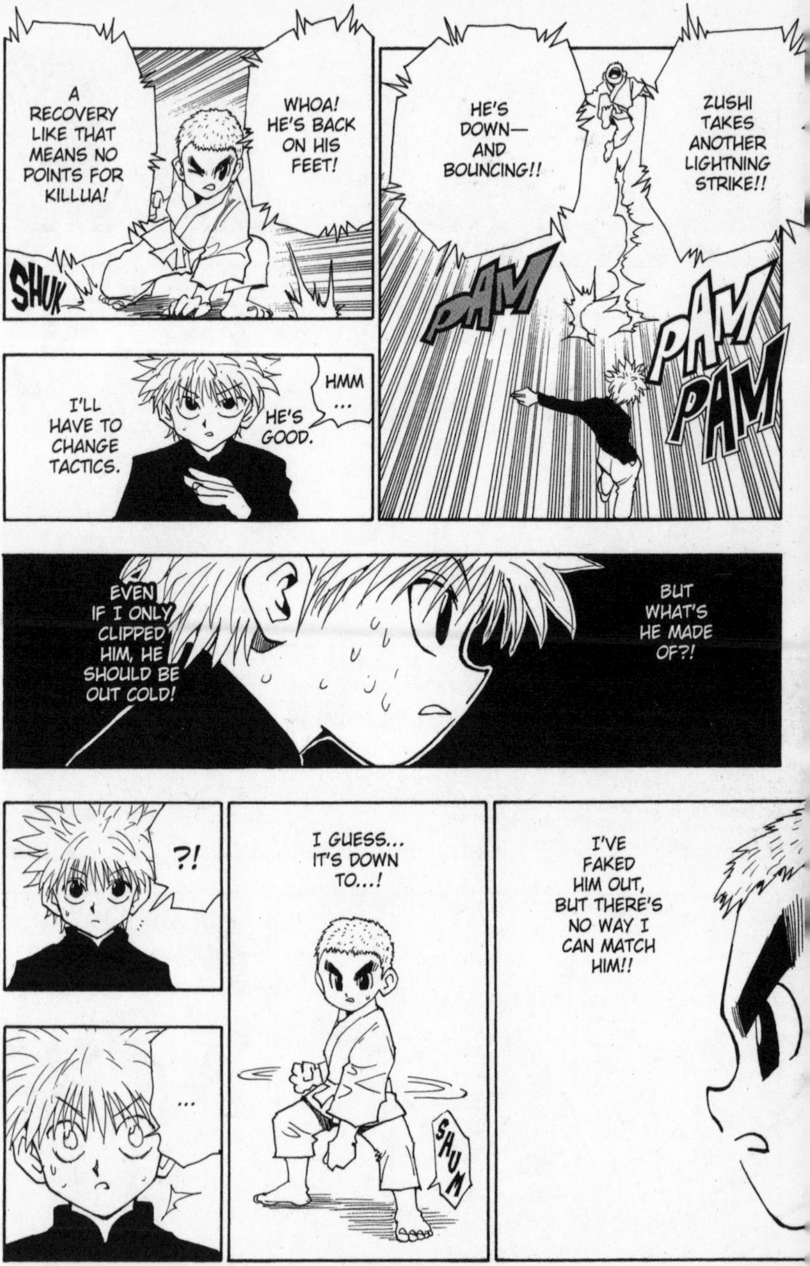
ZUSHI TAKES ANOTHER LIGHTNING STRIKE!!
HE'S DOWN— AND BOUNCING!!
PAM
PAM PAM
WHOA! HE'S BACK ON HIS FEET!
A RECOVERY LIKE THAT MEANS NO POINTS FOR KILLUA!
SHUK
HMM ...
HE'S GOOD.
I'LL HAVE TO CHANGE TACTICS.
BUT WHAT'S HE MADE OF?!
EVEN IF I ONLY CLIPPED HIM, HE SHOULD BE OUT COLD!
I'VE FAKED HIM OUT, BUT THERE'S NO WAY I CAN MATCH HIM!!
I GUESS... IT'S DOWN TO...!
SHUM
?!
...

READ THIS WAY

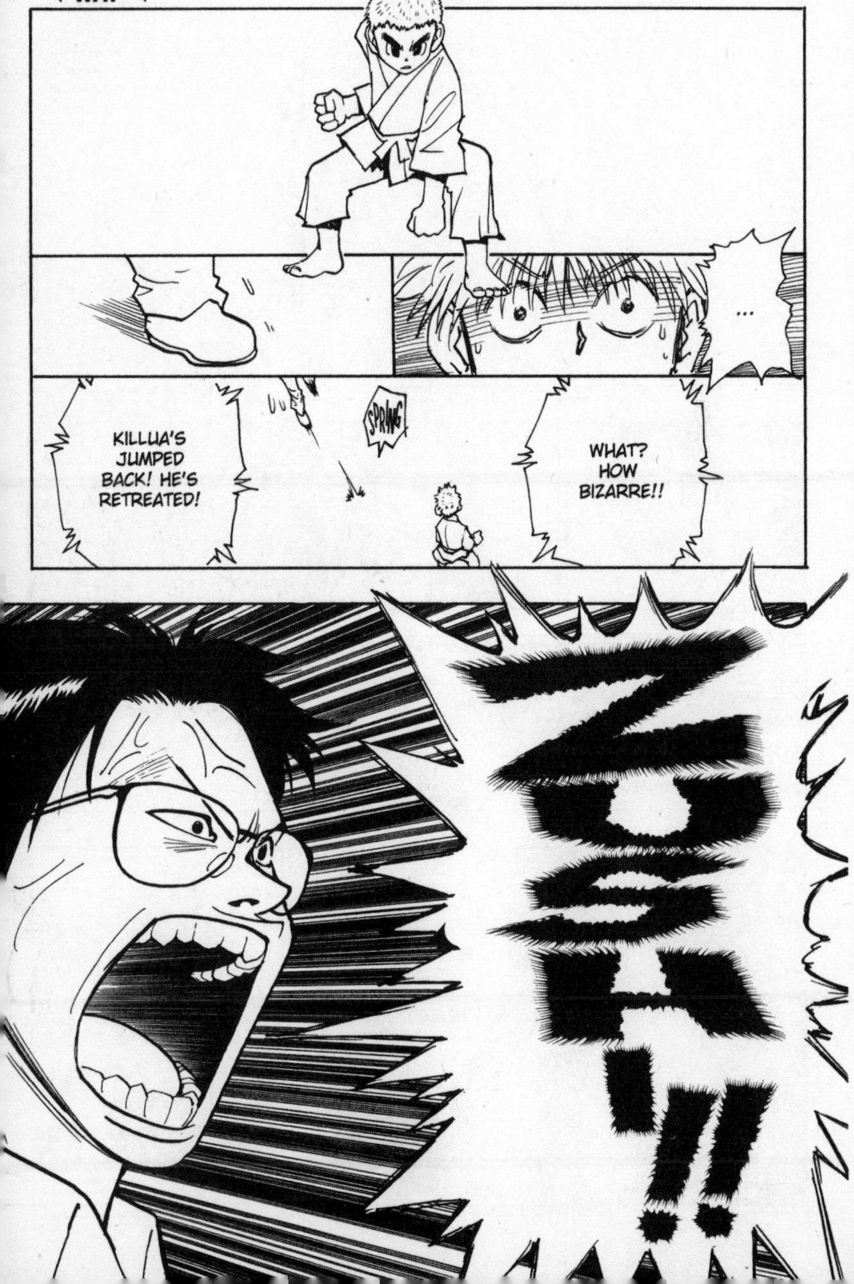
...
WHAT? HOW BIZARRE!!
SPRING
KILLUA'S JUMPED BACK! HE'S RETREATED!

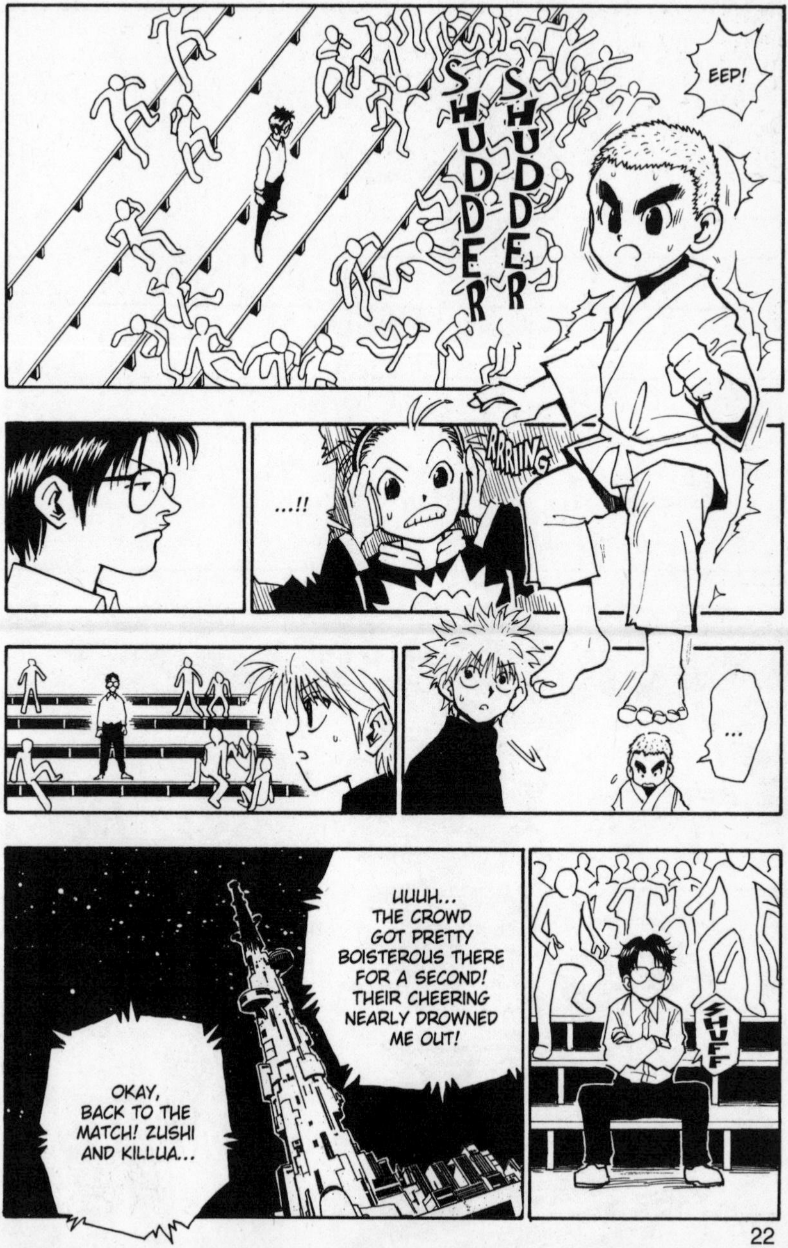
EEP!
SHUDDER SHUDDER
RRRIING
...!!
...
SHUFF
UUUH... THE CROWD GOT PRETTY BOISTEROUS THERE FOR A SECOND! THEIR CHEERING NEARLY DROWNED ME OUT!
OKAY, BACK TO THE MATCH! ZUSHI AND KILLUA...

READ THIS WAY

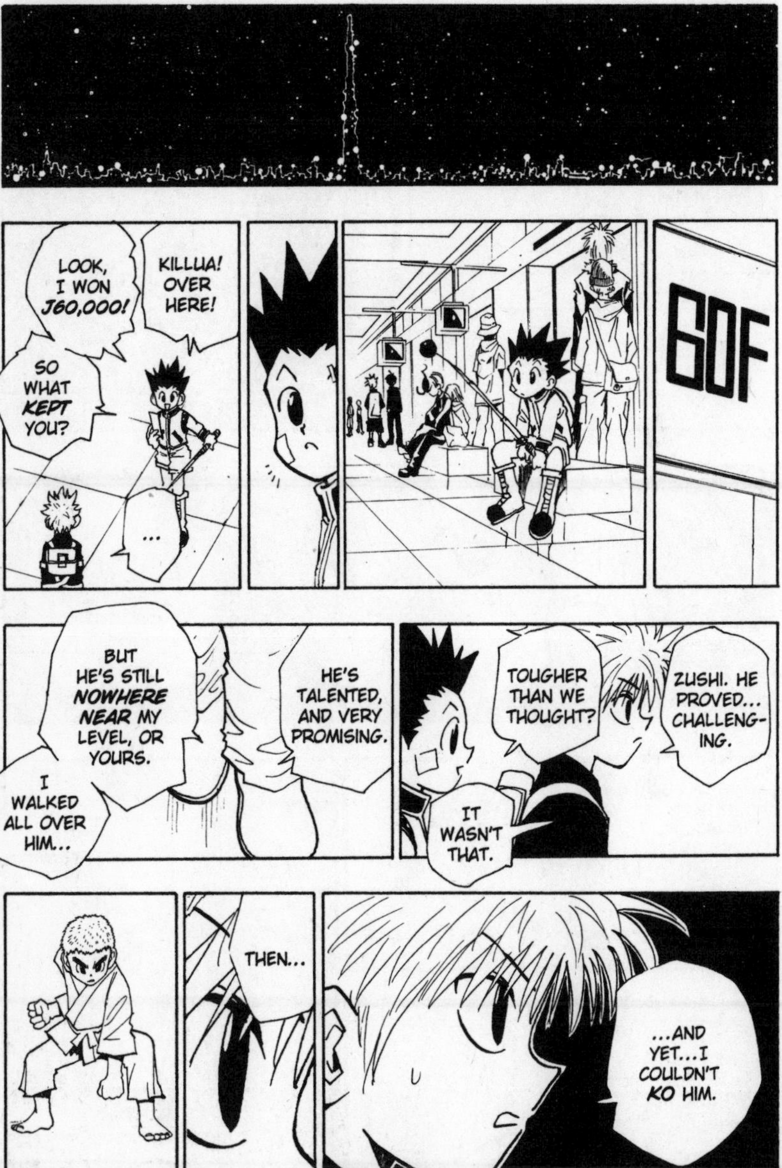
60F
KILLUA! OVER HERE!
LOOK, I WON J60,000!
SO WHAT KEPT YOU?
...
ZUSHI. HE PROVED... CHALLENG-ING.
TOUGHER THAN WE THOUGHT?
IT WASN'T THAT.
HE'S TALENTED, AND VERY PROMISING.
BUT HE'S STILL NOWHERE NEAR MY LEVEL, OR YOURS.
I WALKED ALL OVER HIM...
...AND YET...I COULDN'T KO HIM.
THEN...

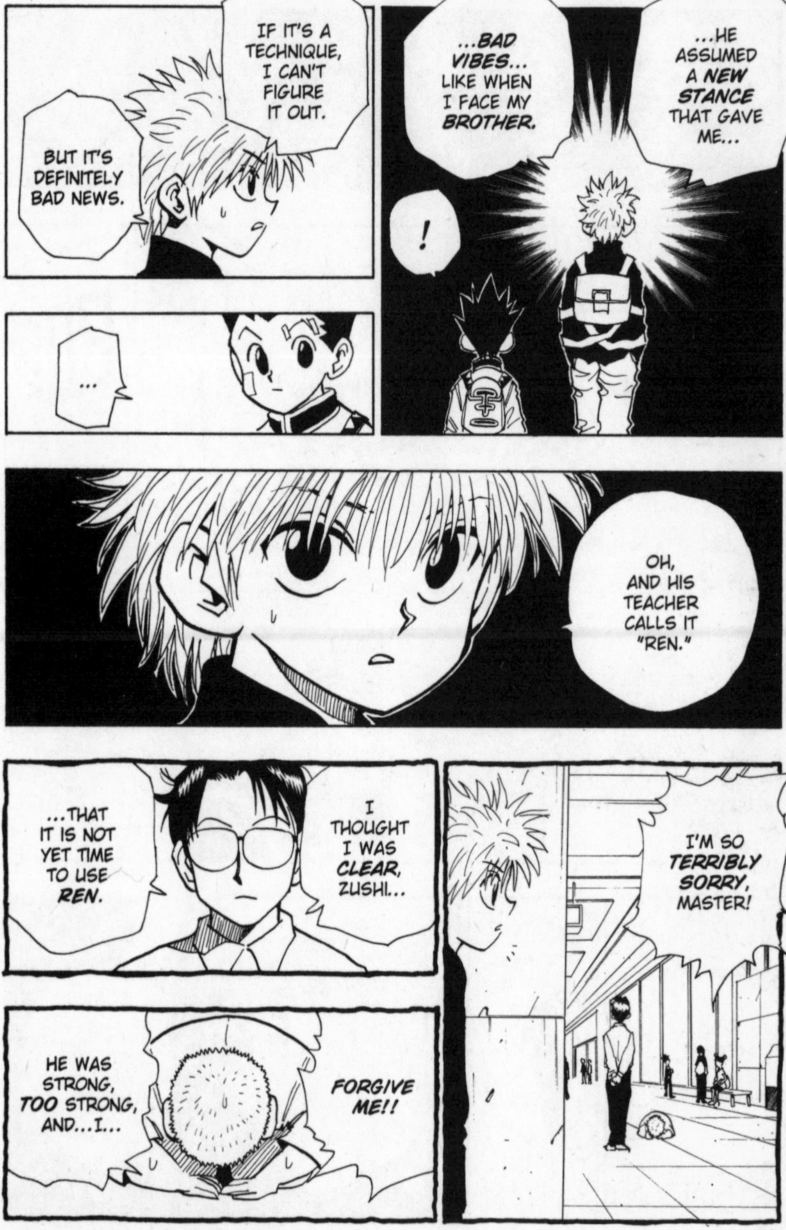
...HE ASSUMED A NEW STANCE THAT GAVE ME...
...BAD VIBES... LIKE WHEN I FACE MY BROTHER.
!
IF IT'S A TECHNIQUE, I CAN'T FIGURE IT OUT.
BUT IT'S DEFINITELY BAD NEWS.
...
OH, AND HIS TEACHER CALLS IT "REN."
I'M SO TERRIBLY SORRY, MASTER!
I THOUGHT I WAS CLEAR, ZUSHI...
...THAT IT IS NOT YET TIME TO USE REN.
FORGIVE ME!!
HE WAS STRONG, TOO STRONG, AND...I...

READ THIS WAY

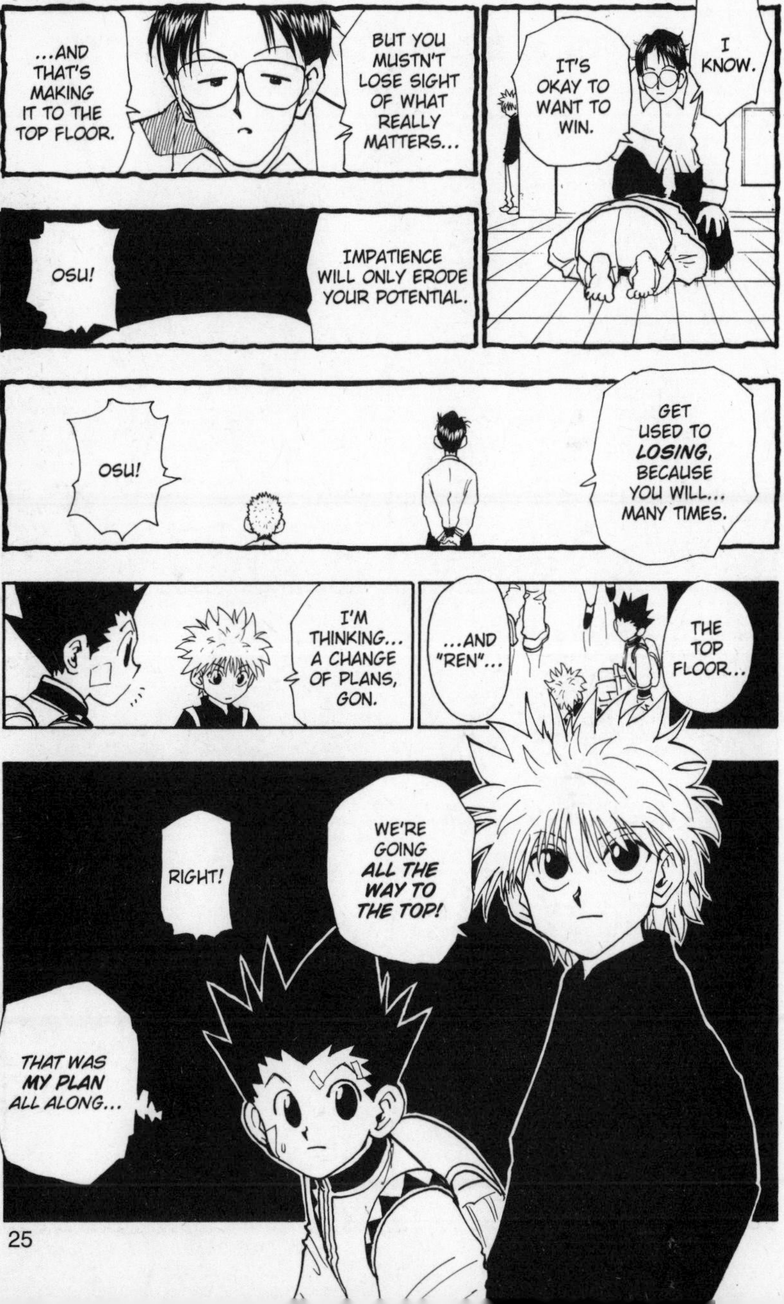
I KNOW.
IT'S OKAY TO WANT TO WIN.
BUT YOU MUSTN'T LOSE SIGHT OF WHAT REALLY MATTERS...
...AND THAT'S MAKING IT TO THE TOP FLOOR.
IMPATIENCE WILL ONLY ERODE YOUR POTENTIAL.
OSU!
GET USED TO ***LOSING***, BECAUSE YOU WILL... MANY TIMES.
OSU!
THE TOP FLOOR...
...AND "REN"...
I'M THINKING... A CHANGE OF PLANS, GON.
WE'RE GOING ***ALL THE WAY TO THE TOP!***
RIGHT!
THAT WAS ***MY PLAN*** ALL ALONG...

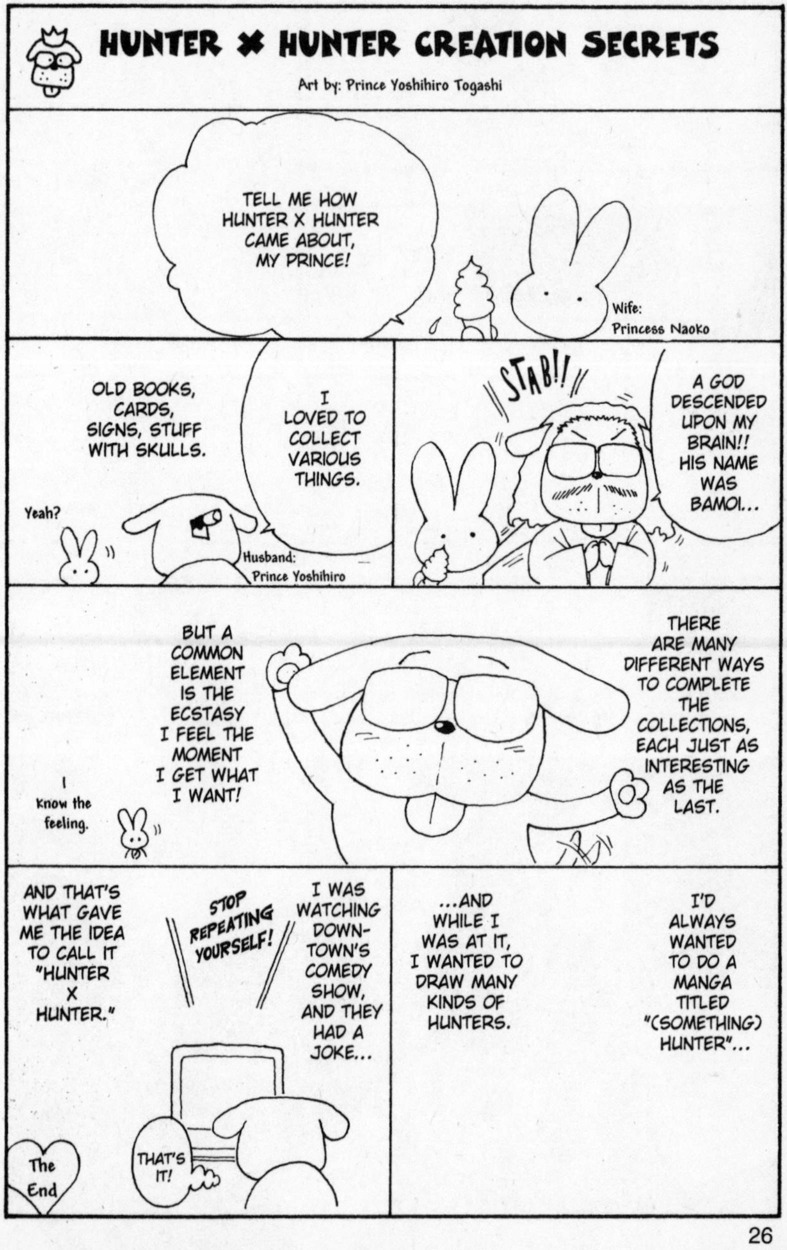
HUNTER × HUNTER CREATION SECRETS
Art by: Prince Yoshihiro Togashi
TELL ME HOW HUNTER X HUNTER CAME ABOUT, MY PRINCE!
Wife: Princess Naoko
STAB!!
A GOD DESCENDED UPON MY BRAIN!! HIS NAME WAS BAMOI...
I LOVED TO COLLECT VARIOUS THINGS.
OLD BOOKS, CARDS, SIGNS, STUFF WITH SKULLS.
Husband: Prince Yoshihiro
Yeah?
THERE ARE MANY DIFFERENT WAYS TO COMPLETE THE COLLECTIONS, EACH JUST AS INTERESTING AS THE LAST.
BUT A COMMON ELEMENT IS THE ECSTASY I FEEL THE MOMENT I GET WHAT I WANT!
I know the feeling.
I'D ALWAYS WANTED TO DO A MANGA TITLED "(SOMETHING) HUNTER"...
...AND WHILE I WAS AT IT, I WANTED TO DRAW MANY KINDS OF HUNTERS.
I WAS WATCHING DOWN-TOWN'S COMEDY SHOW, AND THEY HAD A JOKE...
STOP REPEATING YOURSELF!
AND THAT'S WHAT GAVE ME THE IDEA TO CALL IT "HUNTER X HUNTER."
THAT'S IT!
The End

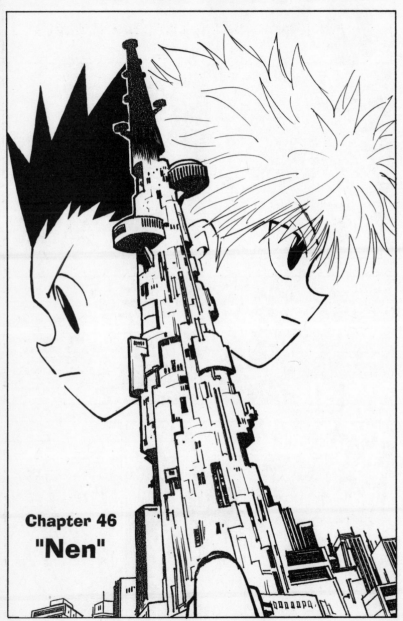

Chapter 46
"Nen"

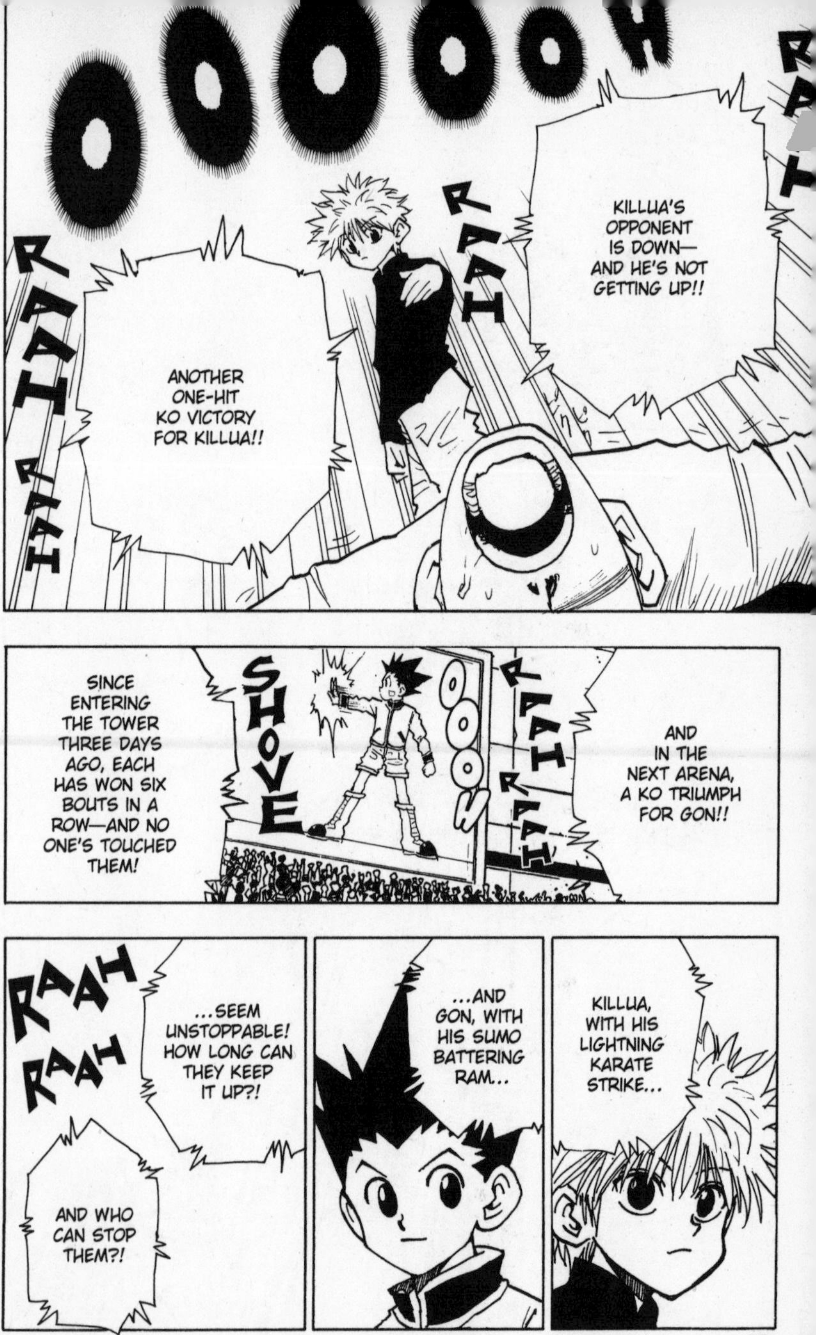
OOOOOOH
KILLUA'S OPPONENT IS DOWN— AND HE'S NOT GETTING UP!!
RAAH
ANOTHER ONE-HIT KO VICTORY FOR KILLUA!!
RAAH RAAH
AND IN THE NEXT ARENA, A KO TRIUMPH FOR GON!!
RAAH RAAH
OOOOH
SHOVE
SINCE ENTERING THE TOWER THREE DAYS AGO, EACH HAS WON SIX BOUTS IN A ROW—AND NO ONE'S TOUCHED THEM!
KILLUA, WITH HIS LIGHTNING KARATE STRIKE...
...AND GON, WITH HIS SUMO BATTERING RAM...
...SEEM UNSTOPPABLE! HOW LONG CAN THEY KEEP IT UP?!
RAAH RAAH
AND WHO CAN STOP THEM?!

READ THIS WAY

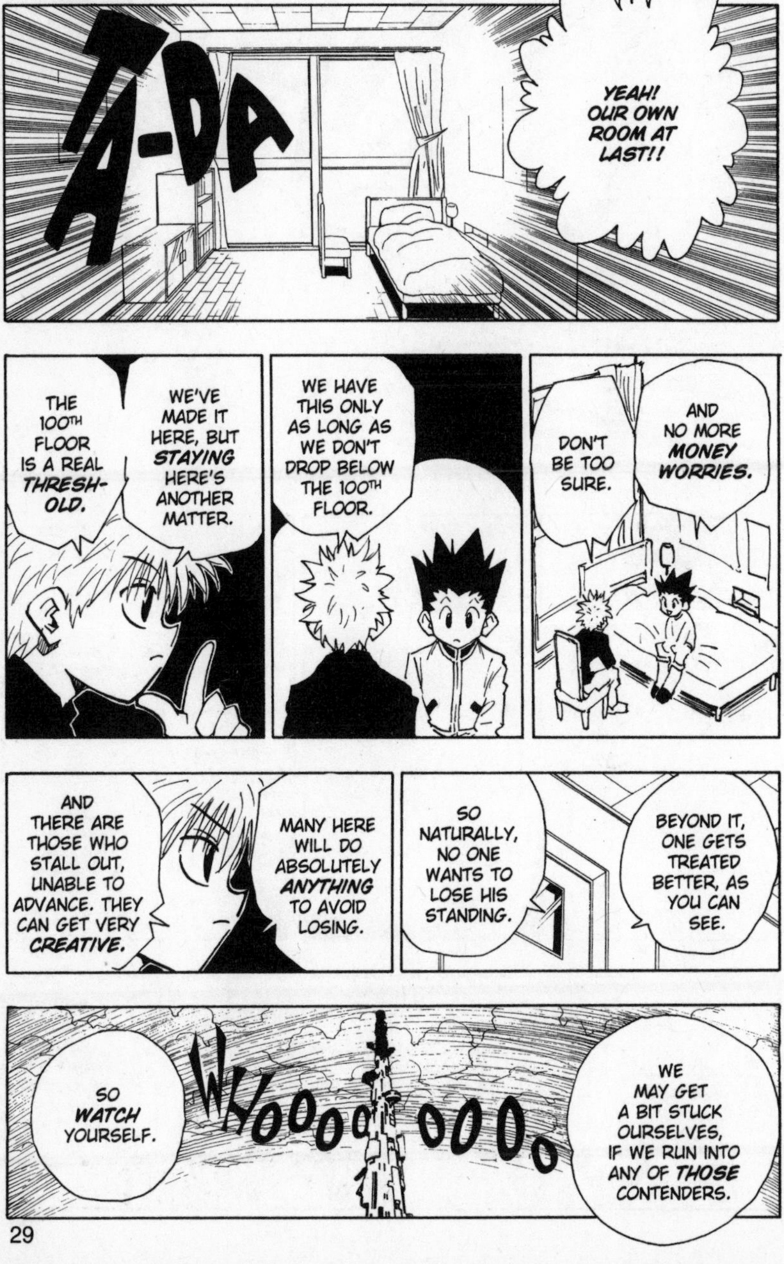

YEAH! OUR OWN ROOM AT LAST!!
TA-DA
AND NO MORE *MONEY WORRIES.*
DON'T BE TOO SURE.
WE HAVE THIS ONLY AS LONG AS WE DON'T DROP BELOW THE 100TH FLOOR.
WE'VE MADE IT HERE, BUT *STAYING* HERE'S ANOTHER MATTER.
THE 100TH FLOOR IS A REAL *THRESH-OLD.*
BEYOND IT, ONE GETS TREATED BETTER, AS YOU CAN SEE.
SO NATURALLY, NO ONE WANTS TO LOSE HIS STANDING.
MANY HERE WILL DO ABSOLUTELY *ANYTHING* TO AVOID LOSING.
AND THERE ARE THOSE WHO STALL OUT, UNABLE TO ADVANCE. THEY CAN GET VERY *CREATIVE.*
WE MAY GET A BIT STUCK OURSELVES, IF WE RUN INTO ANY OF *THOSE* CONTENDERS.
WHOOOOOOOOOOO
SO *WATCH* YOURSELF.

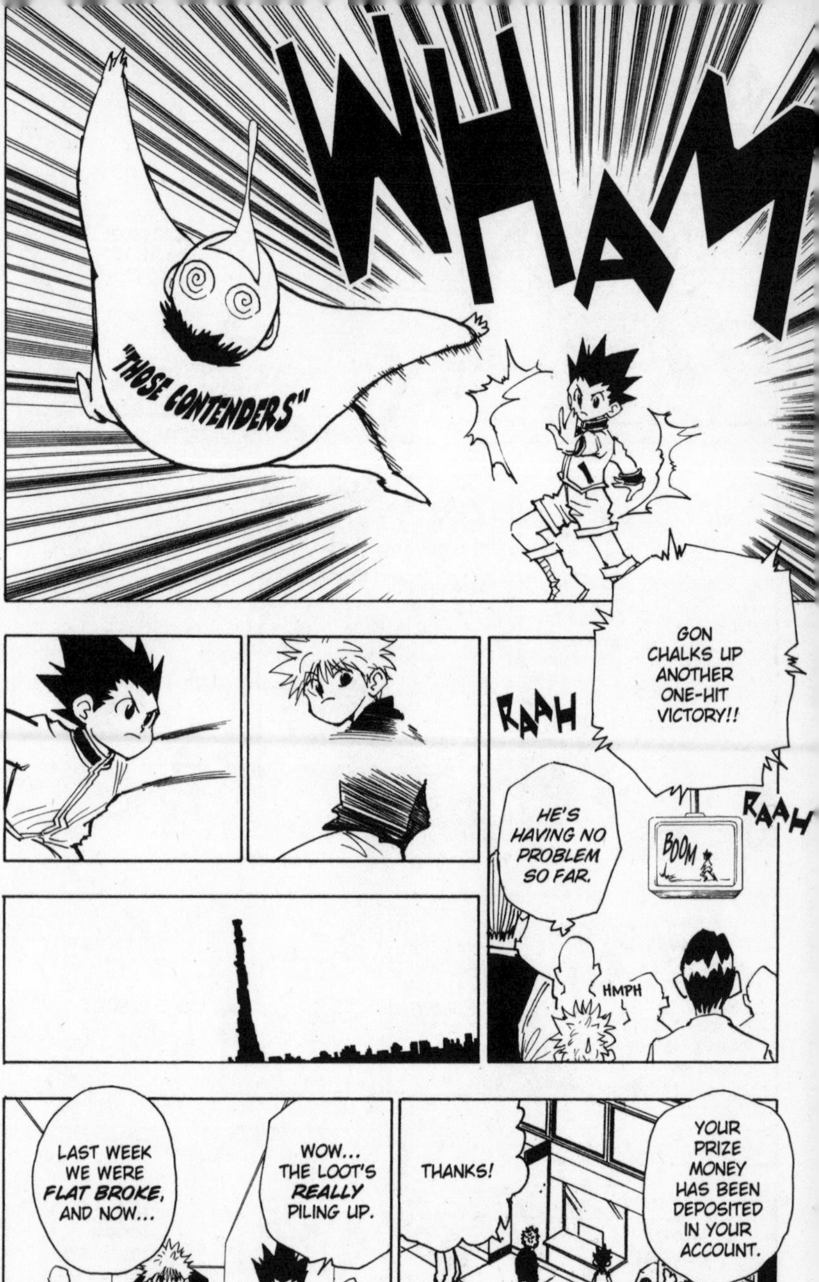
WHAM
"THOSE CONTENDERS"
GON CHALKS UP ANOTHER ONE-HIT VICTORY!!
RAAH
RAAH
BOOM
HE'S HAVING NO PROBLEM SO FAR.
HMPH
YOUR PRIZE MONEY HAS BEEN DEPOSITED IN YOUR ACCOUNT.
THANKS!
WOW... THE LOOT'S REALLY PILING UP.
LAST WEEK WE WERE FLAT BROKE, AND NOW...

READ THIS WAY

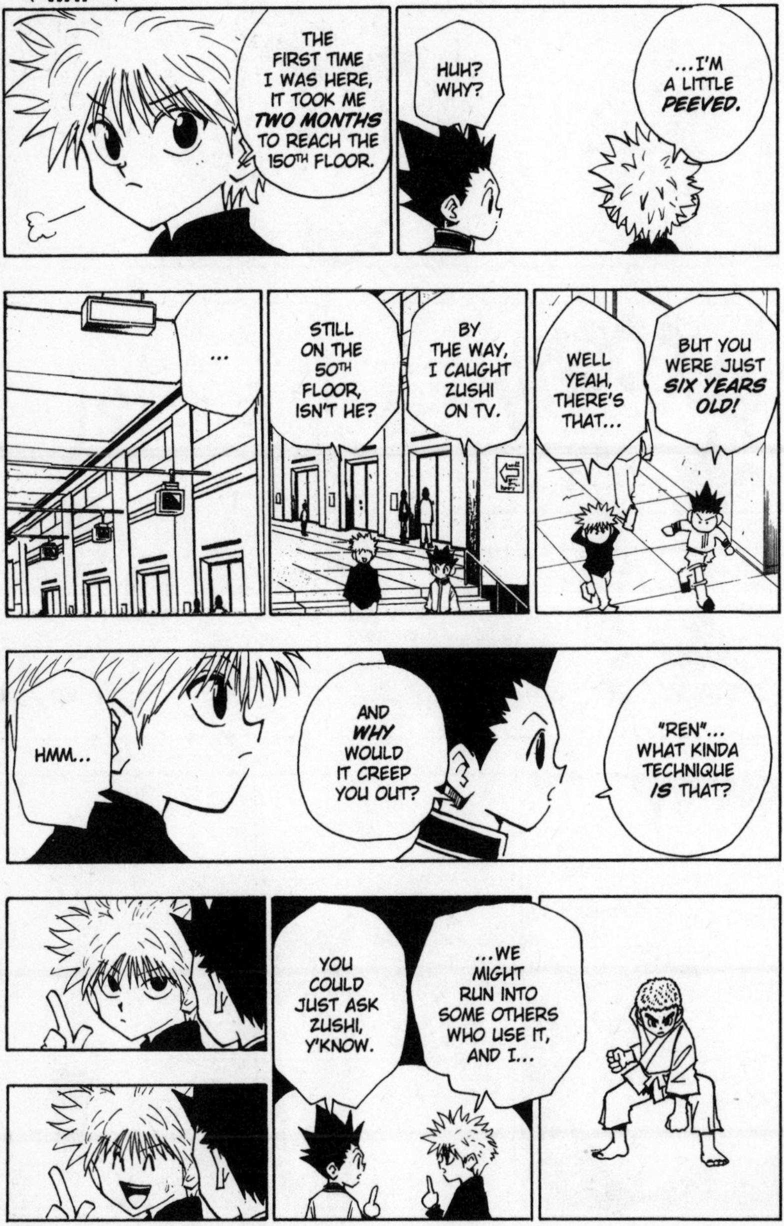
...I'M A LITTLE PEEVED.
HUH? WHY?
THE FIRST TIME I WAS HERE, IT TOOK ME TWO MONTHS TO REACH THE 150TH FLOOR.
BUT YOU WERE JUST SIX YEARS OLD!
WELL YEAH, THERE'S THAT...
BY THE WAY, I CAUGHT ZUSHI ON TV.
STILL ON THE 50TH FLOOR, ISN'T HE?
...
"REN"... WHAT KINDA TECHNIQUE IS THAT?
AND WHY WOULD IT CREEP YOU OUT?
HMM...
...WE MIGHT RUN INTO SOME OTHERS WHO USE IT, AND I...
YOU COULD JUST ASK ZUSHI, Y'KNOW.

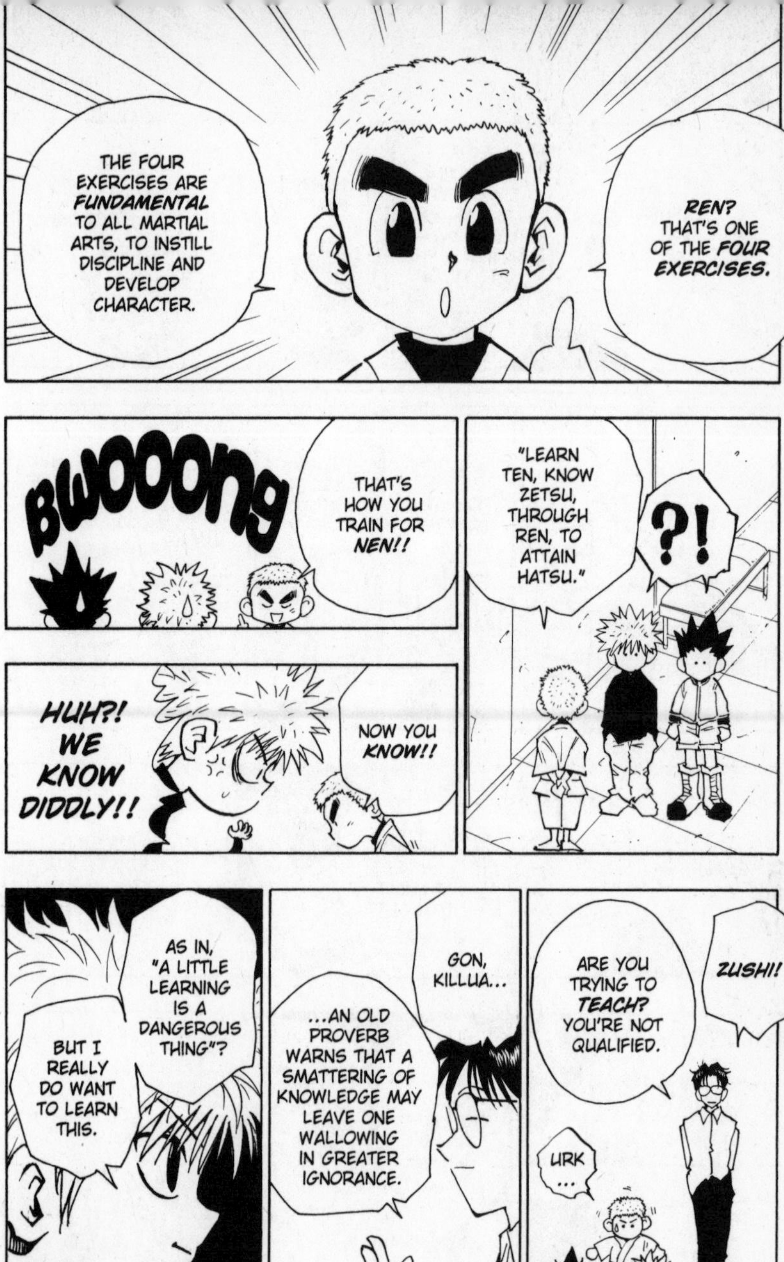
REN? THAT'S ONE OF THE *FOUR EXERCISES.*
THE FOUR EXERCISES ARE *FUNDAMENTAL* TO ALL MARTIAL ARTS, TO INSTILL DISCIPLINE AND DEVELOP CHARACTER.
"LEARN TEN, KNOW ZETSU, THROUGH REN, TO ATTAIN HATSU."
?!
THAT'S HOW YOU TRAIN FOR *NEN!!*
BWOOONG
NOW YOU *KNOW!!*
HUH?! WE KNOW DIDDLY!!
ZUSHI!
ARE YOU TRYING TO *TEACH?* YOU'RE NOT QUALIFIED.
URK ...
GON, KILLUA...
...AN OLD PROVERB WARNS THAT A SMATTERING OF KNOWLEDGE MAY LEAVE ONE WALLOWING IN GREATER IGNORANCE.
AS IN, "A LITTLE LEARNING IS A DANGEROUS THING"?
BUT I REALLY DO WANT TO LEARN THIS.

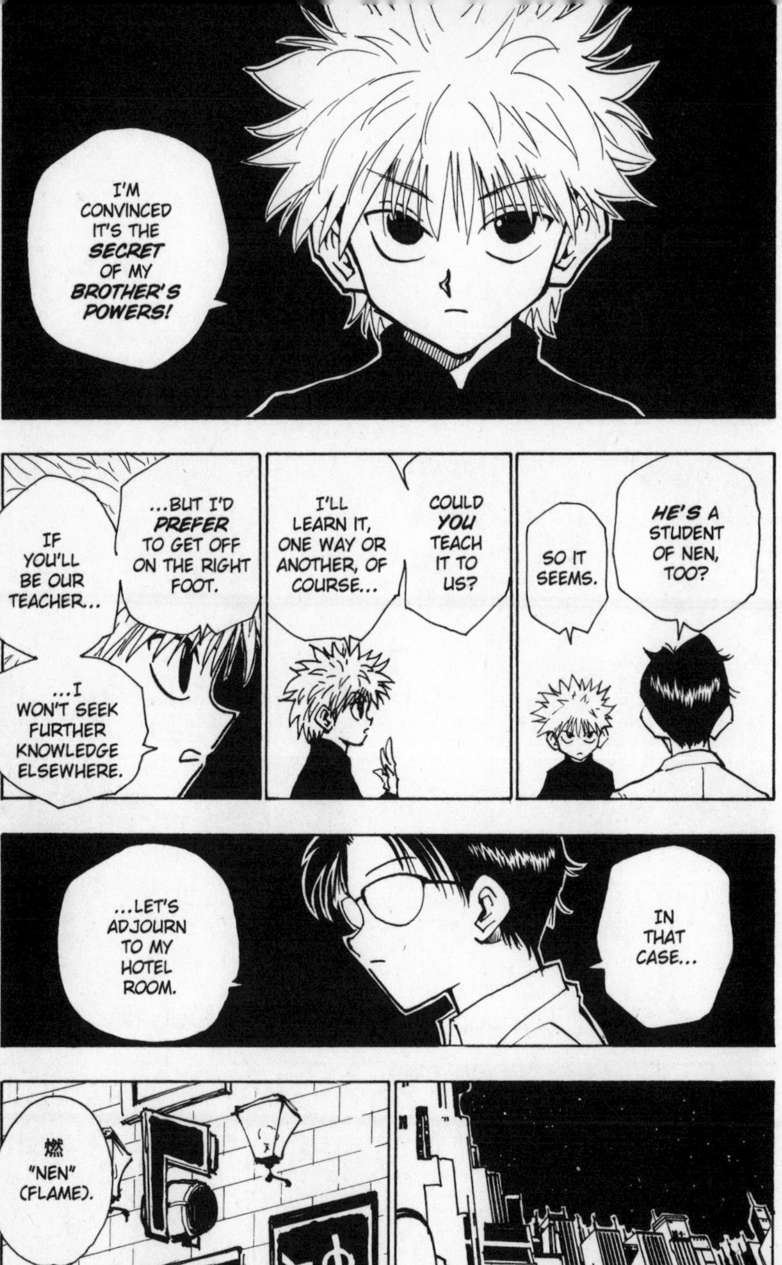
I'M CONVINCED IT'S THE SECRET OF MY BROTHER'S POWERS!
HE'S A STUDENT OF NEN, TOO?
SO IT SEEMS.
COULD YOU TEACH IT TO US?
I'LL LEARN IT, ONE WAY OR ANOTHER, OF COURSE...
...BUT I'D PREFER TO GET OFF ON THE RIGHT FOOT.
IF YOU'LL BE OUR TEACHER...
...I WON'T SEEK FURTHER KNOWLEDGE ELSEWHERE.
IN THAT CASE...
...LET'S ADJOURN TO MY HOTEL ROOM.
燃 "NEN" (FLAME).

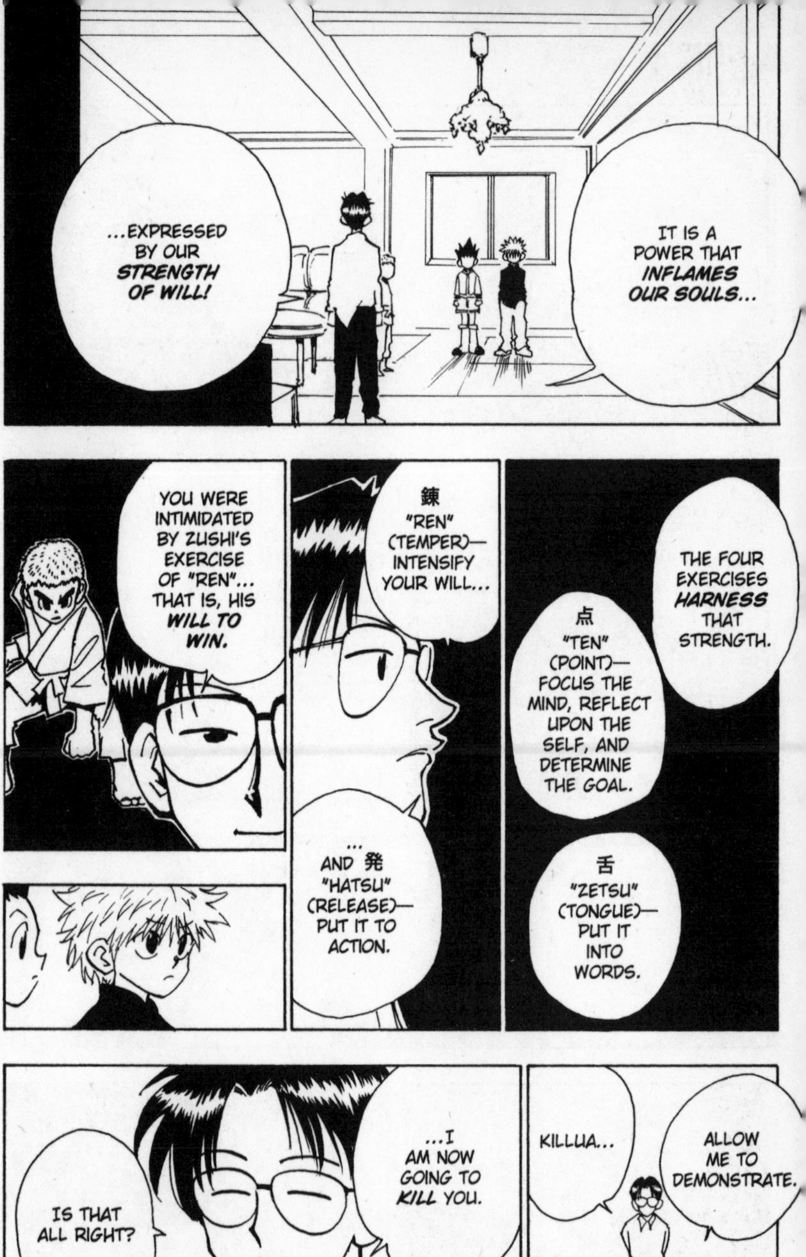
IT IS A POWER THAT INFLAMES OUR SOULS...
...EXPRESSED BY OUR STRENGTH OF WILL!
THE FOUR EXERCISES HARNESS THAT STRENGTH.
点 "TEN" (POINT)—FOCUS THE MIND, REFLECT UPON THE SELF, AND DETERMINE THE GOAL.
舌 "ZETSU" (TONGUE)—PUT IT INTO WORDS.
錬 "REN" (TEMPER)—INTENSIFY YOUR WILL...
...AND 発 "HATSU" (RELEASE)—PUT IT TO ACTION.
YOU WERE INTIMIDATED BY ZUSHI'S EXERCISE OF "REN"... THAT IS, HIS WILL TO WIN.
ALLOW ME TO DEMONSTRATE.
KILLUA...
...I AM NOW GOING TO KILL YOU.
IS THAT ALL RIGHT?

READ THIS WAY

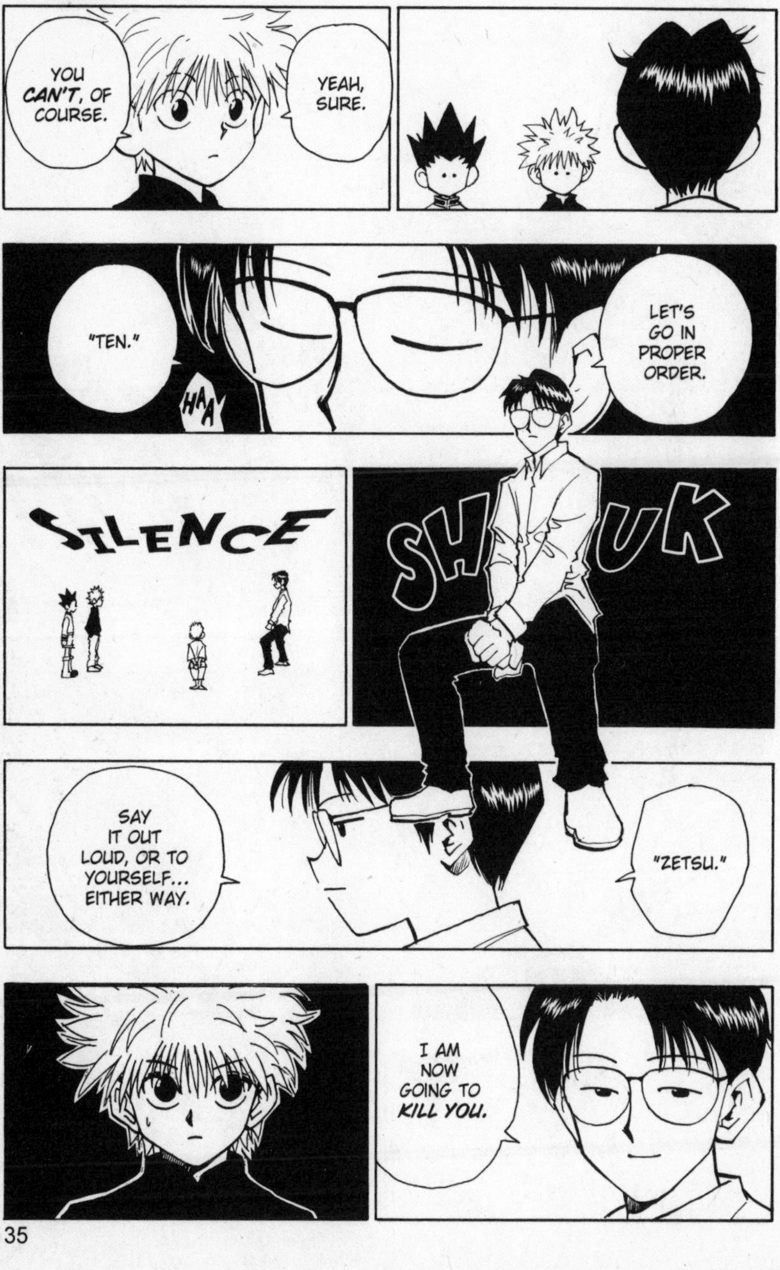
YEAH, SURE.
YOU CAN'T, OF COURSE.
LET'S GO IN PROPER ORDER.
"TEN."
HAA
SH UK
SILENCE
"ZETSU."
SAY IT OUT LOUD, OR TO YOURSELF... EITHER WAY.
I AM NOW GOING TO KILL YOU.

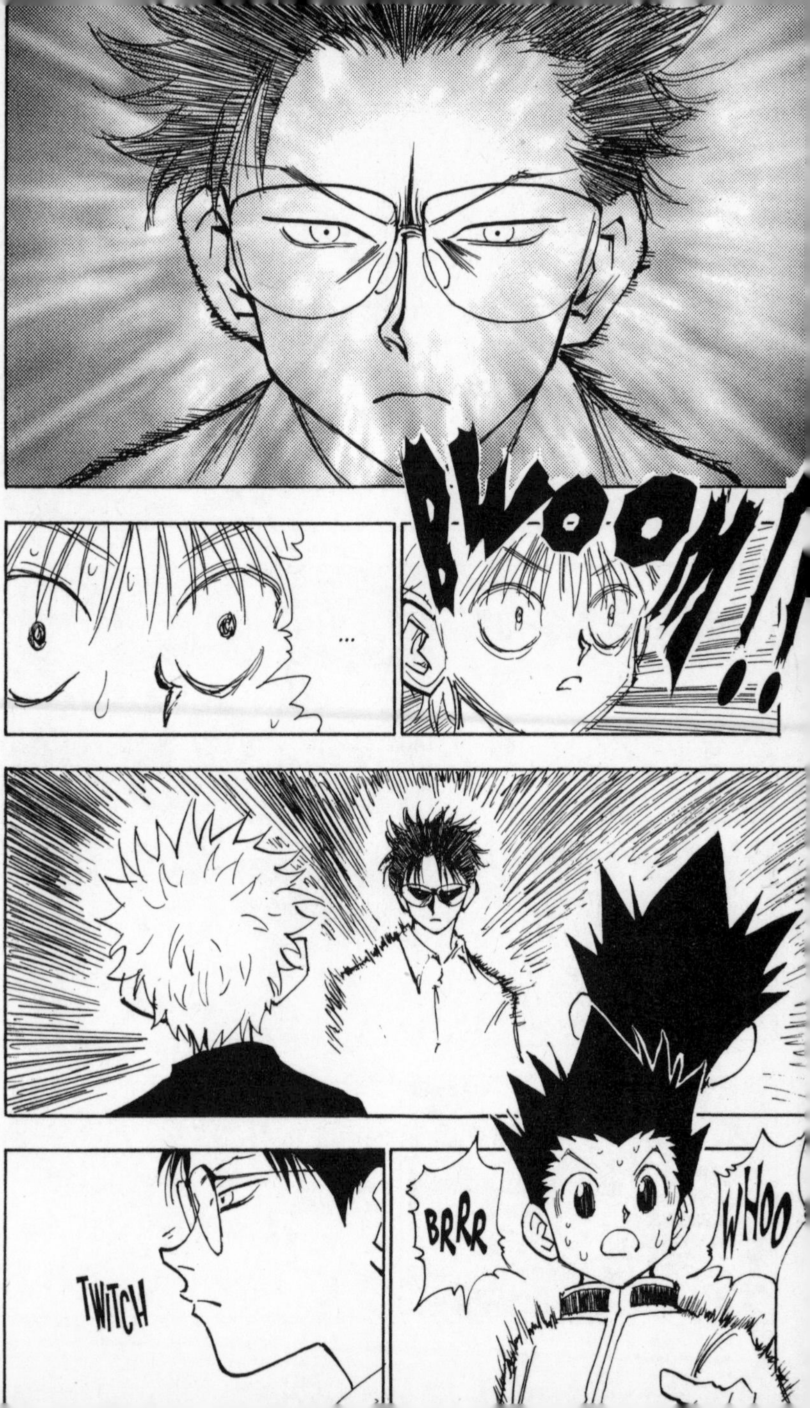
BWOOM!!
...
WHOO
BRRR
TWITCH

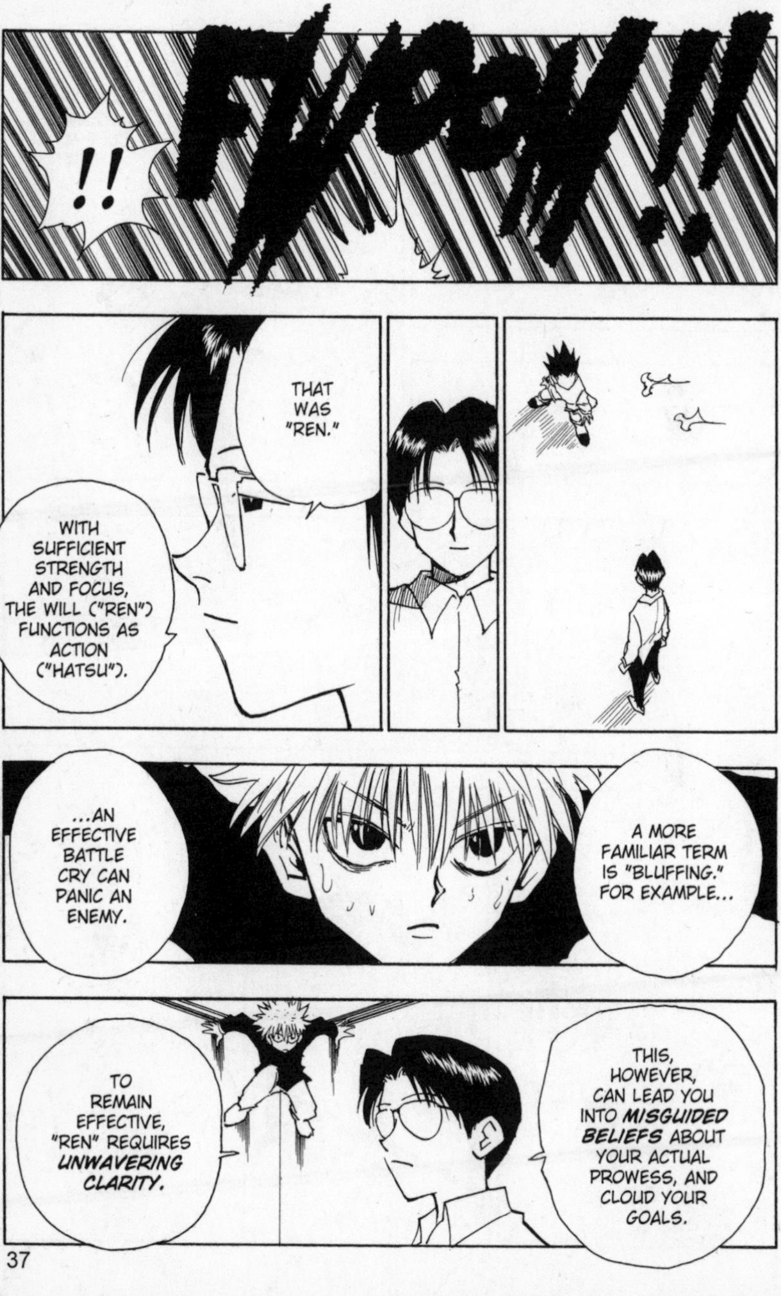
!!
THAT WAS "REN."
WITH SUFFICIENT STRENGTH AND FOCUS, THE WILL ("REN") FUNCTIONS AS ACTION ("HATSU").
A MORE FAMILIAR TERM IS "BLUFFING." FOR EXAMPLE...
...AN EFFECTIVE BATTLE CRY CAN PANIC AN ENEMY.
THIS, HOWEVER, CAN LEAD YOU INTO MISGUIDED BELIEFS ABOUT YOUR ACTUAL PROWESS, AND CLOUD YOUR GOALS.
TO REMAIN EFFECTIVE, "REN" REQUIRES UNWAVERING CLARITY.

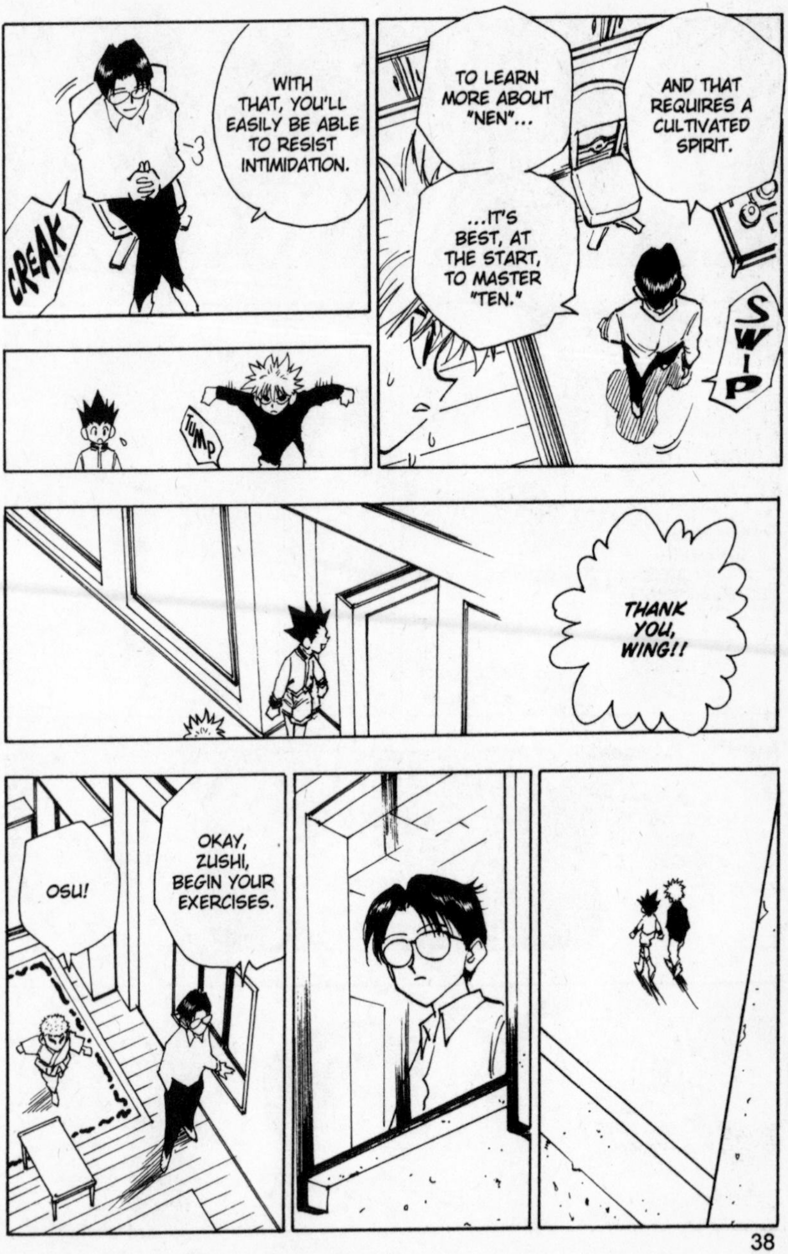
TO LEARN MORE ABOUT "NEN"...
...IT'S BEST, AT THE START, TO MASTER "TEN."
AND THAT REQUIRES A CULTIVATED SPIRIT.
SWIP
WITH THAT, YOU'LL EASILY BE ABLE TO RESIST INTIMIDATION.
CREAK
TUMP
THANK YOU, WING!!
OKAY, ZUSHI, BEGIN YOUR EXERCISES.
OSU!

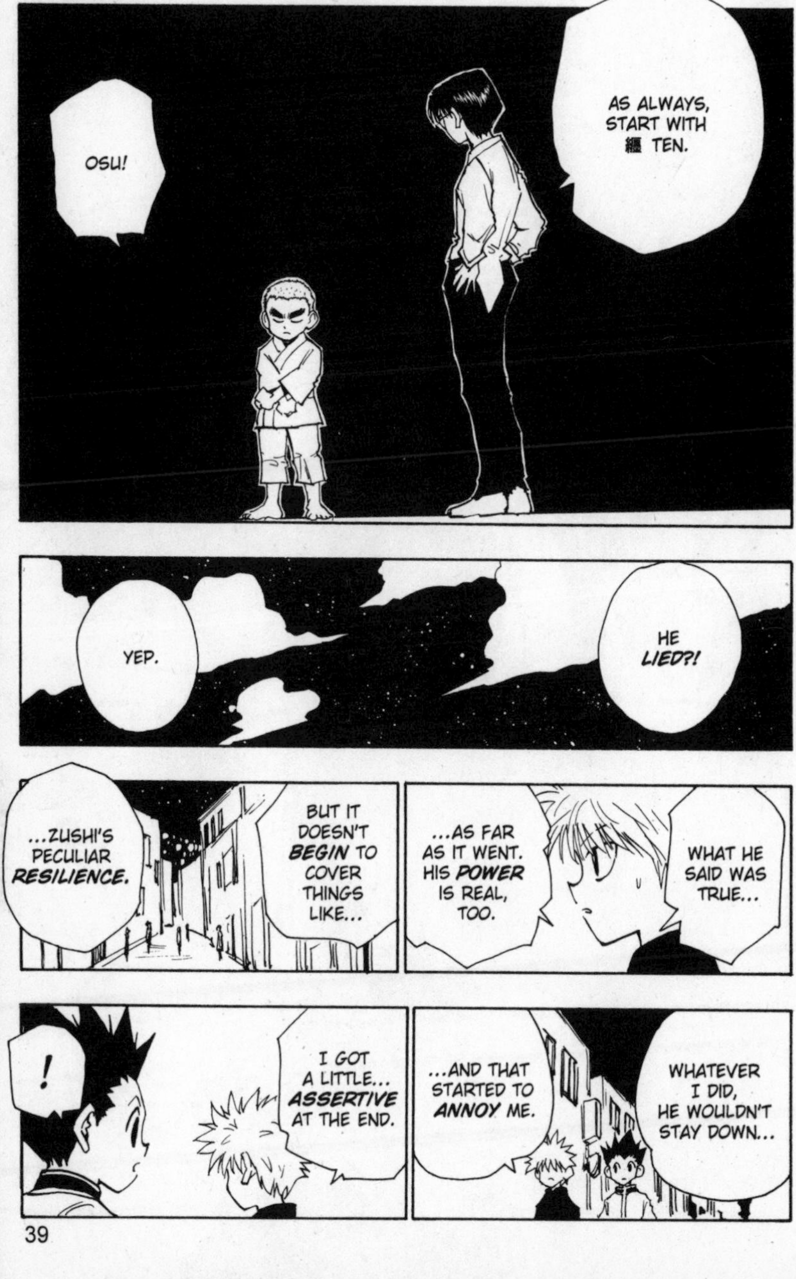
AS ALWAYS, START WITH 纏 TEN.
OSU!
HE LIED?!
YEP.
WHAT HE SAID WAS TRUE...
...AS FAR AS IT WENT. HIS POWER IS REAL, TOO.
BUT IT DOESN'T BEGIN TO COVER THINGS LIKE...
...ZUSHI'S PECULIAR RESILIENCE.
WHATEVER I DID, HE WOULDN'T STAY DOWN...
...AND THAT STARTED TO ANNOY ME.
I GOT A LITTLE... ASSERTIVE AT THE END.
!

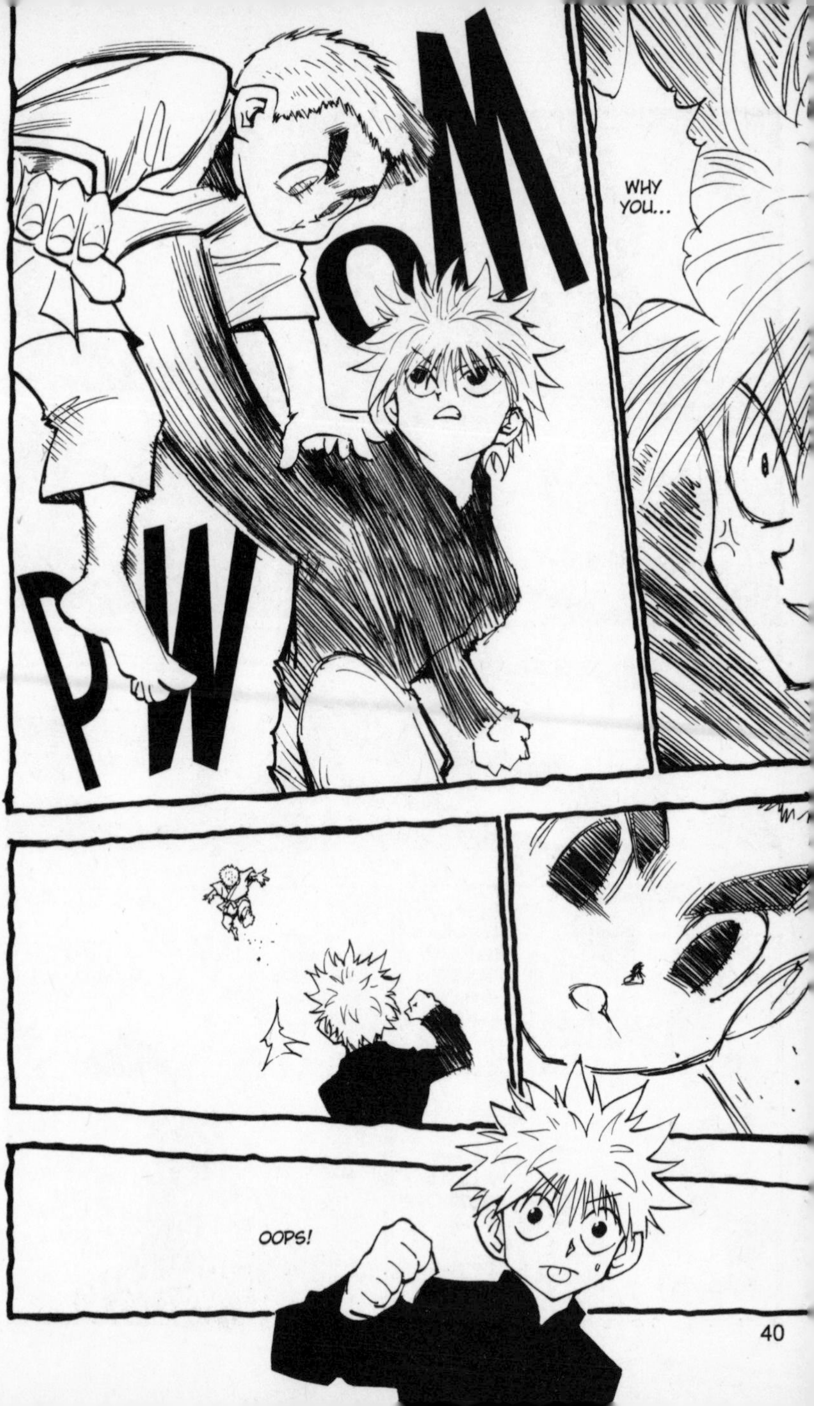
WHY YOU...
OOPS!

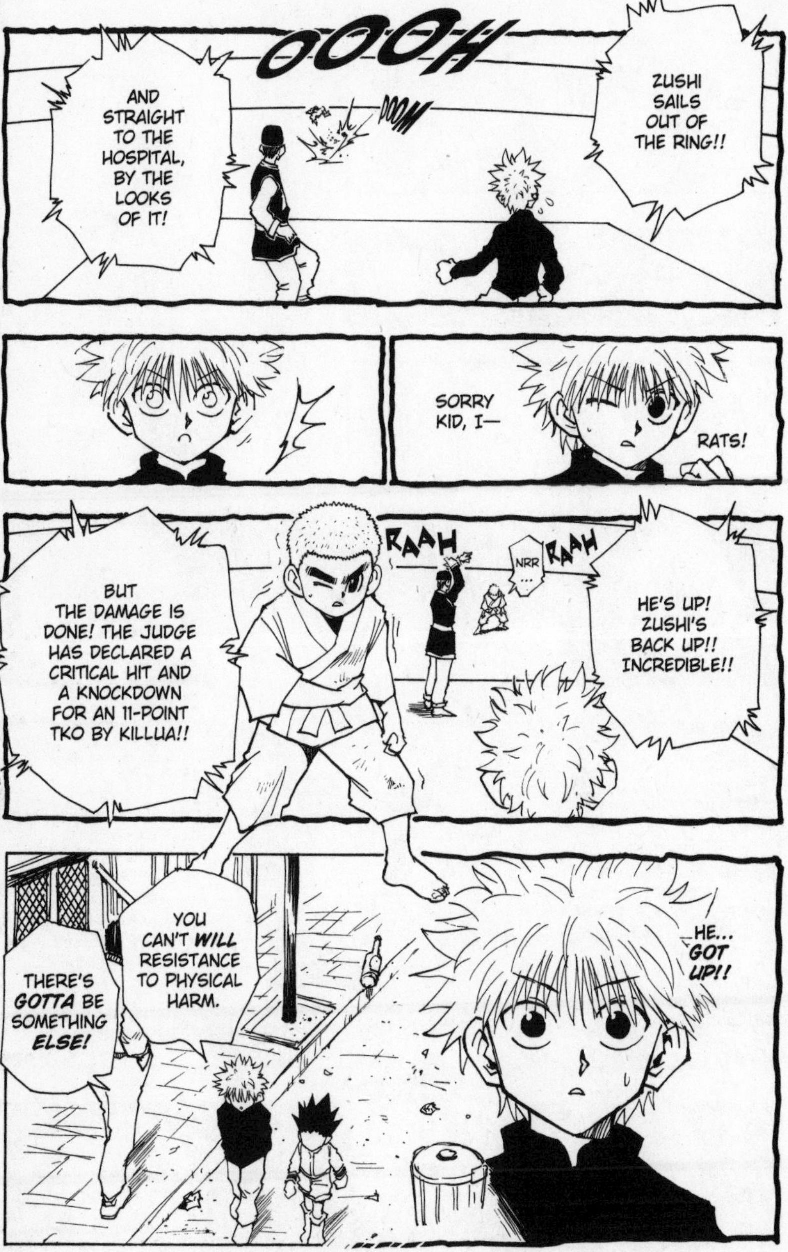
OOOOH
ZUSHI SAILS OUT OF THE RING!!
DOOM
AND STRAIGHT TO THE HOSPITAL, BY THE LOOKS OF IT!
SORRY KID, I—
RATS!
HE'S UP! ZUSHI'S BACK UP!! INCREDIBLE!!
RAAH
NRR ...
RAAH
BUT THE DAMAGE IS DONE! THE JUDGE HAS DECLARED A CRITICAL HIT AND A KNOCKDOWN FOR AN 11-POINT TKO BY KILLUA!!
HE... GOT UP!!
YOU CAN'T WILL RESISTANCE TO PHYSICAL HARM.
THERE'S GOTTA BE SOMETHING ELSE!

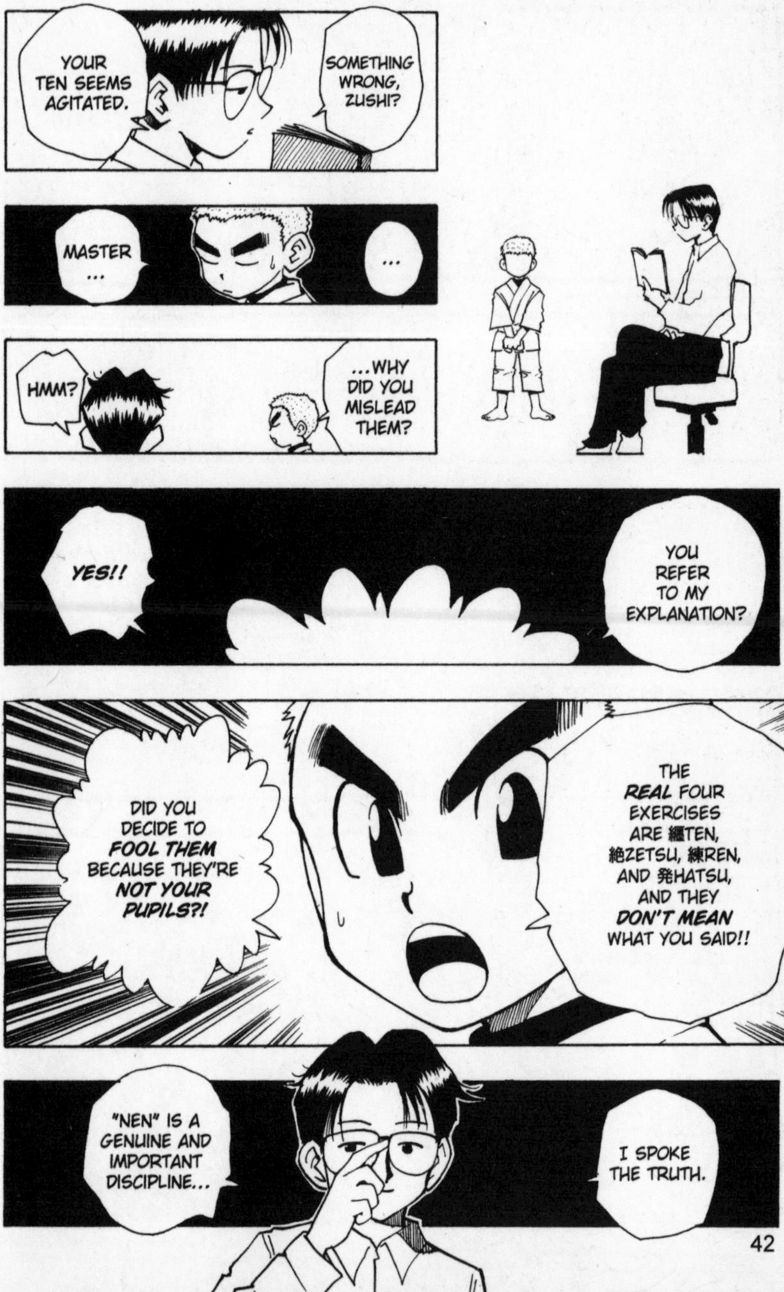

SOMETHING WRONG, ZUSHI?
YOUR TEN SEEMS AGITATED.
...
MASTER ...
...WHY DID YOU MISLEAD THEM?
HMM?
YOU REFER TO MY EXPLANATION?
YES!!
THE REAL FOUR EXERCISES ARE 纏TEN, 絶ZETSU, 練REN, AND 発HATSU, AND THEY DON'T MEAN WHAT YOU SAID!!
DID YOU DECIDE TO FOOL THEM BECAUSE THEY'RE NOT YOUR PUPILS?!
I SPOKE THE TRUTH.
"NEN" IS A GENUINE AND IMPORTANT DISCIPLINE...

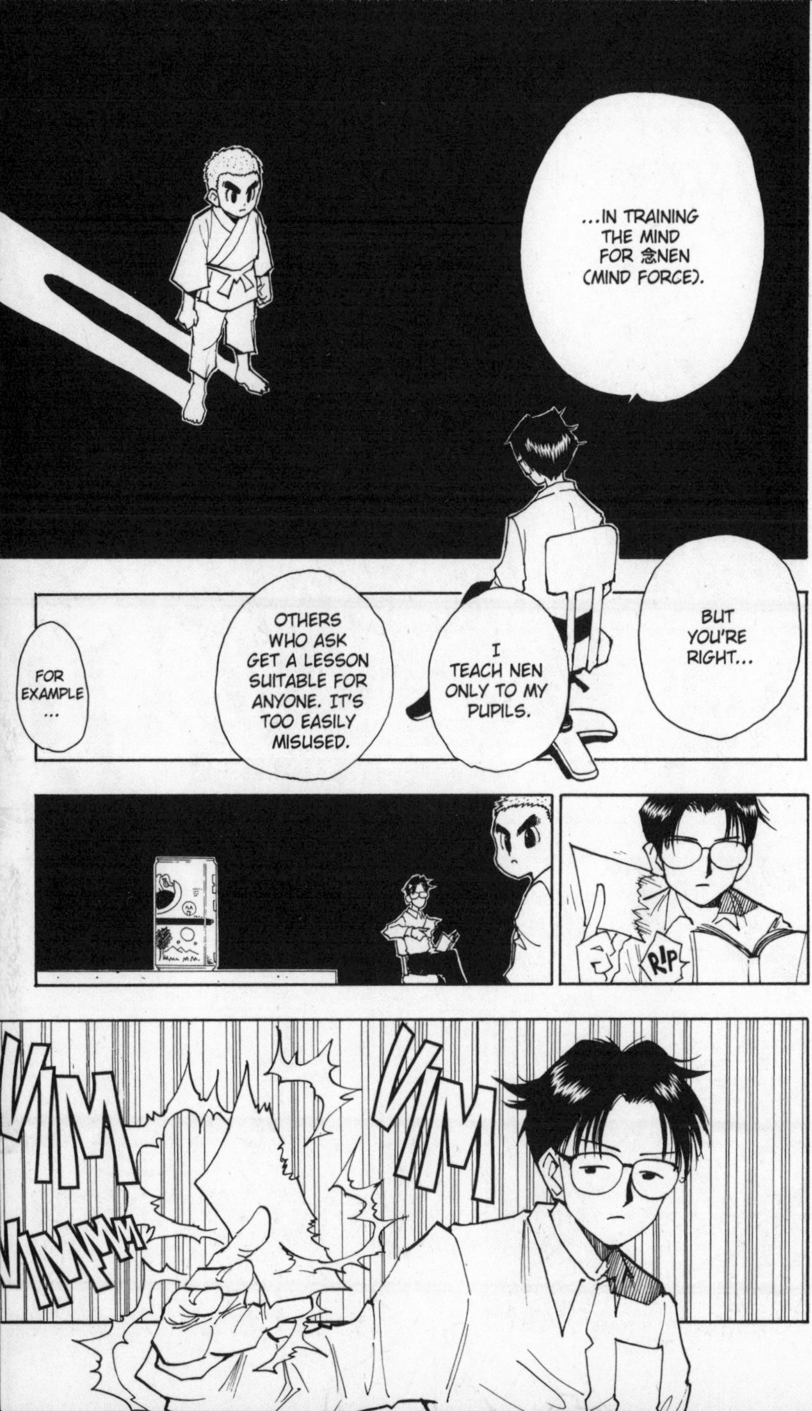
...IN TRAINING THE MIND FOR 念NEN (MIND FORCE).
BUT YOU'RE RIGHT...
I TEACH NEN ONLY TO MY PUPILS.
OTHERS WHO ASK GET A LESSON SUITABLE FOR ANYONE. IT'S TOO EASILY MISUSED.
FOR EXAMPLE ...
RIP
VIM
VIM
VIMMM

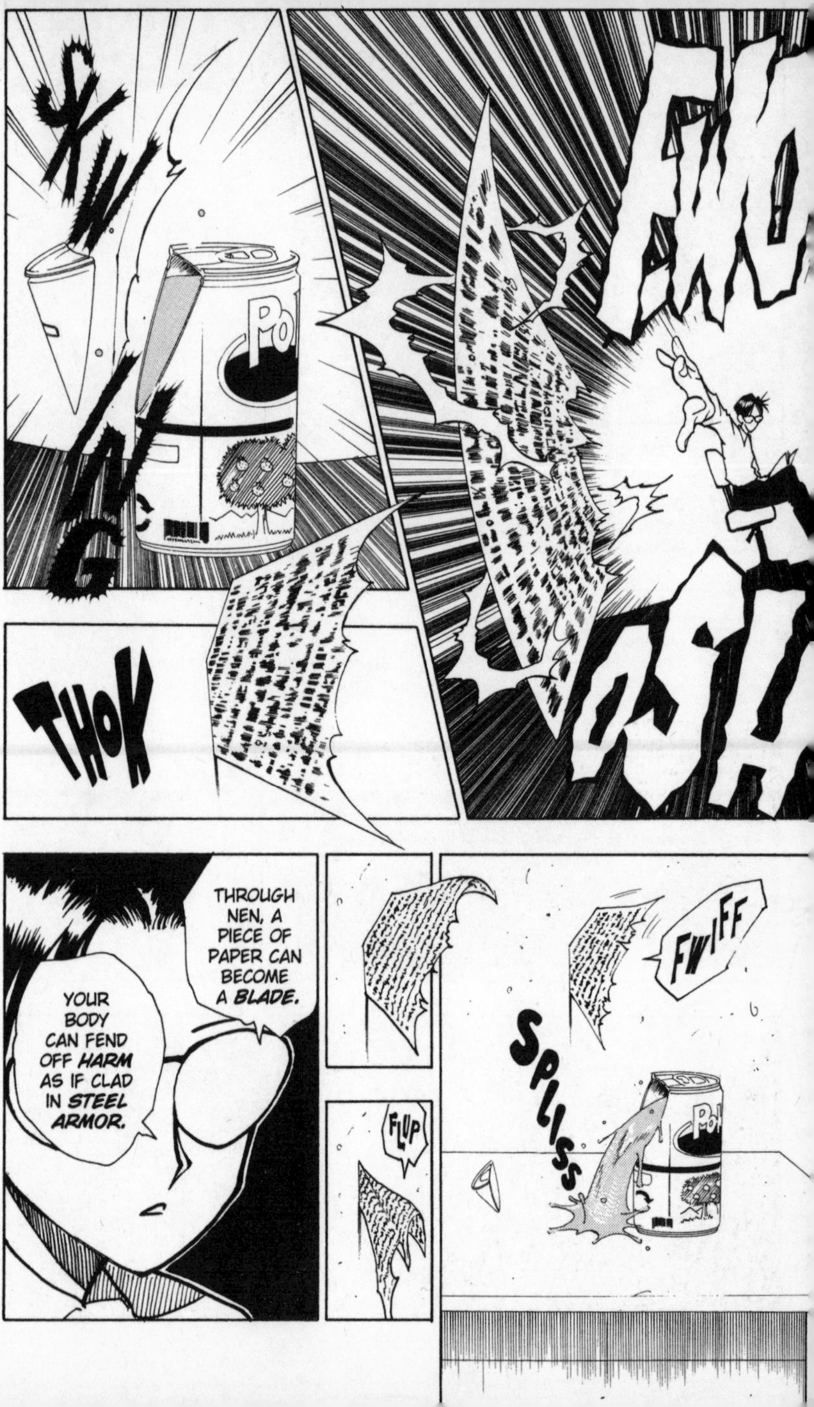
SKWANG
THOK
FWIFF
SPLISS
FLUP
THROUGH NEN, A PIECE OF PAPER CAN BECOME A *BLADE.*
YOUR BODY CAN FEND OFF *HARM* AS IF CLAD IN *STEEL ARMOR.*

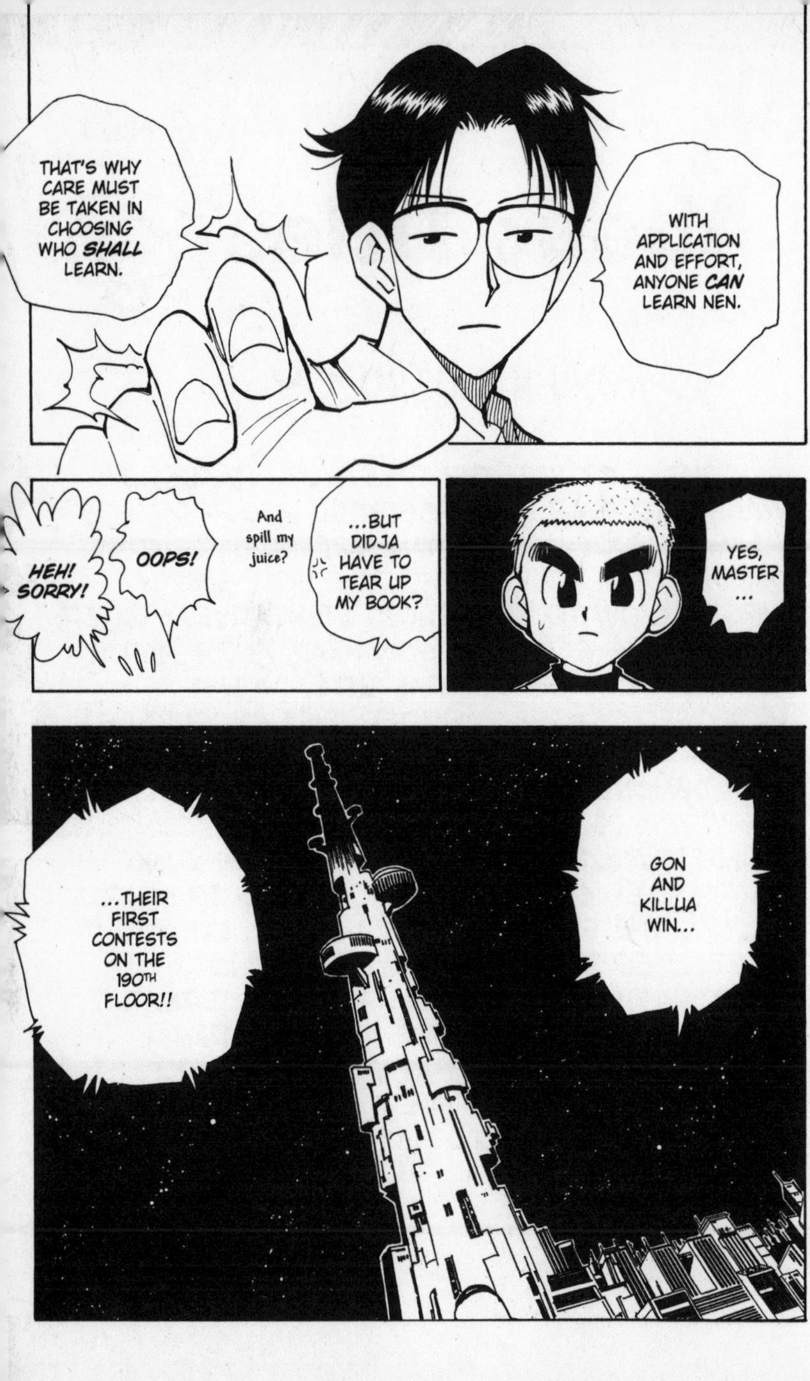
WITH APPLICATION AND EFFORT, ANYONE CAN LEARN NEN.
THAT'S WHY CARE MUST BE TAKEN IN CHOOSING WHO SHALL LEARN.
YES, MASTER ...
...BUT DIDJA HAVE TO TEAR UP MY BOOK?
And spill my juice?
OOPS!
HEH! SORRY!
GON AND KILLUA WIN...
...THEIR FIRST CONTESTS ON THE 190TH FLOOR!!

About Titles

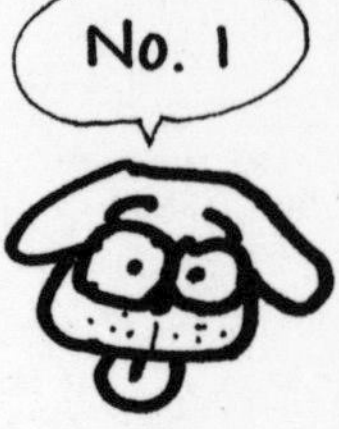
No. 1

~ YUYU HAKUSHO ~

COMING UP WITH THE TITLE "YUYU HAKUSHO" WASN'T SO SIMPLE. I PRESENTED ROUGH DRAFTS TO MY EDITORS AT PLANNING MEETINGS. I HADN'T DECIDED ON A TITLE AT THE TIME, SO I SIMPLY WROTE, "HOW TO BE A GHOST (TENTATIVE)." LATER, WHEN I WAS GIVEN THE GO-AHEAD, AND I HAD TO COME UP WITH THE OFFICIAL TITLE, I FIRST PROPOSED "YUYU-KI" (POLTERGEIST CHRONICLES). I FIGURED THAT EVENTUALLY THERE'D BE BATTLES WITH DEMONS, SO IT WAS A PLAY ON "JOURNEY TO THE WEST" (SAIYU-KI). BUT MY EDITORS COUNTERED, "THERE'S ANOTHER MANGA CALLED 'CHIN-YU-KI' (CHRONICLES OF THE BIZARRE) SLATED TO START AROUND THE SAME TIME. AND HE CAME UP WITH IT FIRST..." SO I OFFERED "YUYU HAKUSHO" (POLTERGEIST REPORT) AS A HASTY ALTERNATIVE. IT DIDN'T REALLY MATTER IF IT WAS "...DEN (LEGEND)" OR "...MONOGATARI (STORY)," BUT "HAKUSHO" WAS WHAT FIRST CAME TO MY MIND. IT WAS ALL IMPROMPTU INSPIRATION.

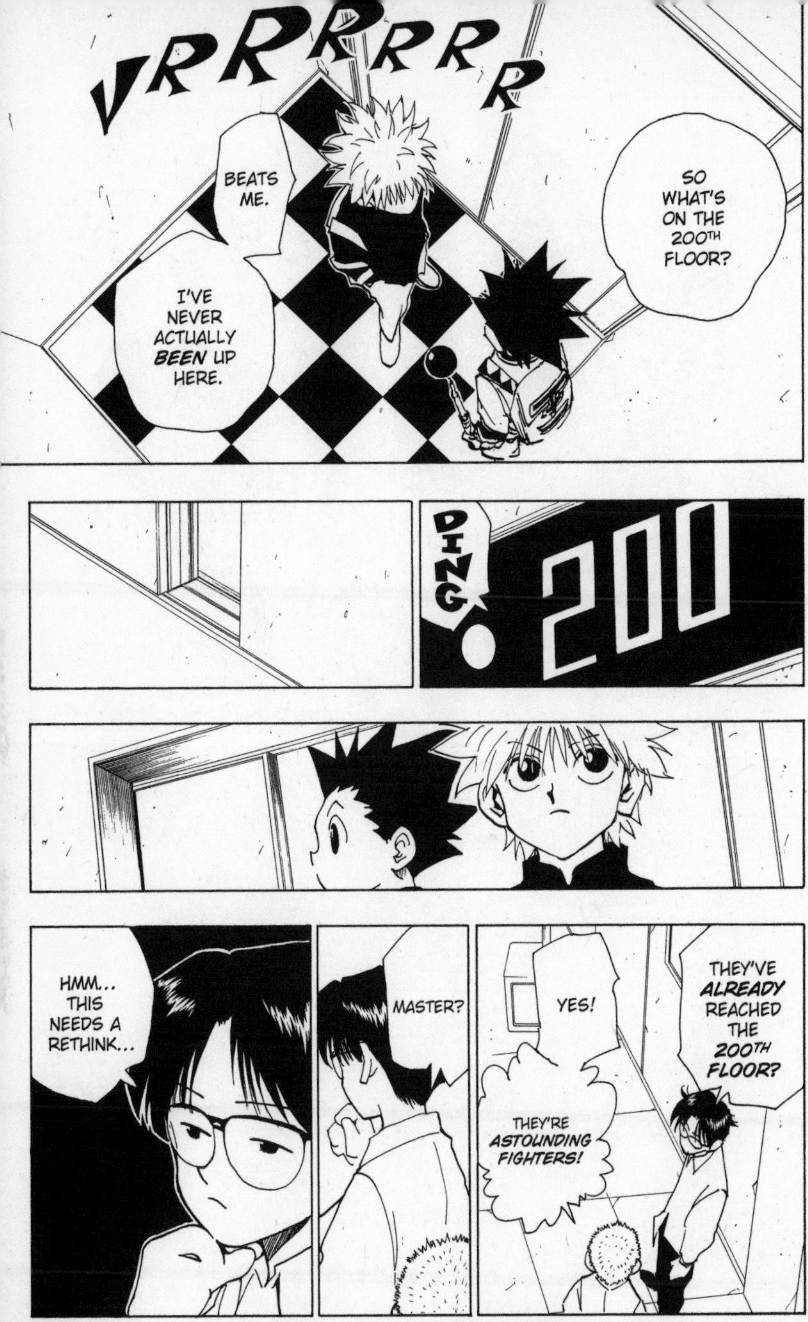
VRRRRRRR
SO WHAT'S ON THE 200TH FLOOR?
BEATS ME.
I'VE NEVER ACTUALLY BEEN UP HERE.
DING
200
THEY'VE ALREADY REACHED THE 200TH FLOOR?
YES!
THEY'RE ASTOUNDING FIGHTERS!
MASTER?
HMM... THIS NEEDS A RETHINK...

Chapter 47 The Invisible Wall

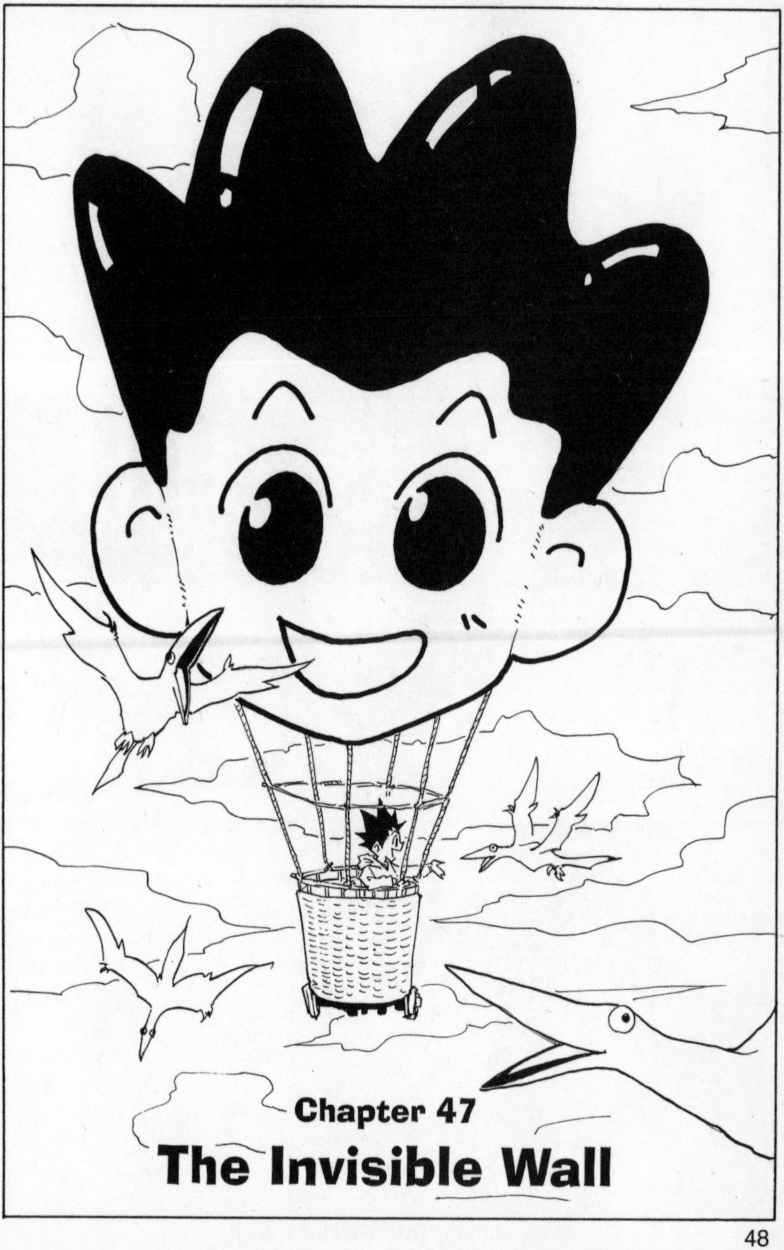

Chapter 47

The Invisible Wall

READ THIS WAY

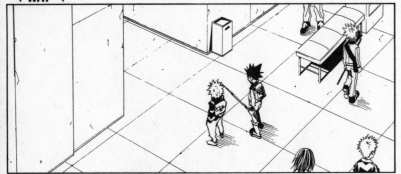

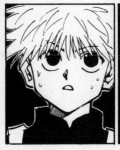

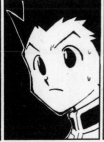

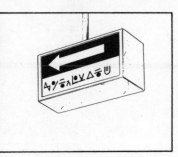

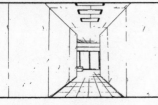

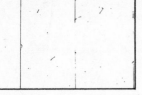

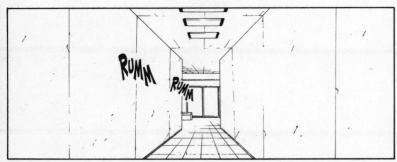

RUMM
RUMM

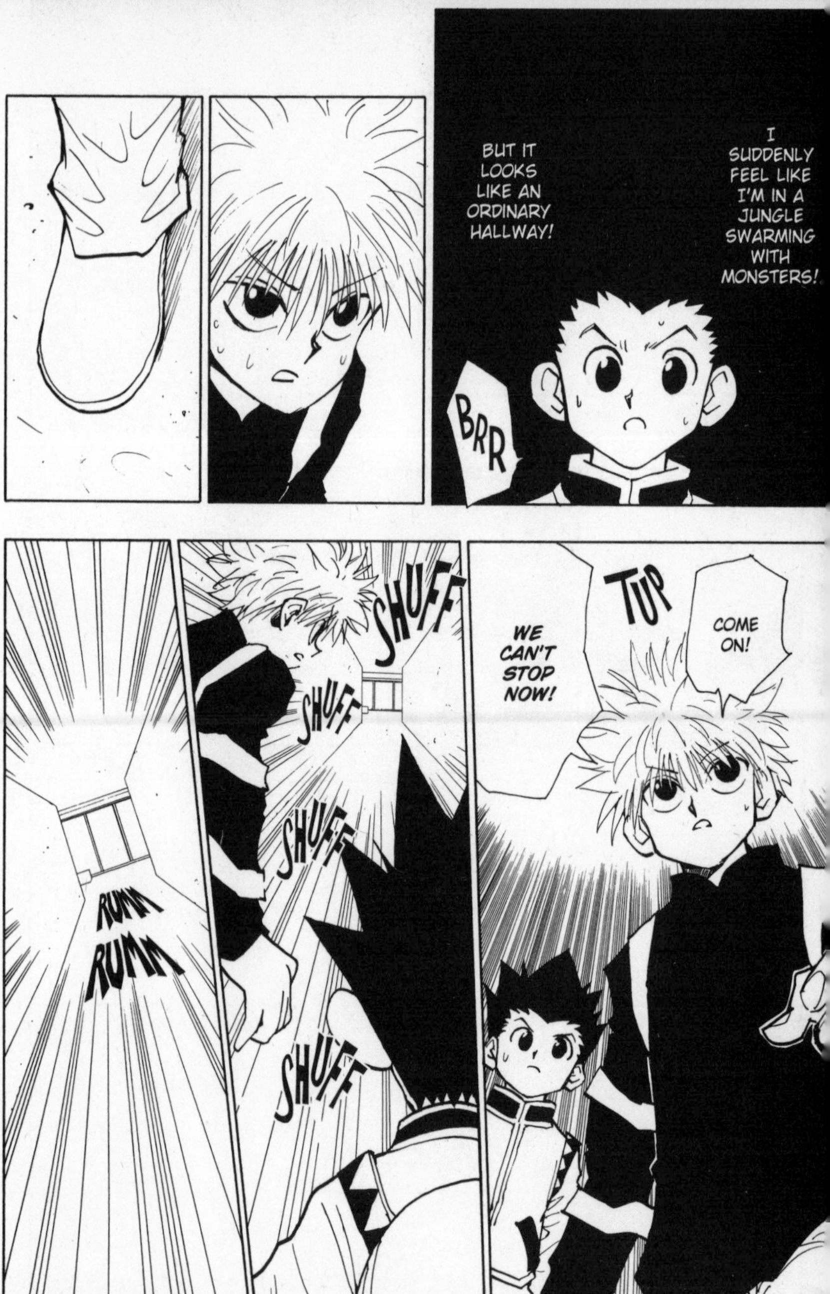
I SUDDENLY FEEL LIKE I'M IN A JUNGLE SWARMING WITH MONSTERS!
BUT IT LOOKS LIKE AN ORDINARY HALLWAY!
BRR
COME ON!
TUP
WE CAN'T STOP NOW!
SHUFF
SHUFF
SHUFF
SHUFF
RUMM
RUMM

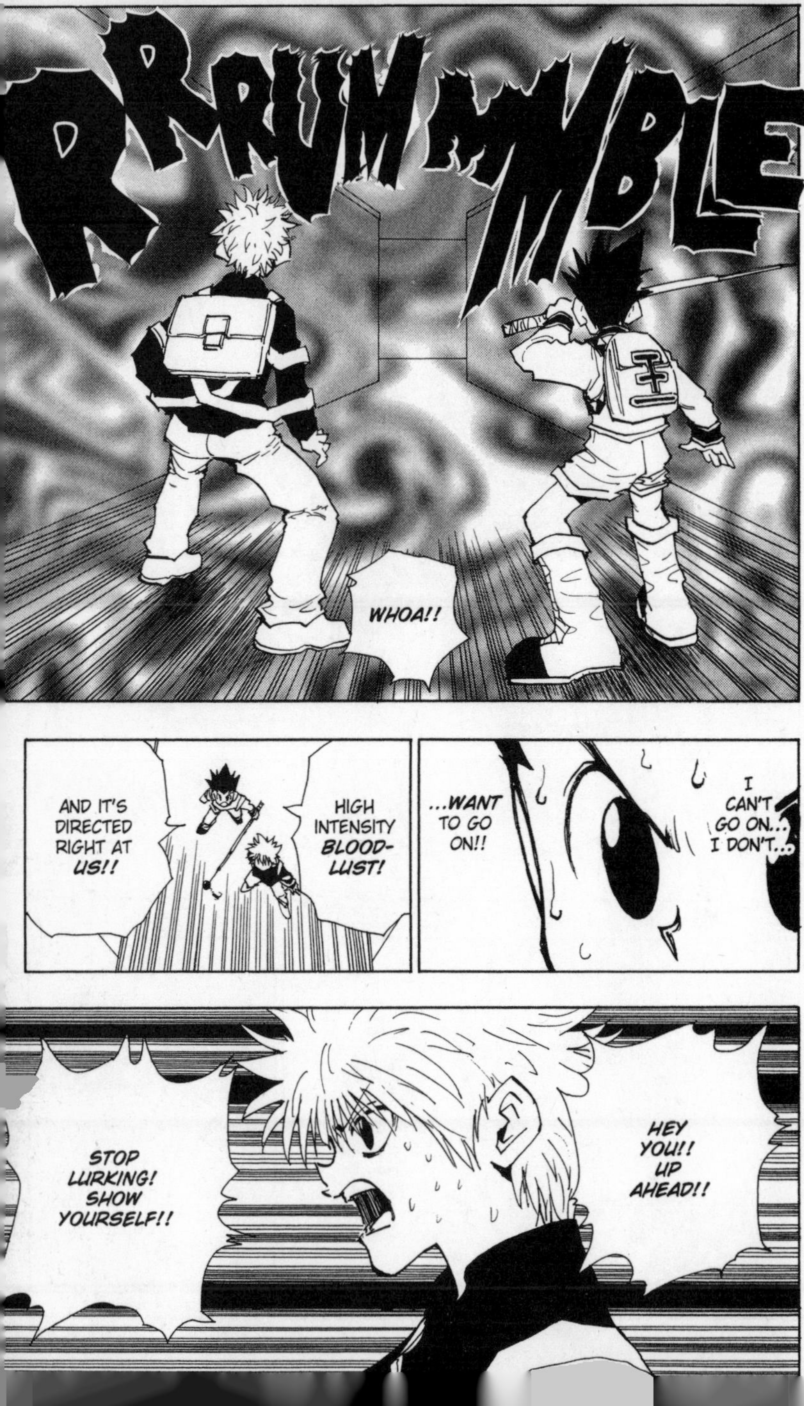
RRRUMMMBLE
WHOA!!
I CAN'T GO ON... I DON'T...
...WANT TO GO ON!!
HIGH INTENSITY BLOOD-LUST!
AND IT'S DIRECTED RIGHT AT US!!
HEY YOU!! UP AHEAD!!
STOP LURKING! SHOW YOURSELF!!

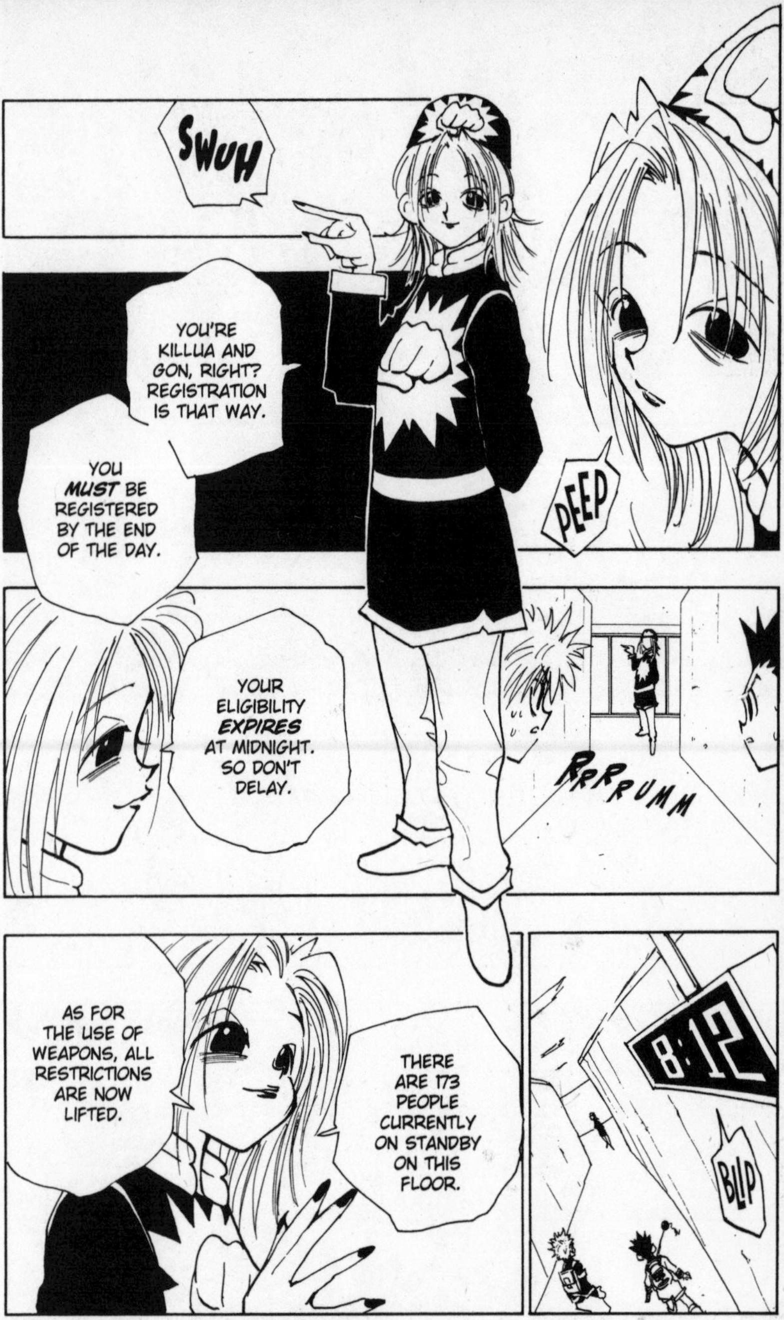
PEEP
SWUH
YOU'RE KILLUA AND GON, RIGHT? REGISTRATION IS THAT WAY.
YOU **MUST** BE REGISTERED BY THE END OF THE DAY.
RRRRUMM
YOUR ELIGIBILITY **EXPIRES** AT MIDNIGHT. SO DON'T DELAY.
8:12
BLIP
THERE ARE 173 PEOPLE CURRENTLY ON STANDBY ON THIS FLOOR.
AS FOR THE USE OF WEAPONS, ALL RESTRICTIONS ARE NOW LIFTED.

READ THIS WAY

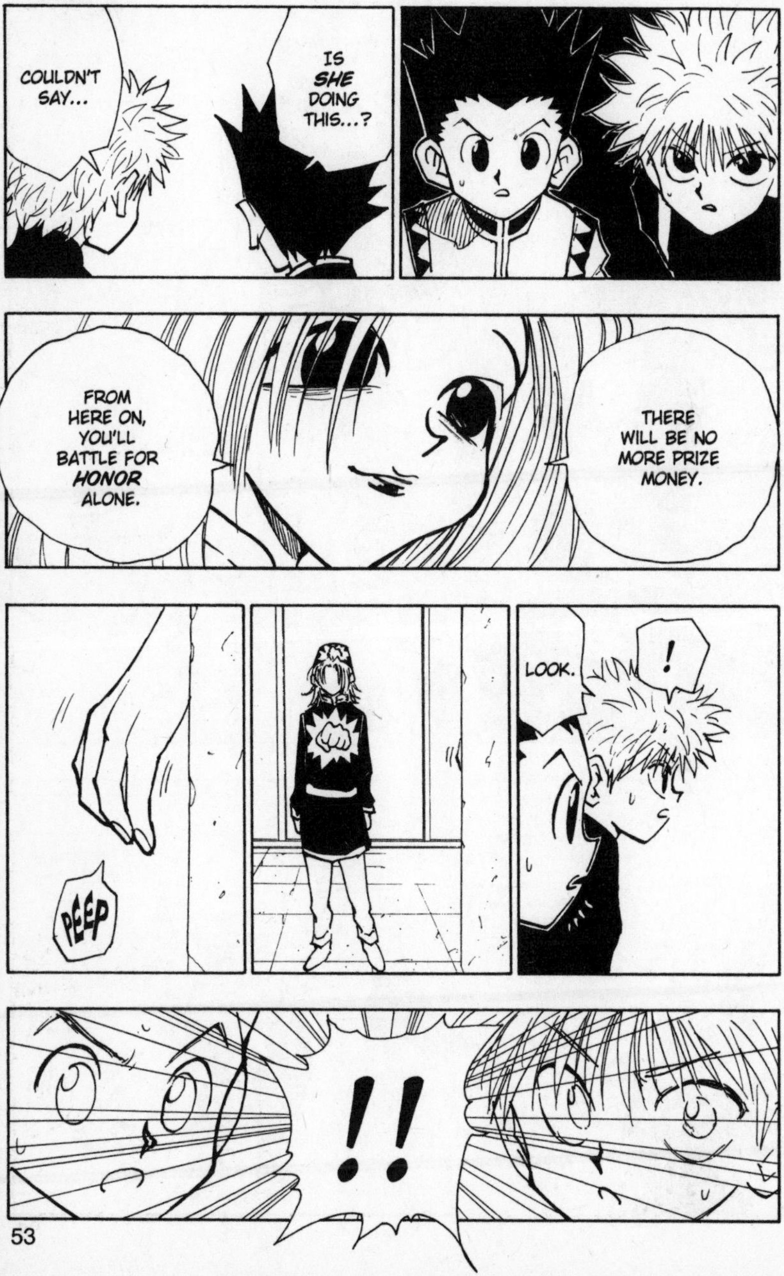
IS *SHE* DOING THIS...?
COULDN'T SAY...
THERE WILL BE NO MORE PRIZE MONEY.
FROM HERE ON, YOU'LL BATTLE FOR *HONOR* ALONE.
!
LOOK.
PEEP
!!

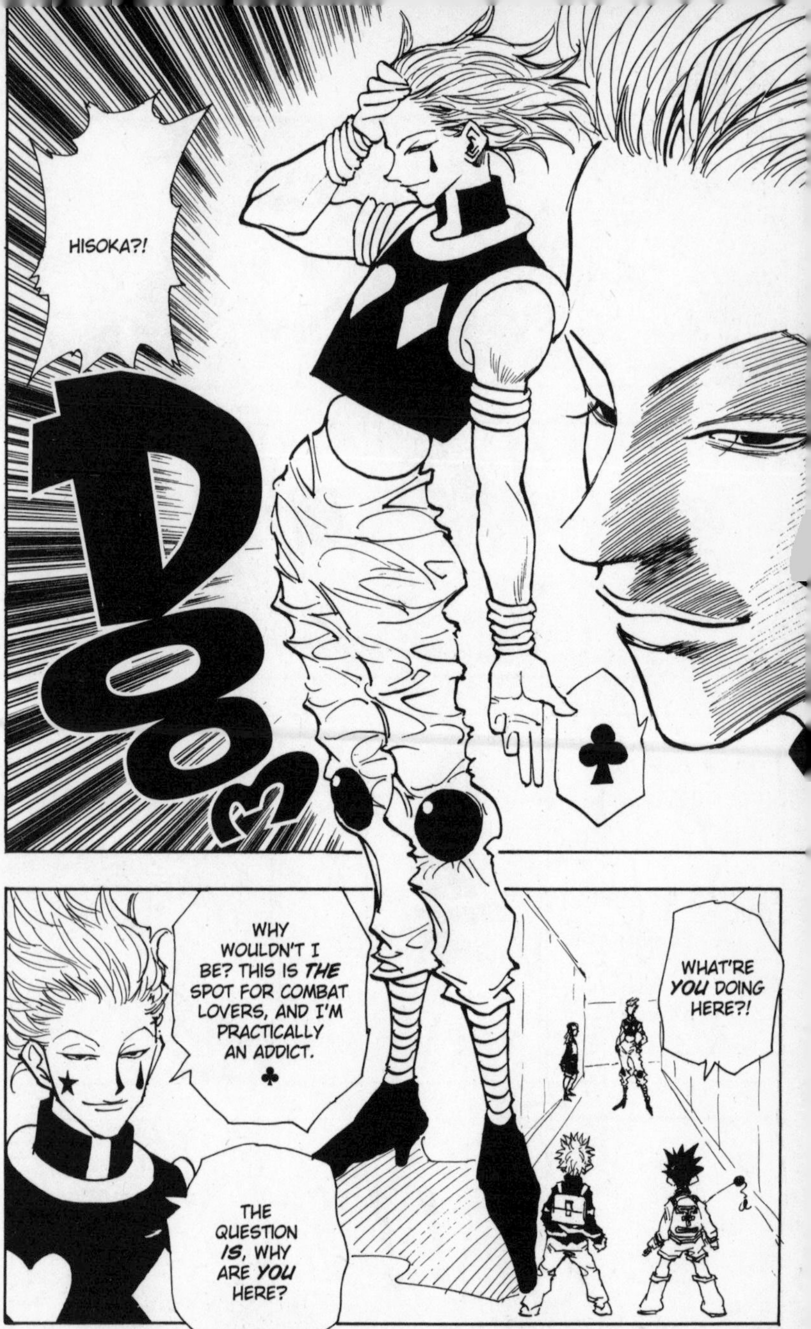
HISOKA?!
DOOM
WHAT'RE *YOU* DOING HERE?!
WHY WOULDN'T I BE? THIS IS *THE* SPOT FOR COMBAT LOVERS, AND I'M PRACTICALLY AN ADDICT. ♣
THE QUESTION *IS*, WHY ARE *YOU* HERE?

READ THIS WAY

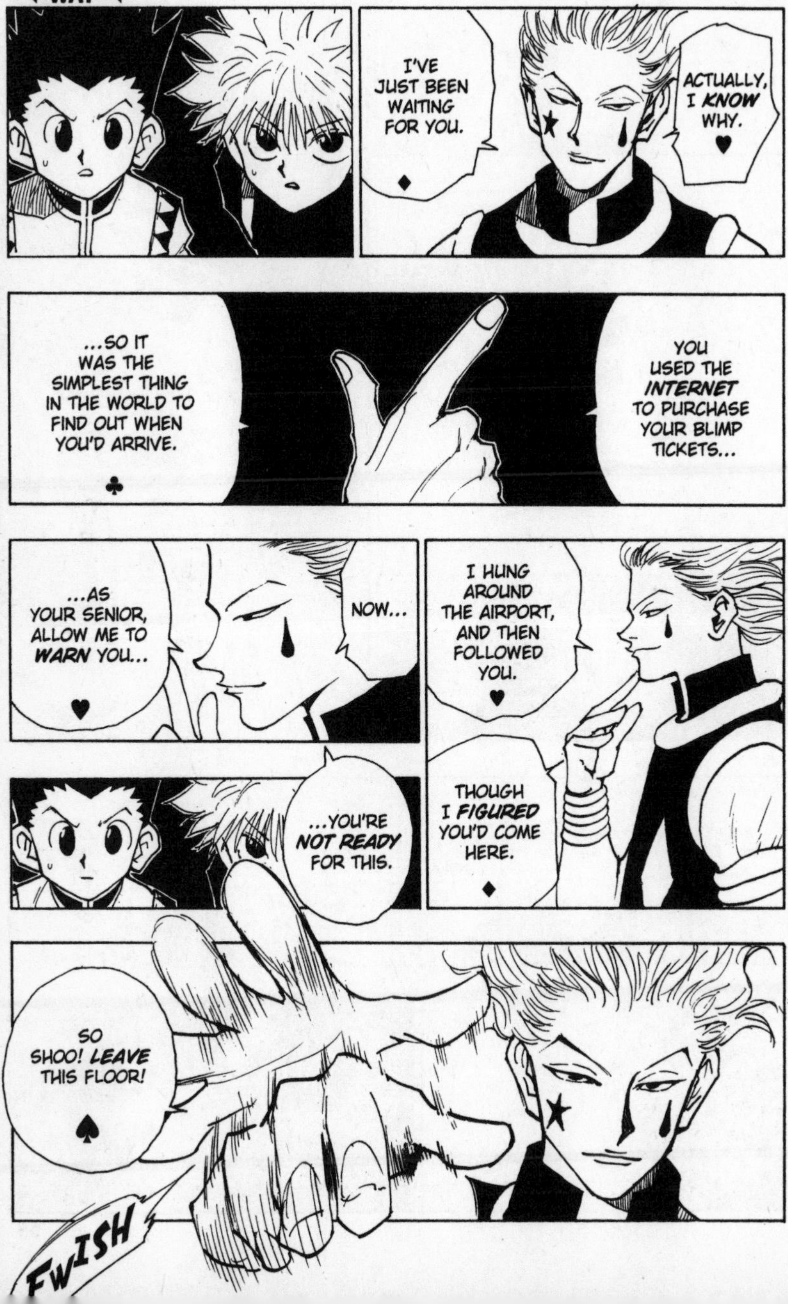
ACTUALLY, I *KNOW* WHY. ♥
I'VE JUST BEEN WAITING FOR YOU. ♦
YOU USED THE *INTERNET* TO PURCHASE YOUR BLIMP TICKETS...
...SO IT WAS THE SIMPLEST THING IN THE WORLD TO FIND OUT WHEN YOU'D ARRIVE. ♣
I HUNG AROUND THE AIRPORT, AND THEN FOLLOWED YOU. ♥
THOUGH I *FIGURED* YOU'D COME HERE. ♦
NOW...
...AS YOUR SENIOR, ALLOW ME TO *WARN* YOU... ♥
...YOU'RE *NOT READY* FOR THIS.
SO SHOO! *LEAVE* THIS FLOOR! ♠
FWISH

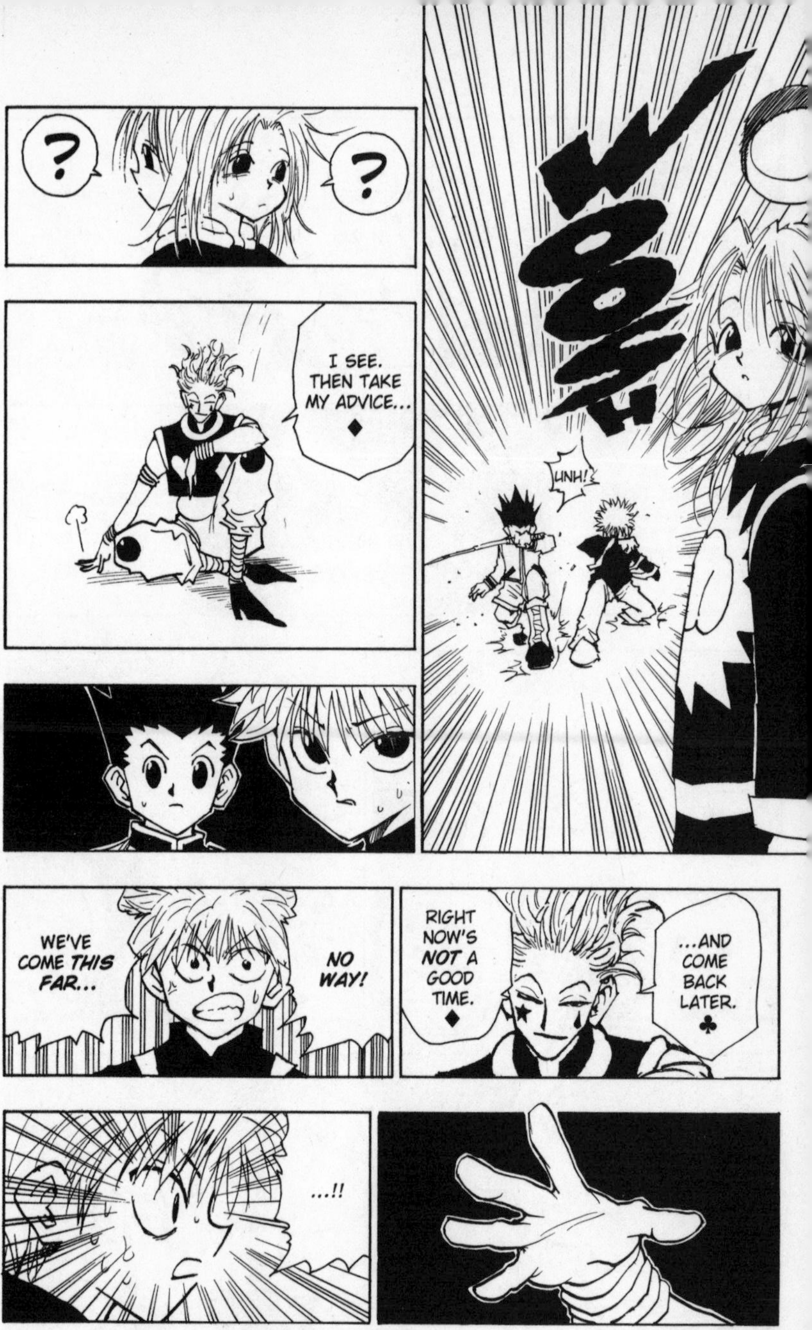
WOOSH
UNH!
?
?
I SEE. THEN TAKE MY ADVICE... ◆
RIGHT NOW'S NOT A GOOD TIME. ◆
...AND COME BACK LATER. ♣
NO WAY!
WE'VE COME THIS FAR...
...!!

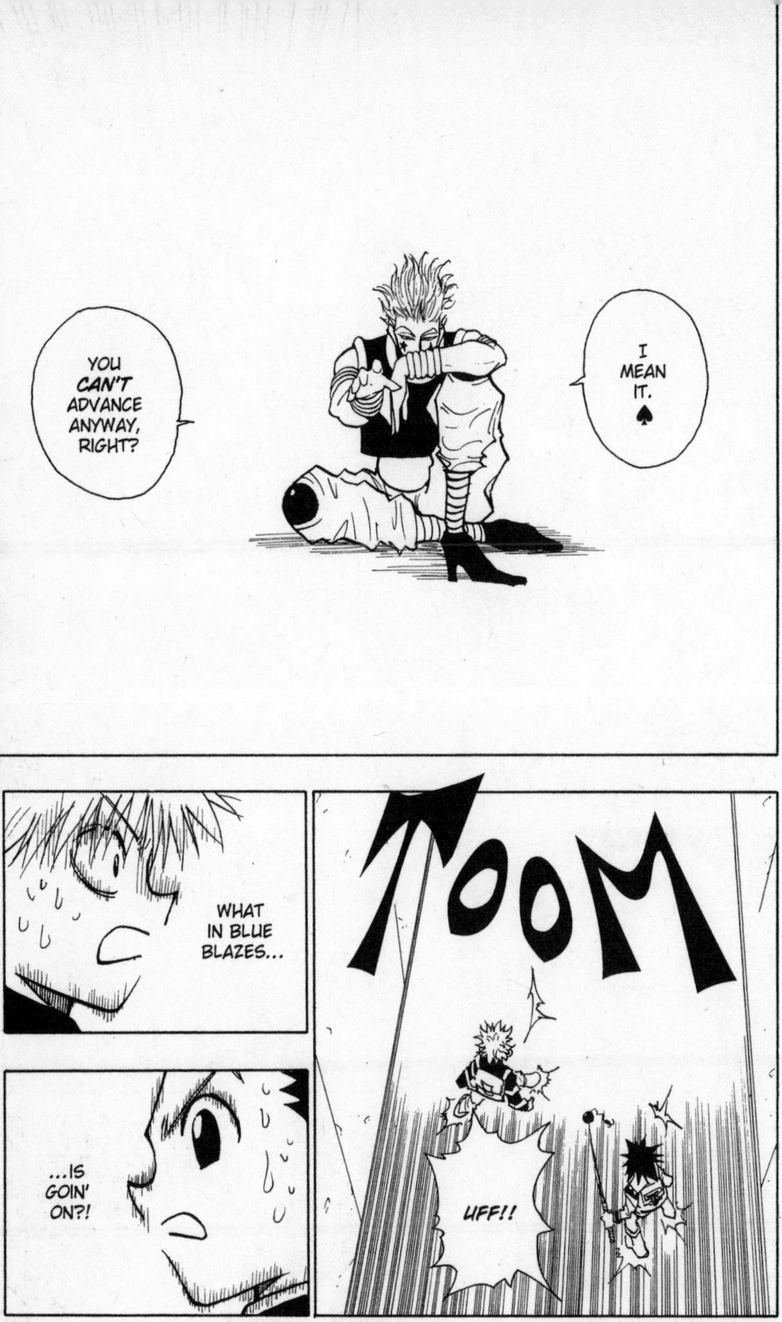
I MEAN IT. ♠
YOU *CAN'T* ADVANCE ANYWAY, RIGHT?
TOOM
UFF!!
WHAT IN BLUE BLAZES...
...IS GOIN' ON?!

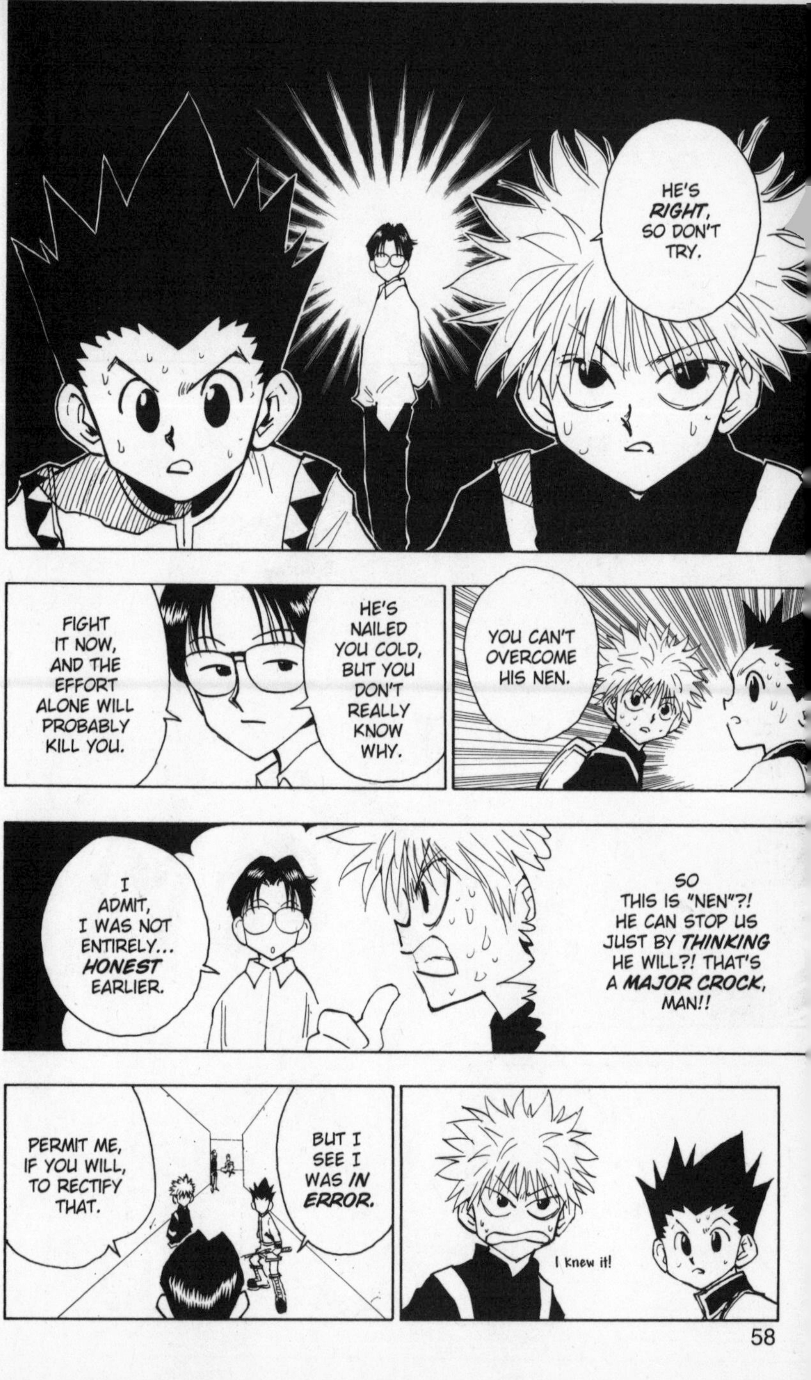

HE'S RIGHT, SO DON'T TRY.
YOU CAN'T OVERCOME HIS NEN.
HE'S NAILED YOU COLD, BUT YOU DON'T REALLY KNOW WHY.
FIGHT IT NOW, AND THE EFFORT ALONE WILL PROBABLY KILL YOU.
SO THIS IS "NEN"?! HE CAN STOP US JUST BY THINKING HE WILL?! THAT'S A MAJOR CROCK, MAN!!
I ADMIT, I WAS NOT ENTIRELY... HONEST EARLIER.
I knew it!
BUT I SEE I WAS IN ERROR.
PERMIT ME, IF YOU WILL, TO RECTIFY THAT.

READ THIS WAY

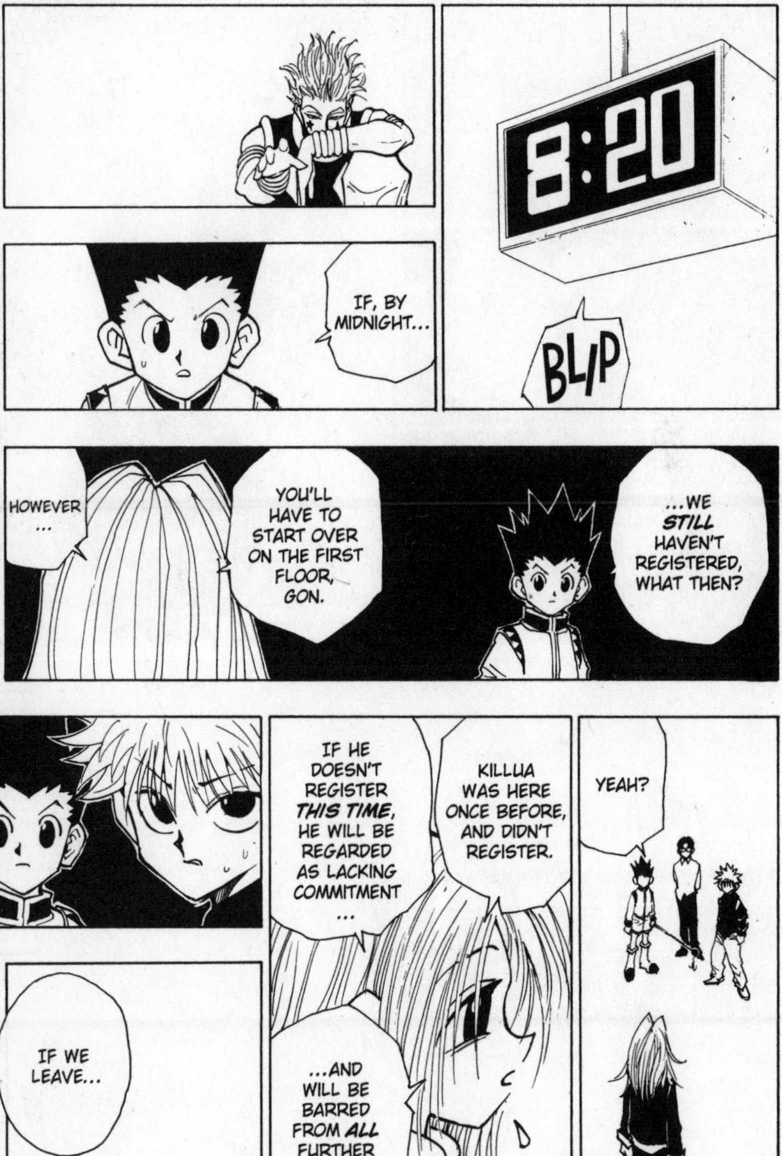
8:20
BLIP
IF, BY MIDNIGHT...
...WE STILL HAVEN'T REGISTERED, WHAT THEN?
YOU'LL HAVE TO START OVER ON THE FIRST FLOOR, GON.
HOWEVER ...
YEAH?
KILLUA WAS HERE ONCE BEFORE, AND DIDN'T REGISTER.
IF HE DOESN'T REGISTER THIS TIME, HE WILL BE REGARDED AS LACKING COMMITMENT ...
...AND WILL BE BARRED FROM ALL FURTHER COMBAT.
IF WE LEAVE...

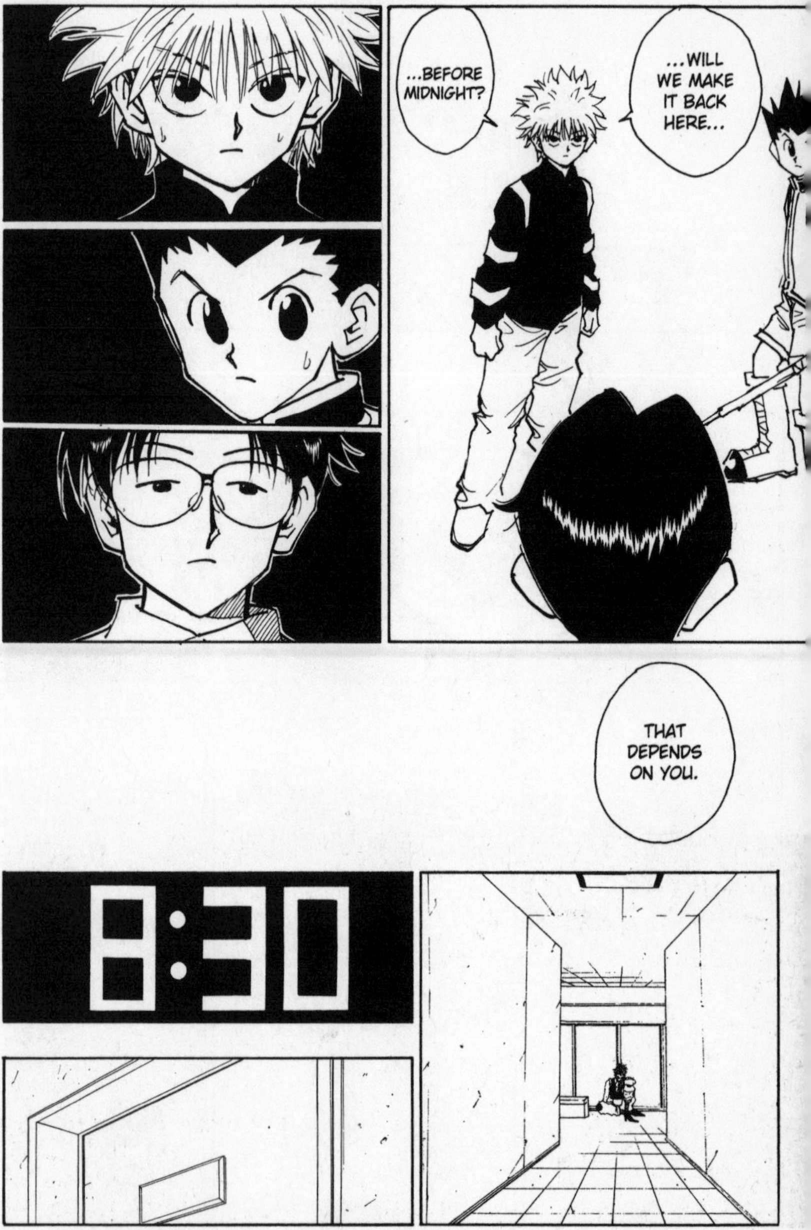
...WILL WE MAKE IT BACK HERE...
...BEFORE MIDNIGHT?
THAT DEPENDS ON YOU.
8:30

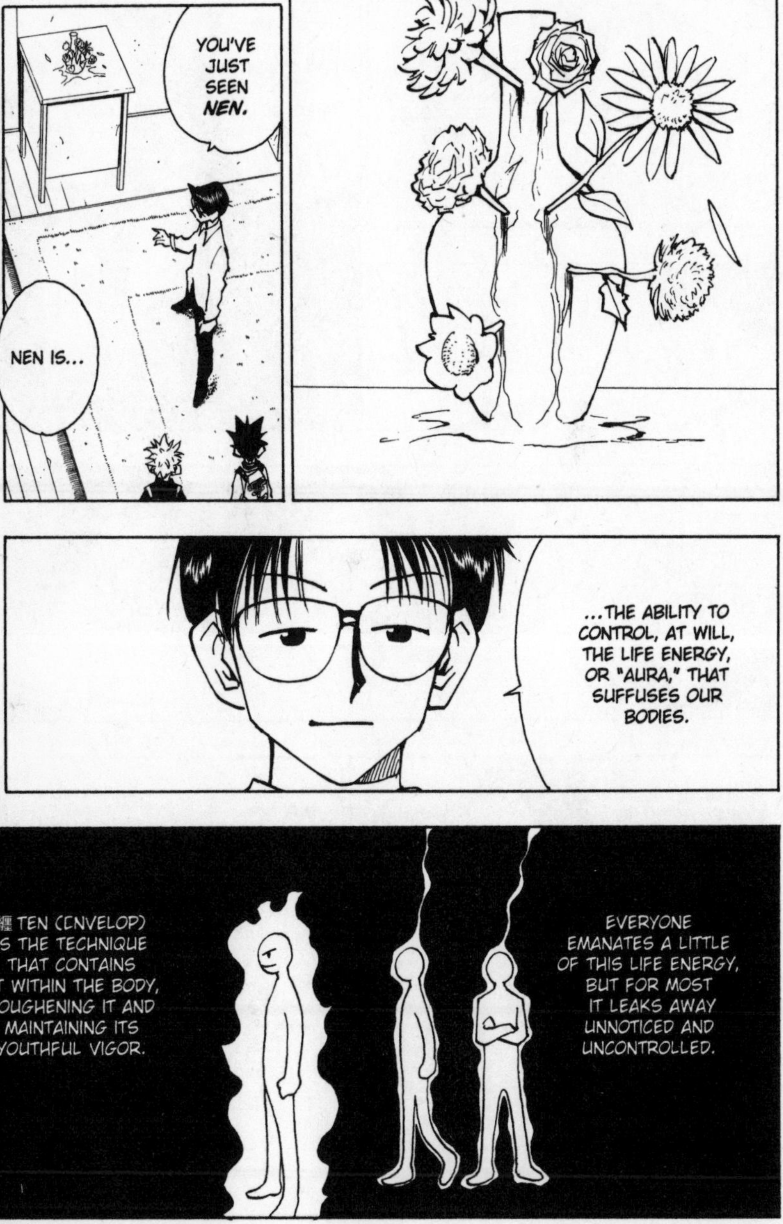

YOU'VE JUST SEEN **NEN.**
NEN IS...
...THE ABILITY TO CONTROL, AT WILL, THE LIFE ENERGY, OR "AURA," THAT SUFFUSES OUR BODIES.
EVERYONE EMANATES A LITTLE OF THIS LIFE ENERGY, BUT FOR MOST IT LEAKS AWAY UNNOTICED AND UNCONTROLLED.
纏 TEN (ENVELOP) IS THE TECHNIQUE THAT CONTAINS IT WITHIN THE BODY, TOUGHENING IT AND MAINTAINING ITS YOUTHFUL VIGOR.

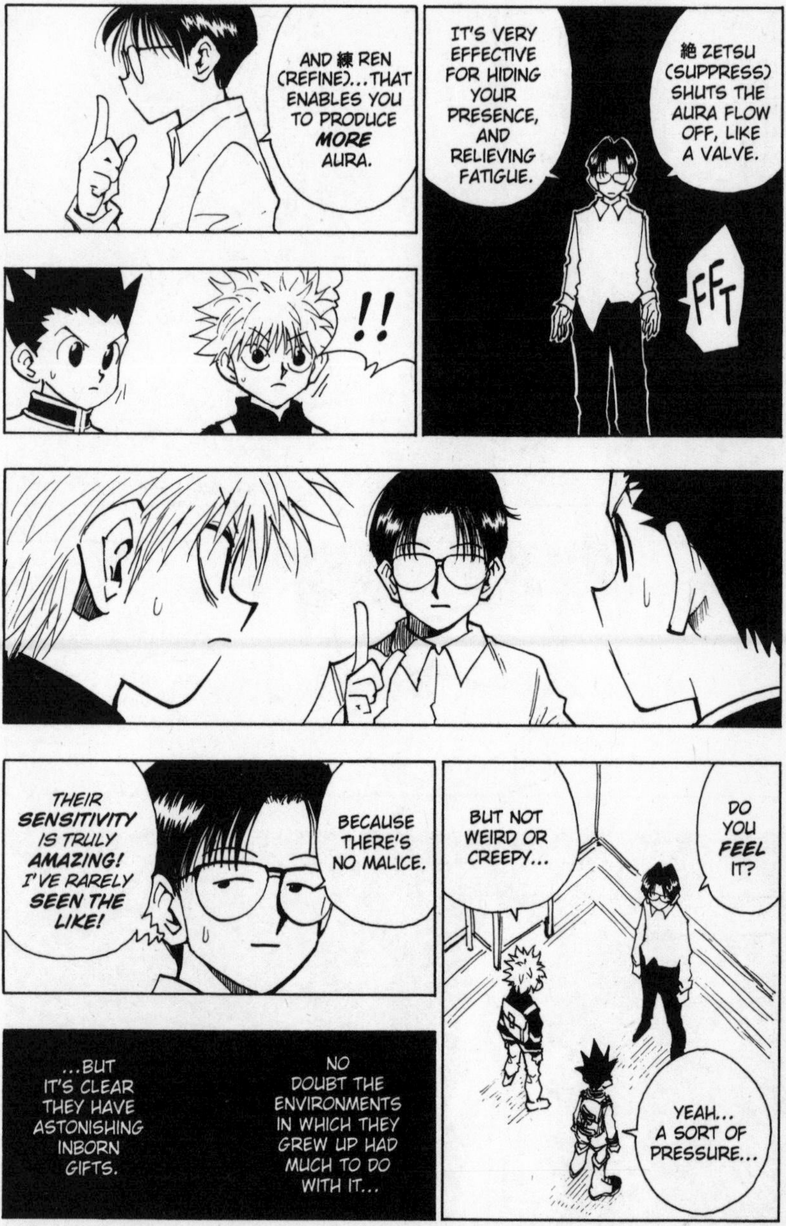
絶 ZETSU (SUPPRESS) SHUTS THE AURA FLOW OFF, LIKE A VALVE.
IT'S VERY EFFECTIVE FOR HIDING YOUR PRESENCE, AND RELIEVING FATIGUE.
FFT
AND 練 REN (REFINE)...THAT ENABLES YOU TO PRODUCE ***MORE*** AURA.
!!
DO YOU ***FEEL*** IT?
BUT NOT WEIRD OR CREEPY...
YEAH... A SORT OF PRESSURE...
BECAUSE THERE'S NO MALICE.
*THEIR **SENSITIVITY** IS TRULY **AMAZING!** I'VE RARELY **SEEN THE LIKE!***
NO DOUBT THE ENVIRONMENTS IN WHICH THEY GREW UP HAD MUCH TO DO WITH IT...
...BUT IT'S CLEAR THEY HAVE ASTONISHING INBORN GIFTS.

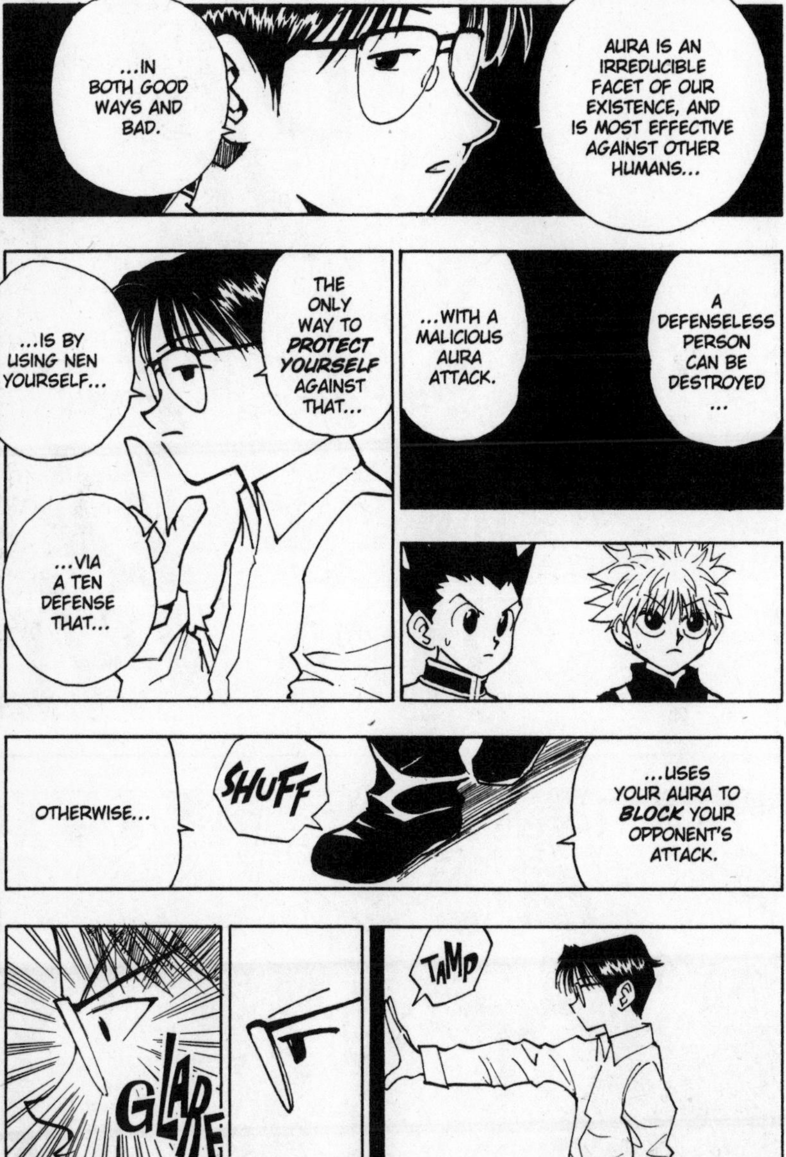
AURA IS AN IRREDUCIBLE FACET OF OUR EXISTENCE, AND IS MOST EFFECTIVE AGAINST OTHER HUMANS...
...IN BOTH GOOD WAYS AND BAD.
A DEFENSELESS PERSON CAN BE DESTROYED ...
...WITH A MALICIOUS AURA ATTACK.
THE ONLY WAY TO PROTECT YOURSELF AGAINST THAT...
...IS BY USING NEN YOURSELF...
...VIA A TEN DEFENSE THAT...
...USES YOUR AURA TO BLOCK YOUR OPPONENT'S ATTACK.
SHUFF
OTHERWISE...
TAMP
GLARE

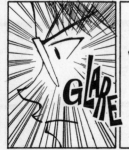

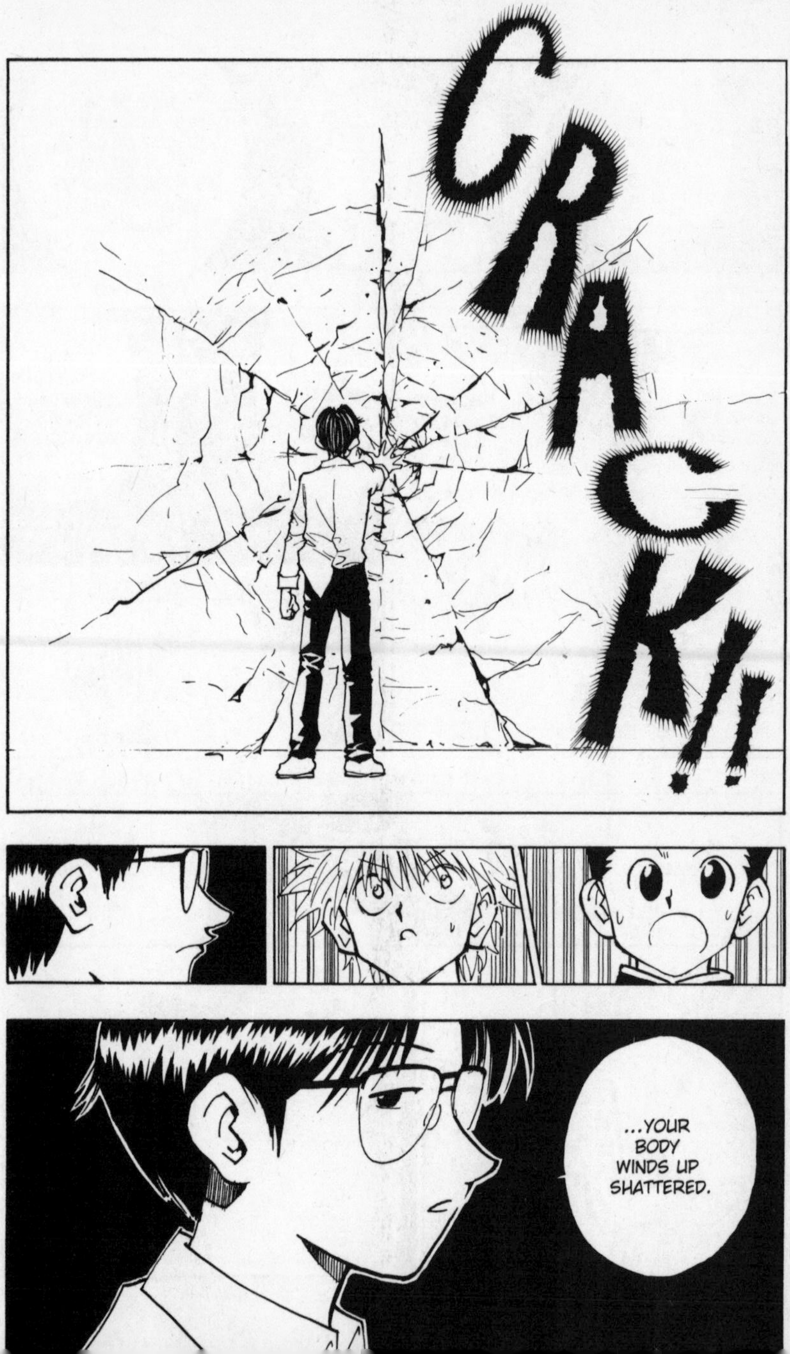
CRACK!!
...YOUR BODY WINDS UP SHATTERED.

READ THIS WAY

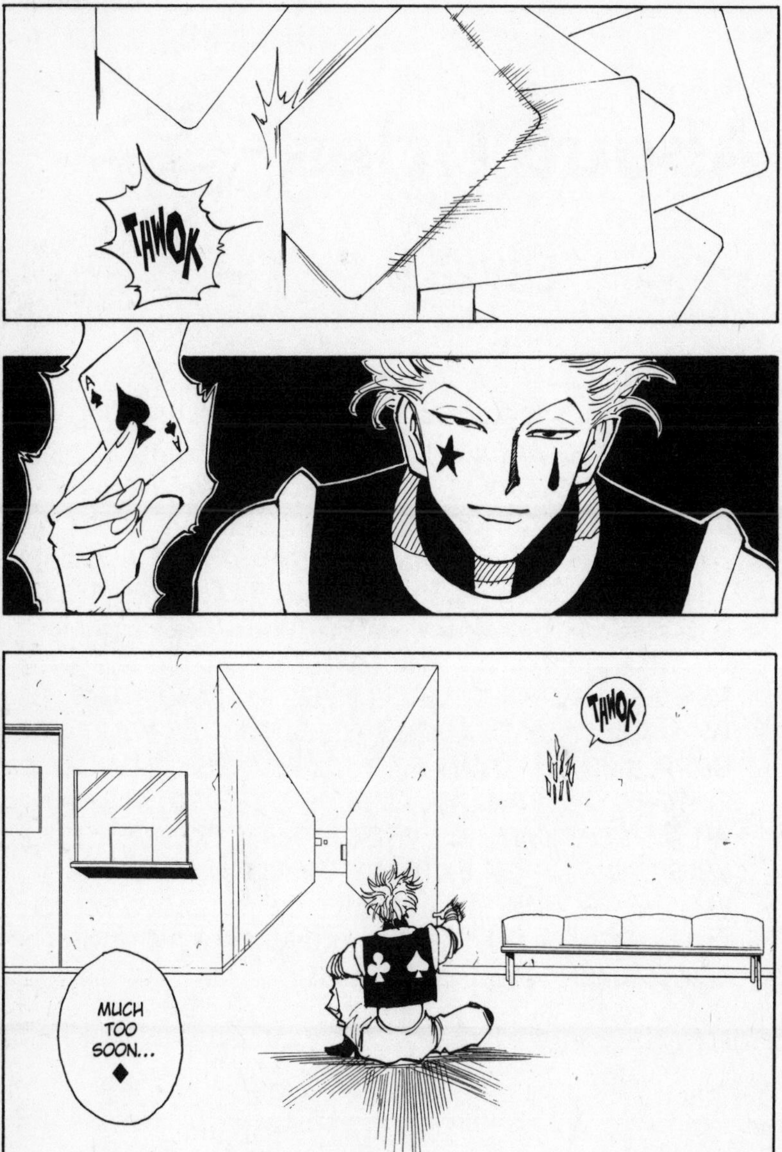
THWOK
THWOK
MUCH TOO SOON... ◆

About Titles

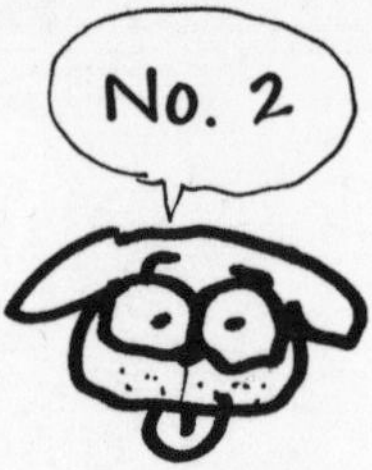
No. 2

~ LEVEL E ~

THIS WASN'T ITS INITIAL TITLE, EITHER. WHEN I GOT THE GO-AHEAD, I ONLY HAD ONE EPISODE'S WORTH OF STORY. I'D PLANNED TO HAVE A DIFFERENT PROTAGONIST EVERY EPISODE (OR EVERY STORY ARC). SINCE IT WAS ABOUT ALIENS, I HAD CALLED IT "ALIEN CRISIS." BUT I WAS TOLD IT SOUNDED TOO STRAIGHTFORWARD, SO I CAME UP WITH "LEVEL E." THE REASON? I'D JUST RENTED A MOVIE TITLED "LEVEL 4". (AND THAT WAS THE ONLY REASON.) ALSO, THE "E" WAS SUPPOSED TO STAND FOR "ALIEN," BUT THEN MY EDITOR POINTED OUT, "ALIEN IS SPELLED WITH AN A." SO I CAME UP WITH A LAME EXCUSE: "I WAS THINKING OF EXTRATERRESTRIAL." BY THE WAY, MY SORRY SKILLS EARN ME 70 OUT OF 200 TOTAL POINTS ON THE JAPANESE FIRST-STAGE ACHIEVEMENT TEST IN ENGLISH.

Chapter 48
Hisoka's Terms

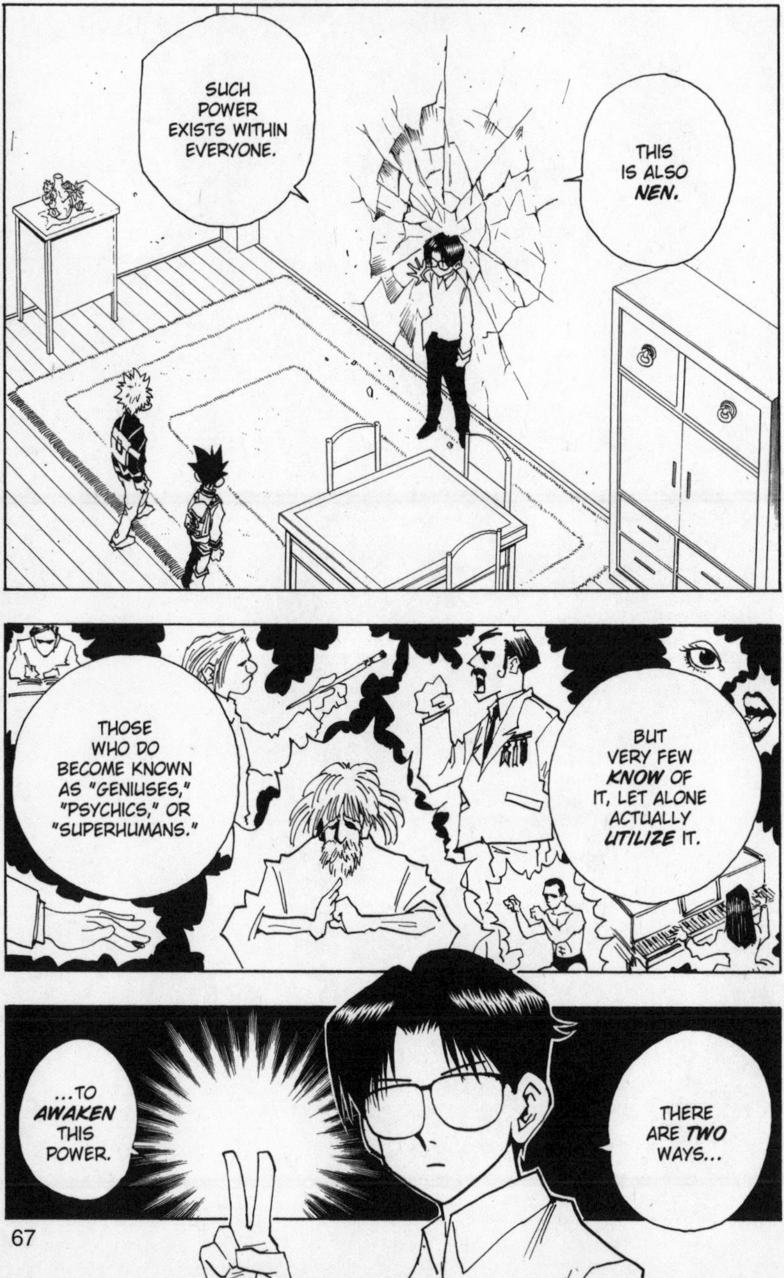
THIS IS ALSO NEN.
SUCH POWER EXISTS WITHIN EVERYONE.
BUT VERY FEW KNOW OF IT, LET ALONE ACTUALLY UTILIZE IT.
THOSE WHO DO BECOME KNOWN AS "GENIUSES," "PSYCHICS," OR "SUPERHUMANS."
THERE ARE TWO WAYS...
...TO AWAKEN THIS POWER.

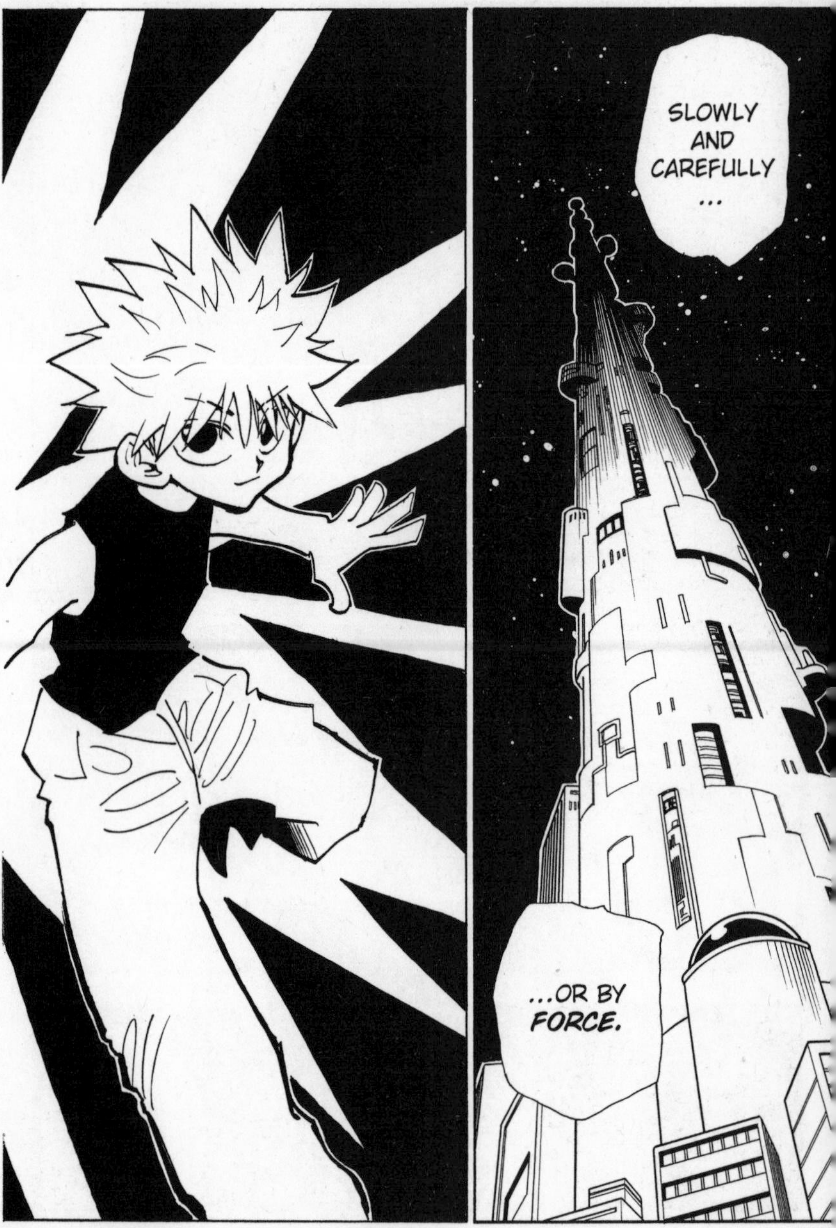
SLOWLY AND CAREFULLY ...
...OR BY FORCE.

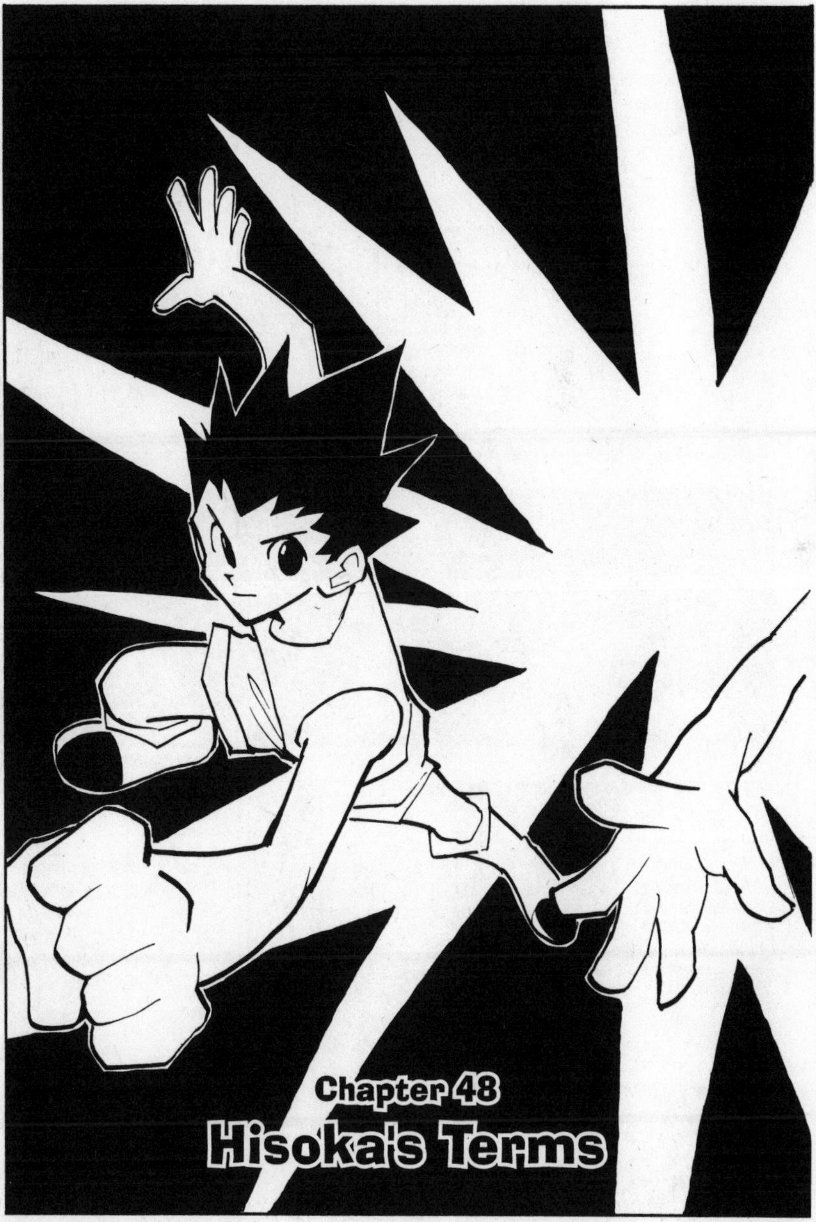
Chapter 48
Hisoka's Terms

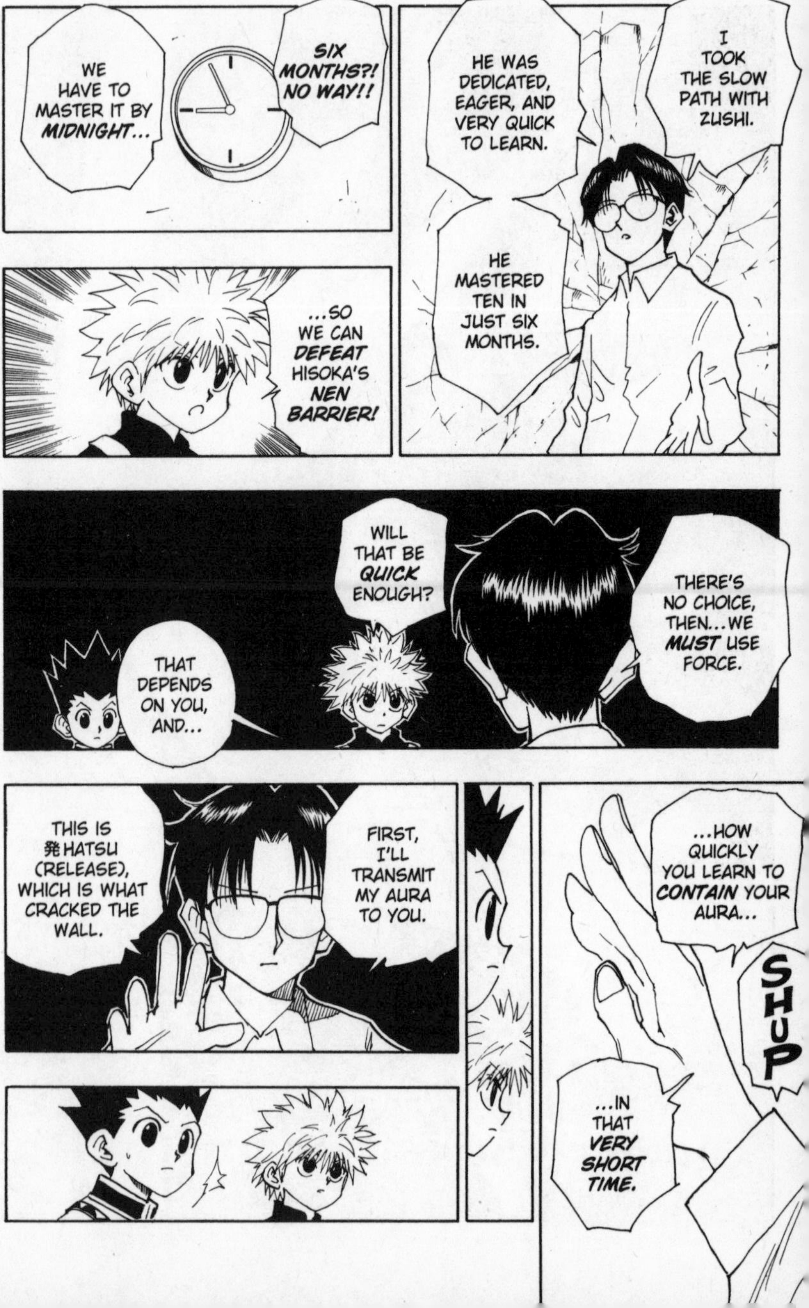
I TOOK THE SLOW PATH WITH ZUSHI.
HE WAS DEDICATED, EAGER, AND VERY QUICK TO LEARN.
HE MASTERED TEN IN JUST SIX MONTHS.
SIX MONTHS?! NO WAY!!
WE HAVE TO MASTER IT BY MIDNIGHT...
...SO WE CAN DEFEAT HISOKA'S NEN BARRIER!
THERE'S NO CHOICE, THEN...WE MUST USE FORCE.
WILL THAT BE QUICK ENOUGH?
THAT DEPENDS ON YOU, AND...
...HOW QUICKLY YOU LEARN TO CONTAIN YOUR AURA...
SHUP
...IN THAT VERY SHORT TIME.
FIRST, I'LL TRANSMIT MY AURA TO YOU.
THIS IS 発 HATSU (RELEASE), WHICH IS WHAT CRACKED THE WALL.

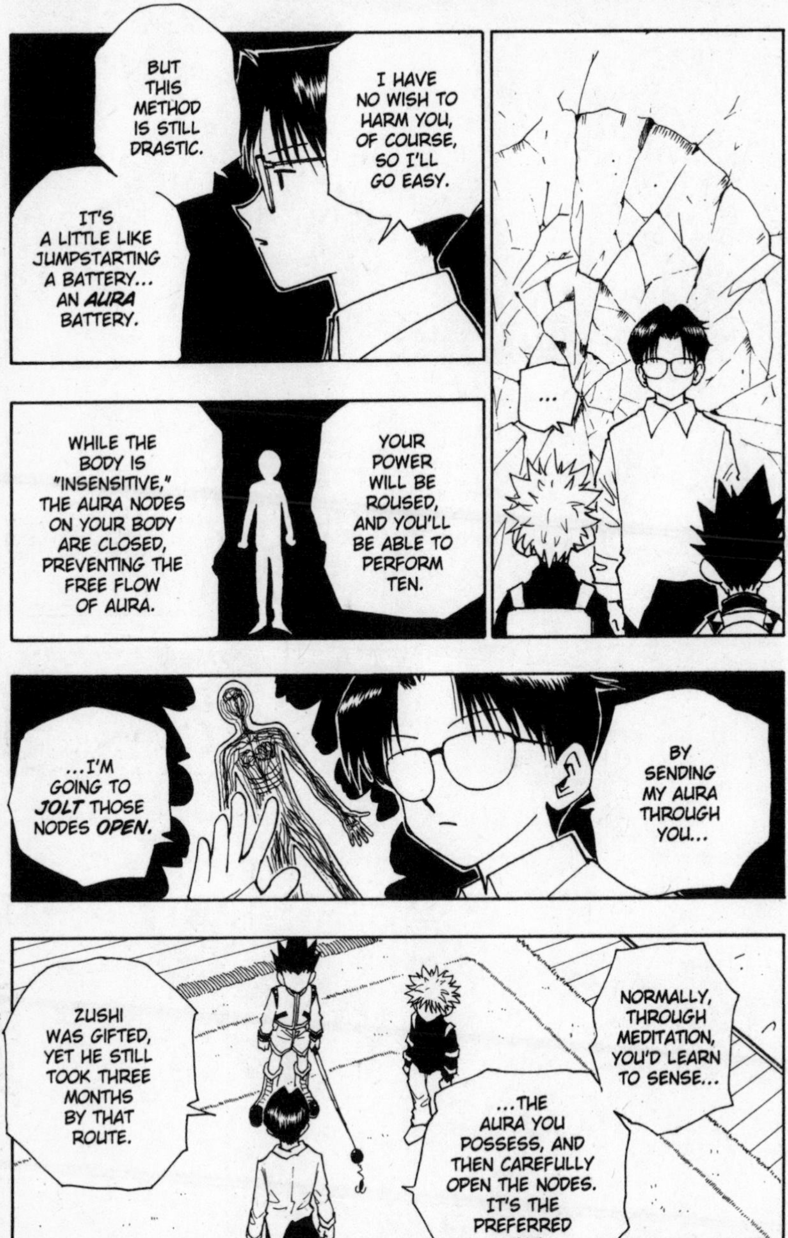
...
I HAVE NO WISH TO HARM YOU, OF COURSE, SO I'LL GO EASY.
BUT THIS METHOD IS STILL DRASTIC.
IT'S A LITTLE LIKE JUMPSTARTING A BATTERY... AN *AURA* BATTERY.
YOUR POWER WILL BE ROUSED, AND YOU'LL BE ABLE TO PERFORM TEN.
WHILE THE BODY IS "INSENSITIVE," THE AURA NODES ON YOUR BODY ARE CLOSED, PREVENTING THE FREE FLOW OF AURA.
BY SENDING MY AURA THROUGH YOU...
...I'M GOING TO *JOLT* THOSE NODES *OPEN*.
NORMALLY, THROUGH MEDITATION, YOU'D LEARN TO SENSE...
...THE AURA YOU POSSESS, AND THEN CAREFULLY OPEN THE NODES. IT'S THE PREFERRED WAY.
ZUSHI WAS GIFTED, YET HE STILL TOOK THREE MONTHS BY THAT ROUTE.

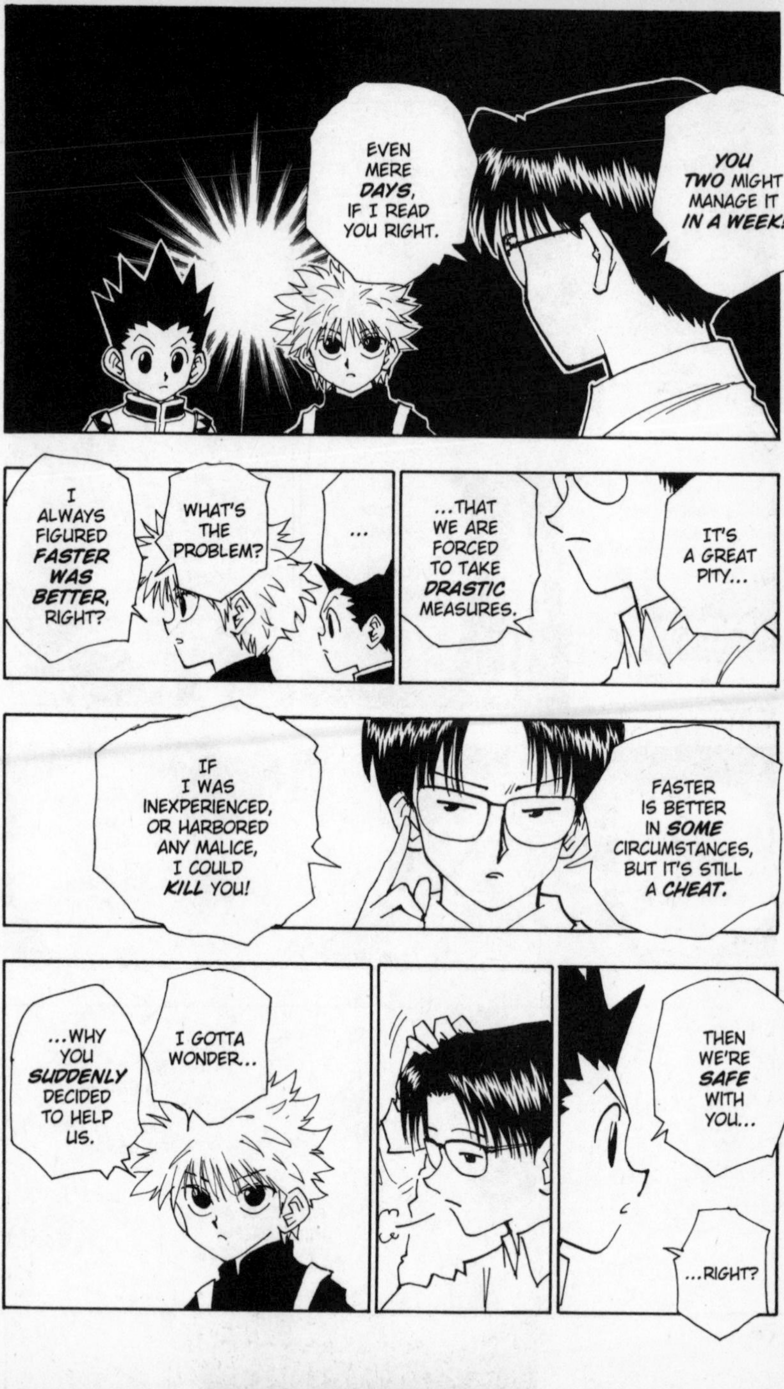
YOU TWO MIGHT MANAGE IT IN A WEEK!
EVEN MERE DAYS, IF I READ YOU RIGHT.
IT'S A GREAT PITY...
...THAT WE ARE FORCED TO TAKE DRASTIC MEASURES.
...
WHAT'S THE PROBLEM?
I ALWAYS FIGURED FASTER WAS BETTER, RIGHT?
FASTER IS BETTER IN SOME CIRCUMSTANCES, BUT IT'S STILL A CHEAT.
IF I WAS INEXPERIENCED, OR HARBORED ANY MALICE, I COULD KILL YOU!
THEN WE'RE SAFE WITH YOU...
...RIGHT?
I GOTTA WONDER...
...WHY YOU SUDDENLY DECIDED TO HELP US.

READ THIS WAY

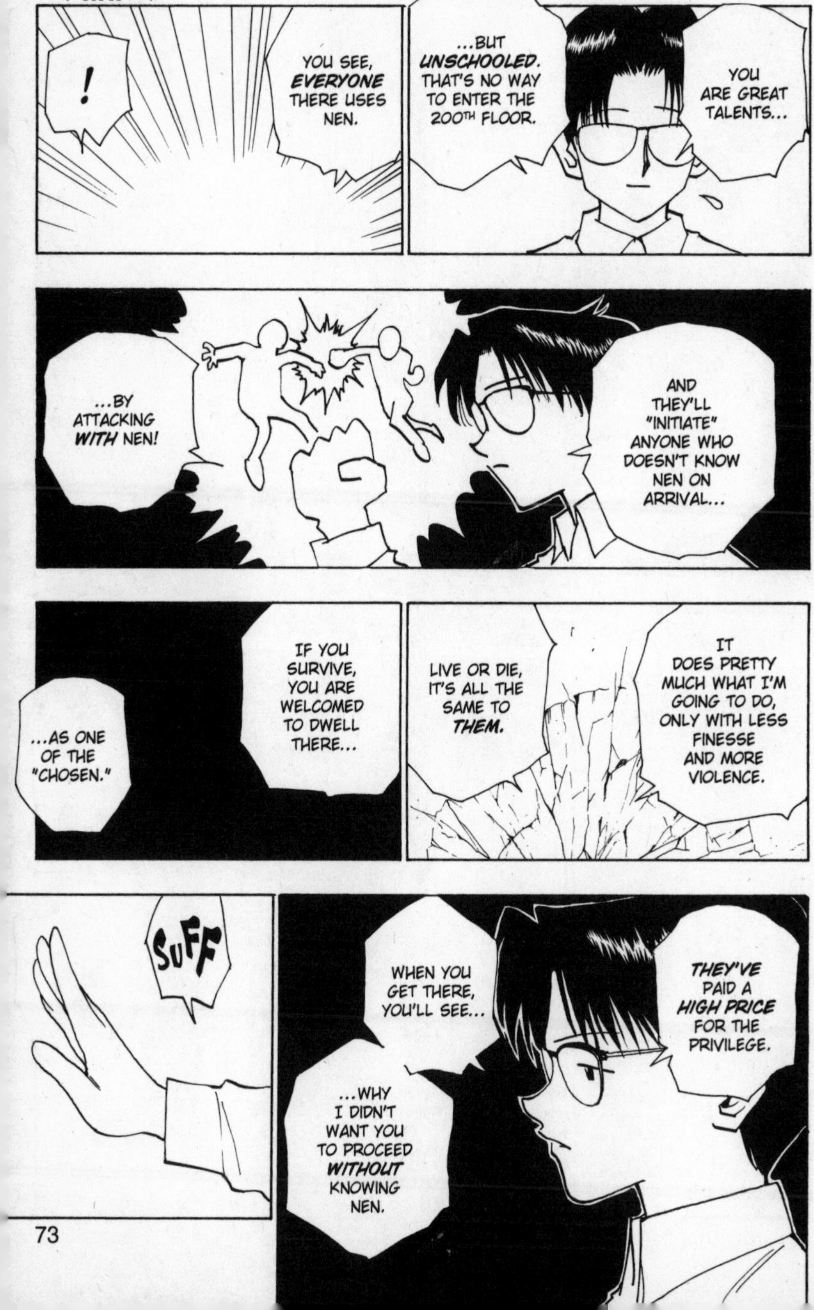
YOU ARE GREAT TALENTS...
...BUT UNSCHOOLED. THAT'S NO WAY TO ENTER THE 200TH FLOOR.
YOU SEE, EVERYONE THERE USES NEN.
!
AND THEY'LL "INITIATE" ANYONE WHO DOESN'T KNOW NEN ON ARRIVAL...
...BY ATTACKING WITH NEN!
IT DOES PRETTY MUCH WHAT I'M GOING TO DO, ONLY WITH LESS FINESSE AND MORE VIOLENCE.
LIVE OR DIE, IT'S ALL THE SAME TO THEM.
IF YOU SURVIVE, YOU ARE WELCOMED TO DWELL THERE...
...AS ONE OF THE "CHOSEN."
THEY'VE PAID A HIGH PRICE FOR THE PRIVILEGE.
WHEN YOU GET THERE, YOU'LL SEE...
...WHY I DIDN'T WANT YOU TO PROCEED WITHOUT KNOWING NEN.
SUFF

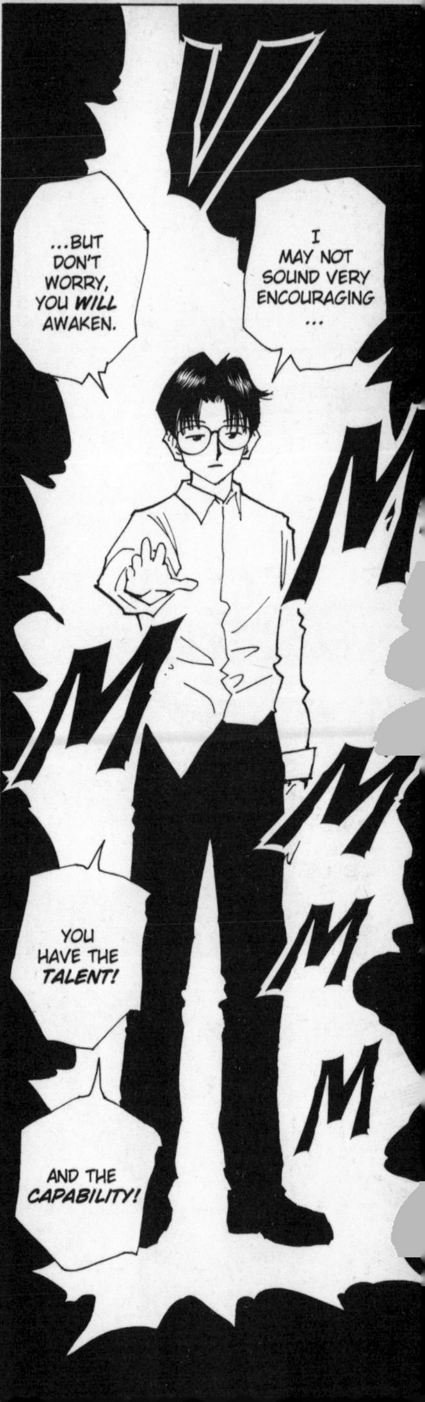
I MAY NOT SOUND VERY ENCOURAGING...
...BUT DON'T WORRY, YOU *WILL* AWAKEN.
YOU HAVE THE *TALENT!*
AND THE *CAPABILITY!*

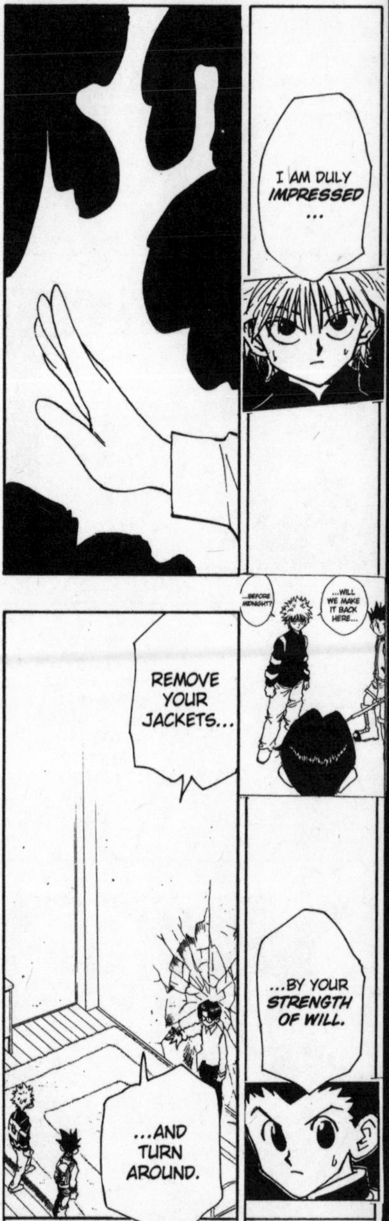
I AM DULY *IMPRESSED*...
...WILL WE MAKE IT BACK HERE...
...BEFORE MIDNIGHT?
...BY YOUR *STRENGTH OF WILL.*
REMOVE YOUR JACKETS...
...AND TURN AROUND.

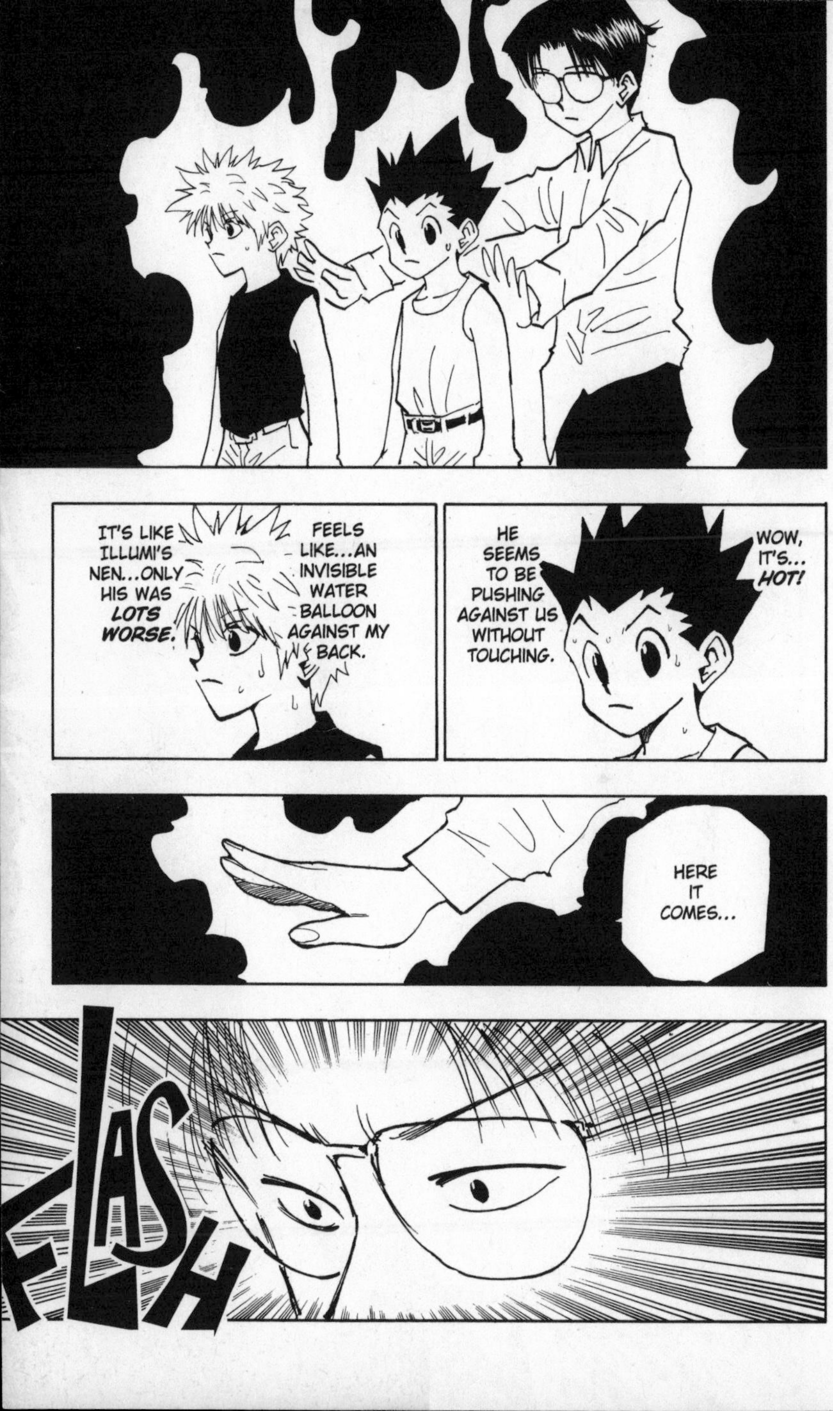
WOW, IT'S... ***HOT!***
HE SEEMS TO BE PUSHING AGAINST US WITHOUT TOUCHING.
FEELS LIKE...AN INVISIBLE WATER BALLOON AGAINST MY BACK.
IT'S LIKE ILLUMI'S NEN...ONLY HIS WAS ***LOTS WORSE.***
HERE IT COMES...
FLASH

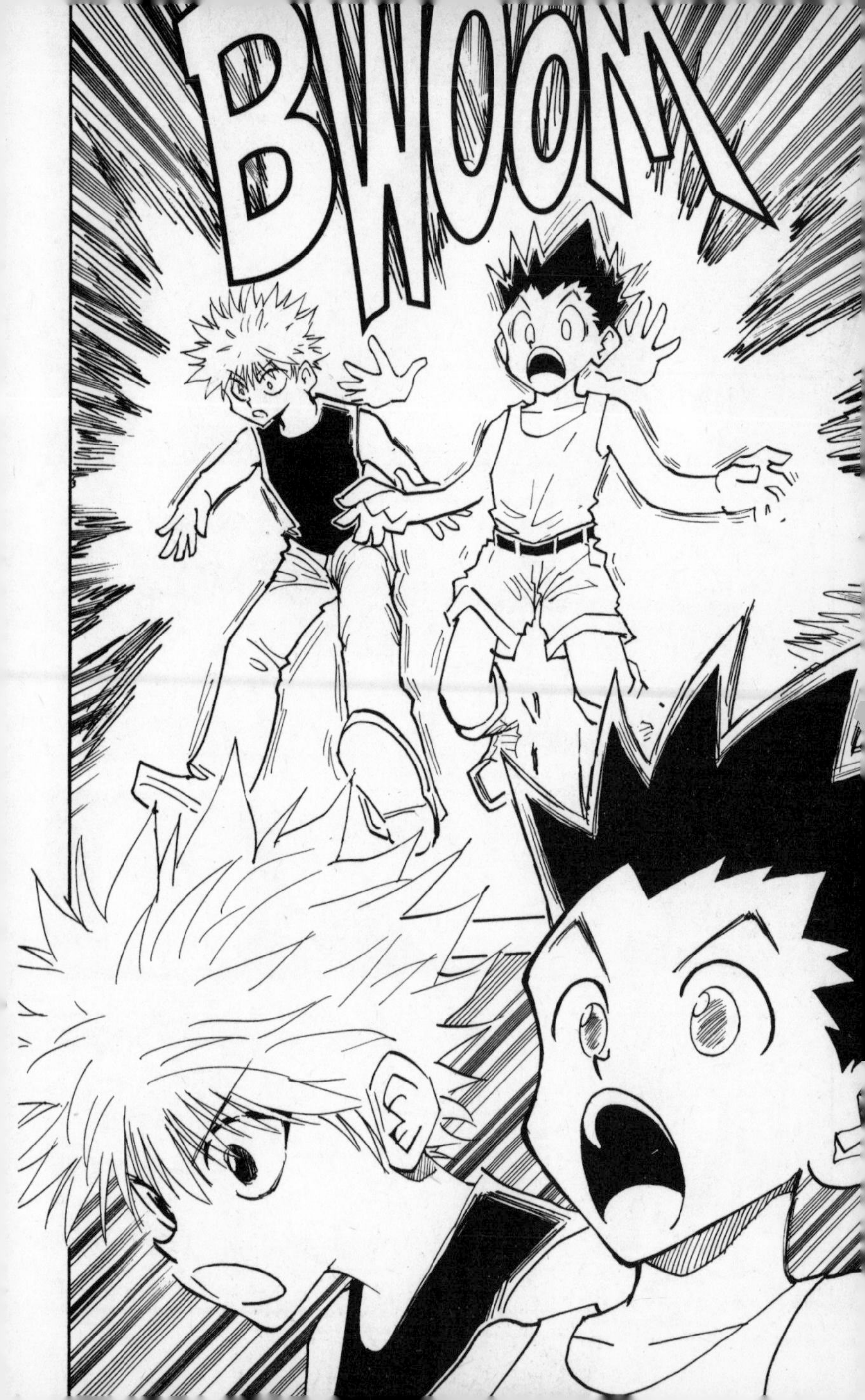
BWOOM

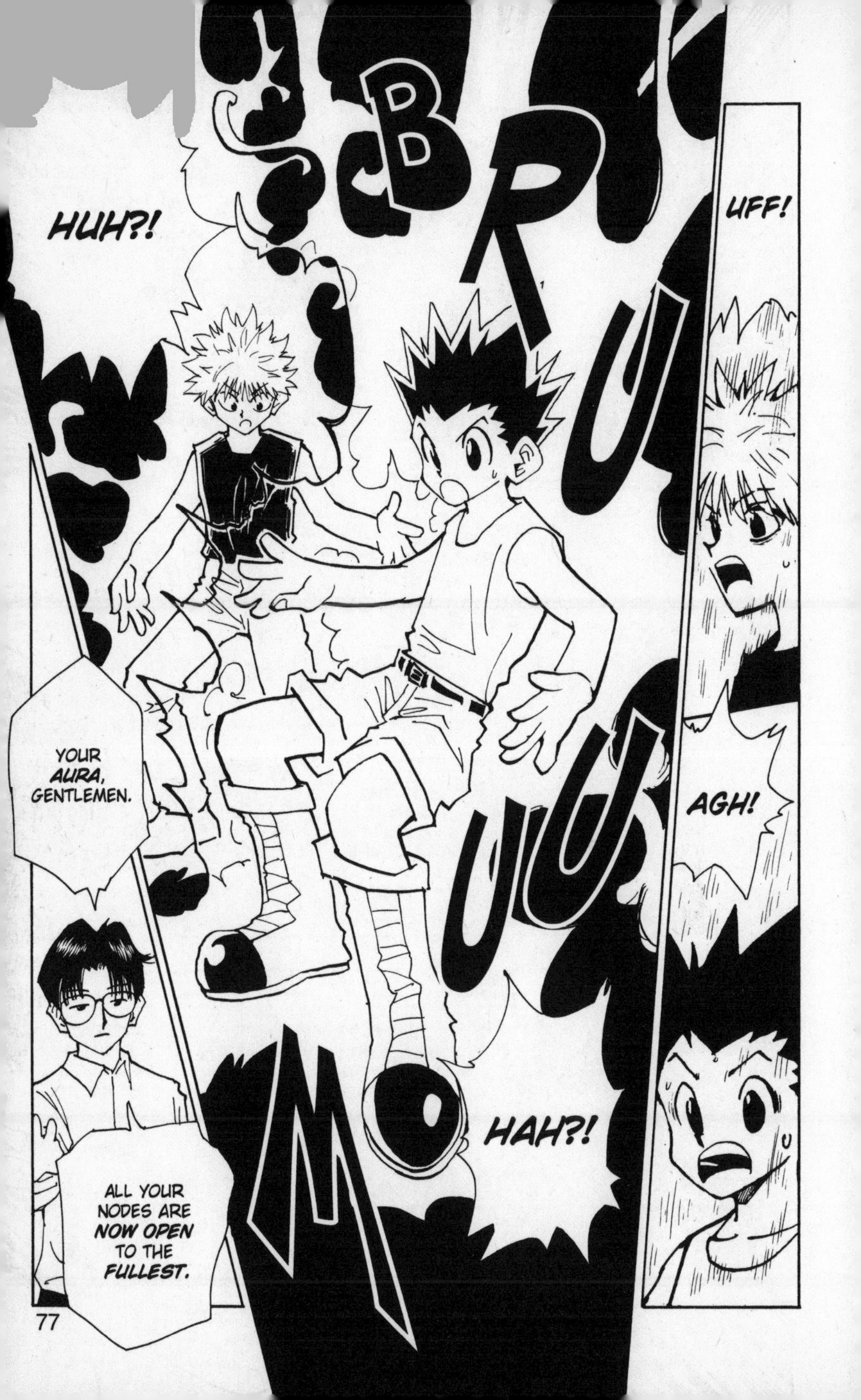
UFF!
AGH!
HAH?!
HUH?!
YOUR AURA, GENTLEMEN.
ALL YOUR NODES ARE NOW OPEN TO THE FULLEST.

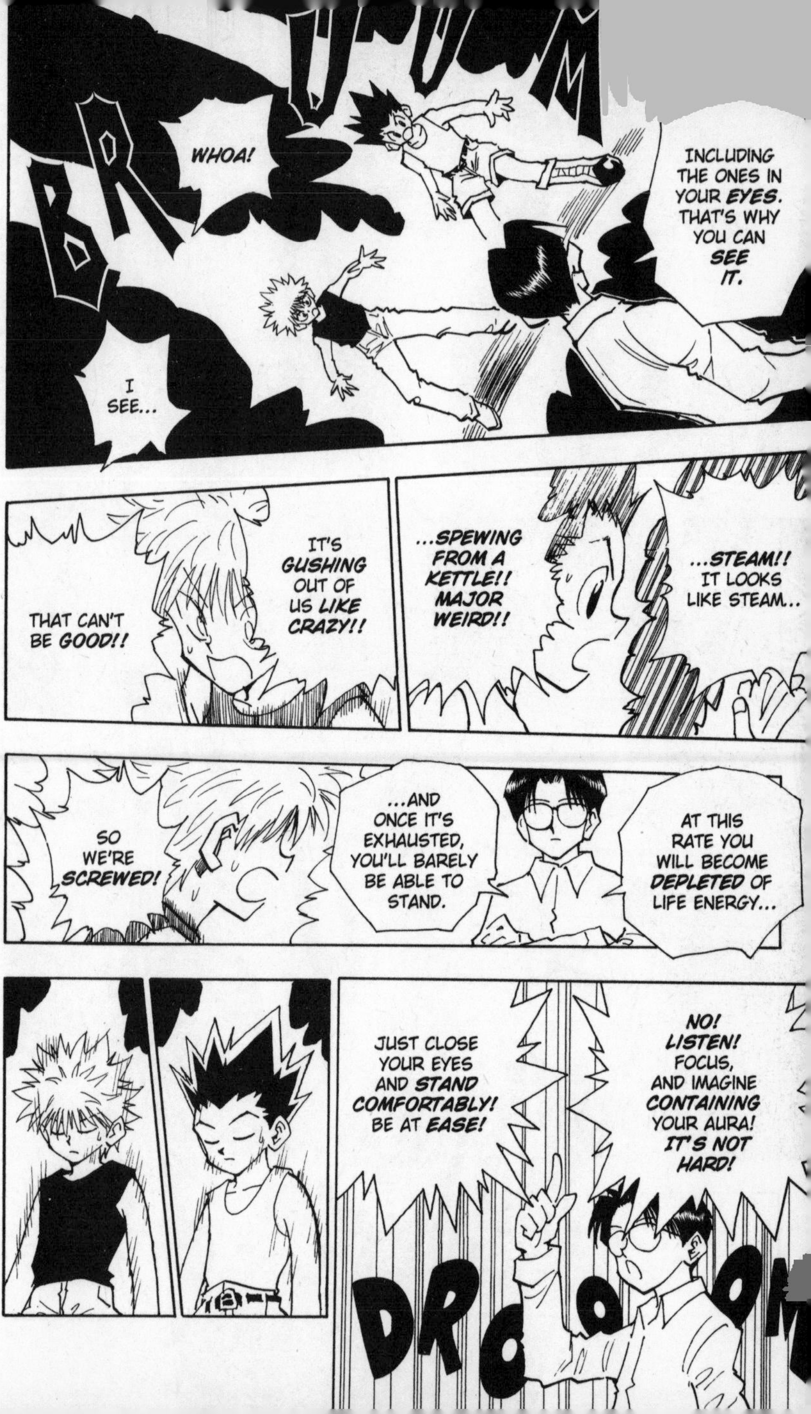
INCLUDING THE ONES IN YOUR EYES. THAT'S WHY YOU CAN SEE IT.
BRUUM
WHOA!
I SEE...
...STEAM!! IT LOOKS LIKE STEAM...
...SPEWING FROM A KETTLE!! MAJOR WEIRD!!
IT'S GUSHING OUT OF US LIKE CRAZY!!
THAT CAN'T BE GOOD!!
AT THIS RATE YOU WILL BECOME DEPLETED OF LIFE ENERGY...
...AND ONCE IT'S EXHAUSTED, YOU'LL BARELY BE ABLE TO STAND.
SO WE'RE SCREWED!
NO! LISTEN! FOCUS, AND IMAGINE CONTAINING YOUR AURA! IT'S NOT HARD!
JUST CLOSE YOUR EYES AND STAND COMFORTABLY! BE AT EASE!
DROOOM

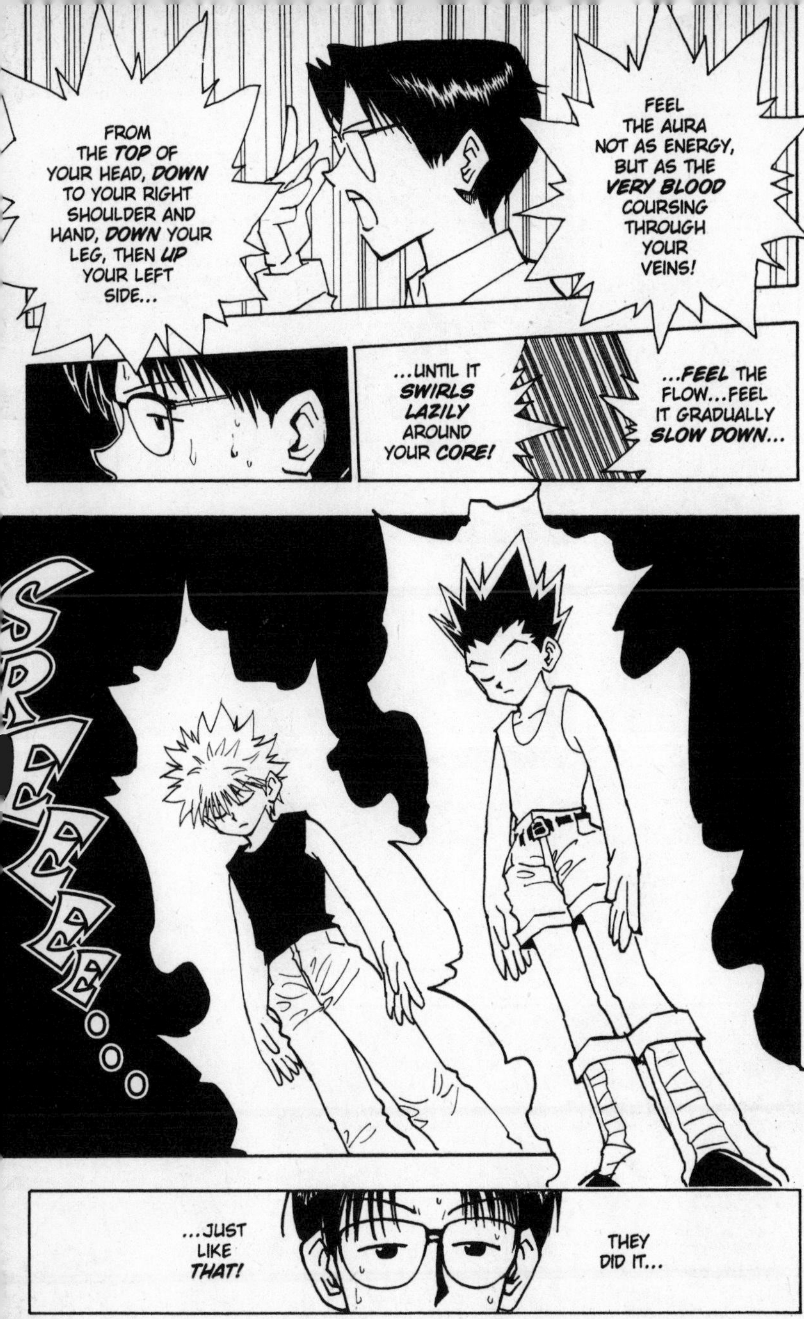
FEEL THE AURA NOT AS ENERGY, BUT AS THE VERY BLOOD COURSING THROUGH YOUR VEINS!
FROM THE TOP OF YOUR HEAD, DOWN TO YOUR RIGHT SHOULDER AND HAND, DOWN YOUR LEG, THEN UP YOUR LEFT SIDE...
...FEEL THE FLOW...FEEL IT GRADUALLY SLOW DOWN...
...UNTIL IT SWIRLS LAZILY AROUND YOUR CORE!
SREEEE...
THEY DID IT...
...JUST LIKE THAT!

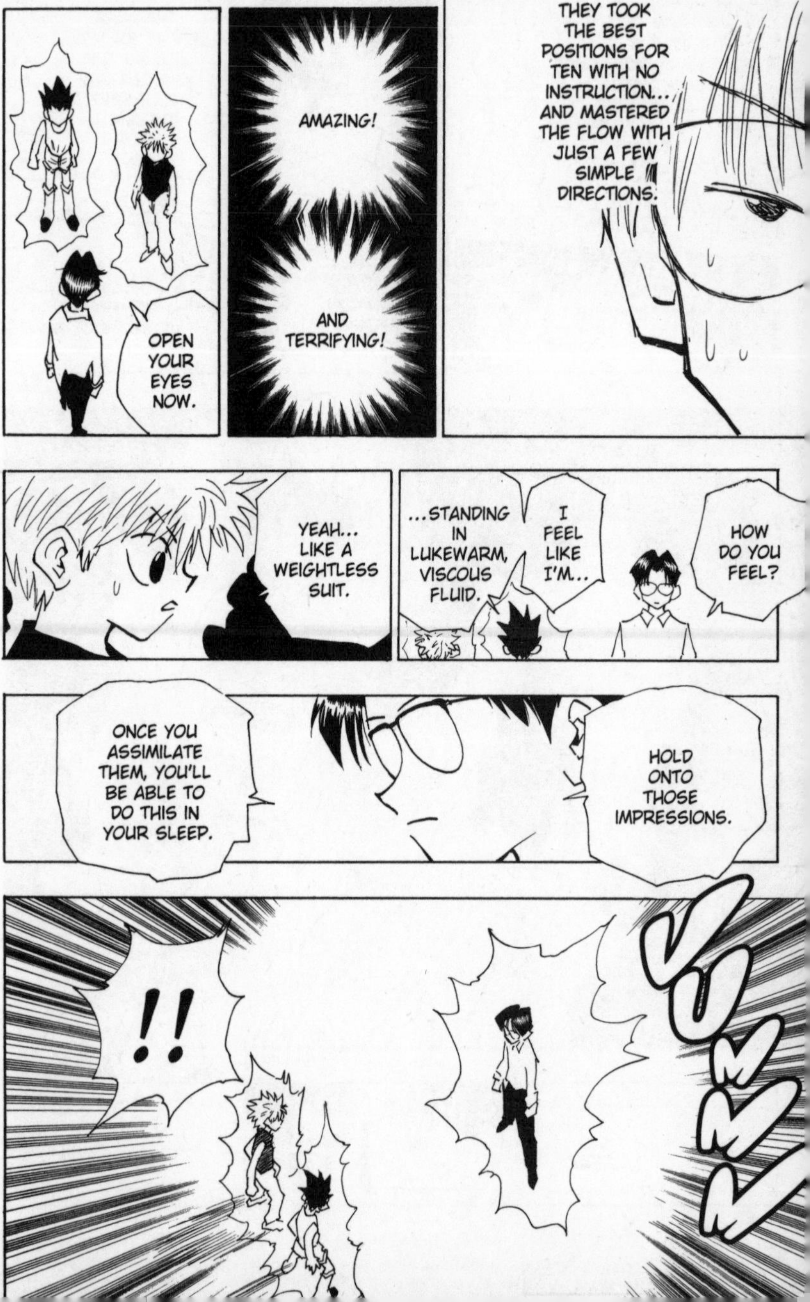
THEY TOOK THE BEST POSITIONS FOR TEN WITH NO INSTRUCTION... AND MASTERED THE FLOW WITH JUST A FEW SIMPLE DIRECTIONS.
AMAZING!
AND TERRIFYING!
OPEN YOUR EYES NOW.
HOW DO YOU FEEL?
I FEEL LIKE I'M...
...STANDING IN LUKEWARM, VISCOUS FLUID.
YEAH... LIKE A WEIGHTLESS SUIT.
HOLD ONTO THOSE IMPRESSIONS.
ONCE YOU ASSIMILATE THEM, YOU'LL BE ABLE TO DO THIS IN YOUR SLEEP.
VUMMM
!!

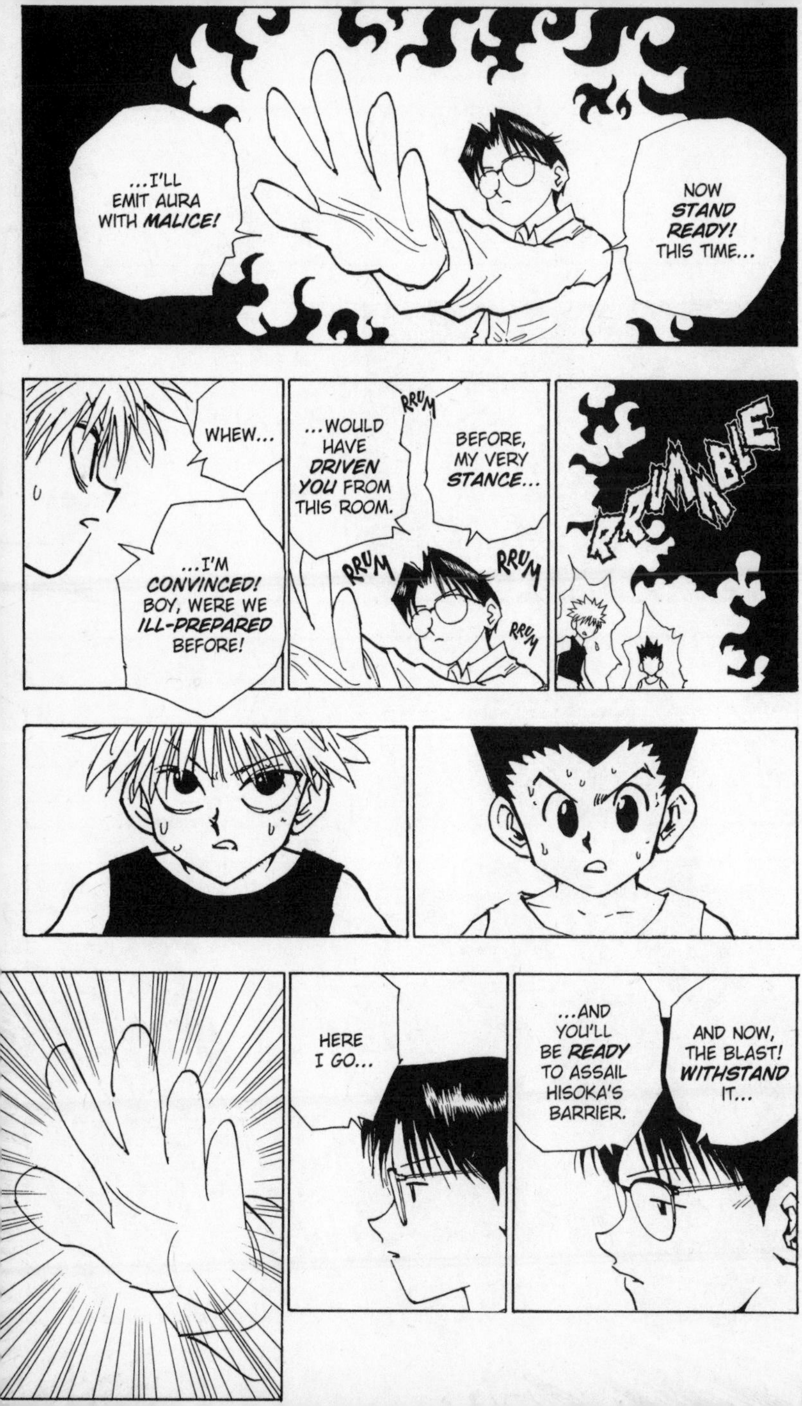

NOW STAND READY! THIS TIME...
...I'LL EMIT AURA WITH MALICE!
RRUMBLE
BEFORE, MY VERY STANCE...
...WOULD HAVE DRIVEN YOU FROM THIS ROOM.
RRUM
RRUM
RRUM
RRUM
WHEW...
...I'M CONVINCED! BOY, WERE WE ILL-PREPARED BEFORE!
AND NOW, THE BLAST! WITHSTAND IT...
...AND YOU'LL BE READY TO ASSAIL HISOKA'S BARRIER.
HERE I GO...

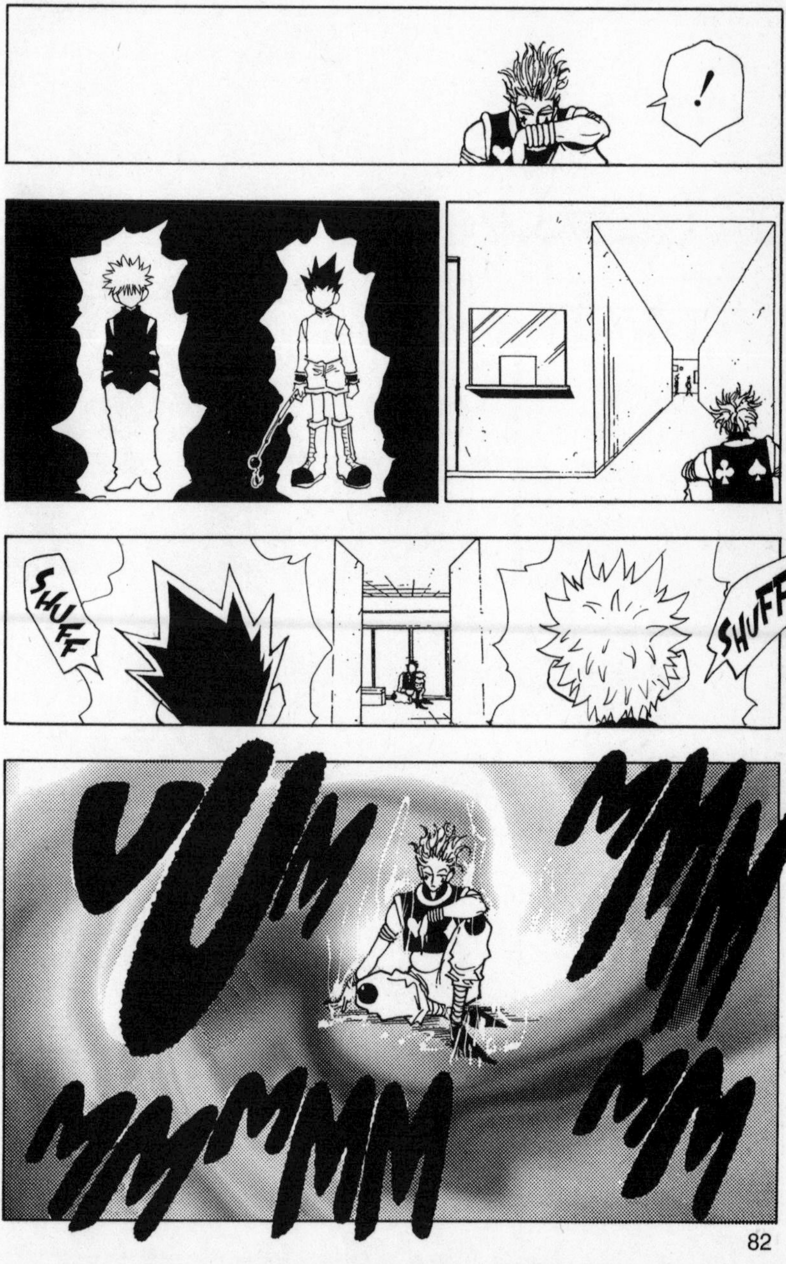
!
SHUFF
SHUFF

READ THIS WAY

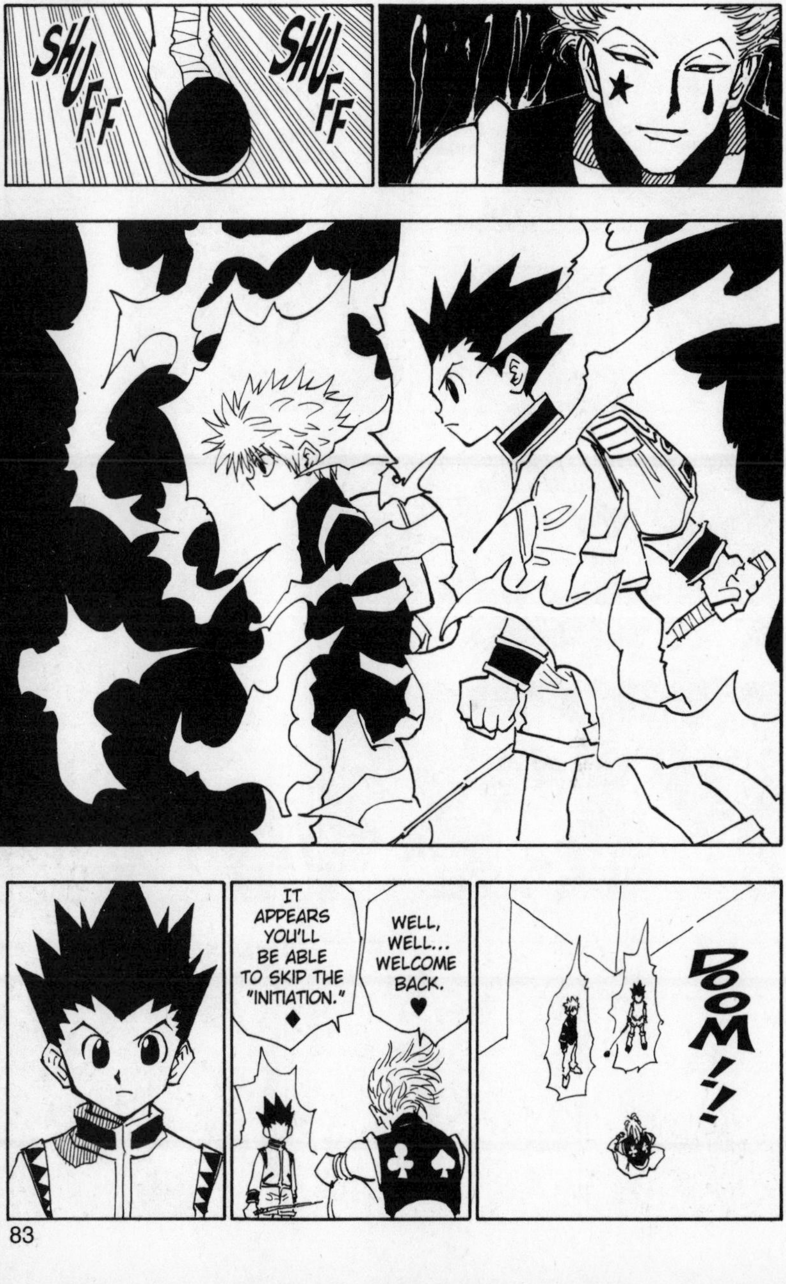
SHUFF
SHUFF
DOOM!!
WELL, WELL... WELCOME BACK. ♥
IT APPEARS YOU'LL BE ABLE TO SKIP THE "INITIATION." ♦

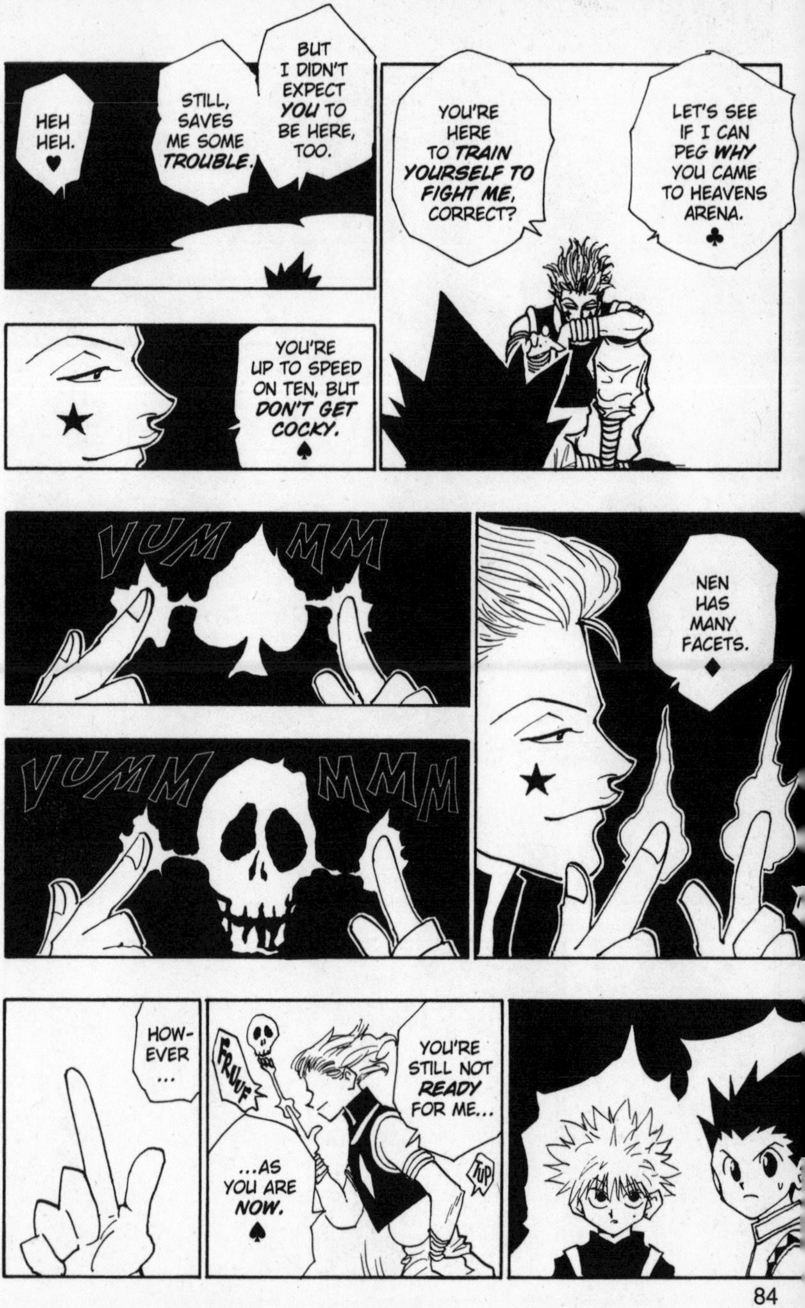
LET'S SEE IF I CAN PEG WHY YOU CAME TO HEAVENS ARENA. ♣
YOU'RE HERE TO TRAIN YOURSELF TO FIGHT ME, CORRECT?
BUT I DIDN'T EXPECT YOU TO BE HERE, TOO.
STILL, SAVES ME SOME TROUBLE.
HEH HEH. ♥
YOU'RE UP TO SPEED ON TEN, BUT DON'T GET COCKY. ♠
NEN HAS MANY FACETS. ♦
VUM MM
VUMM MMM
YOU'RE STILL NOT READY FOR ME...
FRUUF
TUP
...AS YOU ARE NOW. ♠
HOW-EVER ...

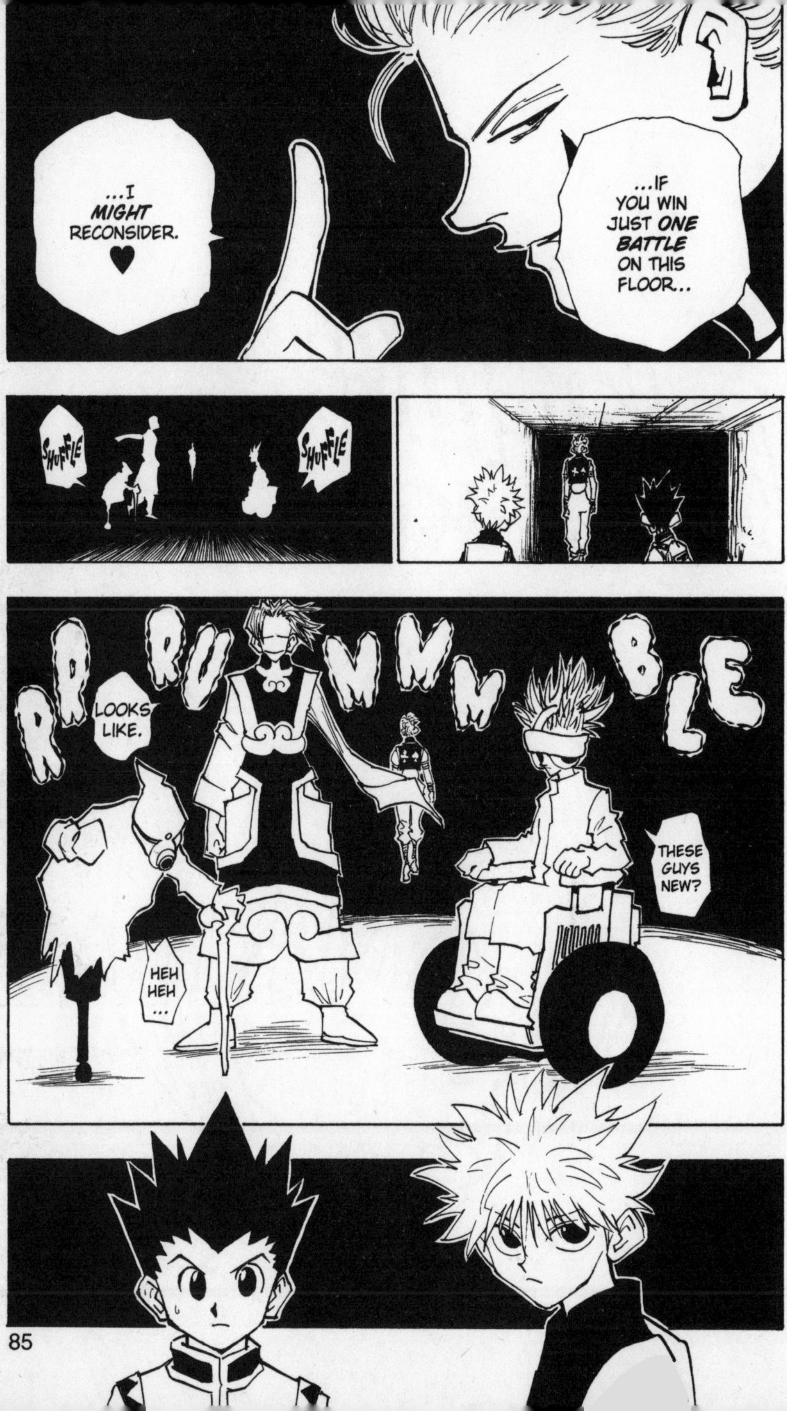
...IF YOU WIN JUST ONE BATTLE ON THIS FLOOR...
...I MIGHT RECONSIDER. ♥
SHUFFLE
SHUFFLE
RRRUMMMBLE
THESE GUYS NEW?
LOOKS LIKE.
HEH HEH...

Color-me-
Kurapika

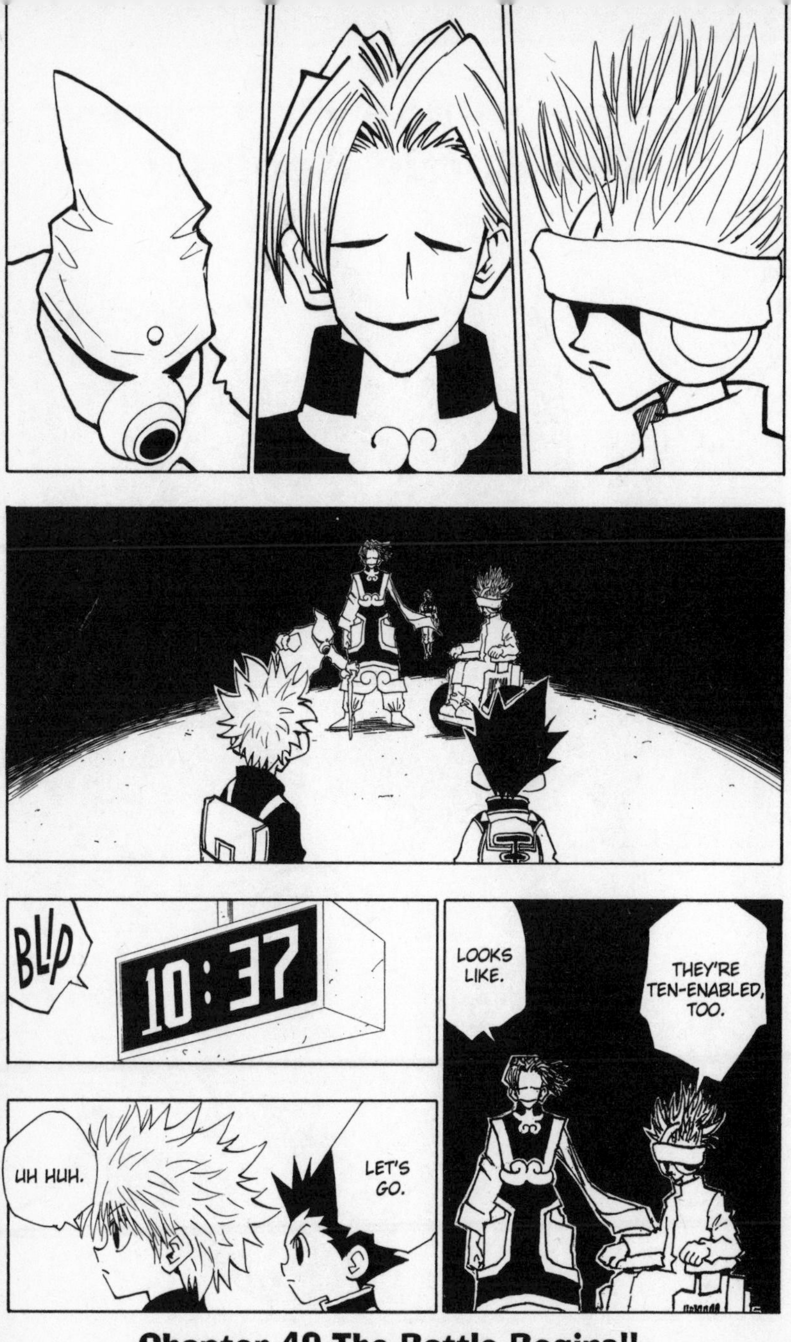
THEY'RE TEN-ENABLED, TOO.
LOOKS LIKE.
BLIP
10:37
LET'S GO.
UH HUH.

Chapter 49 The Battle Begins!!

Chapter 49

The Battle Begins!!

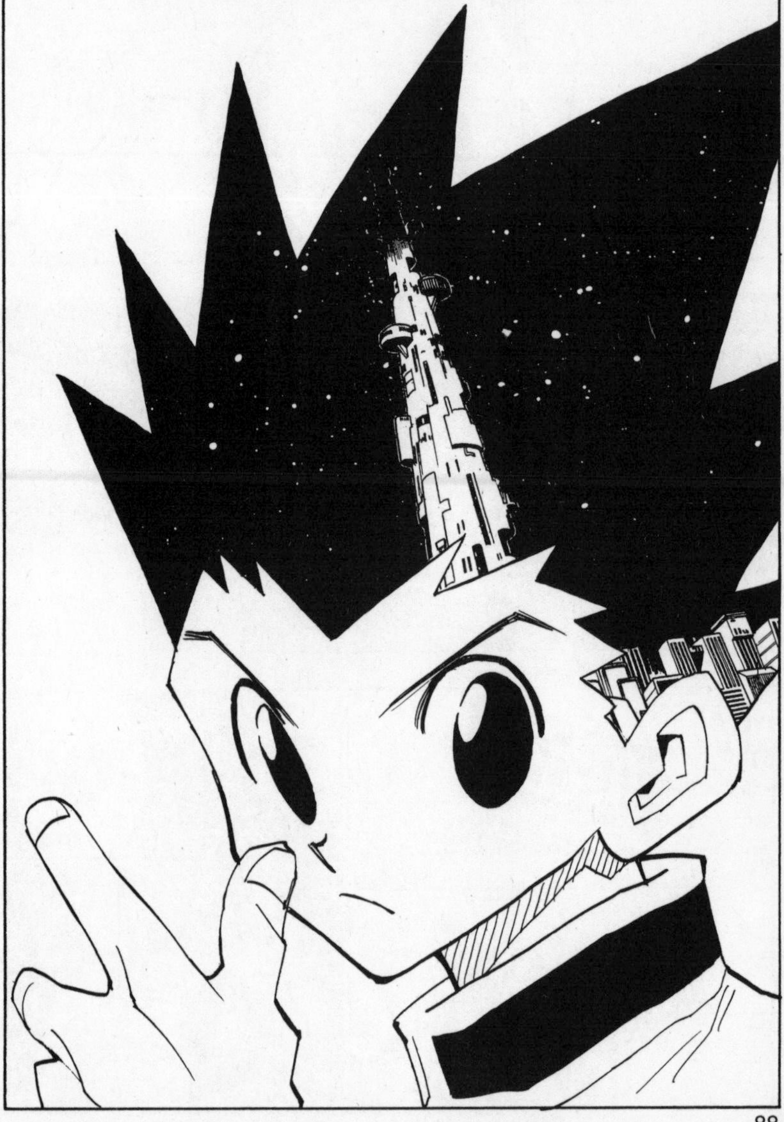

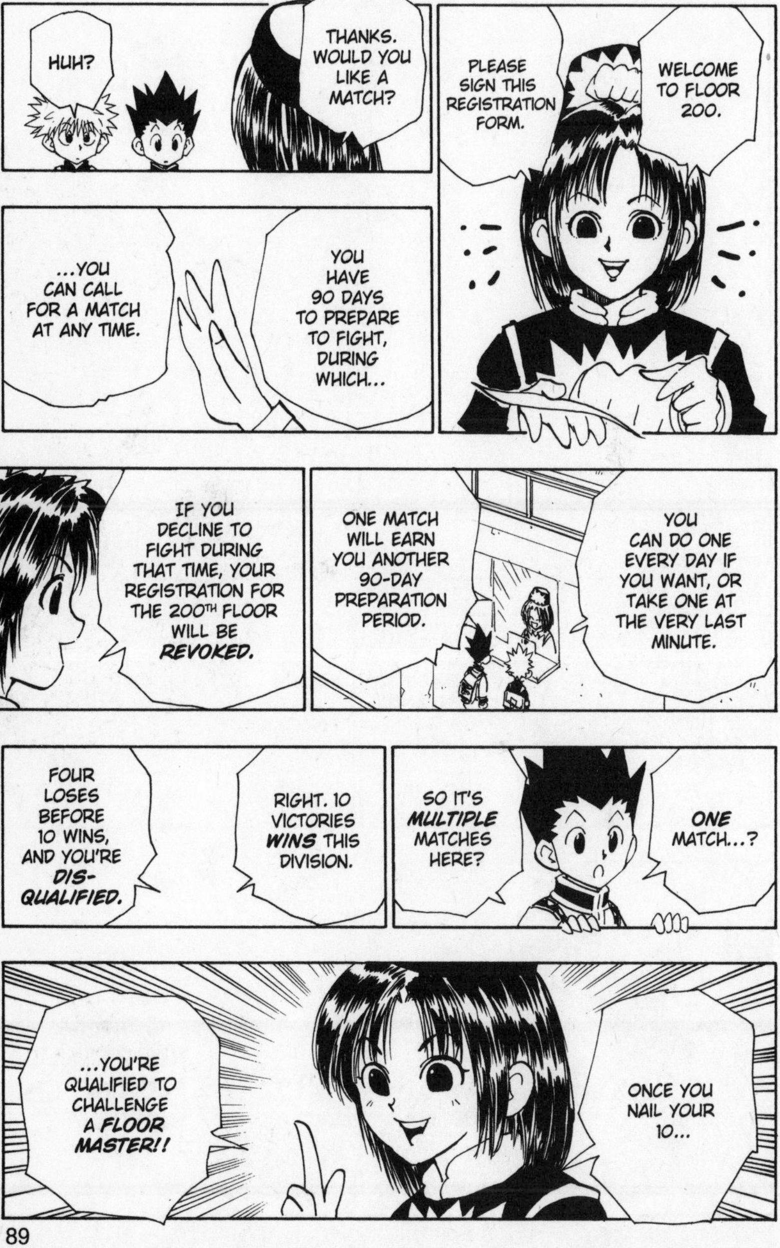
WELCOME TO FLOOR 200.
PLEASE SIGN THIS REGISTRATION FORM.
THANKS. WOULD YOU LIKE A MATCH?
HUH?
YOU HAVE 90 DAYS TO PREPARE TO FIGHT, DURING WHICH...
...YOU CAN CALL FOR A MATCH AT ANY TIME.
YOU CAN DO ONE EVERY DAY IF YOU WANT, OR TAKE ONE AT THE VERY LAST MINUTE.
ONE MATCH WILL EARN YOU ANOTHER 90-DAY PREPARATION PERIOD.
IF YOU DECLINE TO FIGHT DURING THAT TIME, YOUR REGISTRATION FOR THE 200TH FLOOR WILL BE ***REVOKED.***
ONE MATCH...?
SO IT'S ***MULTIPLE*** MATCHES HERE?
RIGHT. 10 VICTORIES ***WINS*** THIS DIVISION.
FOUR LOSES BEFORE 10 WINS, AND YOU'RE ***DIS-QUALIFIED.***
ONCE YOU NAIL YOUR 10...
...YOU'RE QUALIFIED TO CHALLENGE A ***FLOOR MASTER!!***

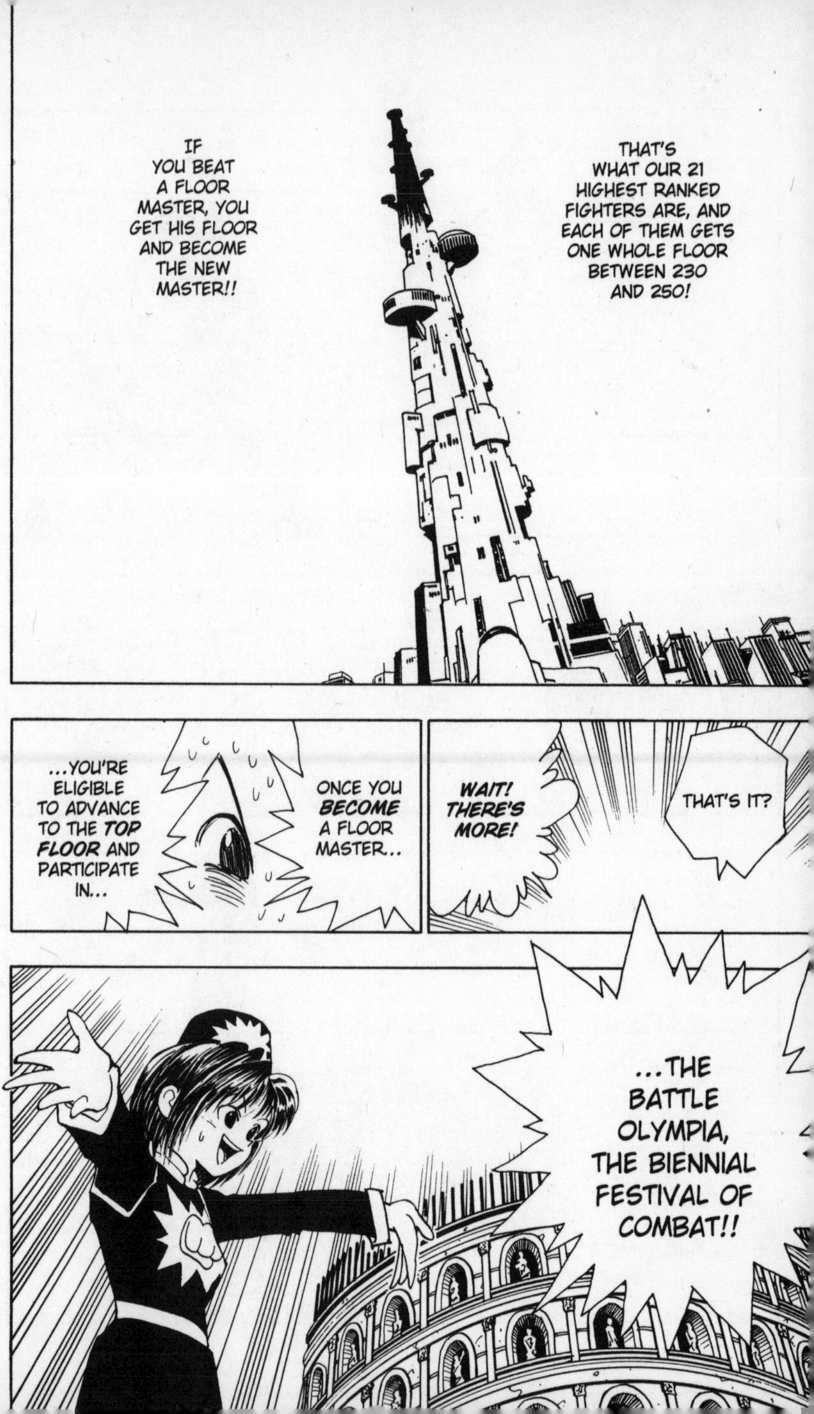
THAT'S WHAT OUR 21 HIGHEST RANKED FIGHTERS ARE, AND EACH OF THEM GETS ONE WHOLE FLOOR BETWEEN 230 AND 250!
IF YOU BEAT A FLOOR MASTER, YOU GET HIS FLOOR AND BECOME THE NEW MASTER!!
THAT'S IT?
WAIT! THERE'S MORE!
ONCE YOU BECOME A FLOOR MASTER...
...YOU'RE ELIGIBLE TO ADVANCE TO THE TOP FLOOR AND PARTICIPATE IN...
...THE BATTLE OLYMPIA, THE BIENNIAL FESTIVAL OF COMBAT!!

READ THIS WAY

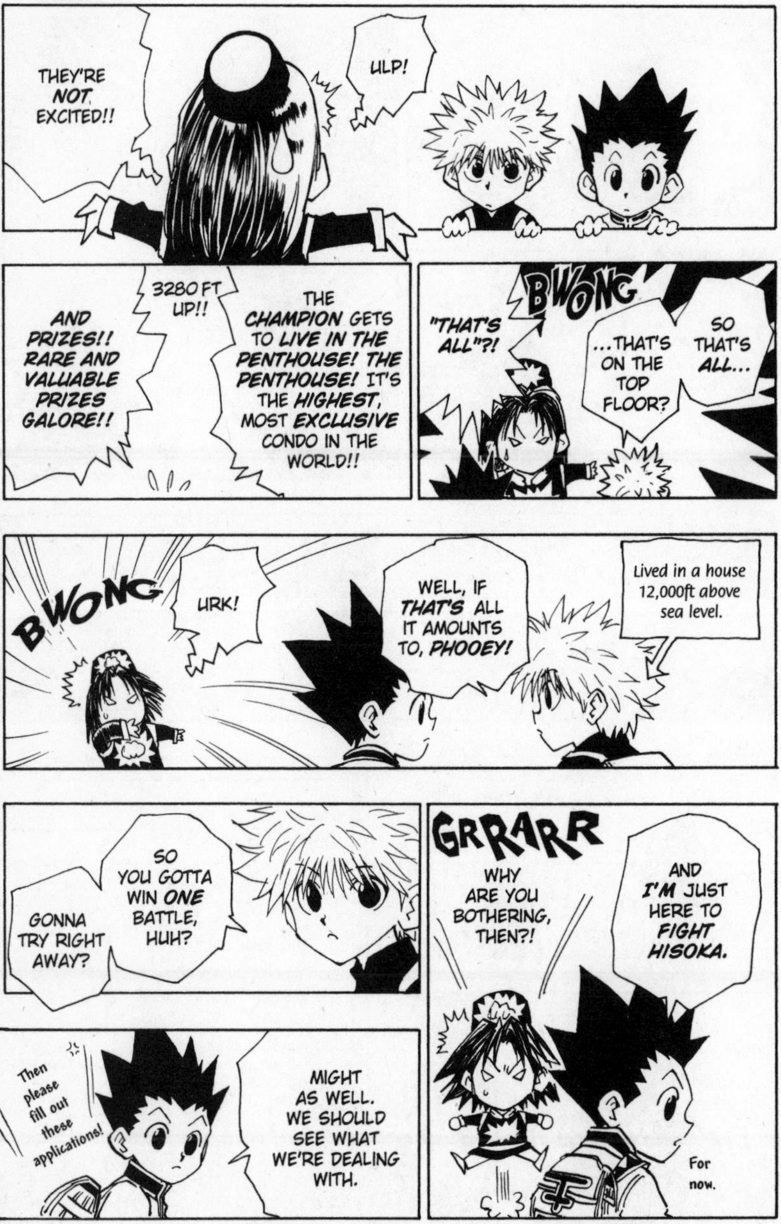

ULP!
THEY'RE NOT EXCITED!!
SO THAT'S ALL...
...THAT'S ON THE TOP FLOOR?
BWONG
"THAT'S ALL"?!
THE CHAMPION GETS TO LIVE IN THE PENTHOUSE! THE PENTHOUSE! IT'S THE HIGHEST, MOST EXCLUSIVE CONDO IN THE WORLD!!
3280 FT UP!!
AND PRIZES!! RARE AND VALUABLE PRIZES GALORE!!
Lived in a house 12,000ft above sea level.
WELL, IF THAT'S ALL IT AMOUNTS TO, PHOOEY!
URK!
BWONG
AND I'M JUST HERE TO FIGHT HISOKA.
GRRARR
WHY ARE YOU BOTHERING, THEN?!
For now.
SO YOU GOTTA WIN ONE BATTLE, HUH?
GONNA TRY RIGHT AWAY?
MIGHT AS WELL. WE SHOULD SEE WHAT WE'RE DEALING WITH.
Then please fill out these applications!

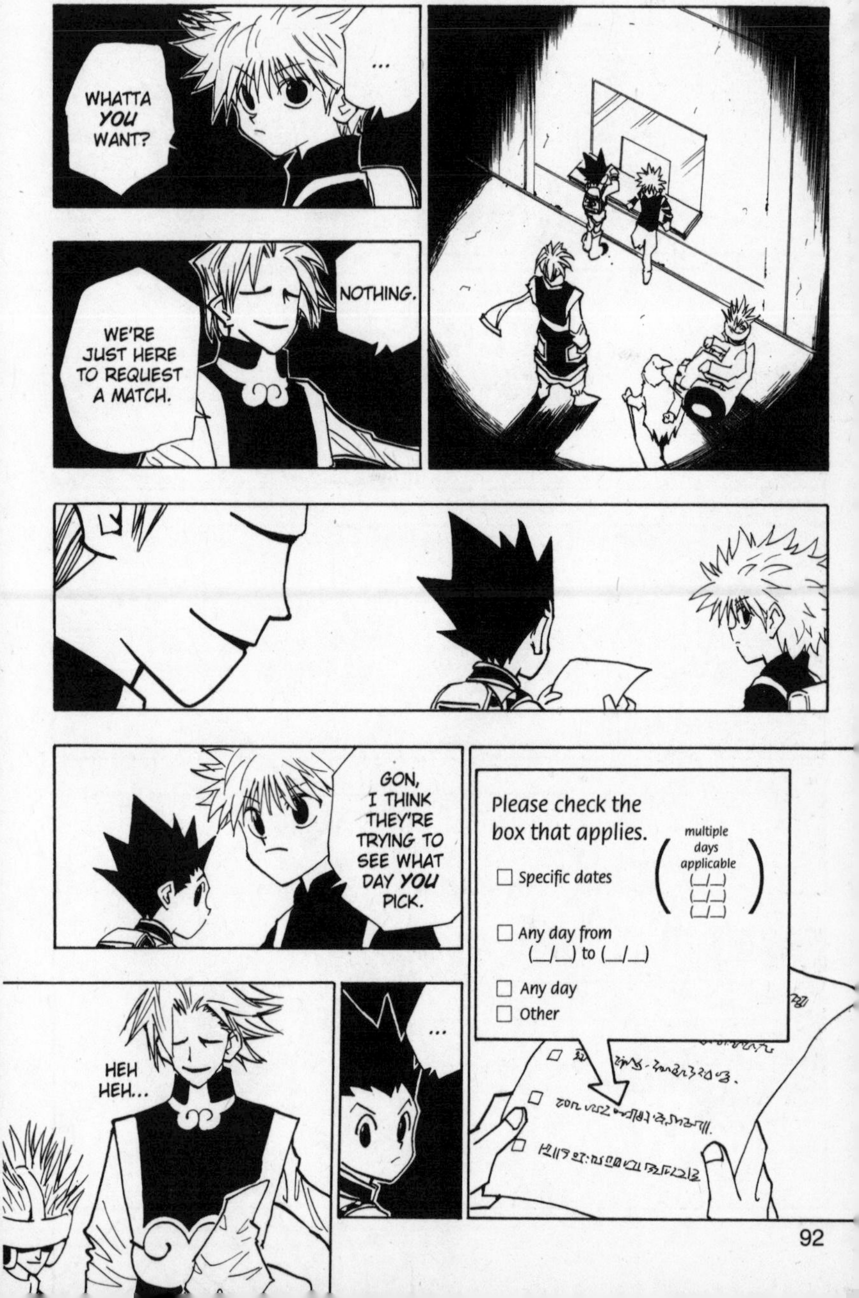
...
WHATTA YOU WANT?
NOTHING.
WE'RE JUST HERE TO REQUEST A MATCH.
Please check the box that applies.
multiple days applicable
(__/__)
(__/__)
(__/__)
☐ Specific dates
☐ Any day from (__/__) to (__/__)
☐ Any day
☐ Other
GON, I THINK THEY'RE TRYING TO SEE WHAT DAY YOU PICK.
...
HEH HEH...

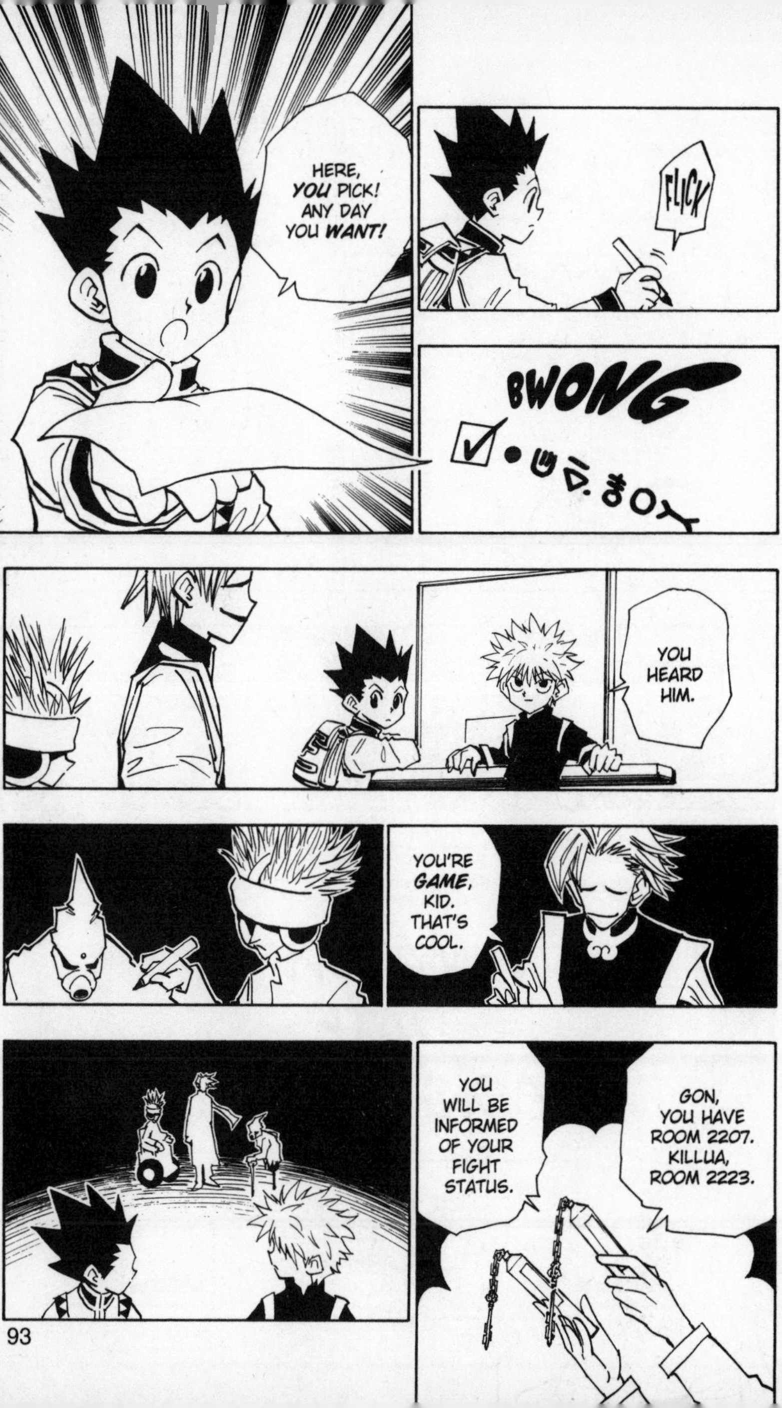
FLICK
BWONG
HERE, YOU PICK! ANY DAY YOU WANT!
YOU HEARD HIM.
YOU'RE GAME, KID. THAT'S COOL.
GON, YOU HAVE ROOM 2207. KILLUA, ROOM 2223.
YOU WILL BE INFORMED OF YOUR FIGHT STATUS.

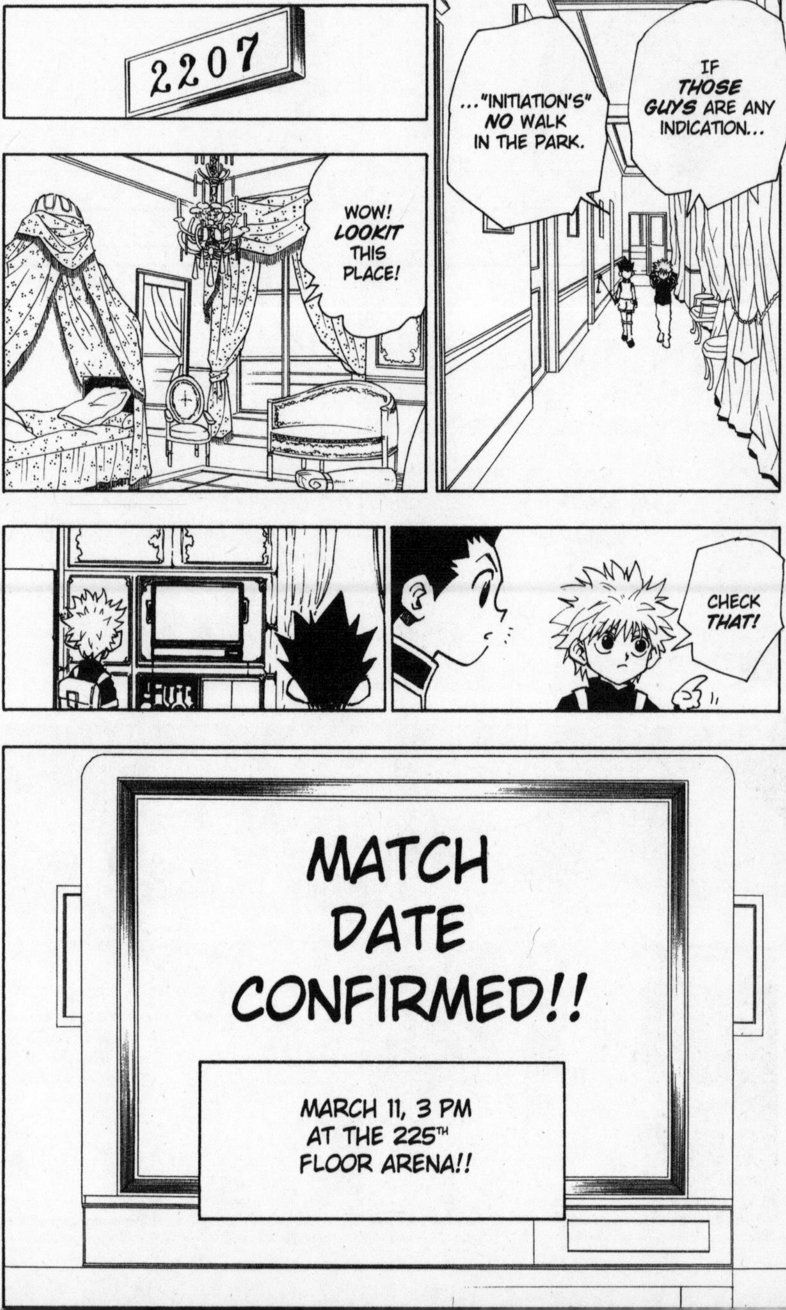
IF THOSE GUYS ARE ANY INDICATION...
..."INITIATION'S" NO WALK IN THE PARK.
2207
WOW! LOOKIT THIS PLACE!
CHECK THAT!
MATCH DATE CONFIRMED!!
MARCH 11, 3 PM AT THE 225TH FLOOR ARENA!!

READ THIS WAY

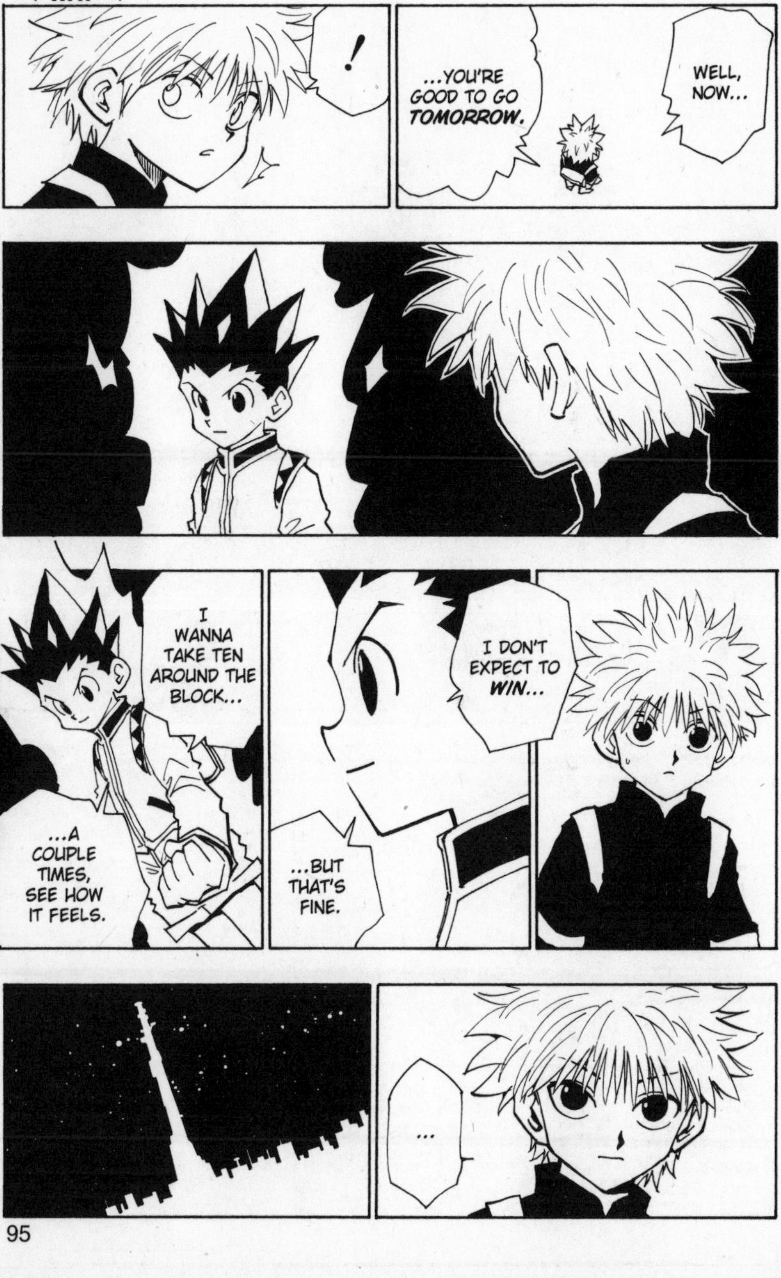
WELL, NOW...
...YOU'RE GOOD TO GO TOMORROW.
!
I DON'T EXPECT TO WIN...
...BUT THAT'S FINE.
I WANNA TAKE TEN AROUND THE BLOCK...
...A COUPLE TIMES, SEE HOW IT FEELS.
...

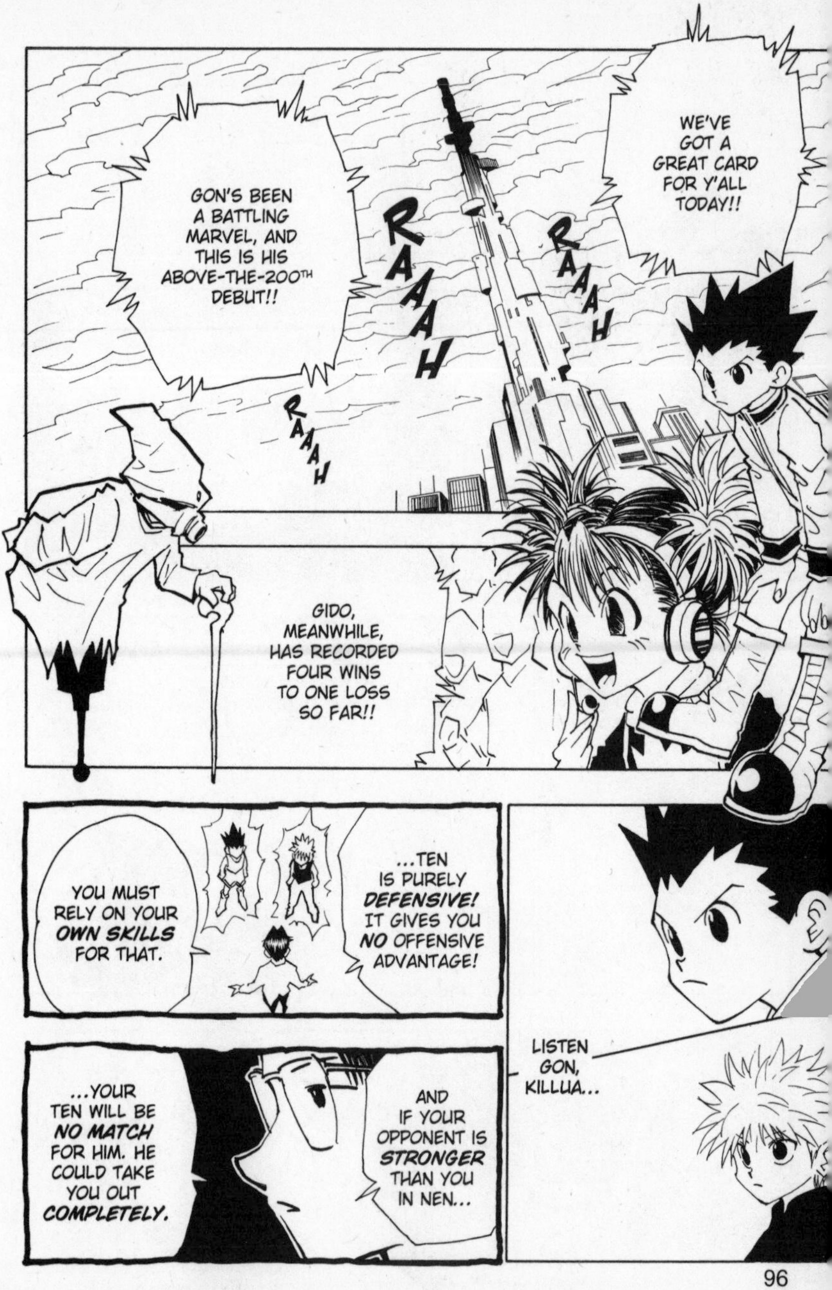
WE'VE GOT A GREAT CARD FOR Y'ALL TODAY!!
RAAAAH
RAAAAH
GON'S BEEN A BATTLING MARVEL, AND THIS IS HIS ABOVE-THE-200TH DEBUT!!
RAAAAH
GIDO, MEANWHILE, HAS RECORDED FOUR WINS TO ONE LOSS SO FAR!!
LISTEN GON, KILLUA...
...TEN IS PURELY DEFENSIVE! IT GIVES YOU NO OFFENSIVE ADVANTAGE!
YOU MUST RELY ON YOUR OWN SKILLS FOR THAT.
AND IF YOUR OPPONENT IS STRONGER THAN YOU IN NEN...
...YOUR TEN WILL BE NO MATCH FOR HIM. HE COULD TAKE YOU OUT COMPLETELY.

READ THIS WAY

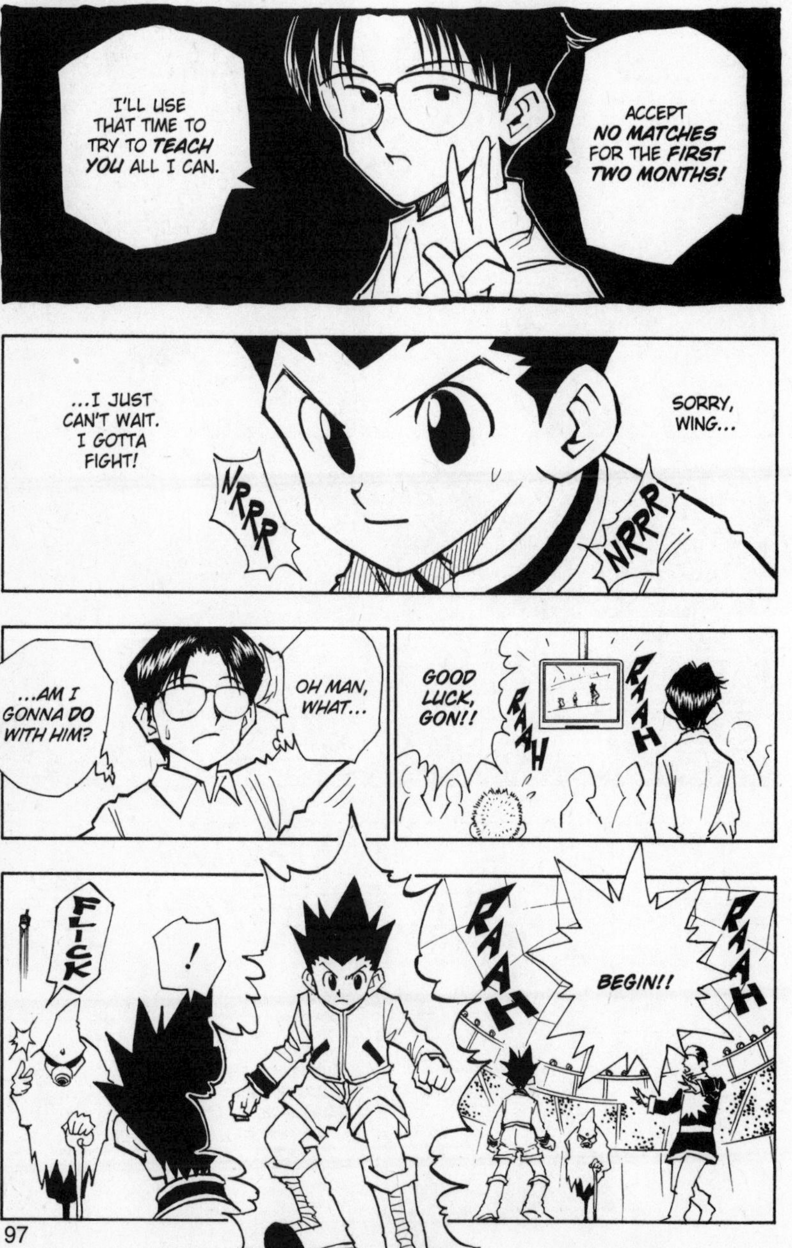
ACCEPT NO MATCHES FOR THE FIRST TWO MONTHS!
I'LL USE THAT TIME TO TRY TO TEACH YOU ALL I CAN.
SORRY, WING...
NRRR
NRRR
...I JUST CAN'T WAIT. I GOTTA FIGHT!
RAAH
GOOD LUCK, GON!!
RAAH
OH MAN, WHAT...
...AM I GONNA DO WITH HIM?
RAAAH
BEGIN!!
RAAAH
!
FLICK

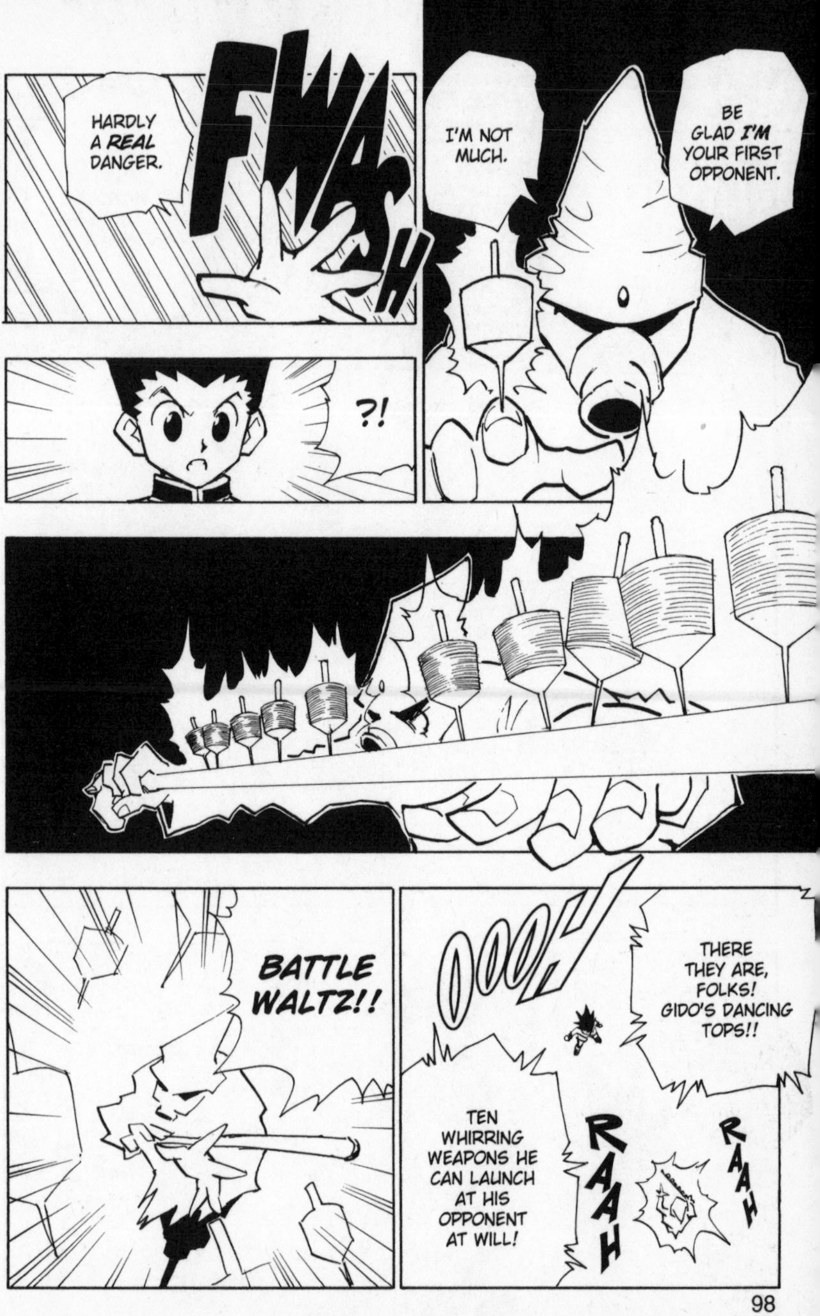
BE GLAD I'M YOUR FIRST OPPONENT.
I'M NOT MUCH.
HARDLY A REAL DANGER.
FWASH
?!
OOOH
THERE THEY ARE, FOLKS! GIDO'S DANCING TOPS!!
RAAAH
RAAAH
TEN WHIRRING WEAPONS HE CAN LAUNCH AT HIS OPPONENT AT WILL!
BATTLE WALTZ!!

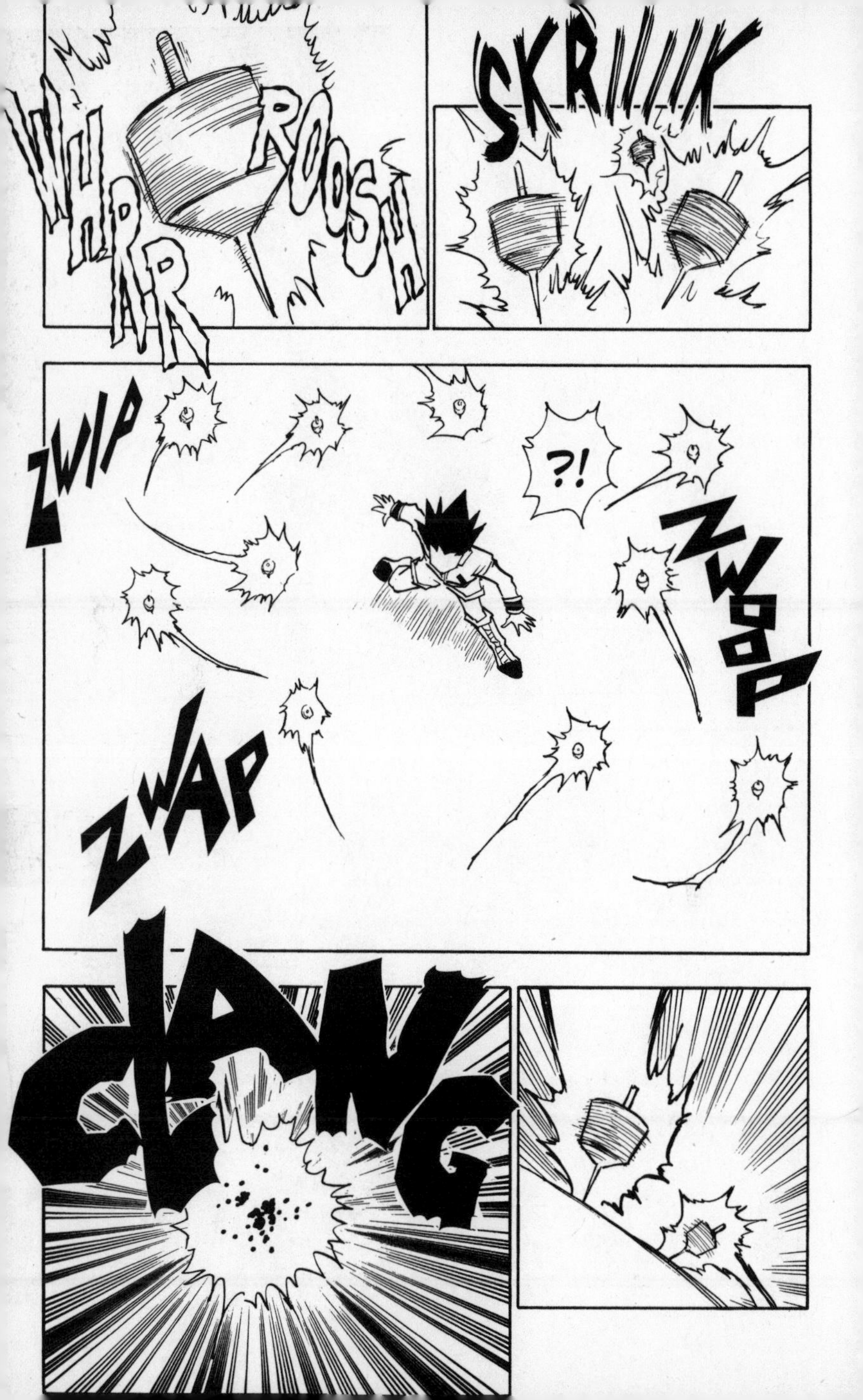
SKRIIIK
WHIRR
ROOSH
?!
NWOOP
ZWIP
ZWAP
CLANG

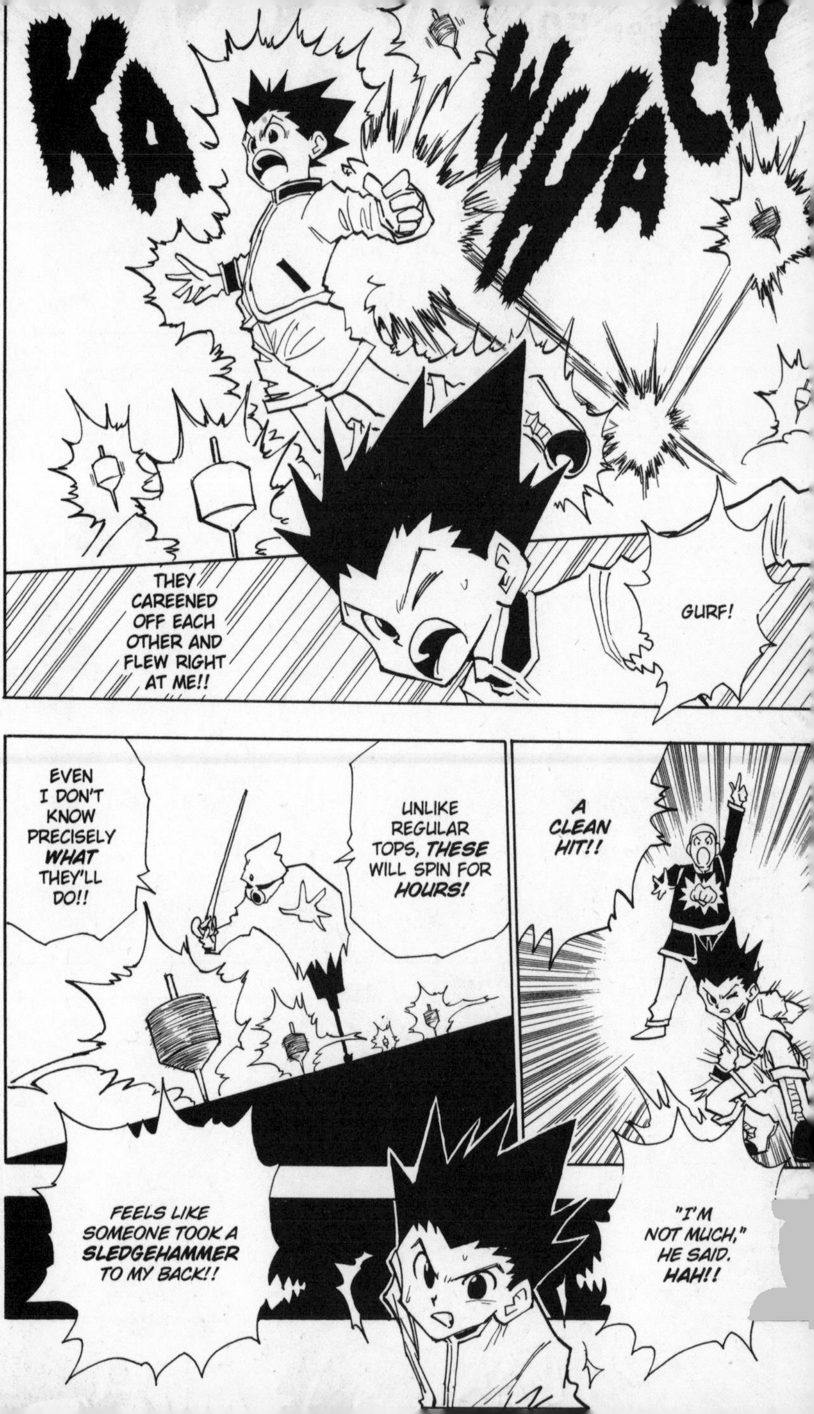
KA-WHACK
GURF!
THEY CAREENED OFF EACH OTHER AND FLEW RIGHT AT ME!!
A CLEAN HIT!!
UNLIKE REGULAR TOPS, *THESE* WILL SPIN FOR *HOURS!*
EVEN I DON'T KNOW PRECISELY *WHAT* THEY'LL DO!!
"I'M NOT MUCH," HE SAID. *HAH!!*
FEELS LIKE SOMEONE TOOK A ***SLEDGEHAMMER*** *TO MY BACK!!*

Chapter 50
"Zetsu"

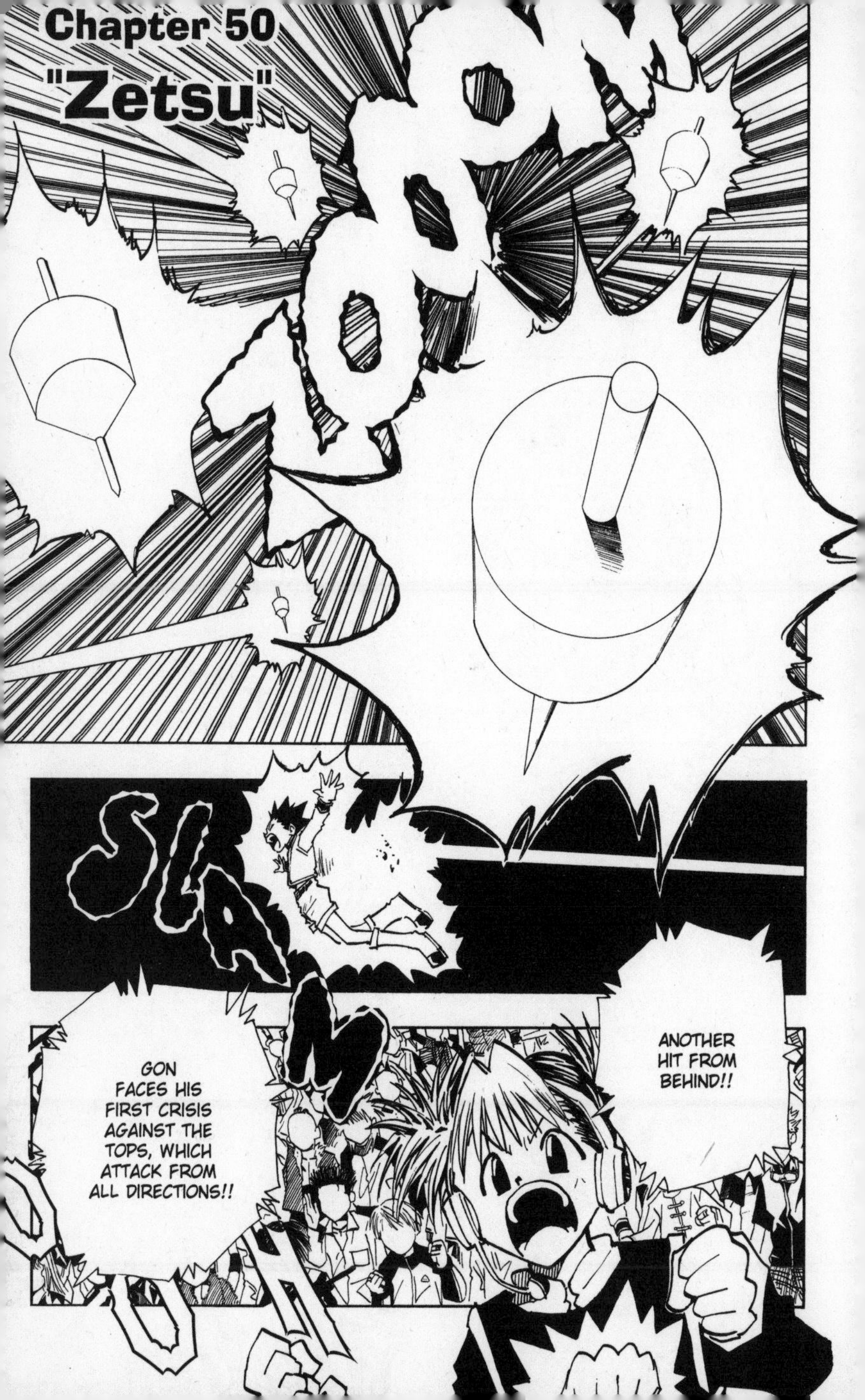
SLAM
ANOTHER HIT FROM BEHIND!!
GON FACES HIS FIRST CRISIS AGAINST THE TOPS, WHICH ATTACK FROM ALL DIRECTIONS!!

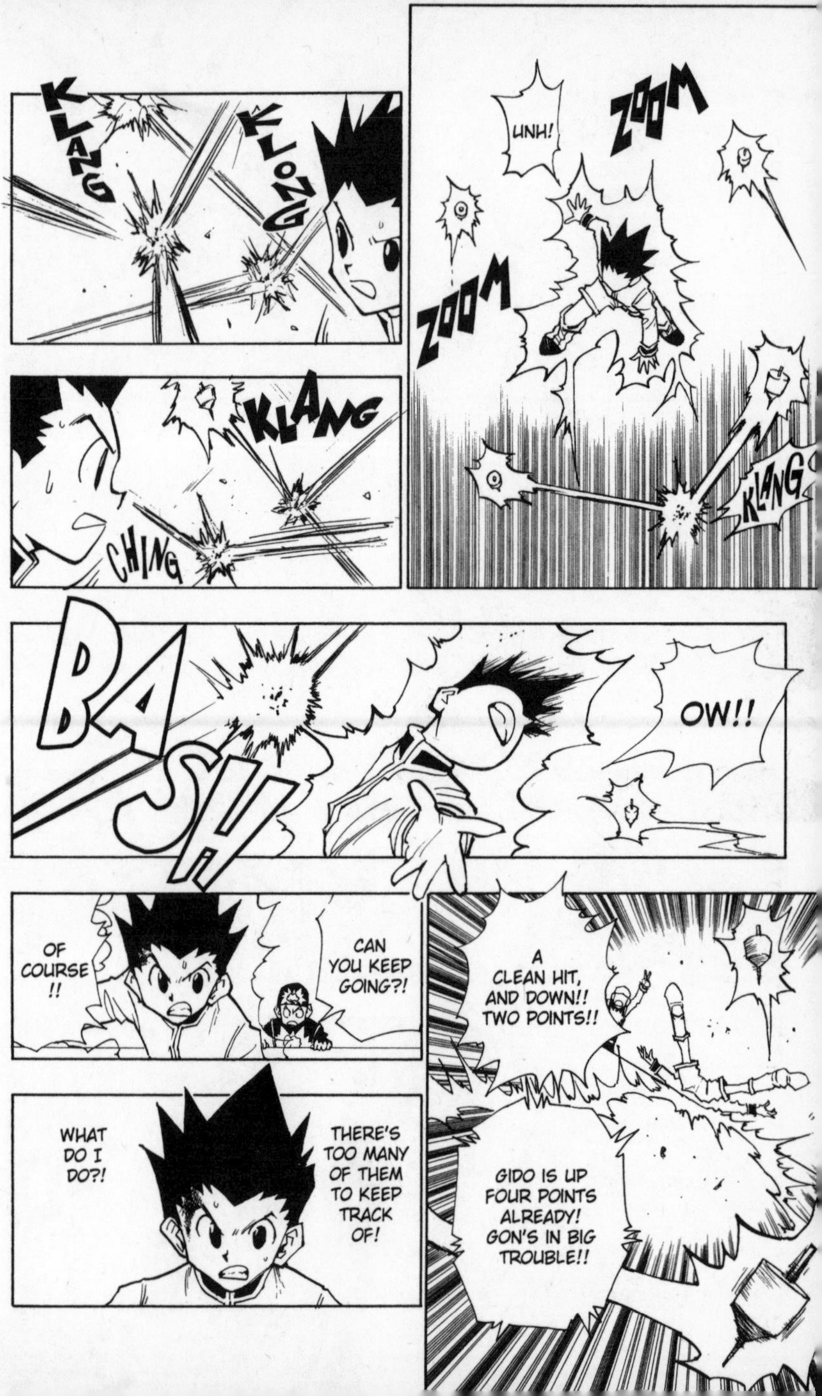
ZOOM
UNH!
ZOOM
KLANG
KLONG
KLANG
KLANG
CHING
OW!!
BASH
A CLEAN HIT, AND DOWN!! TWO POINTS!!
GIDO IS UP FOUR POINTS ALREADY! GON'S IN BIG TROUBLE!!
CAN YOU KEEP GOING?!
OF COURSE!!
THERE'S TOO MANY OF THEM TO KEEP TRACK OF!
WHAT DO I DO?!

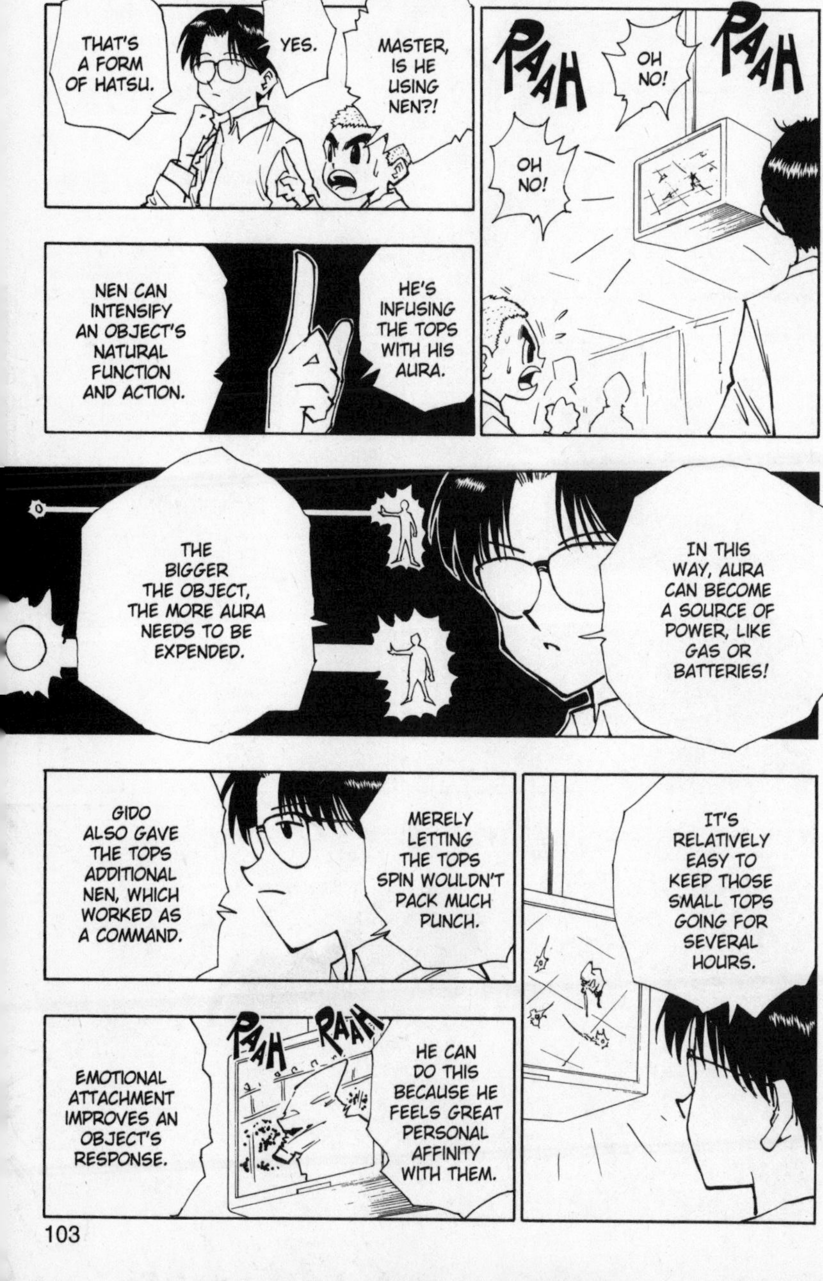
RAAH
OH NO!
RAAH
OH NO!
MASTER, IS HE USING NEN?!
YES.
THAT'S A FORM OF HATSU.
HE'S INFUSING THE TOPS WITH HIS AURA.
NEN CAN INTENSIFY AN OBJECT'S NATURAL FUNCTION AND ACTION.
IN THIS WAY, AURA CAN BECOME A SOURCE OF POWER, LIKE GAS OR BATTERIES!
THE BIGGER THE OBJECT, THE MORE AURA NEEDS TO BE EXPENDED.
IT'S RELATIVELY EASY TO KEEP THOSE SMALL TOPS GOING FOR SEVERAL HOURS.
MERELY LETTING THE TOPS SPIN WOULDN'T PACK MUCH PUNCH.
GIDO ALSO GAVE THE TOPS ADDITIONAL NEN, WHICH WORKED AS A COMMAND.
HE CAN DO THIS BECAUSE HE FEELS GREAT PERSONAL AFFINITY WITH THEM.
RAAH
RAAH
EMOTIONAL ATTACHMENT IMPROVES AN OBJECT'S RESPONSE.

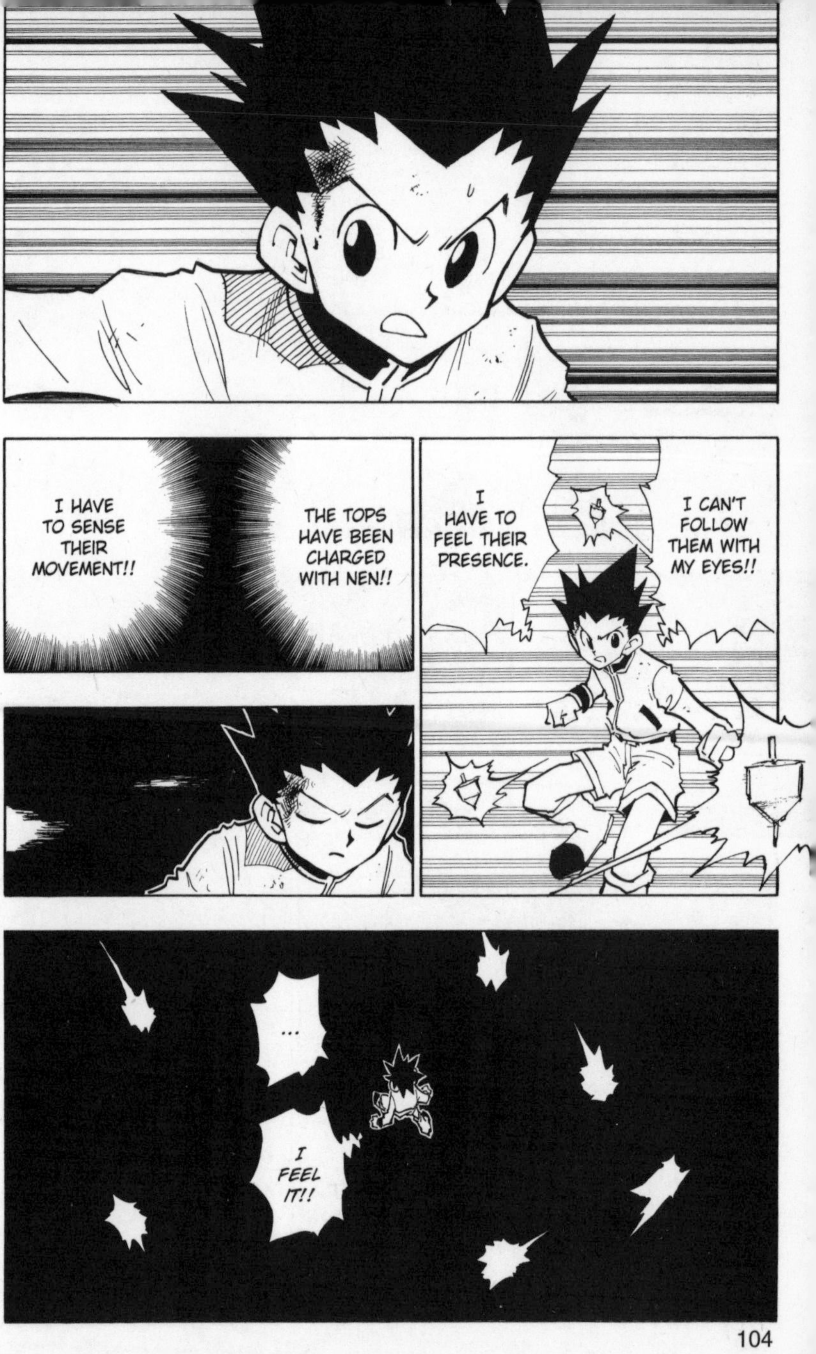
I CAN'T FOLLOW THEM WITH MY EYES!!
I HAVE TO FEEL THEIR PRESENCE.
THE TOPS HAVE BEEN CHARGED WITH NEN!!
I HAVE TO SENSE THEIR MOVEMENT!!
...
I FEEL IT!!

READ THIS WAY

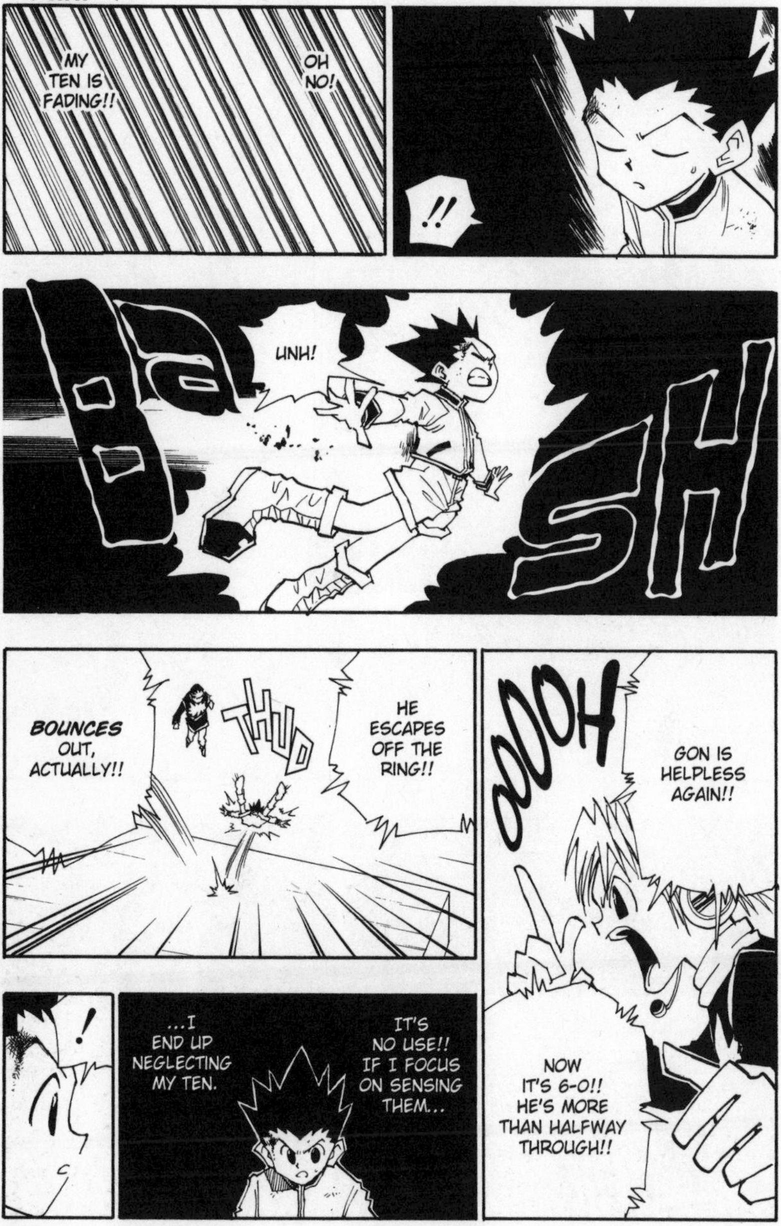
!!
OH NO!
MY TEN IS FADING!!
UNH!
BASH
OOOOH
GON IS HELPLESS AGAIN!!
NOW IT'S 6-0!! HE'S MORE THAN HALFWAY THROUGH!!
HE ESCAPES OFF THE RING!!
THUD
BOUNCES OUT, ACTUALLY!!
IT'S NO USE!! IF I FOCUS ON SENSING THEM...
...I END UP NEGLECTING MY TEN.
!

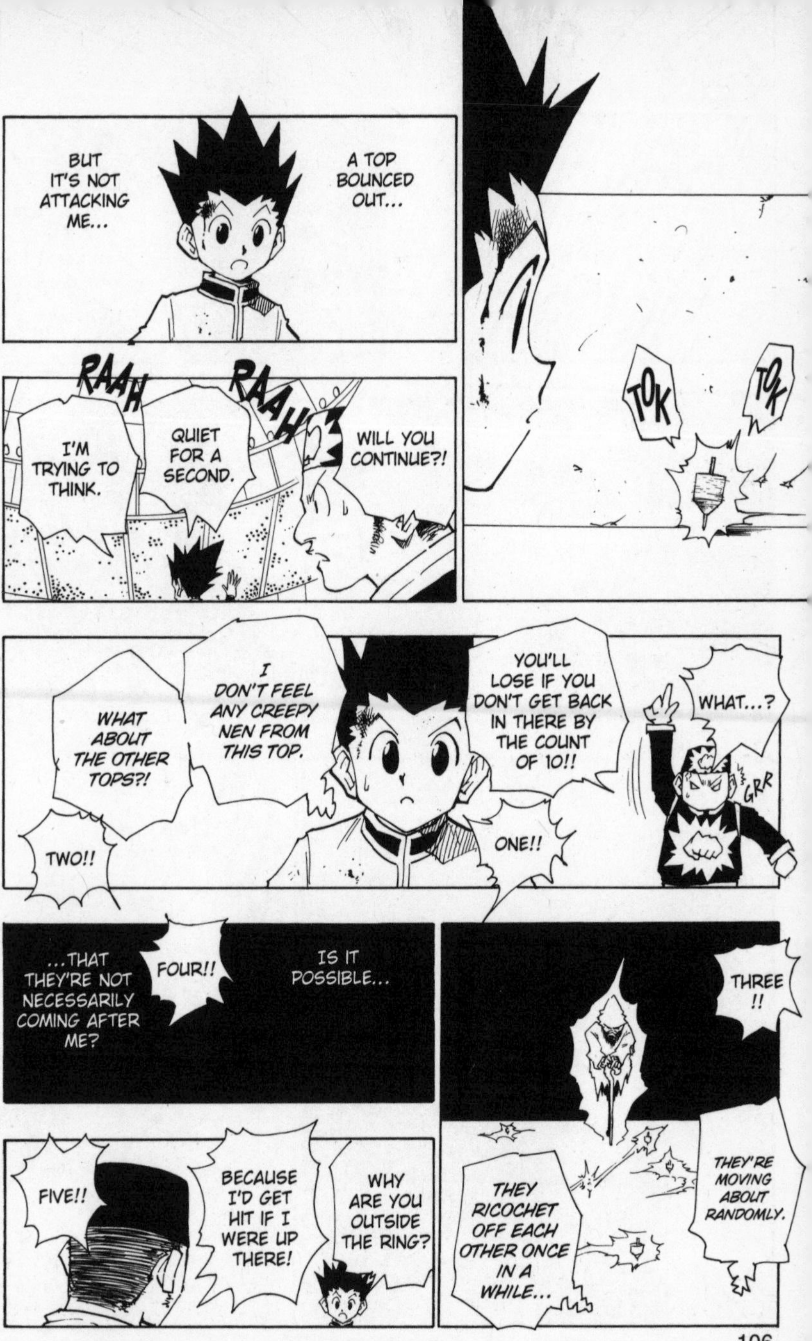
TOK
TOK
A TOP BOUNCED OUT...
BUT IT'S NOT ATTACKING ME...
WILL YOU CONTINUE?!
RAAH
QUIET FOR A SECOND.
RAAH
I'M TRYING TO THINK.
WHAT...?
GRR
YOU'LL LOSE IF YOU DON'T GET BACK IN THERE BY THE COUNT OF 10!!
ONE!!
I DON'T FEEL ANY CREEPY NEN FROM THIS TOP.
WHAT ABOUT THE OTHER TOPS?!
TWO!!
THREE !!
THEY'RE MOVING ABOUT RANDOMLY.
THEY RICOCHET OFF EACH OTHER ONCE IN A WHILE...
IS IT POSSIBLE...
FOUR!!
...THAT THEY'RE NOT NECESSARILY COMING AFTER ME?
WHY ARE YOU OUTSIDE THE RING?
BECAUSE I'D GET HIT IF I WERE UP THERE!
FIVE!!

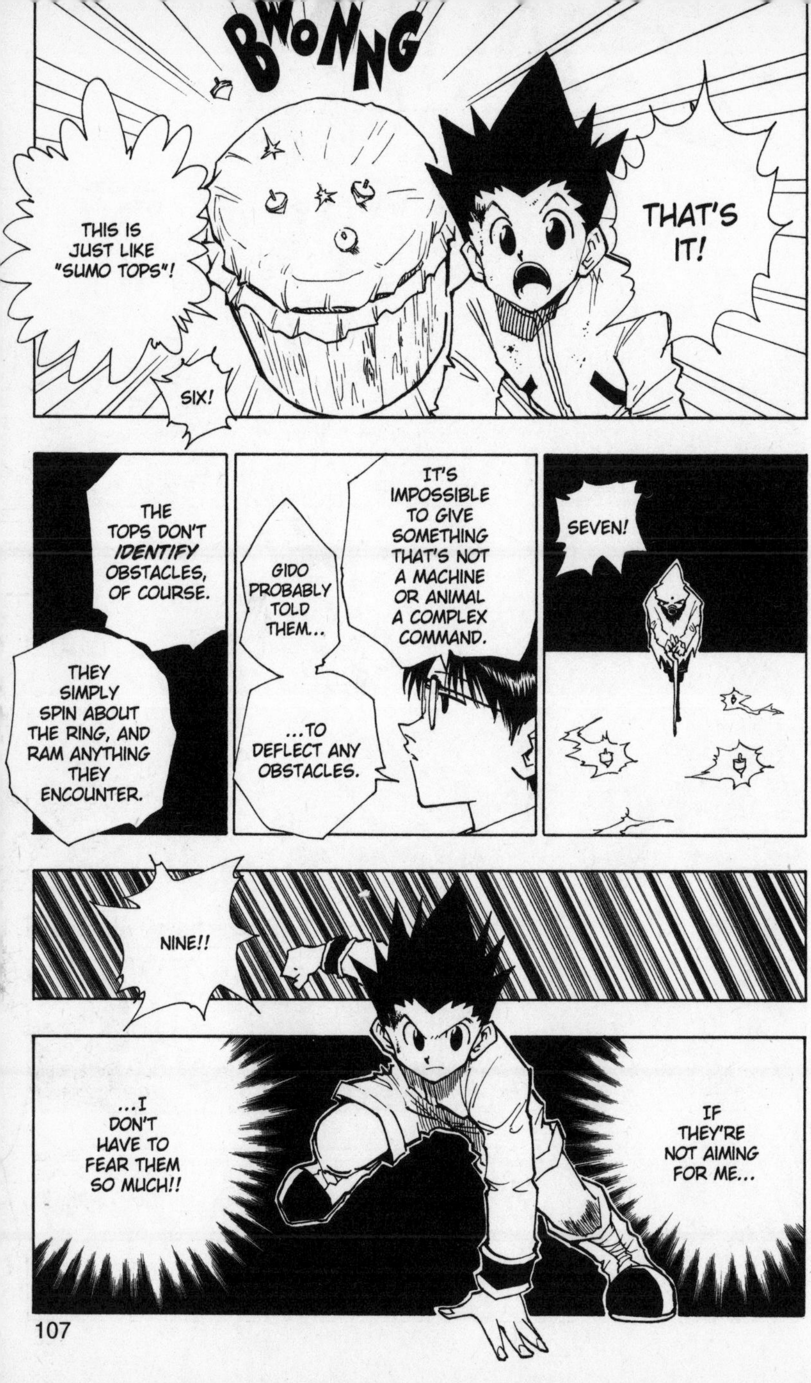
BWONNG
THAT'S IT!
THIS IS JUST LIKE "SUMO TOPS"!
SIX!
SEVEN!
IT'S IMPOSSIBLE TO GIVE SOMETHING THAT'S NOT A MACHINE OR ANIMAL A COMPLEX COMMAND.
GIDO PROBABLY TOLD THEM...
...TO DEFLECT ANY OBSTACLES.
THE TOPS DON'T *IDENTIFY* OBSTACLES, OF COURSE.
THEY SIMPLY SPIN ABOUT THE RING, AND RAM ANYTHING THEY ENCOUNTER.
NINE!!
IF THEY'RE NOT AIMING FOR ME...
...I DON'T HAVE TO FEAR THEM SO MUCH!!

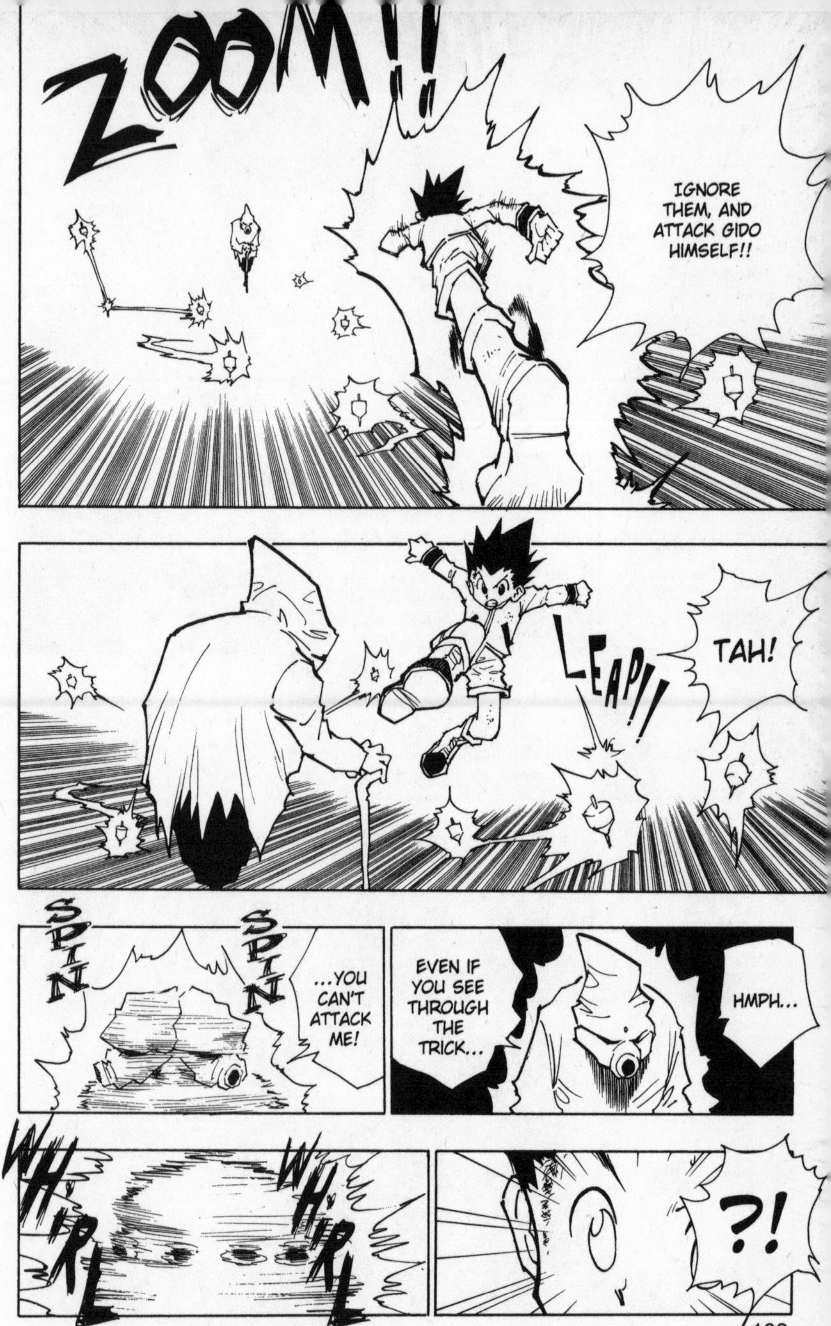
ZOOM!!
IGNORE THEM, AND ATTACK GIDO HIMSELF!!
TAH!
LEAP!!
HMPH...
EVEN IF YOU SEE THROUGH THE TRICK...
...YOU CAN'T ATTACK ME!
SPIN
SPIN
?!
WHIRL
WHIRL

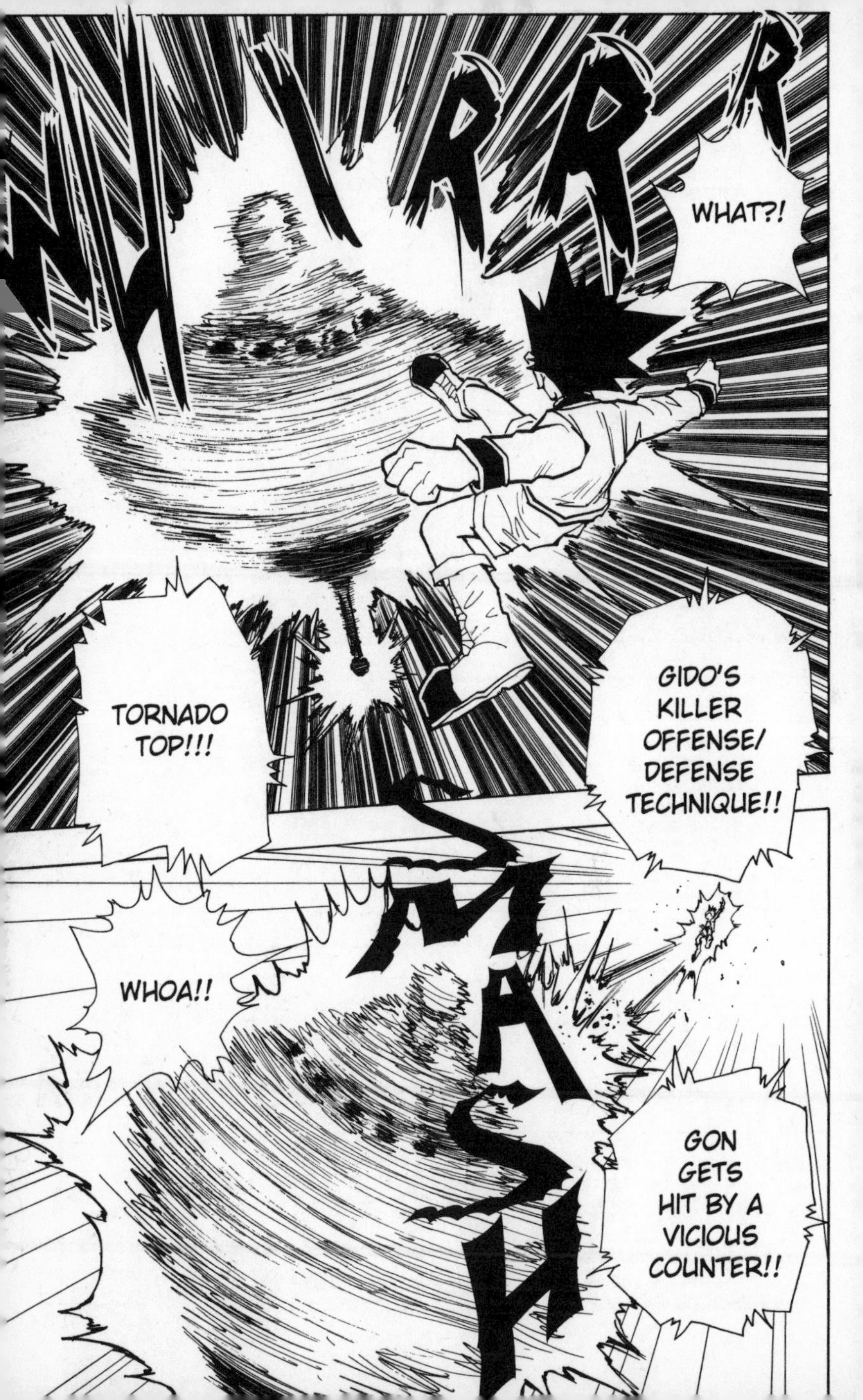
WHAT?!
GIDO'S KILLER OFFENSE/DEFENSE TECHNIQUE!!
TORNADO TOP!!!
SMASH
GON GETS HIT BY A VICIOUS COUNTER!!
WHOA!!

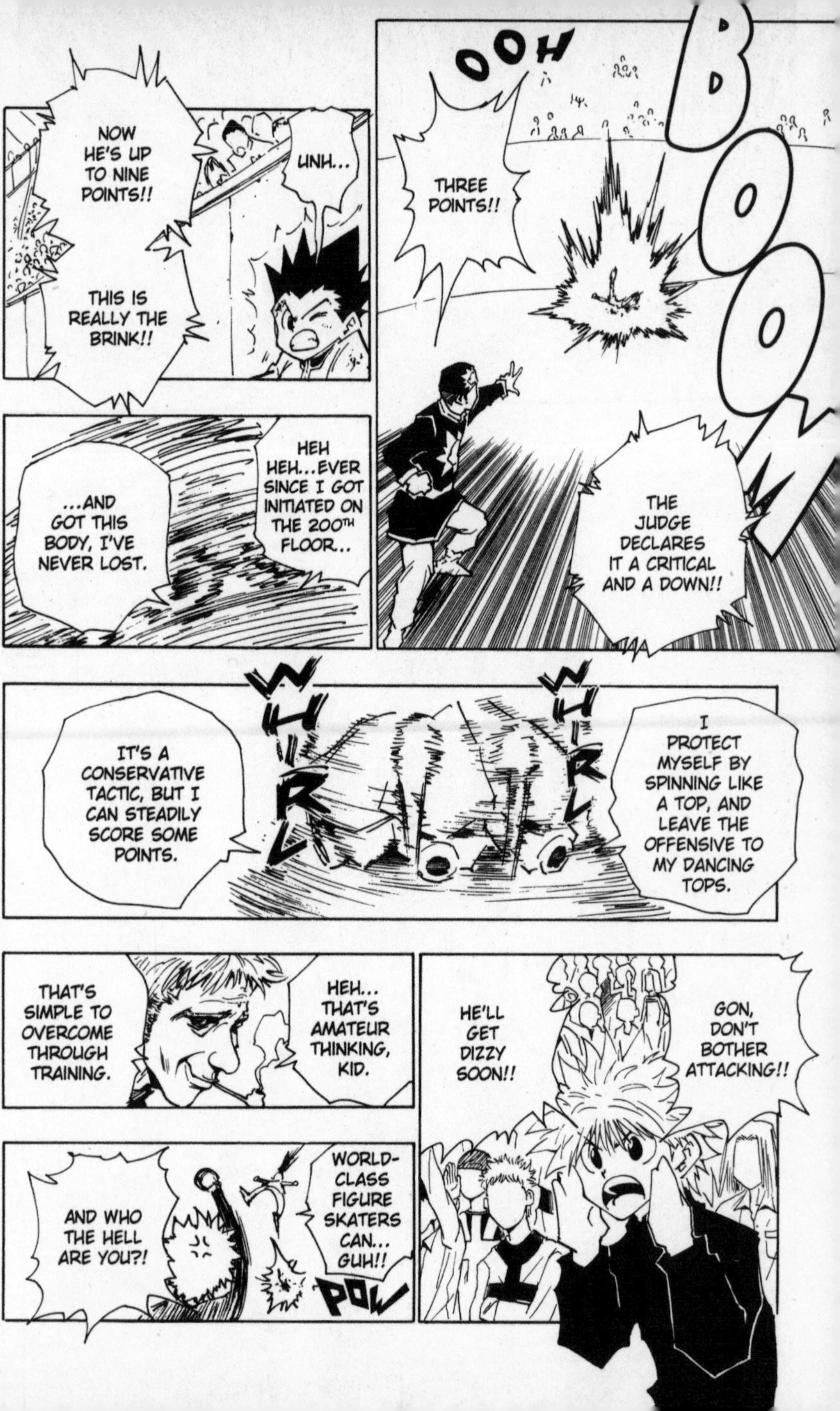
BOOOOM
OOH
THREE POINTS!!
THE JUDGE DECLARES IT A CRITICAL AND A DOWN!!
UNH...
NOW HE'S UP TO NINE POINTS!!
THIS IS REALLY THE BRINK!!
HEH HEH...EVER SINCE I GOT INITIATED ON THE 200TH FLOOR...
...AND GOT THIS BODY, I'VE NEVER LOST.
I PROTECT MYSELF BY SPINNING LIKE A TOP, AND LEAVE THE OFFENSIVE TO MY DANCING TOPS.
WHIRL
WHIRL
IT'S A CONSERVATIVE TACTIC, BUT I CAN STEADILY SCORE SOME POINTS.
GON, DON'T BOTHER ATTACKING!!
HE'LL GET DIZZY SOON!!
HEH... THAT'S AMATEUR THINKING, KID.
THAT'S SIMPLE TO OVERCOME THROUGH TRAINING.
WORLD-CLASS FIGURE SKATERS CAN... GUH!!
POW
AND WHO THE HELL ARE YOU?!

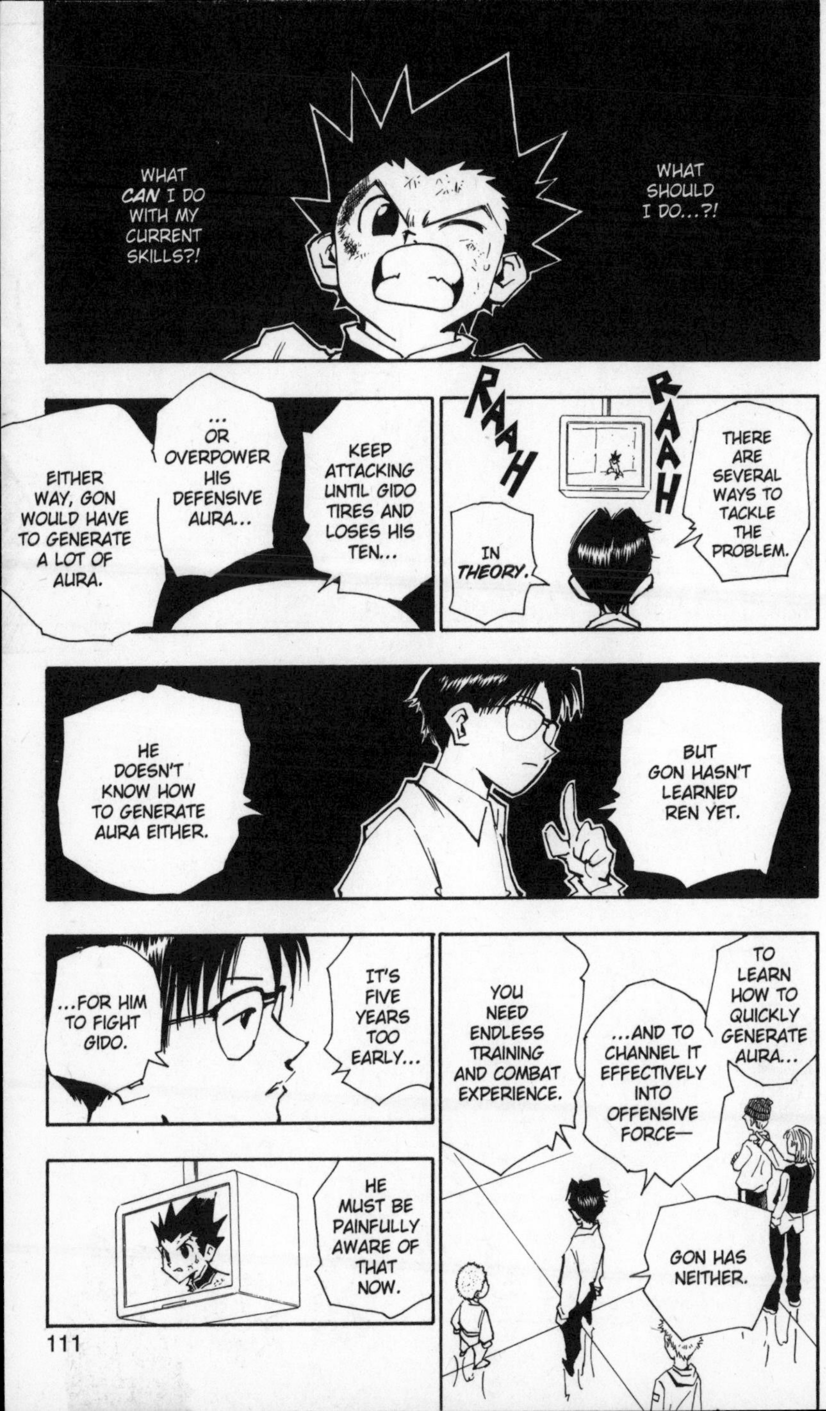
WHAT SHOULD I DO...?!
WHAT *CAN* I DO WITH MY CURRENT SKILLS?!
RAAAH
THERE ARE SEVERAL WAYS TO TACKLE THE PROBLEM.
RAAAH
IN *THEORY*.
KEEP ATTACKING UNTIL GIDO TIRES AND LOSES HIS TEN...
...OR OVERPOWER HIS DEFENSIVE AURA...
EITHER WAY, GON WOULD HAVE TO GENERATE A LOT OF AURA.
BUT GON HASN'T LEARNED REN YET.
HE DOESN'T KNOW HOW TO GENERATE AURA EITHER.
TO LEARN HOW TO QUICKLY GENERATE AURA...
...AND TO CHANNEL IT EFFECTIVELY INTO OFFENSIVE FORCE—
YOU NEED ENDLESS TRAINING AND COMBAT EXPERIENCE.
GON HAS NEITHER.
IT'S FIVE YEARS TOO EARLY...
...FOR HIM TO FIGHT GIDO.
HE MUST BE PAINFULLY AWARE OF THAT NOW.

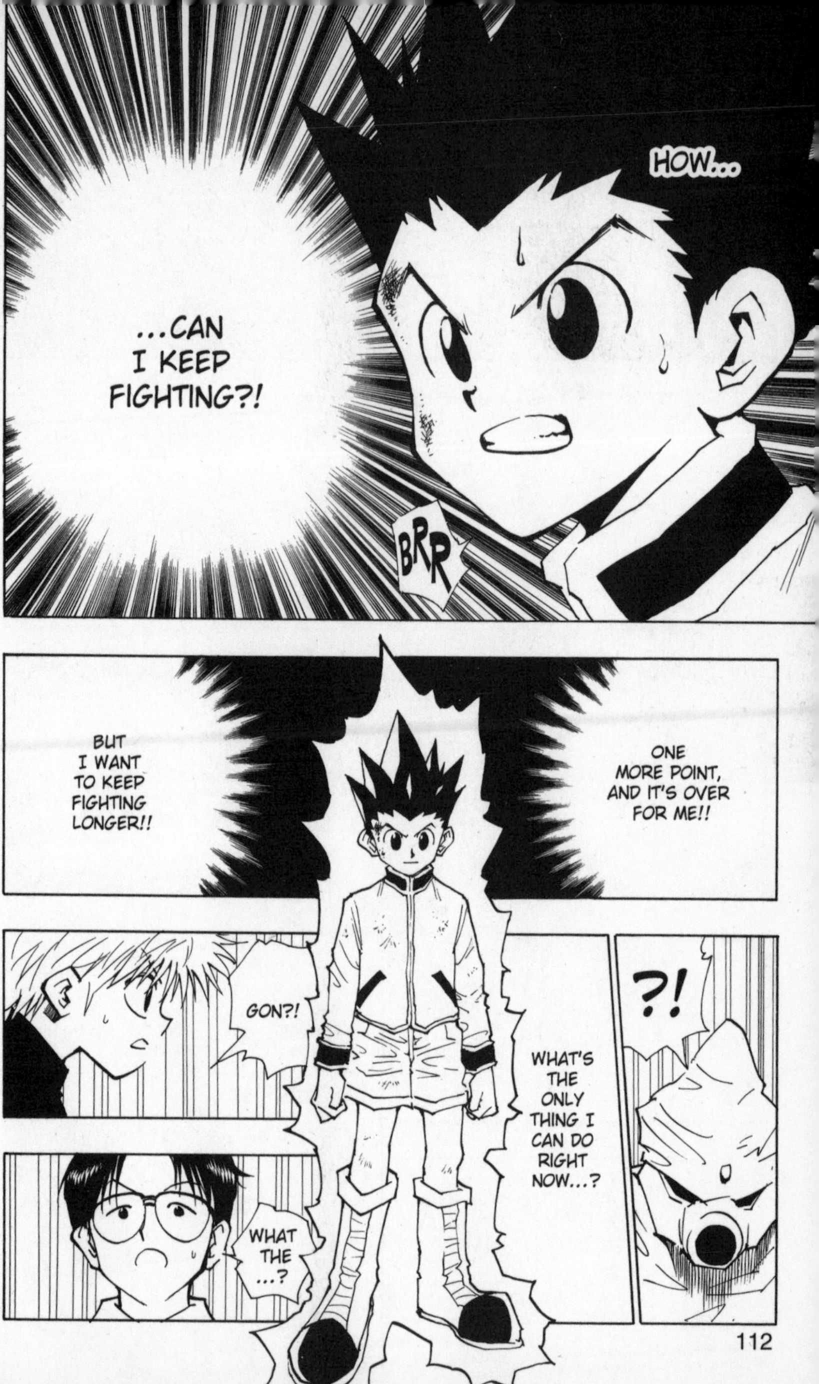
HOW...
...CAN I KEEP FIGHTING?!
BRR
ONE MORE POINT, AND IT'S OVER FOR ME!!
BUT I WANT TO KEEP FIGHTING LONGER!!
?!
WHAT'S THE ONLY THING I CAN DO RIGHT NOW...?
GON?!
WHAT THE ...?

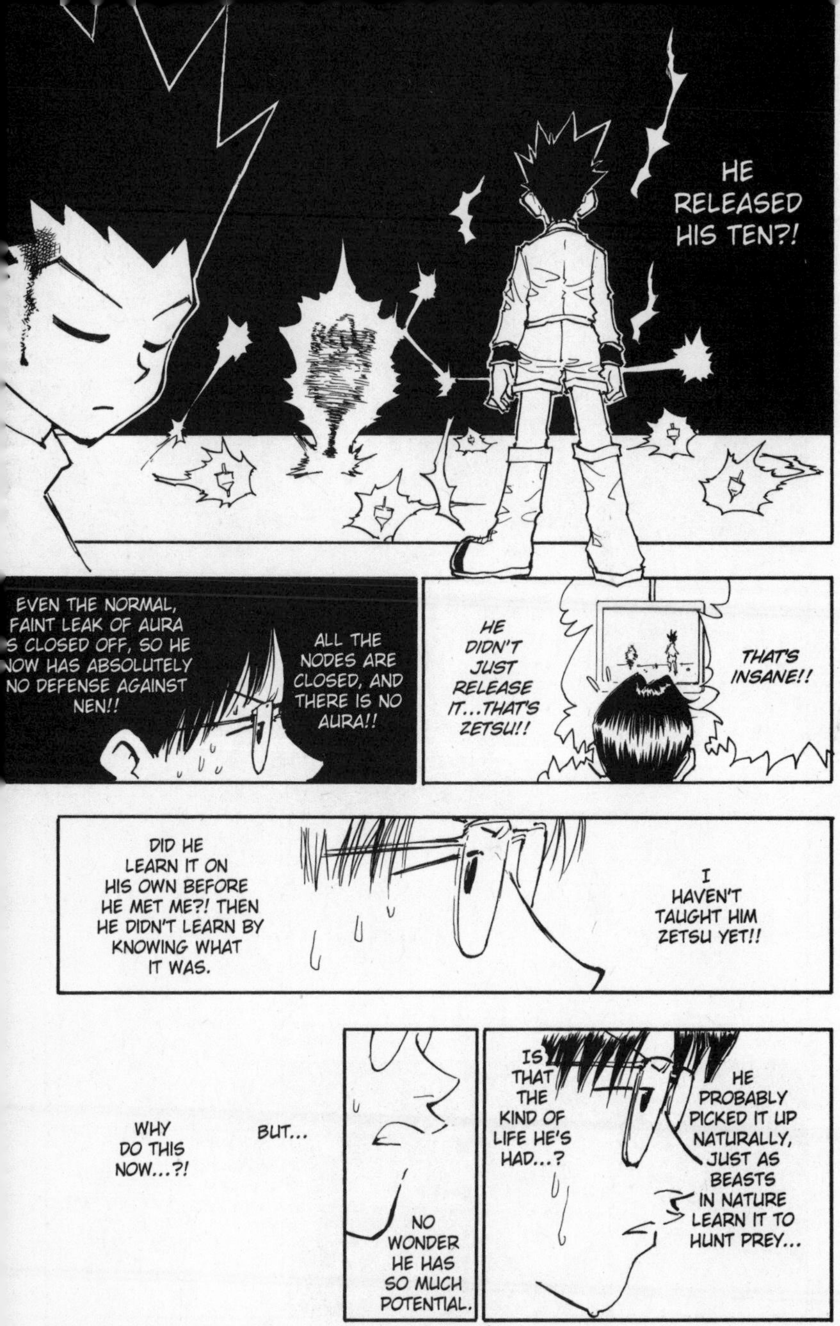
HE RELEASED HIS TEN?!
THAT'S INSANE!!
HE DIDN'T JUST RELEASE IT...THAT'S ZETSU!!
ALL THE NODES ARE CLOSED, AND THERE IS NO AURA!!
EVEN THE NORMAL, FAINT LEAK OF AURA S CLOSED OFF, SO HE NOW HAS ABSOLUTELY NO DEFENSE AGAINST NEN!!
I HAVEN'T TAUGHT HIM ZETSU YET!!
DID HE LEARN IT ON HIS OWN BEFORE HE MET ME?! THEN HE DIDN'T LEARN BY KNOWING WHAT IT WAS.
HE PROBABLY PICKED IT UP NATURALLY, JUST AS BEASTS IN NATURE LEARN IT TO HUNT PREY...
IS THAT THE KIND OF LIFE HE'S HAD...?
NO WONDER HE HAS SO MUCH POTENTIAL.
BUT...
WHY DO THIS NOW...?!

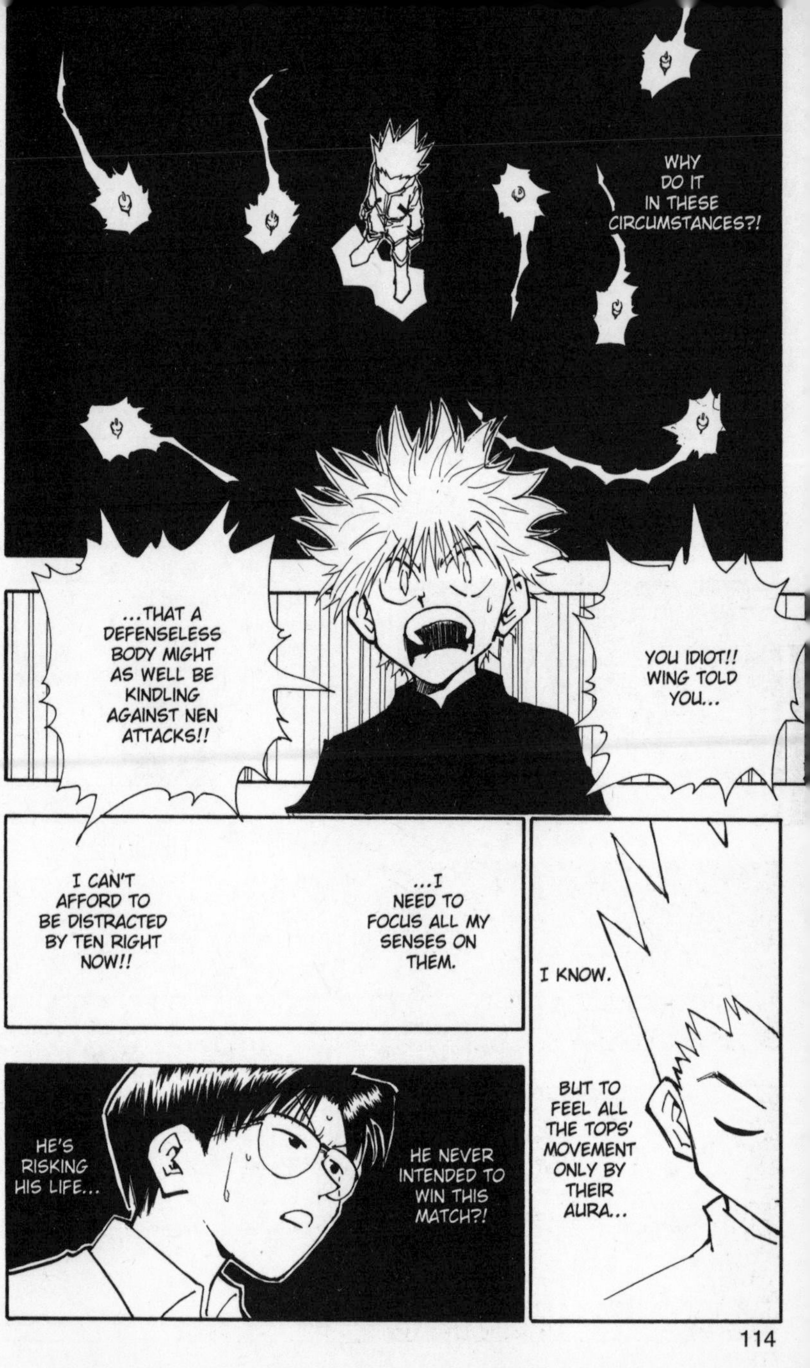
WHY DO IT IN THESE CIRCUMSTANCES?!
YOU IDIOT!! WING TOLD YOU...
...THAT A DEFENSELESS BODY MIGHT AS WELL BE KINDLING AGAINST NEN ATTACKS!!
I KNOW.
BUT TO FEEL ALL THE TOPS' MOVEMENT ONLY BY THEIR AURA...
...I NEED TO FOCUS ALL MY SENSES ON THEM.
I CAN'T AFFORD TO BE DISTRACTED BY TEN RIGHT NOW!!
HE NEVER INTENDED TO WIN THIS MATCH?!
HE'S RISKING HIS LIFE...

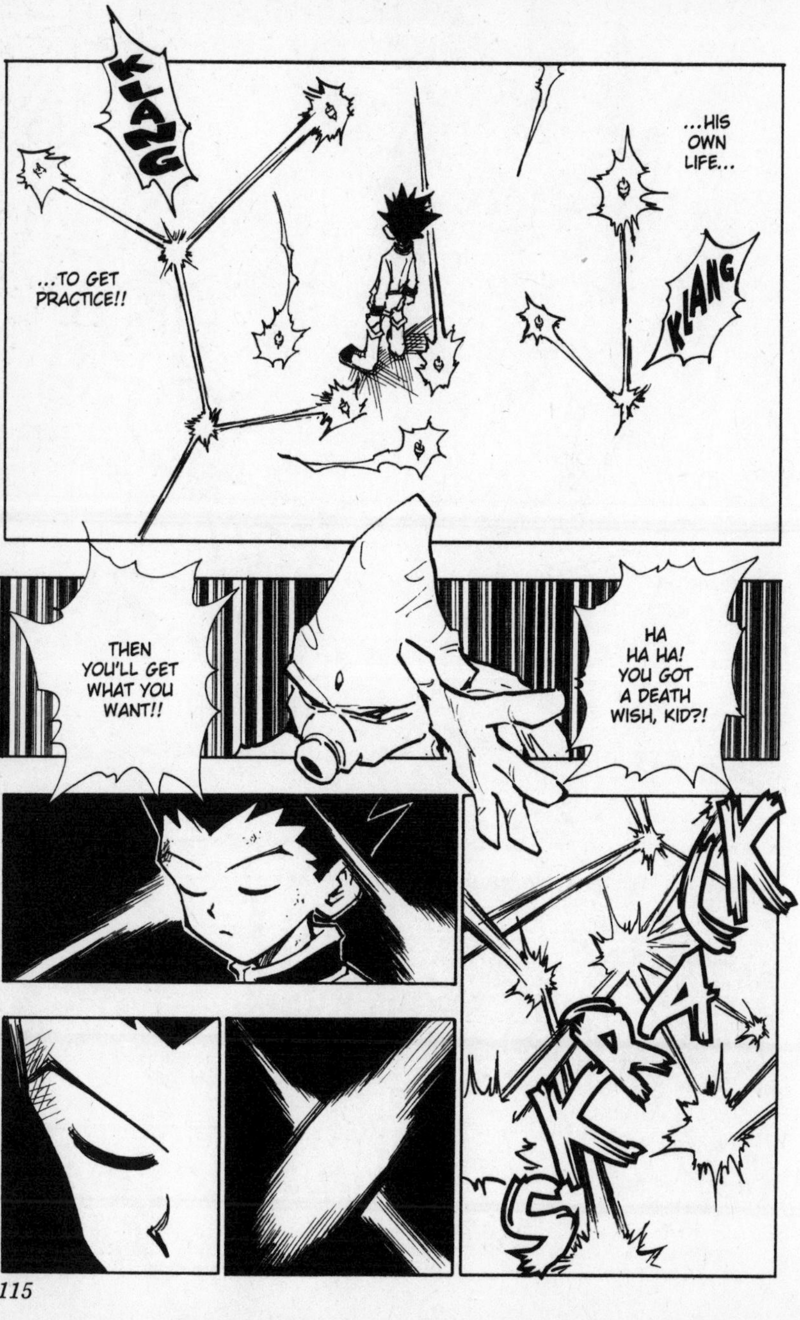
...HIS OWN LIFE...
KLANG
KLANG
...TO GET PRACTICE!!
HA HA HA! YOU GOT A DEATH WISH, KID?!
THEN YOU'LL GET WHAT YOU WANT!!
SKRAKK

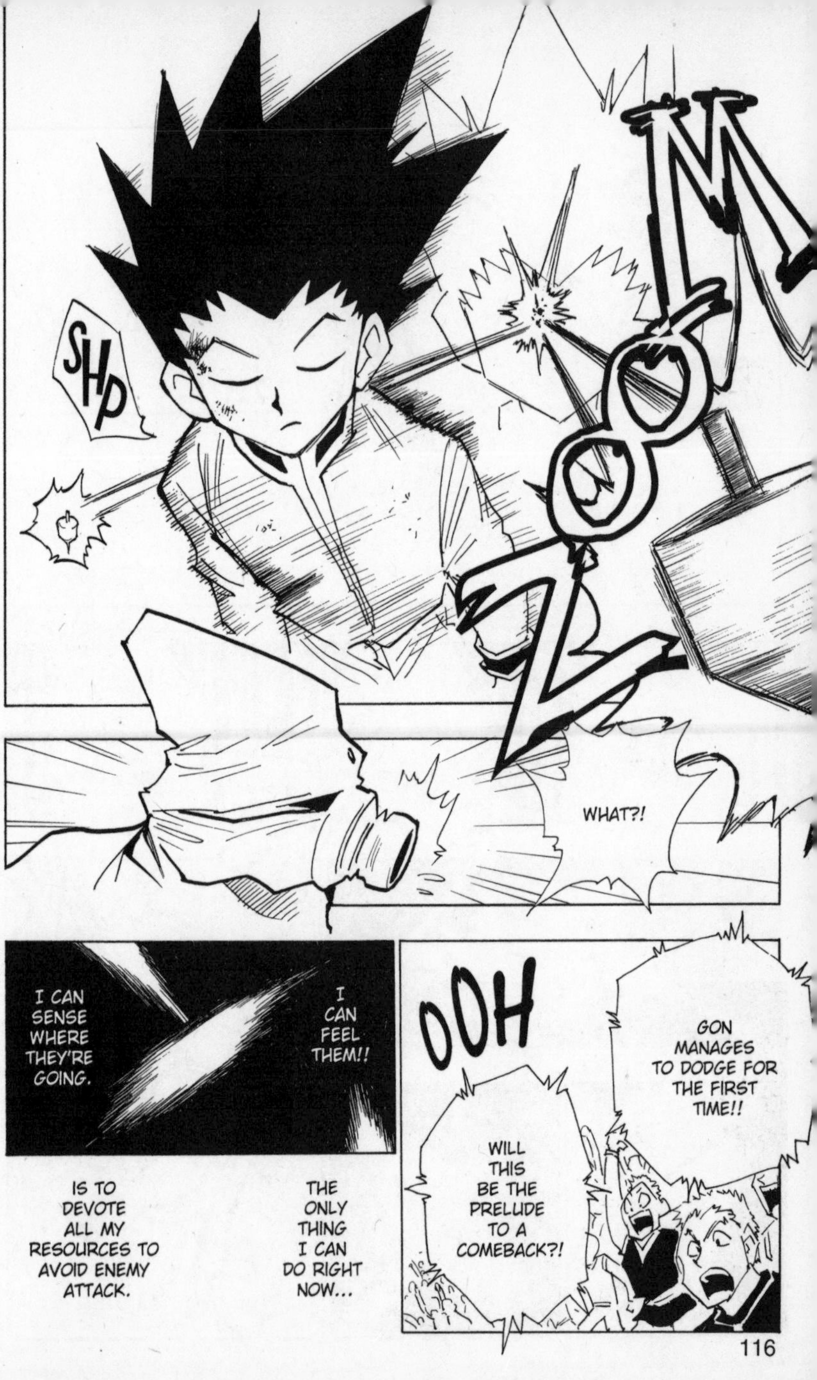
SHP
ZOOOM
WHAT?!
OOH
GON MANAGES TO DODGE FOR THE FIRST TIME!!
WILL THIS BE THE PRELUDE TO A COMEBACK?!
I CAN FEEL THEM!!
I CAN SENSE WHERE THEY'RE GOING.
THE ONLY THING I CAN DO RIGHT NOW...
IS TO DEVOTE ALL MY RESOURCES TO AVOID ENEMY ATTACK.

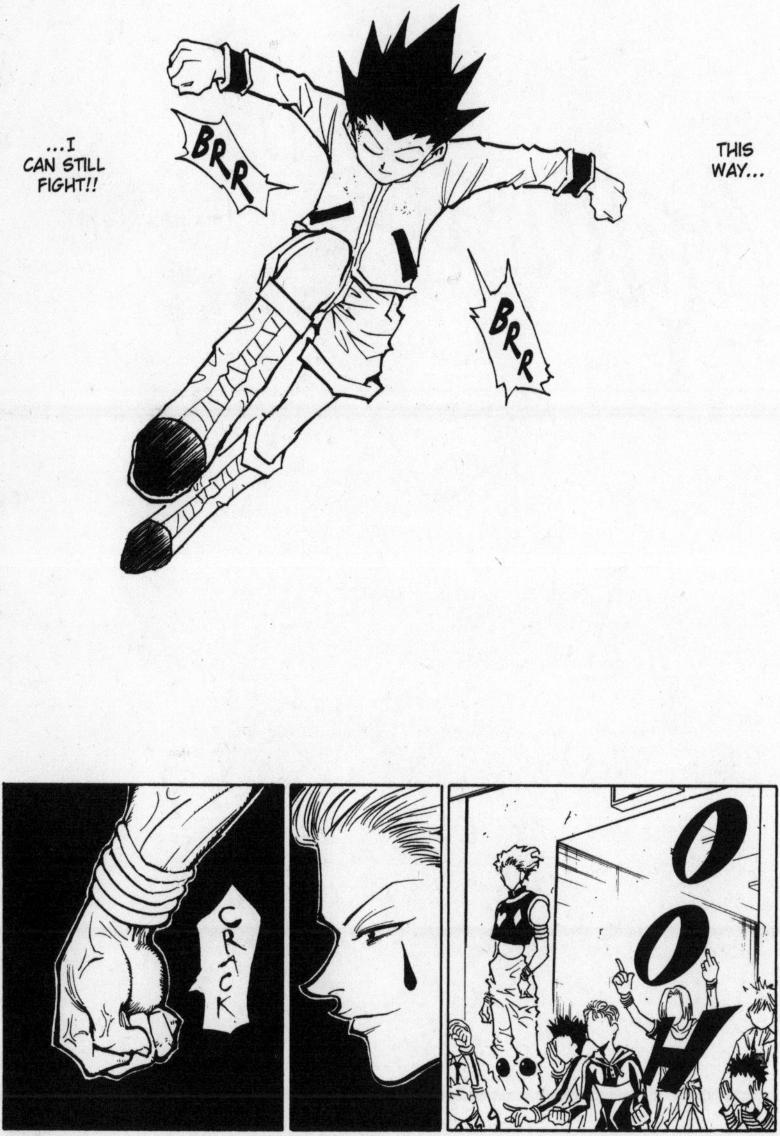

THIS WAY...
...I CAN STILL FIGHT!!
BRR
BRR
OOH
CRACK

Color-me-Gon

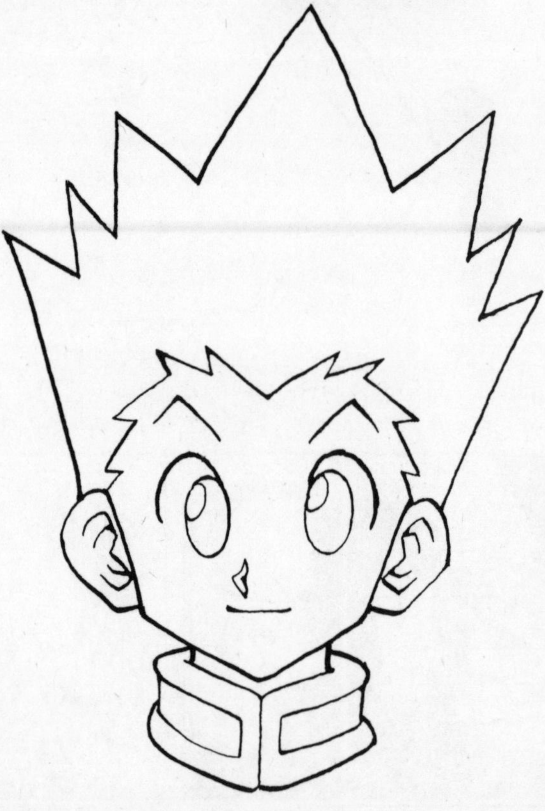

Chapter 51 "Ten"

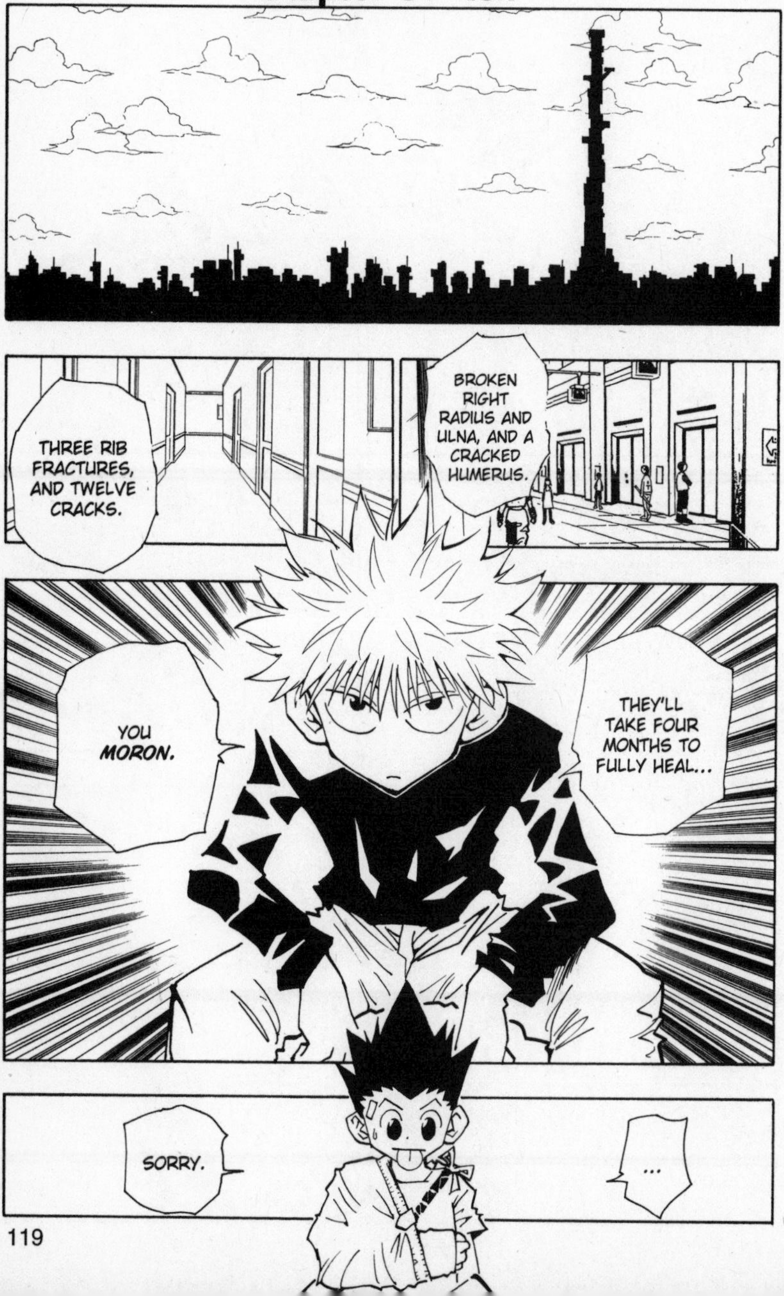
BROKEN RIGHT RADIUS AND ULNA, AND A CRACKED HUMERUS.
THREE RIB FRACTURES, AND TWELVE CRACKS.
THEY'LL TAKE FOUR MONTHS TO FULLY HEAL...
YOU *MORON.*
...
SORRY.

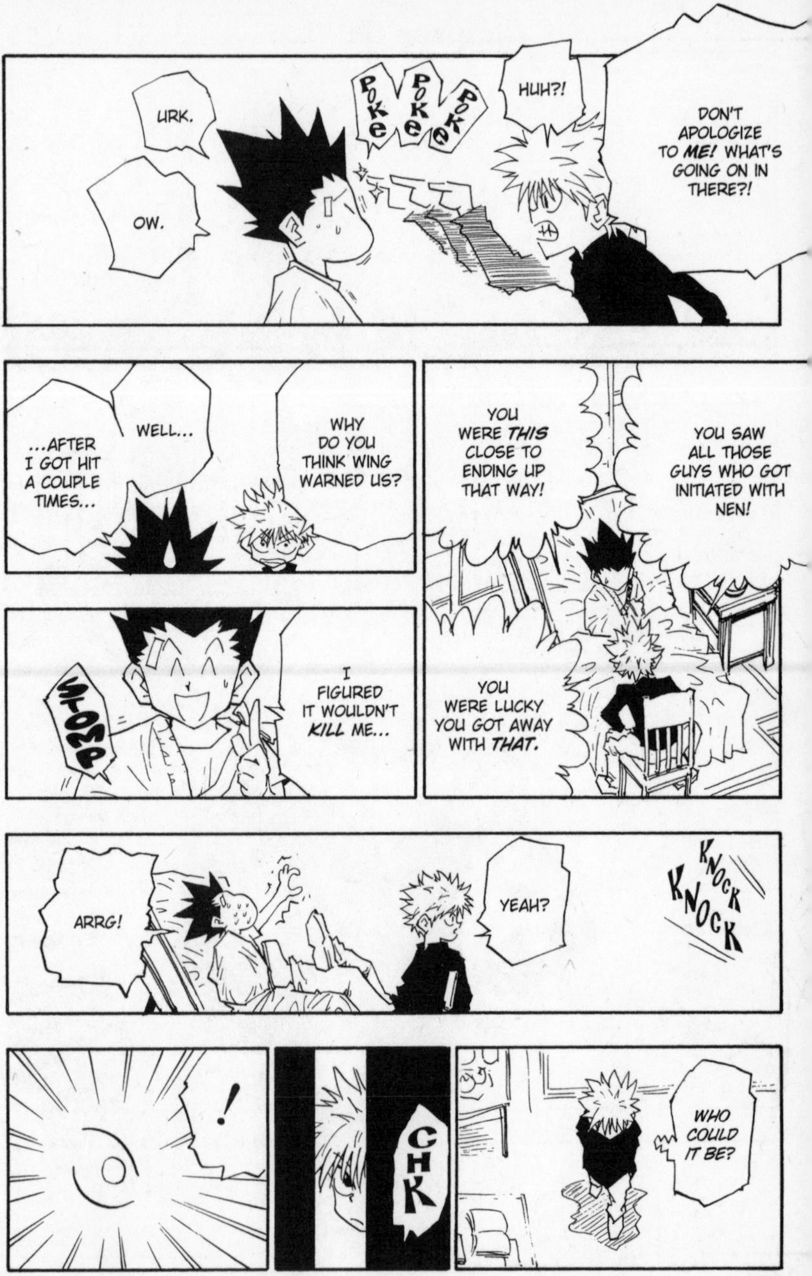

DON'T APOLOGIZE TO *ME!* WHAT'S GOING ON IN THERE?!
HUH?!
POKE
POKE
POKE
URK.
OW.
YOU SAW ALL THOSE GUYS WHO GOT INITIATED WITH NEN!
YOU WERE *THIS* CLOSE TO ENDING UP THAT WAY!
YOU WERE LUCKY YOU GOT AWAY WITH *THAT.*
WHY DO YOU THINK WING WARNED US?
WELL...
...AFTER I GOT HIT A COUPLE TIMES...
I FIGURED IT WOULDN'T *KILL* ME...
STOMP
KNOCK KNOCK
YEAH?
ARRG!
WHO COULD IT BE?
CHK
!

Chapter 51
"Ten"

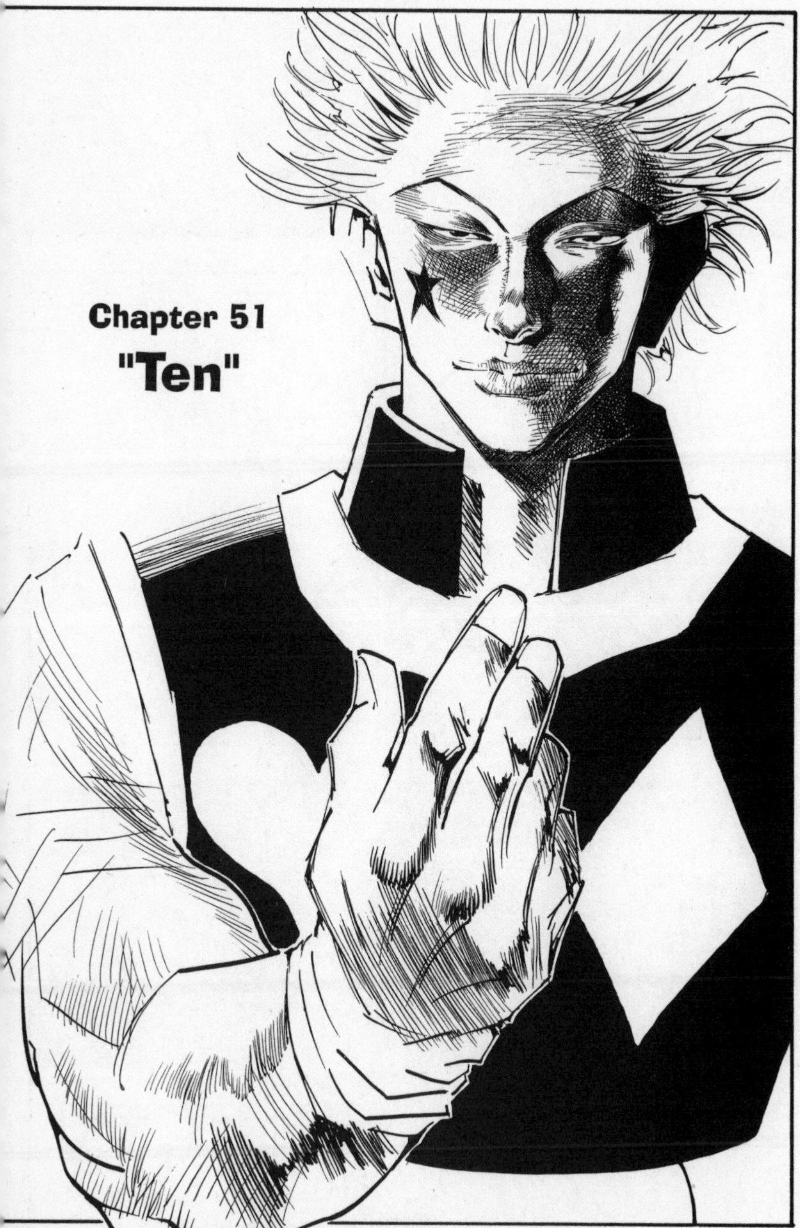

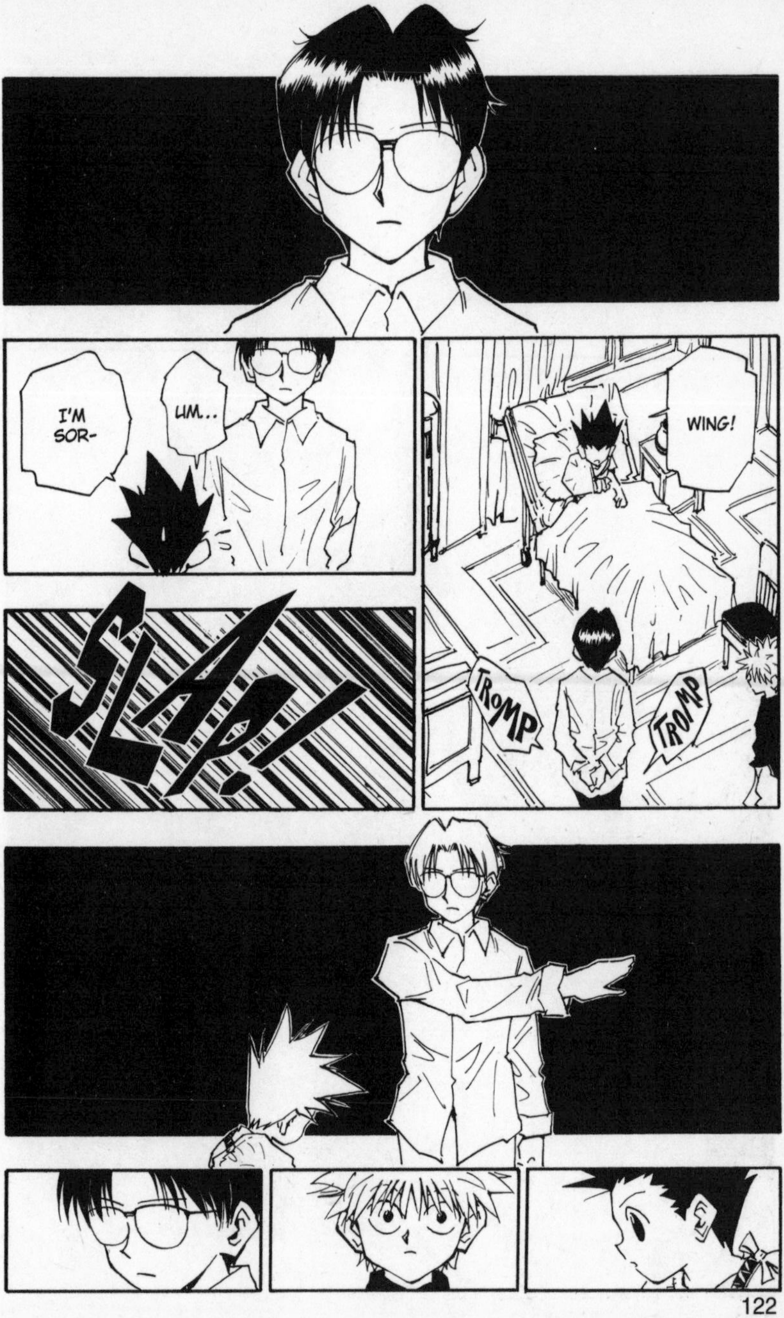
WING!
TROMP
TROMP
UM...
I'M SOR-
SLAP!

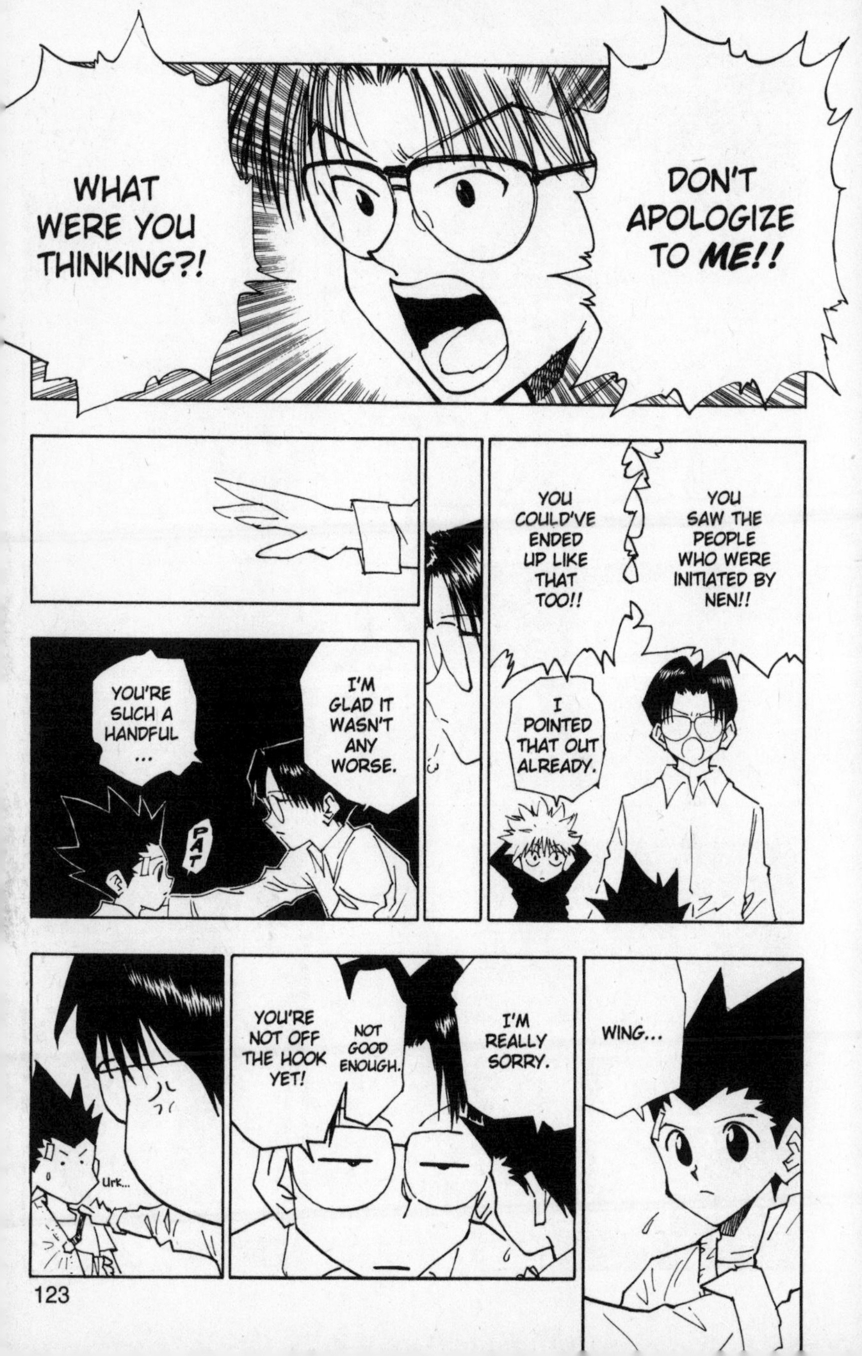
DON'T APOLOGIZE TO ME!!
WHAT WERE YOU THINKING?!
YOU SAW THE PEOPLE WHO WERE INITIATED BY NEN!!
YOU COULD'VE ENDED UP LIKE THAT TOO!!
I POINTED THAT OUT ALREADY.
I'M GLAD IT WASN'T ANY WORSE.
YOU'RE SUCH A HANDFUL ...
PAT
WING...
I'M REALLY SORRY.
NOT GOOD ENOUGH.
YOU'RE NOT OFF THE HOOK YET!
Urk...

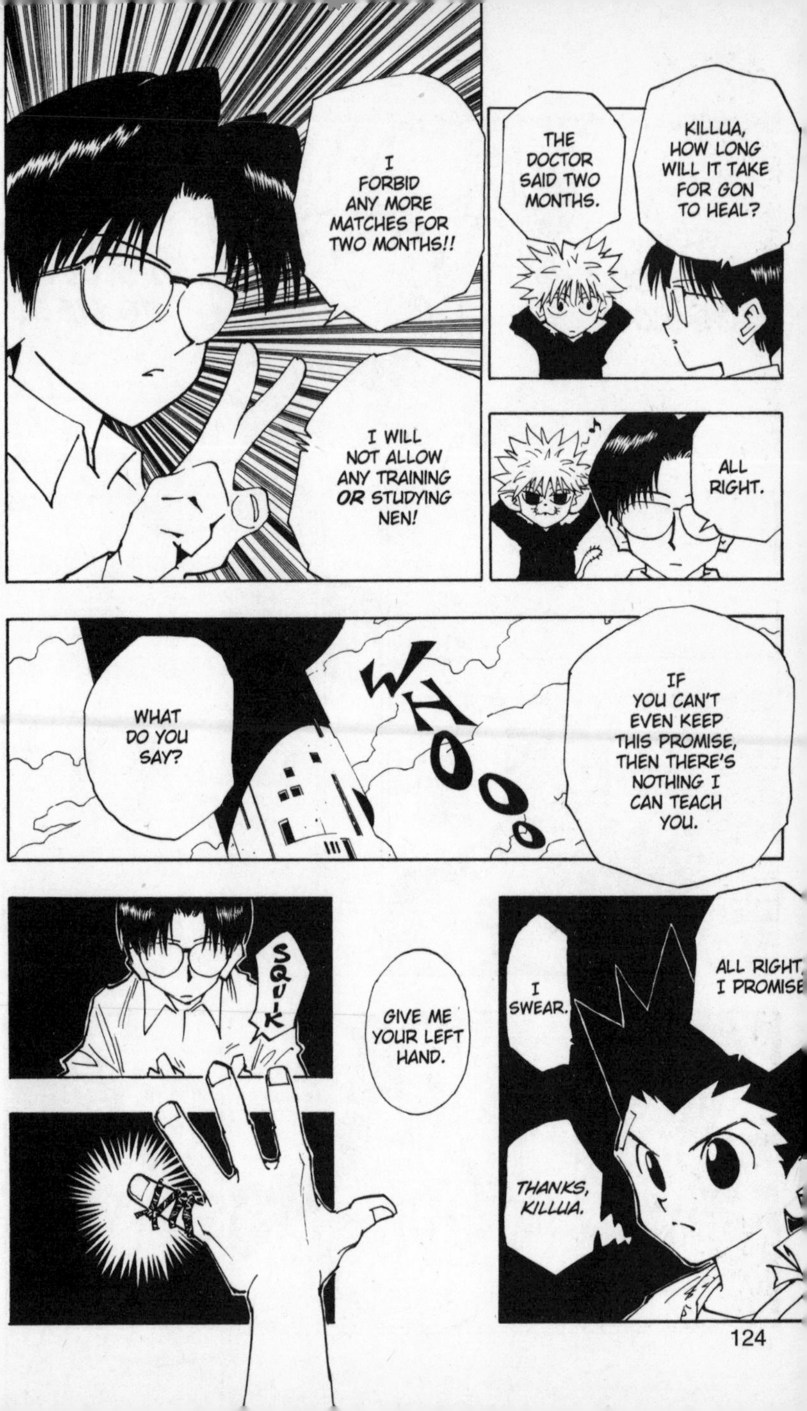
KILLUA, HOW LONG WILL IT TAKE FOR GON TO HEAL?
THE DOCTOR SAID TWO MONTHS.
ALL RIGHT.
I FORBID ANY MORE MATCHES FOR TWO MONTHS!!
I WILL NOT ALLOW ANY TRAINING OR STUDYING NEN!
IF YOU CAN'T EVEN KEEP THIS PROMISE, THEN THERE'S NOTHING I CAN TEACH YOU.
WHOOO
WHAT DO YOU SAY?
ALL RIGHT, I PROMISE
I SWEAR.
THANKS, KILLUA.
SQUIK
GIVE ME YOUR LEFT HAND.

READ THIS WAY

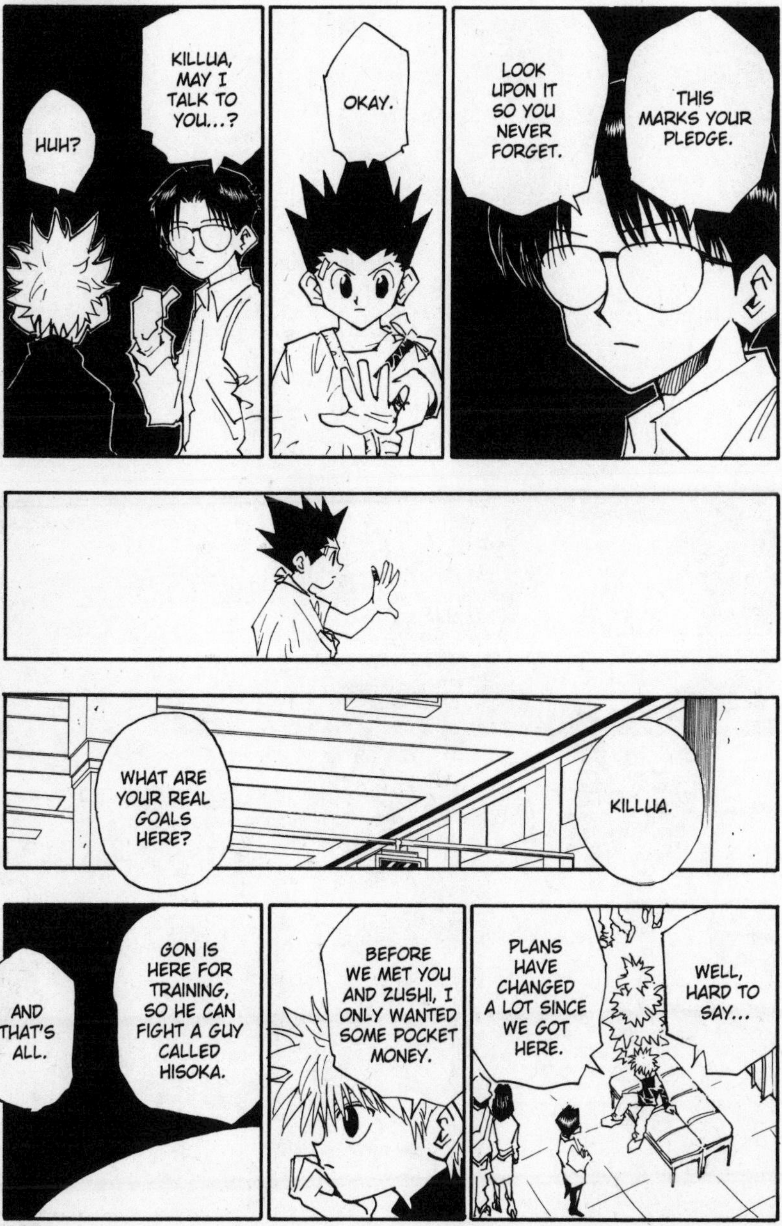
THIS MARKS YOUR PLEDGE.
LOOK UPON IT SO YOU NEVER FORGET.
OKAY.
KILLUA, MAY I TALK TO YOU...?
HUH?
KILLUA.
WHAT ARE YOUR REAL GOALS HERE?
WELL, HARD TO SAY...
PLANS HAVE CHANGED A LOT SINCE WE GOT HERE.
BEFORE WE MET YOU AND ZUSHI, I ONLY WANTED SOME POCKET MONEY.
GON IS HERE FOR TRAINING, SO HE CAN FIGHT A GUY CALLED HISOKA.
AND THAT'S ALL.

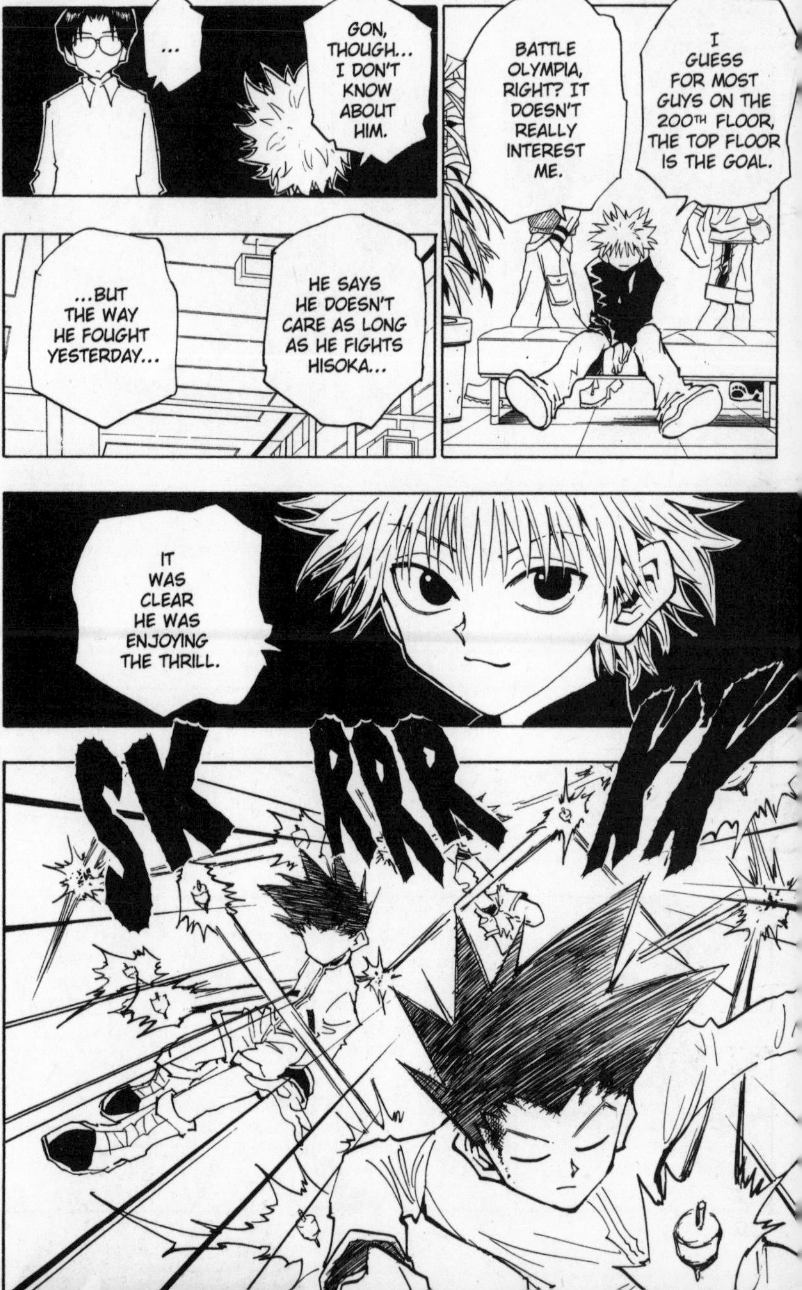
I GUESS FOR MOST GUYS ON THE 200TH FLOOR, THE TOP FLOOR IS THE GOAL.
BATTLE OLYMPIA, RIGHT? IT DOESN'T REALLY INTEREST ME.
GON, THOUGH... I DON'T KNOW ABOUT HIM.
...
HE SAYS HE DOESN'T CARE AS LONG AS HE FIGHTS HISOKA...
...BUT THE WAY HE FOUGHT YESTERDAY...
IT WAS CLEAR HE WAS ENJOYING THE THRILL.
SKRRR

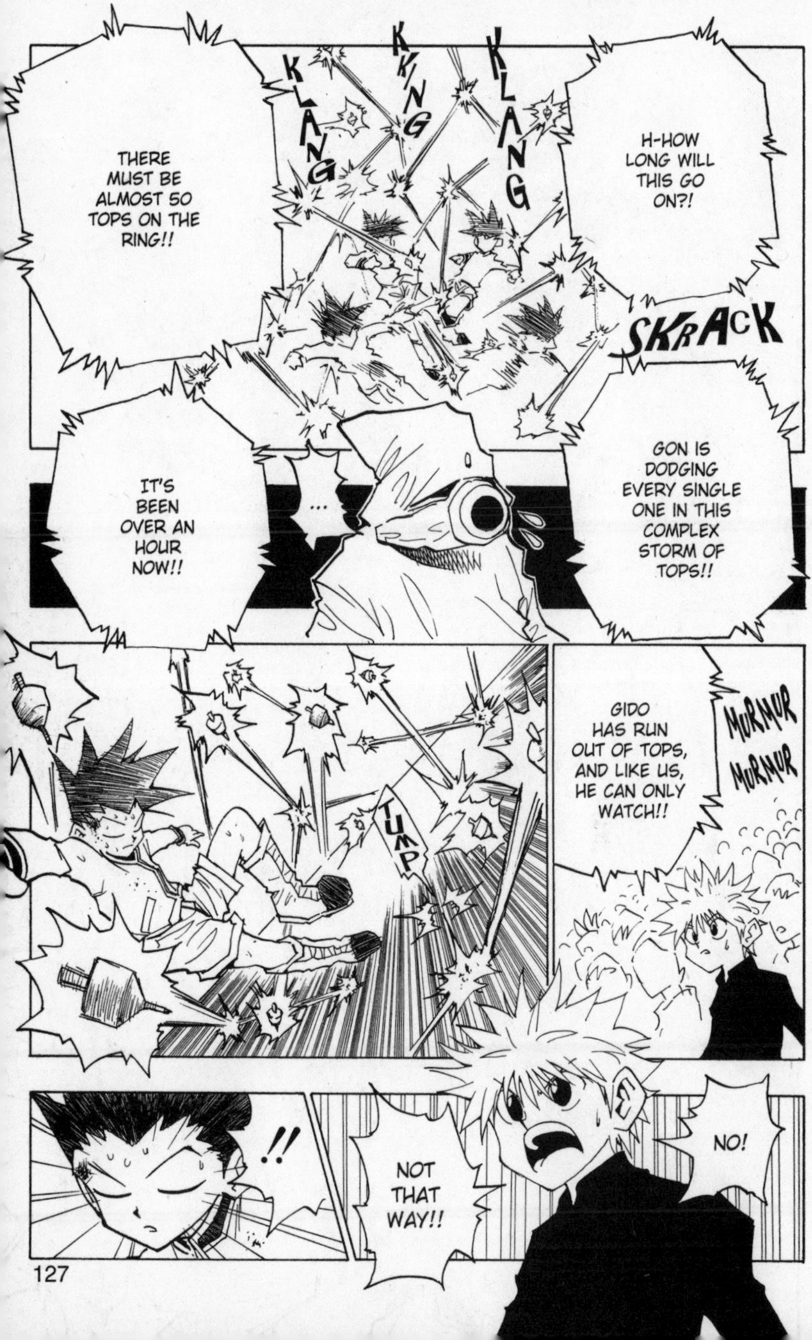
H-HOW LONG WILL THIS GO ON?!
KLANG
KKING
KLANG
THERE MUST BE ALMOST 50 TOPS ON THE RING!!
SKRACK
GON IS DODGING EVERY SINGLE ONE IN THIS COMPLEX STORM OF TOPS!!
...
IT'S BEEN OVER AN HOUR NOW!!
MURMUR
MURMUR
GIDO HAS RUN OUT OF TOPS, AND LIKE US, HE CAN ONLY WATCH!!
TUMP
NO!
NOT THAT WAY!!
!!

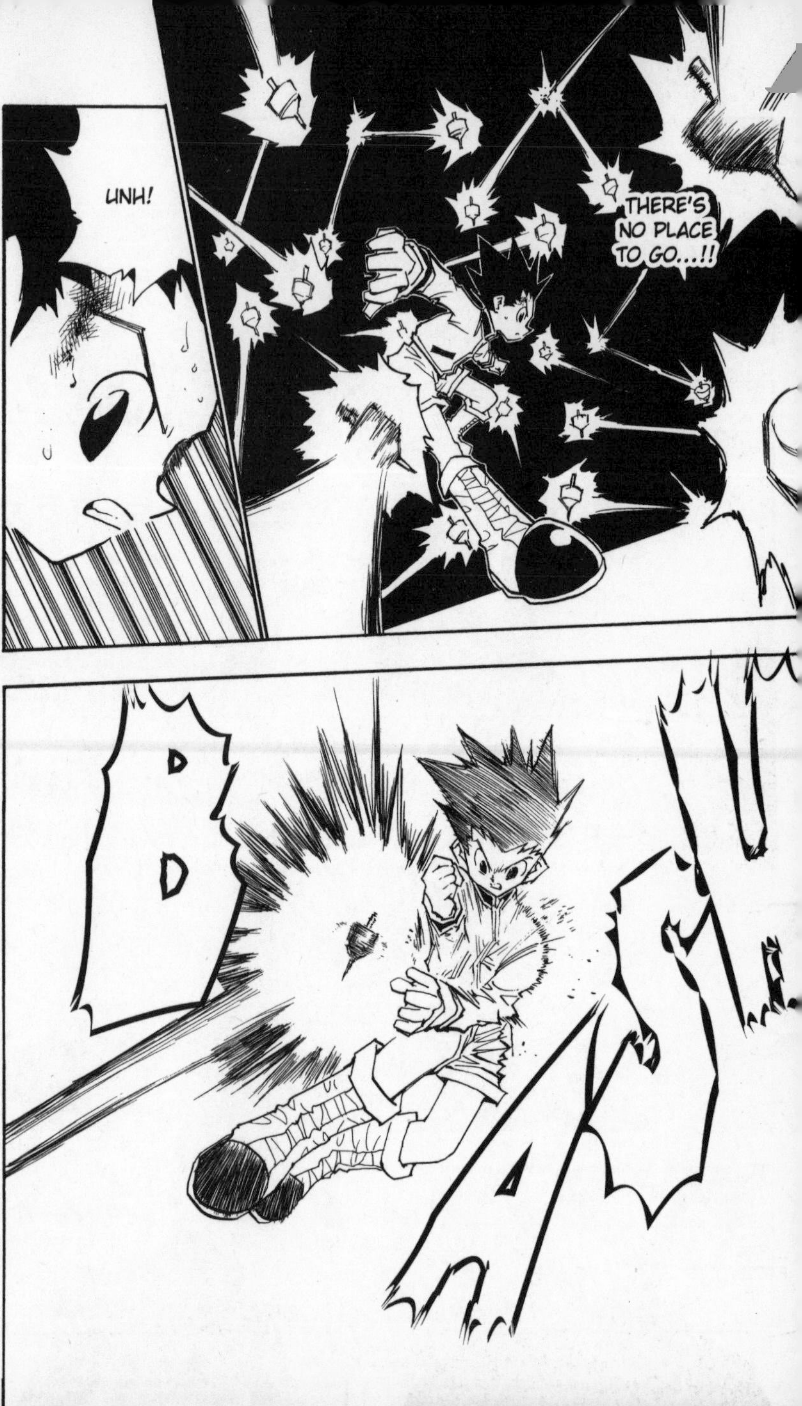
THERE'S NO PLACE TO GO...!!
UNH!

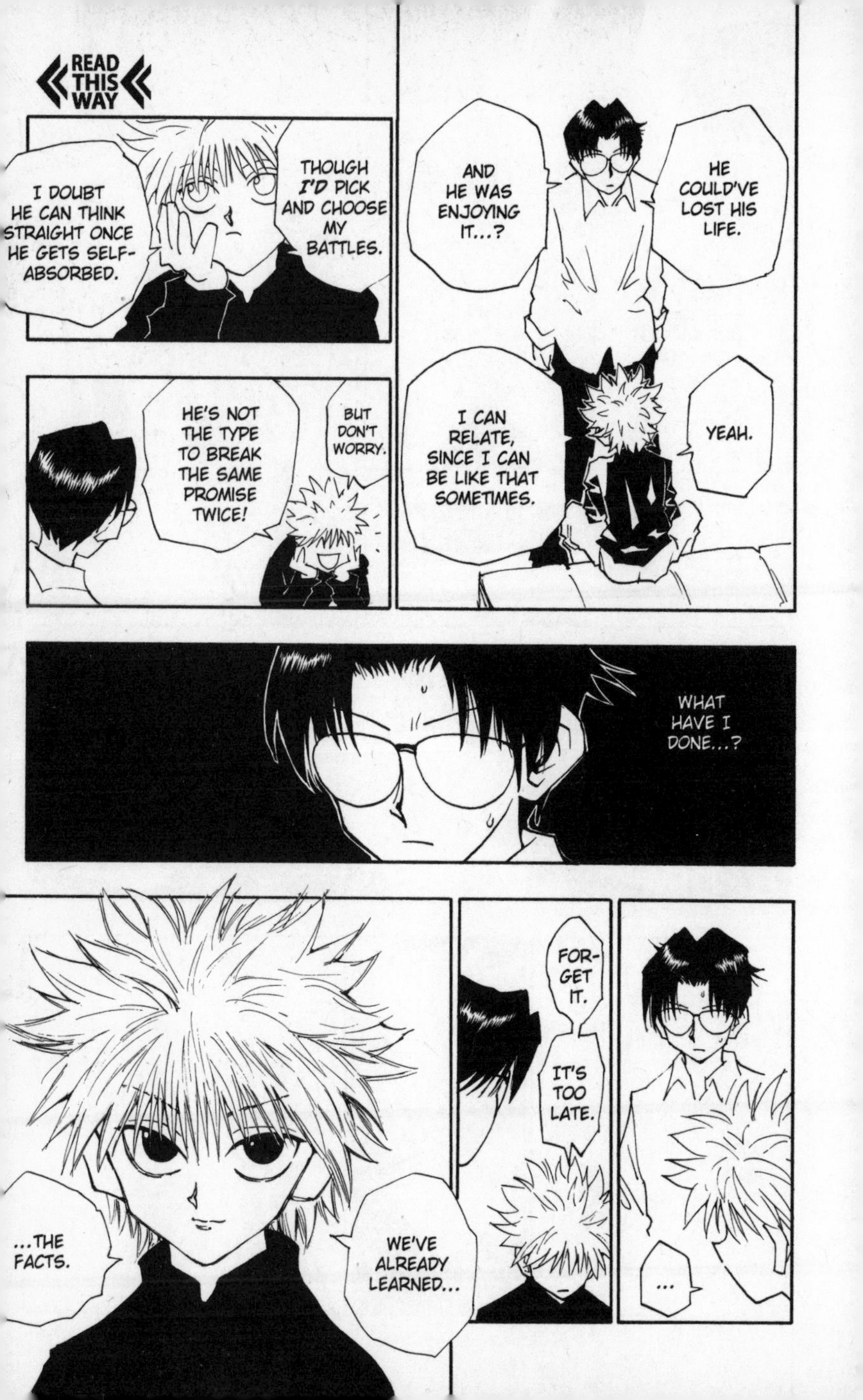
READ THIS WAY
HE COULD'VE LOST HIS LIFE.
AND HE WAS ENJOYING IT...?
YEAH.
I CAN RELATE, SINCE I CAN BE LIKE THAT SOMETIMES.
THOUGH *I'D* PICK AND CHOOSE MY BATTLES.
I DOUBT HE CAN THINK STRAIGHT ONCE HE GETS SELF-ABSORBED.
BUT DON'T WORRY.
HE'S NOT THE TYPE TO BREAK THE SAME PROMISE TWICE!
WHAT HAVE I DONE...?
...
FOR-GET IT.
IT'S TOO LATE.
WE'VE ALREADY LEARNED...
...THE FACTS.

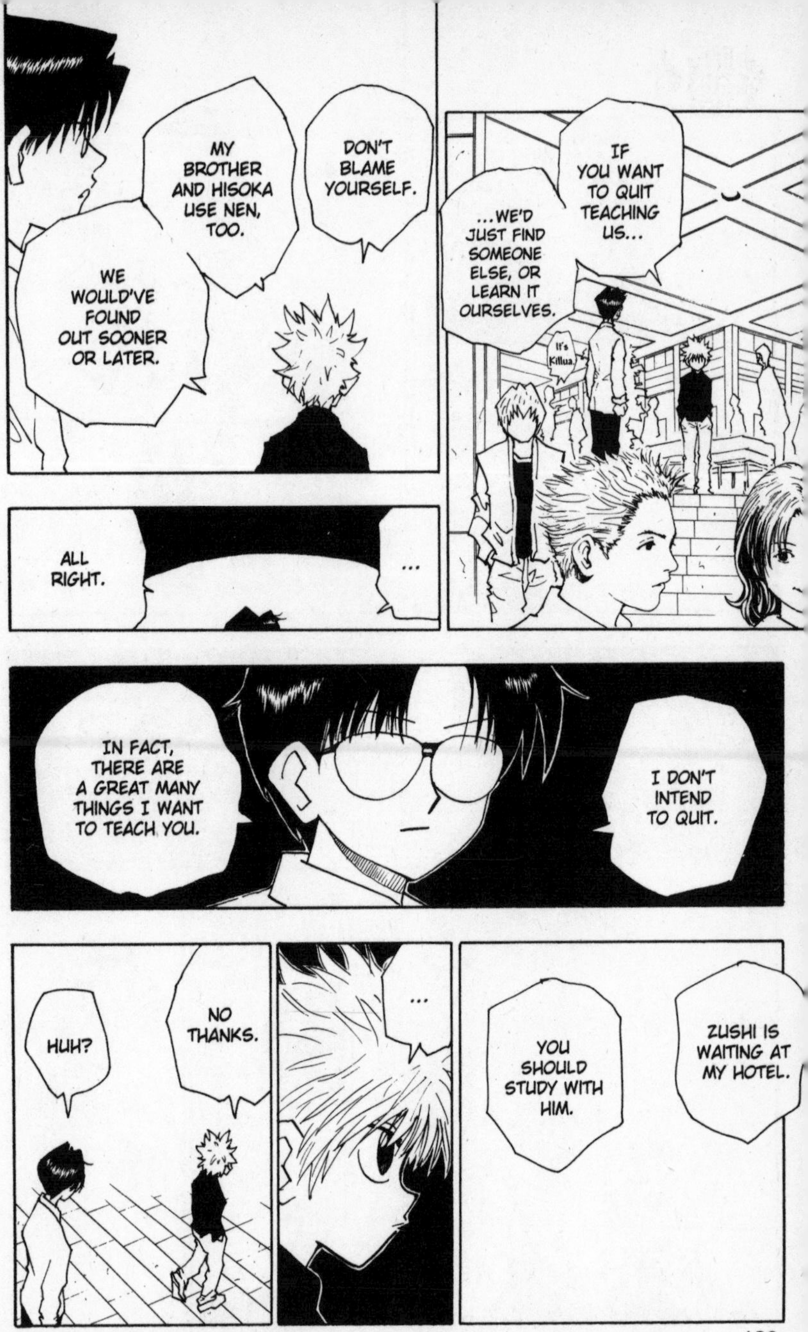
IF YOU WANT TO QUIT TEACHING US...
...WE'D JUST FIND SOMEONE ELSE, OR LEARN IT OURSELVES.
It's Killua.
DON'T BLAME YOURSELF.
MY BROTHER AND HISOKA USE NEN, TOO.
WE WOULD'VE FOUND OUT SOONER OR LATER.
...
ALL RIGHT.
I DON'T INTEND TO QUIT.
IN FACT, THERE ARE A GREAT MANY THINGS I WANT TO TEACH YOU.
ZUSHI IS WAITING AT MY HOTEL.
YOU SHOULD STUDY WITH HIM.
...
NO THANKS.
HUH?

READ THIS WAY

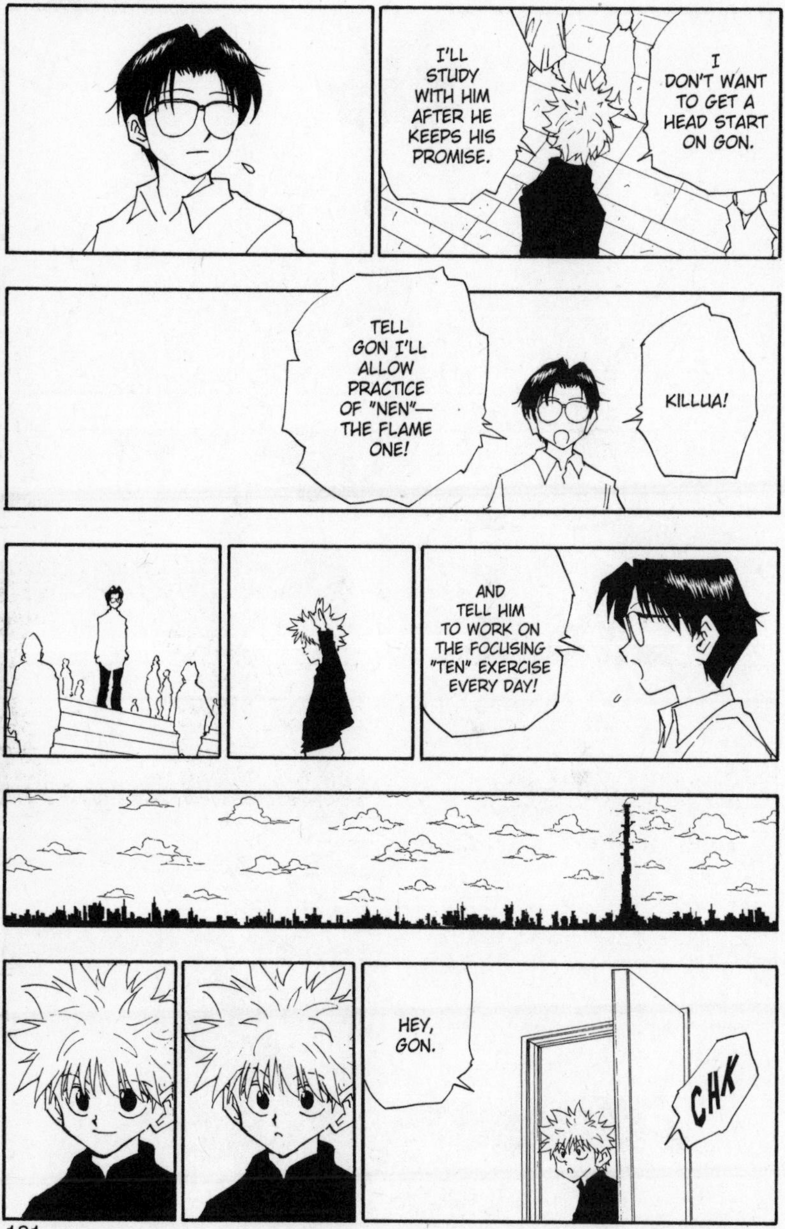
I DON'T WANT TO GET A HEAD START ON GON.
I'LL STUDY WITH HIM AFTER HE KEEPS HIS PROMISE.
KILLUA!
TELL GON I'LL ALLOW PRACTICE OF "NEN"—THE FLAME ONE!
AND TELL HIM TO WORK ON THE FOCUSING "TEN" EXERCISE EVERY DAY!
CHK
HEY, GON.

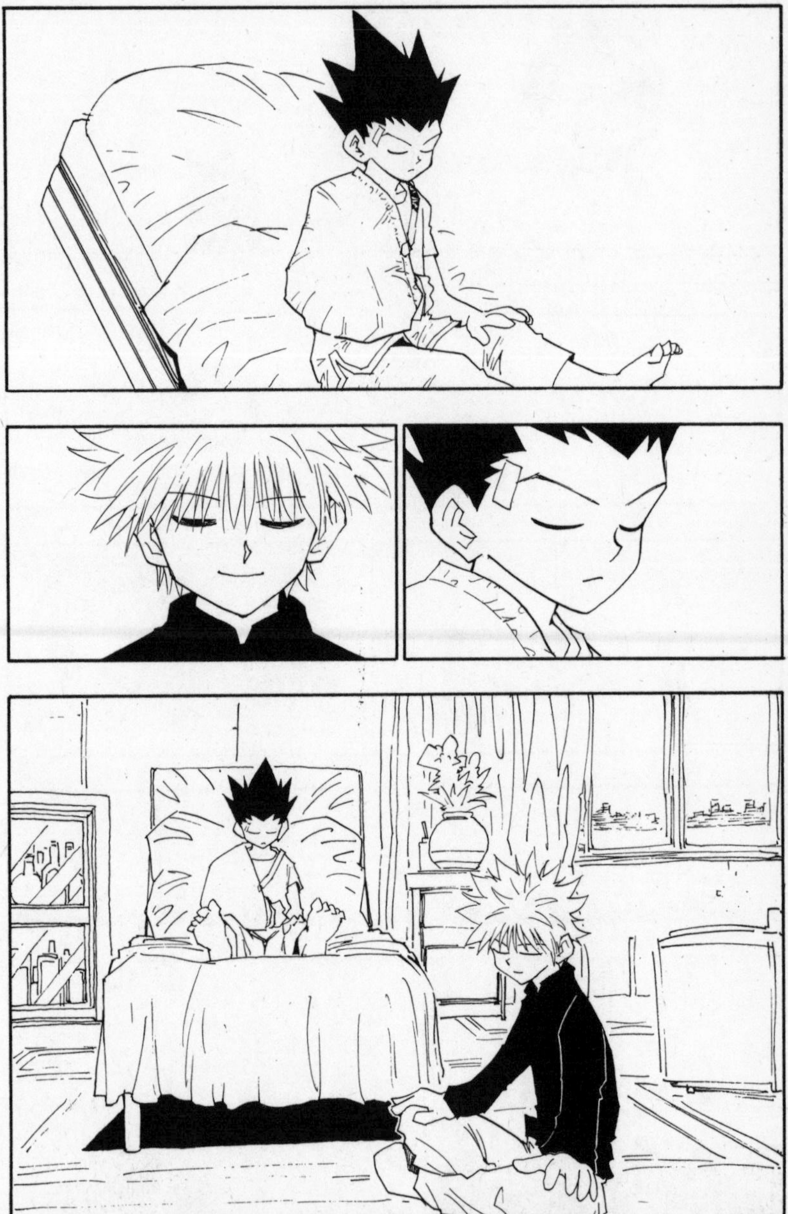

READ THIS WAY

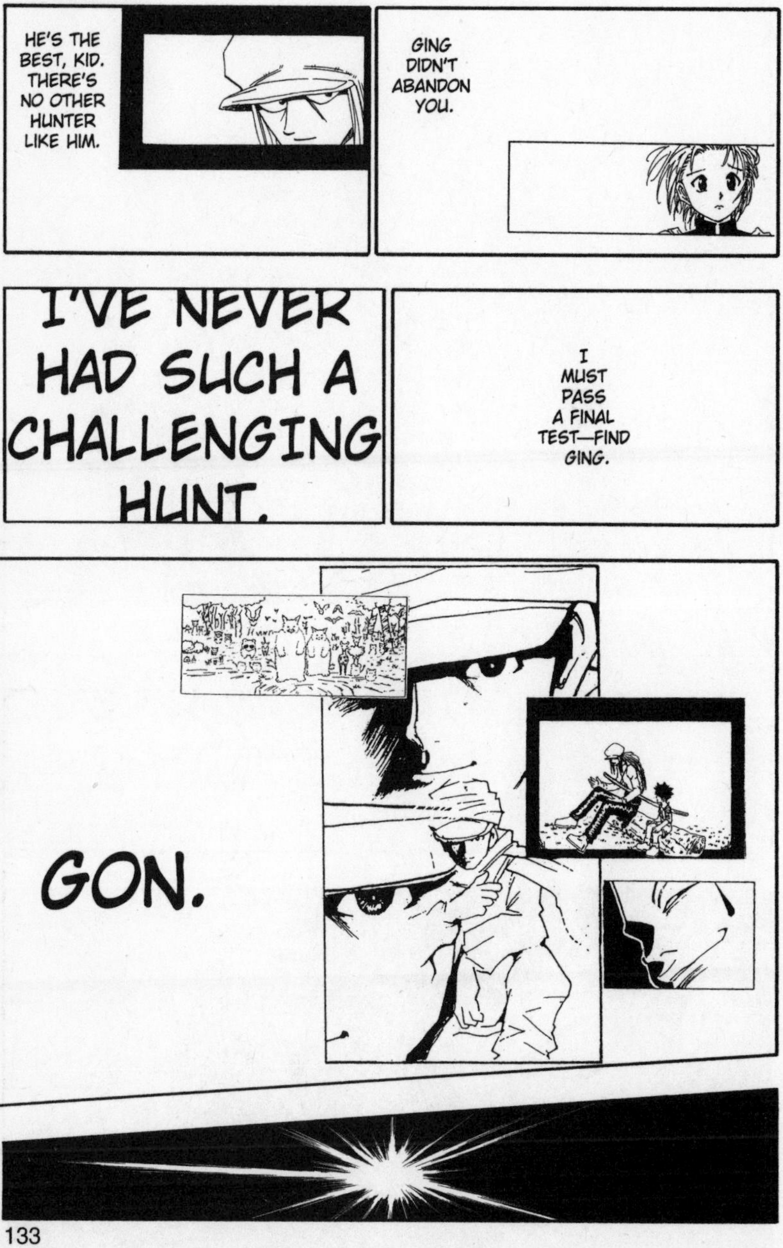

GING DIDN'T ABANDON YOU.
HE'S THE BEST, KID. THERE'S NO OTHER HUNTER LIKE HIM.
I MUST PASS A FINAL TEST—FIND GING.
I'VE NEVER HAD SUCH A CHALLENGING HUNT.
GON.

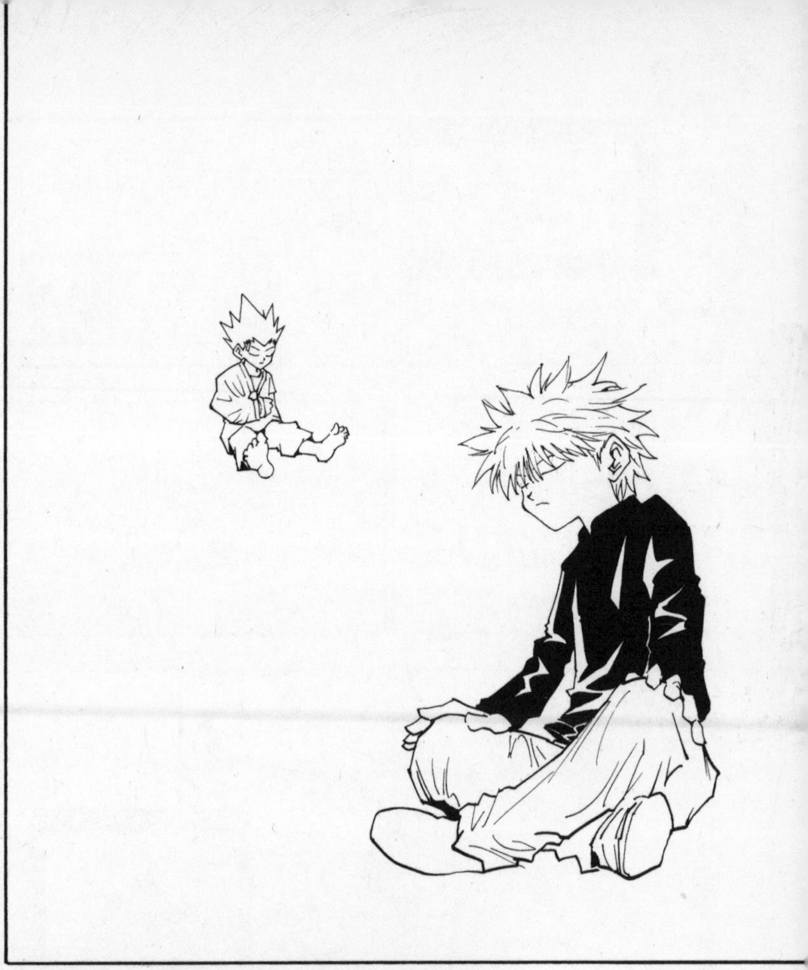
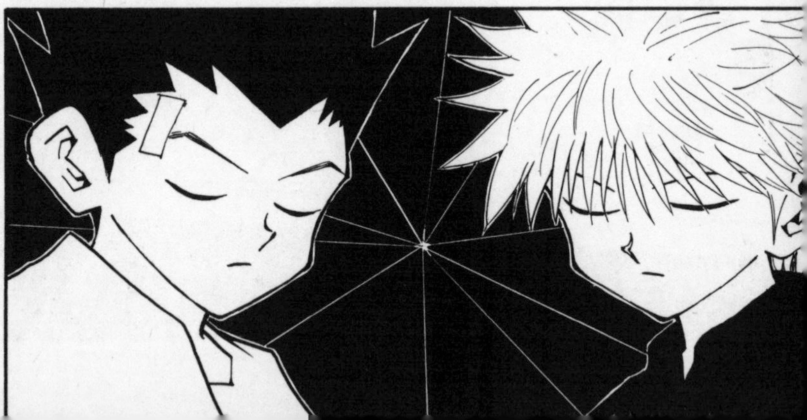

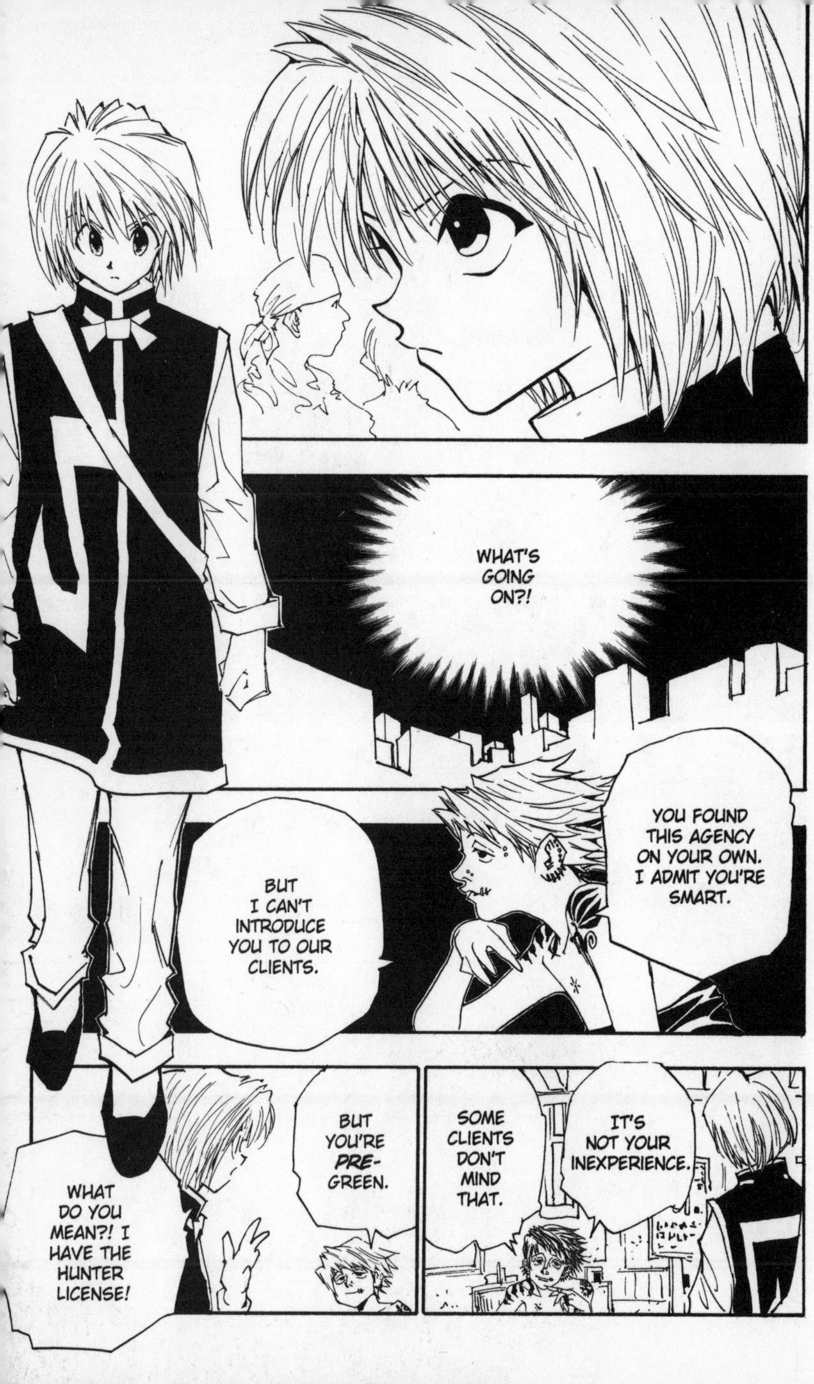
WHAT'S GOING ON?!
YOU FOUND THIS AGENCY ON YOUR OWN. I ADMIT YOU'RE SMART.
BUT I CAN'T INTRODUCE YOU TO OUR CLIENTS.
IT'S NOT YOUR INEXPERIENCE.
SOME CLIENTS DON'T MIND THAT.
BUT YOU'RE *PRE*-GREEN.
WHAT DO YOU MEAN?! I HAVE THE HUNTER LICENSE!

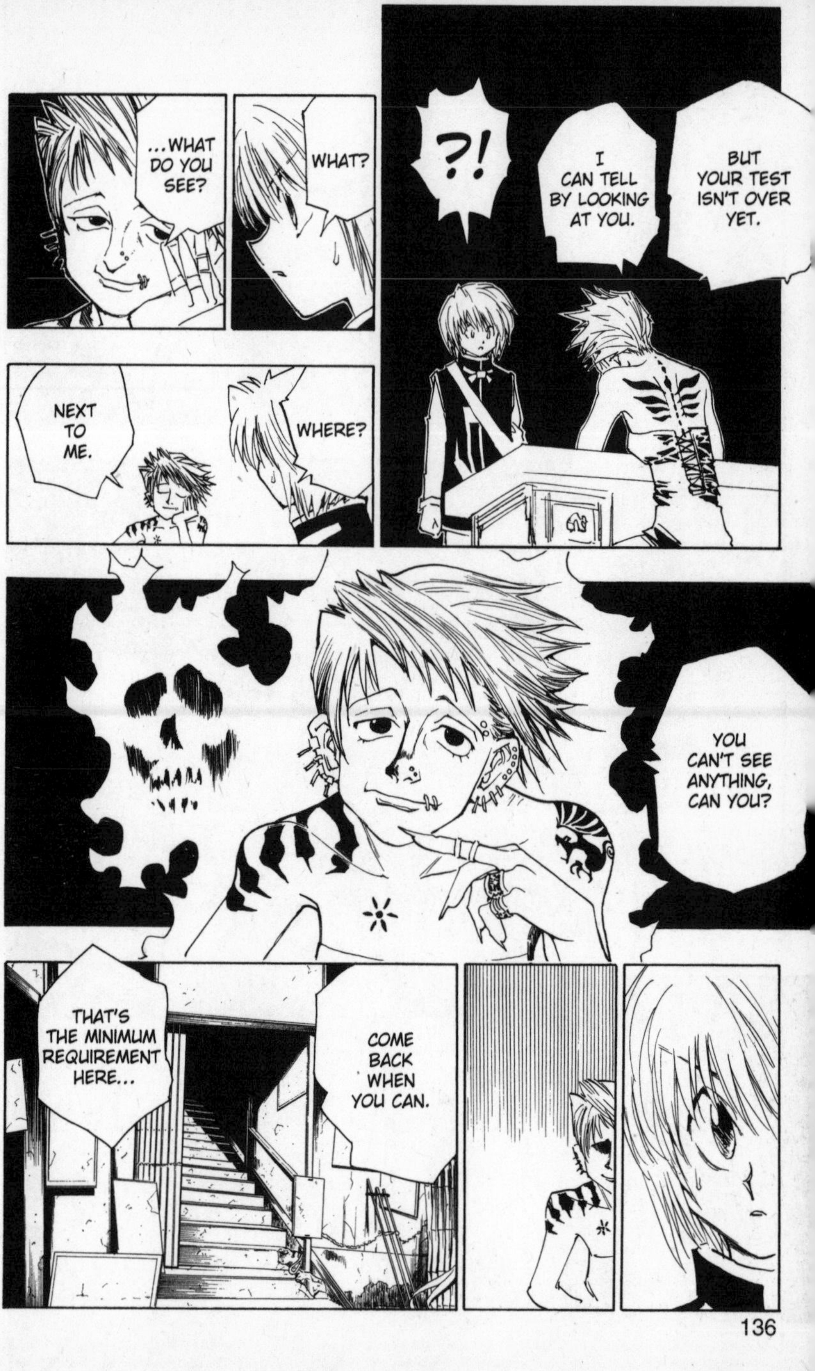
BUT YOUR TEST ISN'T OVER YET.
I CAN TELL BY LOOKING AT YOU.
?!
WHAT?
...WHAT DO YOU SEE?
WHERE?
NEXT TO ME.
YOU CAN'T SEE ANYTHING, CAN YOU?
THAT'S THE MINIMUM REQUIREMENT HERE...
COME BACK WHEN YOU CAN.

READ THIS WAY

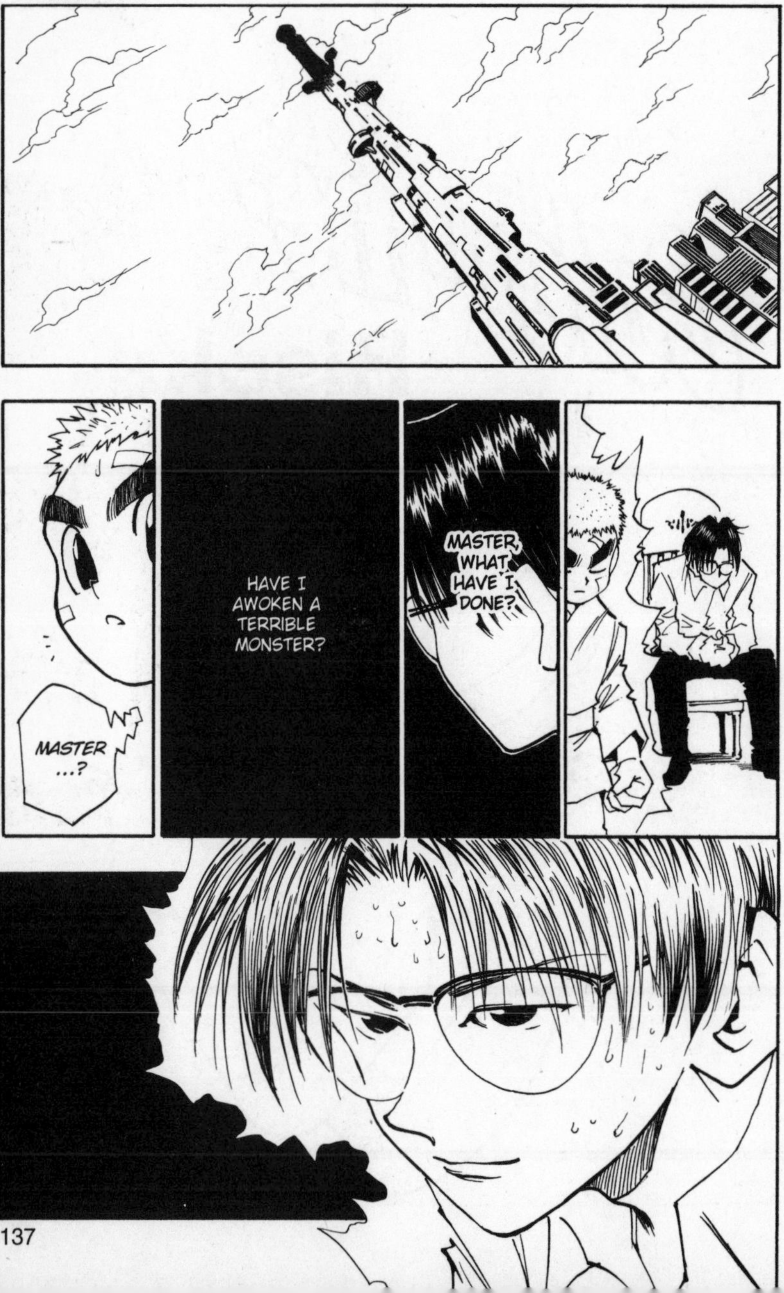

MASTER, WHAT HAVE I DONE?
HAVE I AWOKEN A TERRIBLE MONSTER?
MASTER ...?

Color-me-
Hisoka

Chapter 52
Kastro

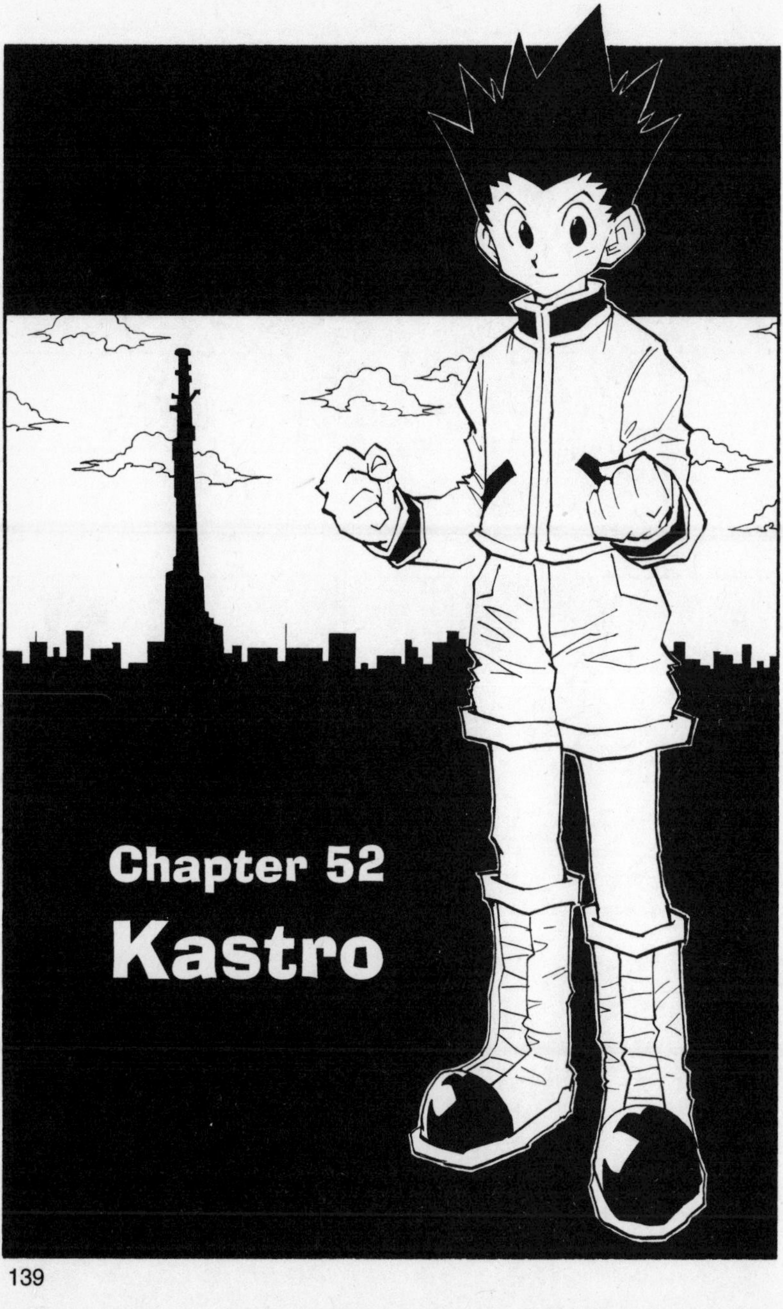

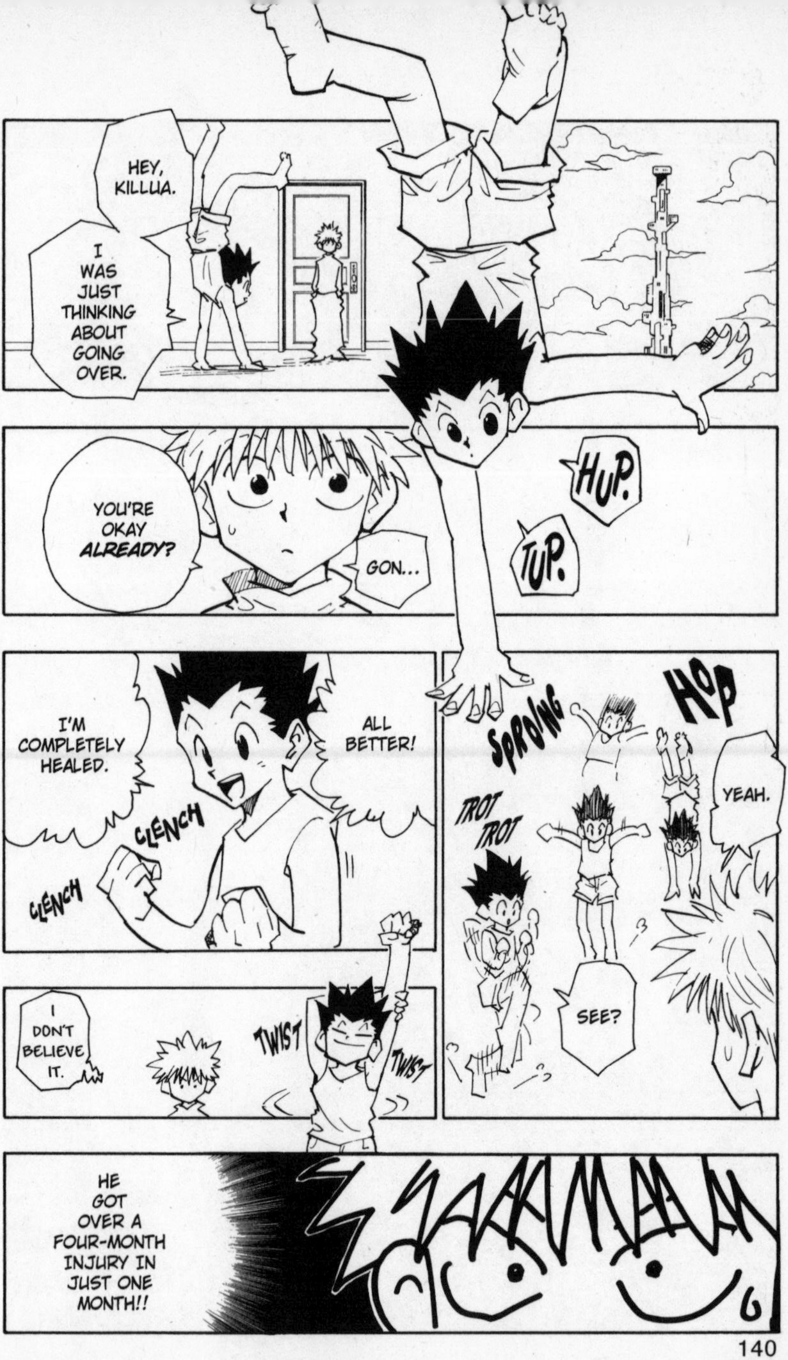
HEY, KILLUA.
I WAS JUST THINKING ABOUT GOING OVER.
HUP.
TUP.
GON...
YOU'RE OKAY ALREADY?
HOP
YEAH.
SPROING
TROT TROT
SEE?
ALL BETTER!
I'M COMPLETELY HEALED.
CLENCH
CLENCH
TWIST
TWIST
I DON'T BELIEVE IT.
HE GOT OVER A FOUR-MONTH INJURY IN JUST ONE MONTH!!

READ THIS WAY

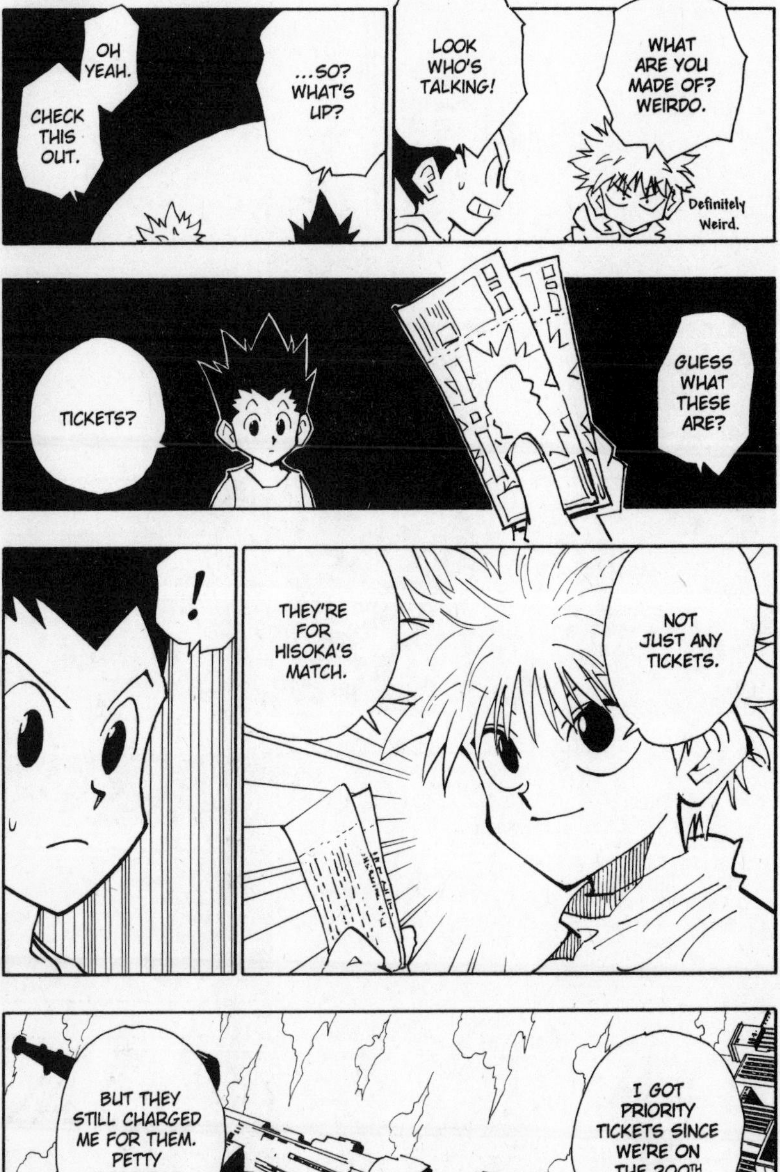

WHAT ARE YOU MADE OF? WEIRDO.
Definitely Weird.
LOOK WHO'S TALKING!
...SO? WHAT'S UP?
OH YEAH.
CHECK THIS OUT.
GUESS WHAT THESE ARE?
TICKETS?
NOT JUST ANY TICKETS.
THEY'RE FOR HISOKA'S MATCH.
!
I GOT PRIORITY TICKETS SINCE WE'RE ON THE 200TH FLOOR.
BUT THEY STILL CHARGED ME FOR THEM. PETTY BASTARDS.

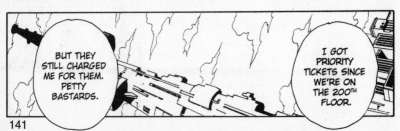

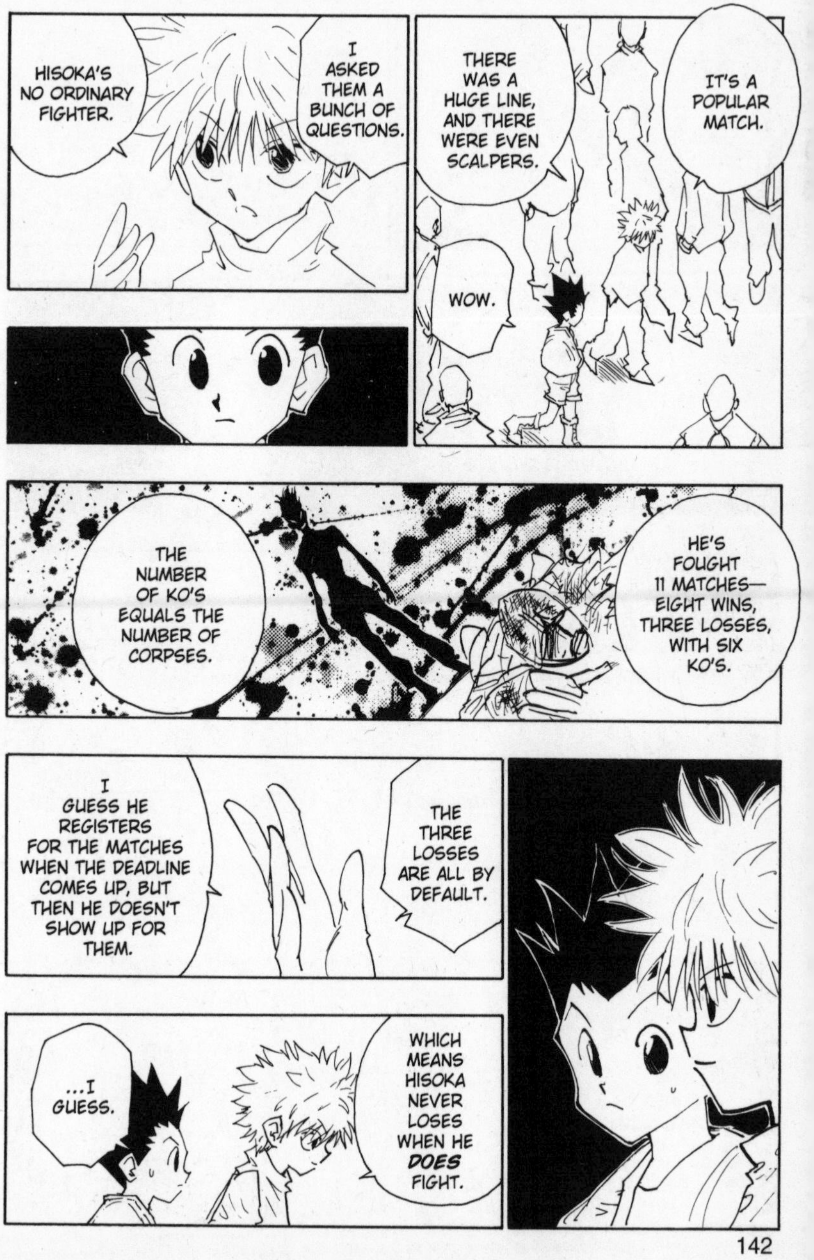
IT'S A POPULAR MATCH.
THERE WAS A HUGE LINE, AND THERE WERE EVEN SCALPERS.
WOW.
I ASKED THEM A BUNCH OF QUESTIONS.
HISOKA'S NO ORDINARY FIGHTER.
HE'S FOUGHT 11 MATCHES— EIGHT WINS, THREE LOSSES, WITH SIX KO'S.
THE NUMBER OF KO'S EQUALS THE NUMBER OF CORPSES.
THE THREE LOSSES ARE ALL BY DEFAULT.
I GUESS HE REGISTERS FOR THE MATCHES WHEN THE DEADLINE COMES UP, BUT THEN HE DOESN'T SHOW UP FOR THEM.
WHICH MEANS HISOKA NEVER LOSES WHEN HE **DOES** FIGHT.
...I GUESS.

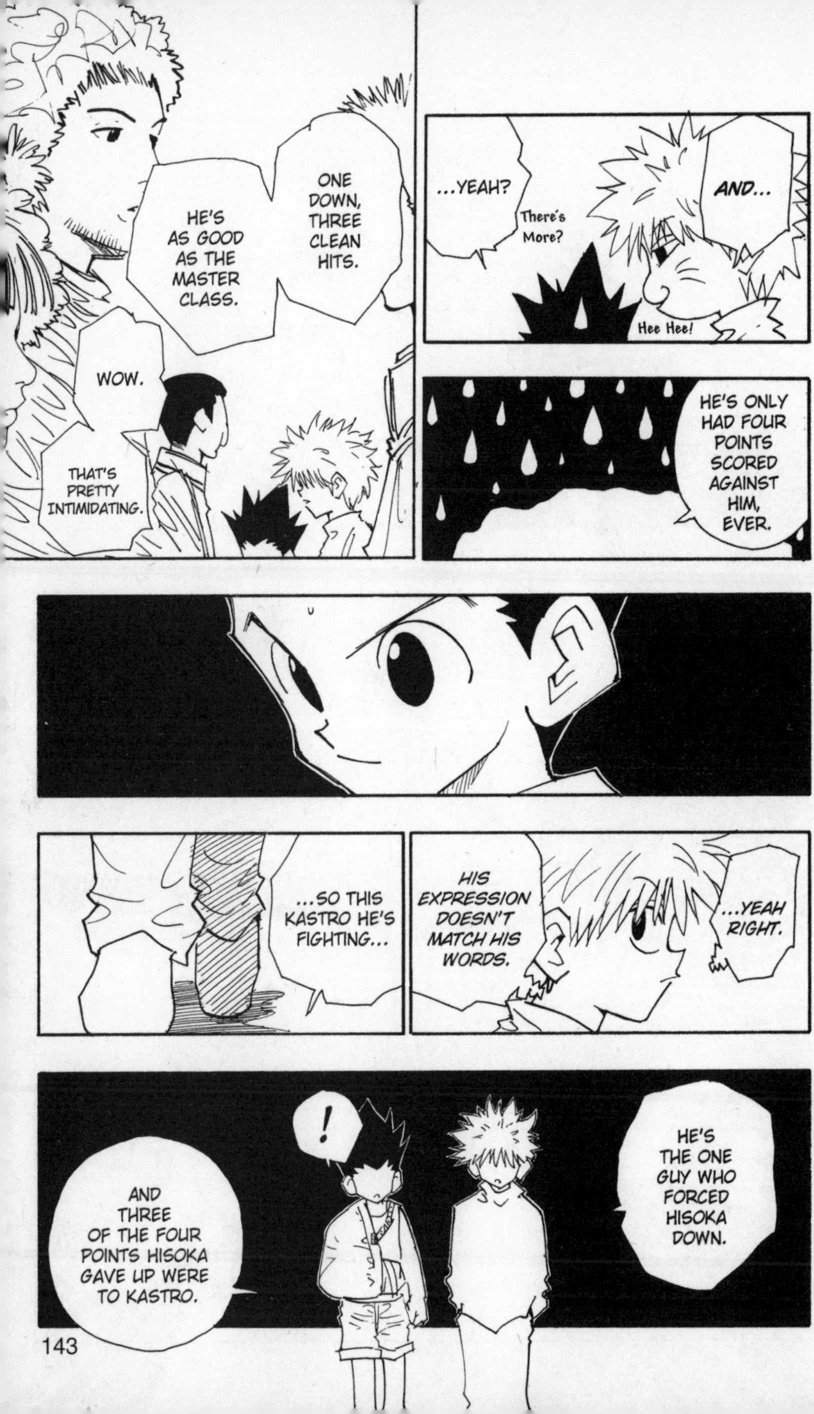
AND...
...YEAH?
There's More?
Hee Hee!
HE'S ONLY HAD FOUR POINTS SCORED AGAINST HIM, EVER.
ONE DOWN, THREE CLEAN HITS.
HE'S AS GOOD AS THE MASTER CLASS.
WOW.
THAT'S PRETTY INTIMIDATING.
...YEAH RIGHT.
HIS EXPRESSION DOESN'T MATCH HIS WORDS.
...SO THIS KASTRO HE'S FIGHTING...
HE'S THE ONE GUY WHO FORCED HISOKA DOWN.
!
AND THREE OF THE FOUR POINTS HISOKA GAVE UP WERE TO KASTRO.

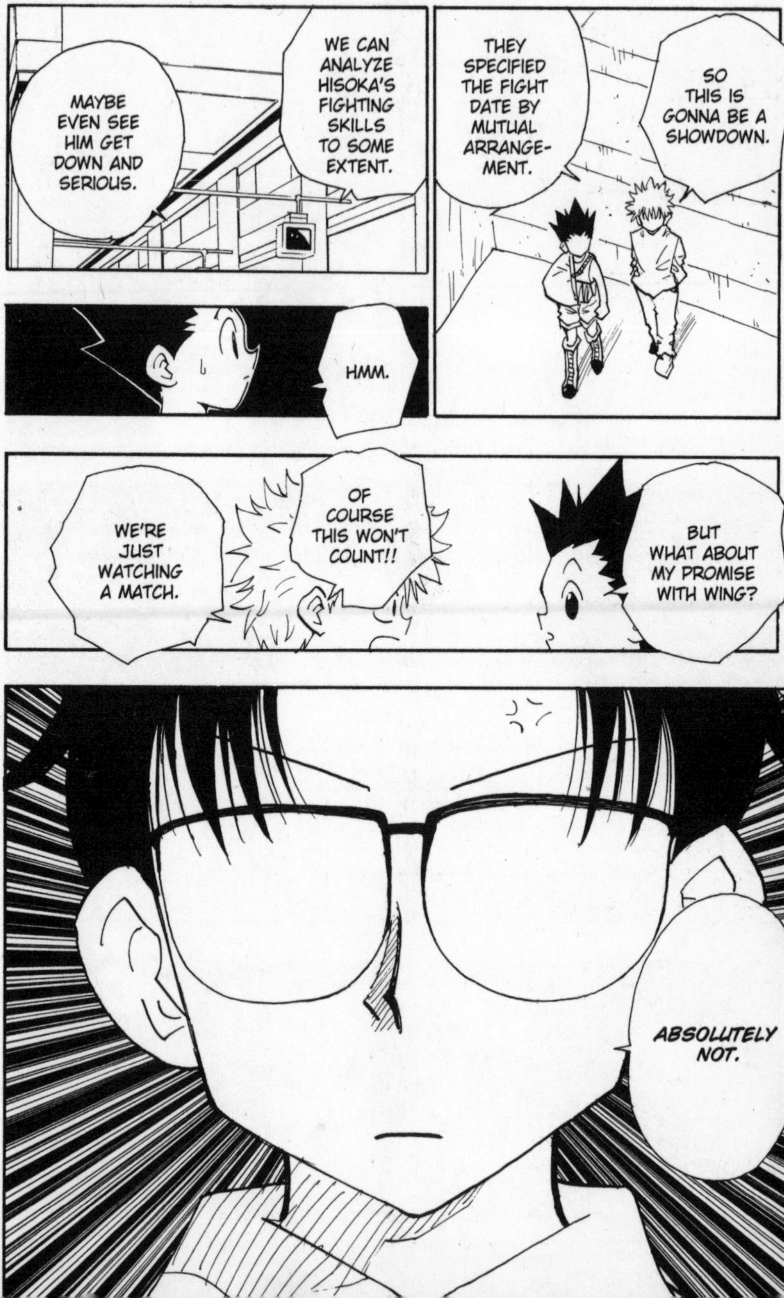
SO THIS IS GONNA BE A SHOWDOWN.
THEY SPECIFIED THE FIGHT DATE BY MUTUAL ARRANGE-MENT.
WE CAN ANALYZE HISOKA'S FIGHTING SKILLS TO SOME EXTENT.
MAYBE EVEN SEE HIM GET DOWN AND SERIOUS.
HMM.
BUT WHAT ABOUT MY PROMISE WITH WING?
OF COURSE THIS WON'T COUNT!!
WE'RE JUST WATCHING A MATCH.
ABSOLUTELY NOT.

READ THIS WAY

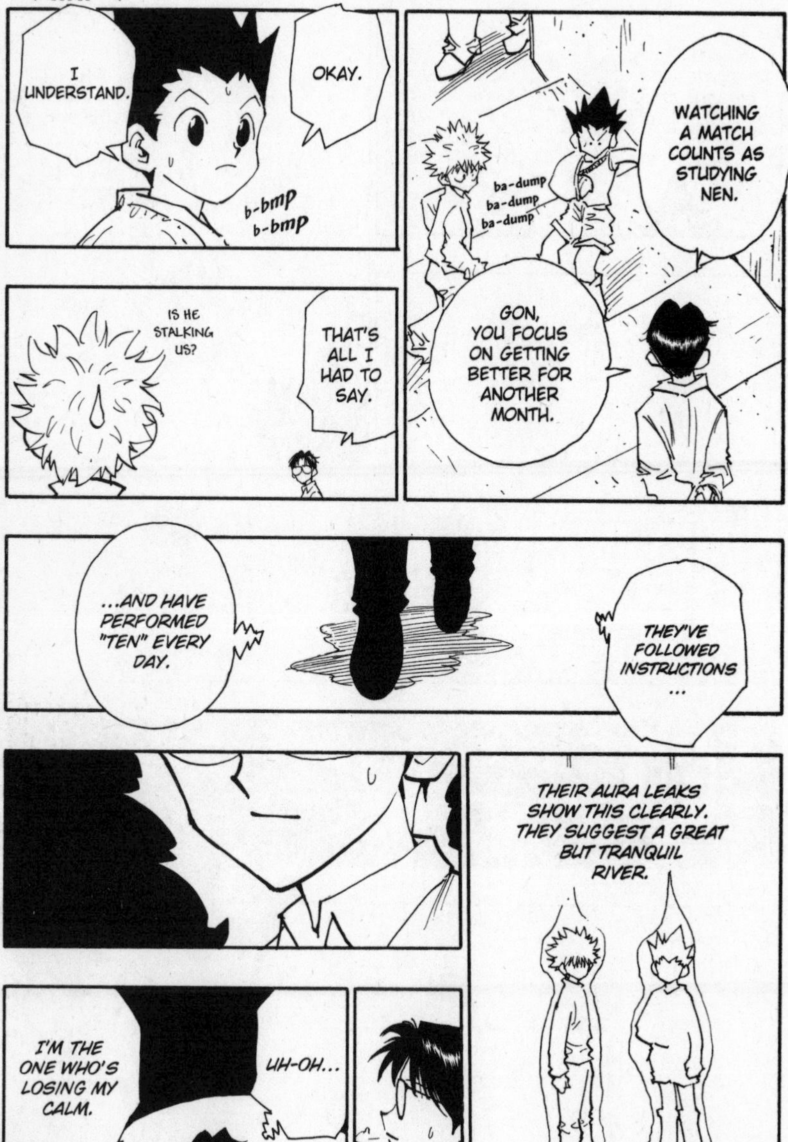

WATCHING A MATCH COUNTS AS STUDYING NEN.
ba-dump
ba-dump
ba-dump
GON, YOU FOCUS ON GETTING BETTER FOR ANOTHER MONTH.
OKAY.
I UNDERSTAND.
b-bmp
b-bmp
THAT'S ALL I HAD TO SAY.
IS HE STALKING US?
THEY'VE FOLLOWED INSTRUCTIONS ...
...AND HAVE PERFORMED "TEN" EVERY DAY.
THEIR AURA LEAKS SHOW THIS CLEARLY. THEY SUGGEST A GREAT BUT TRANQUIL RIVER.
UH-OH...
I'M THE ONE WHO'S LOSING MY CALM.

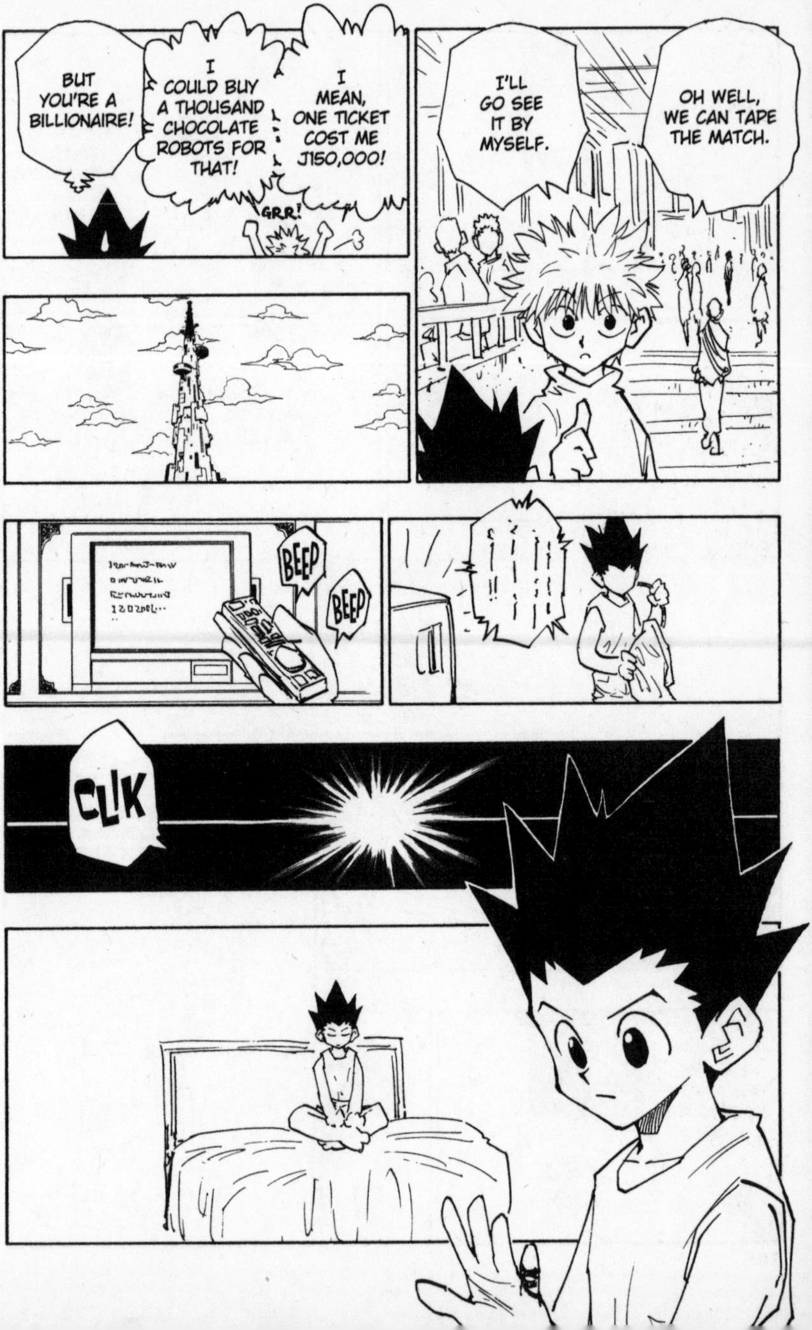
OH WELL, WE CAN TAPE THE MATCH.
I'LL GO SEE IT BY MYSELF.
I MEAN, ONE TICKET COST ME J150,000!
I COULD BUY A THOUSAND CHOCOLATE ROBOTS FOR THAT!
BUT YOU'RE A BILLIONAIRE!
GRR!
!!
BEEP
BEEP
CLIK

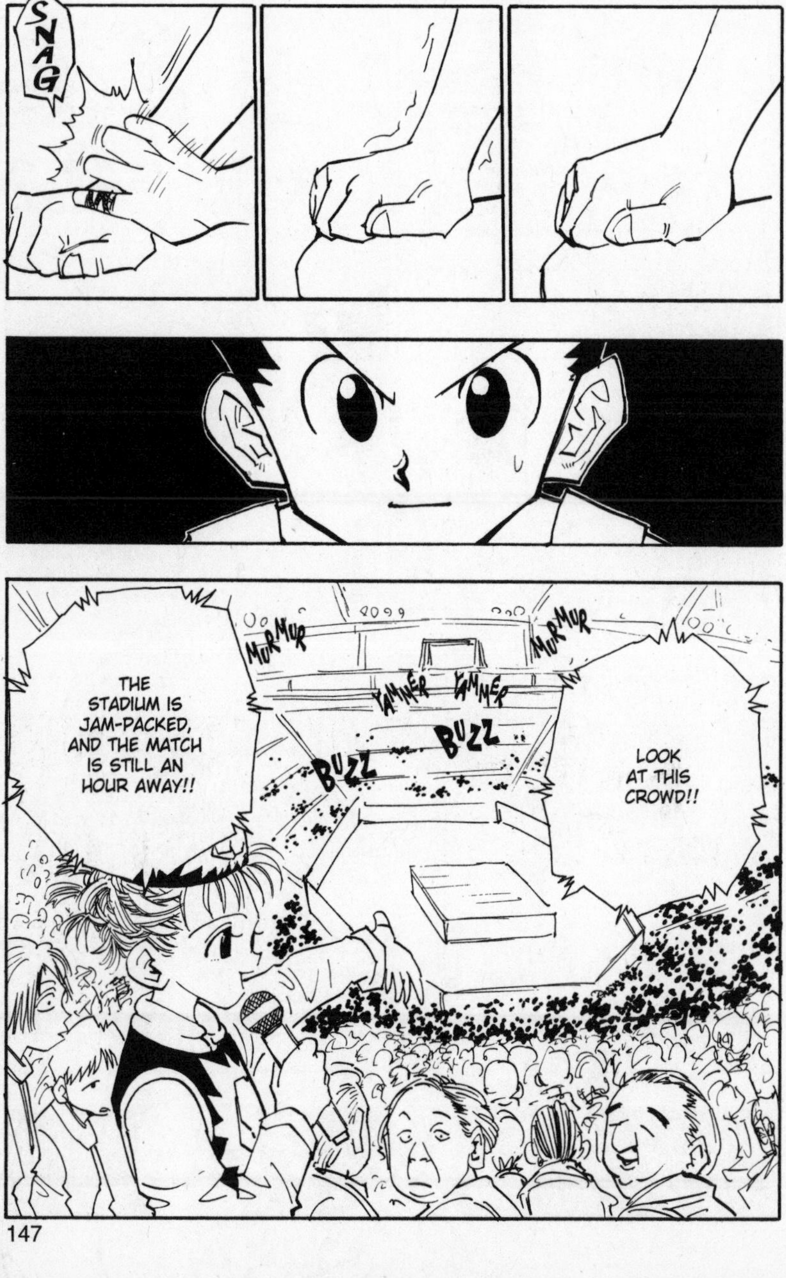
SNAG
MURMUR
YAMMER
YAMMER
MURMUR
BUZZ
LOOK AT THIS CROWD!!
BUZZ
THE STADIUM IS JAM-PACKED, AND THE MATCH IS STILL AN HOUR AWAY!!

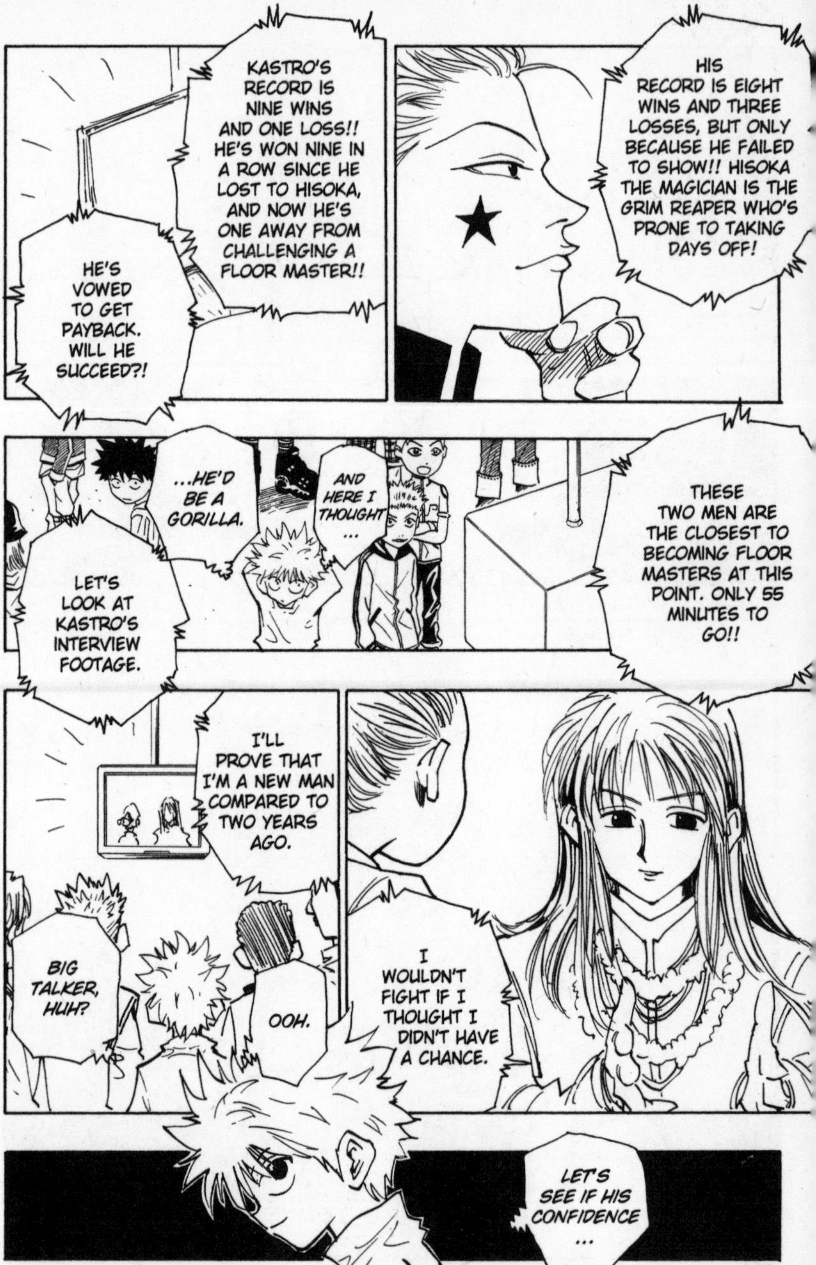
HIS RECORD IS EIGHT WINS AND THREE LOSSES, BUT ONLY BECAUSE HE FAILED TO SHOW!! HISOKA THE MAGICIAN IS THE GRIM REAPER WHO'S PRONE TO TAKING DAYS OFF!
KASTRO'S RECORD IS NINE WINS AND ONE LOSS!! HE'S WON NINE IN A ROW SINCE HE LOST TO HISOKA, AND NOW HE'S ONE AWAY FROM CHALLENGING A FLOOR MASTER!!
HE'S VOWED TO GET PAYBACK. WILL HE SUCCEED?!
THESE TWO MEN ARE THE CLOSEST TO BECOMING FLOOR MASTERS AT THIS POINT. ONLY 55 MINUTES TO GO!!
AND HERE I THOUGHT ...
...HE'D BE A GORILLA.
LET'S LOOK AT KASTRO'S INTERVIEW FOOTAGE.
I WOULDN'T FIGHT IF I THOUGHT I DIDN'T HAVE A CHANCE.
I'LL PROVE THAT I'M A NEW MAN COMPARED TO TWO YEARS AGO.
OOH.
BIG TALKER, HUH?
LET'S SEE IF HIS CONFIDENCE ...

READ THIS WAY

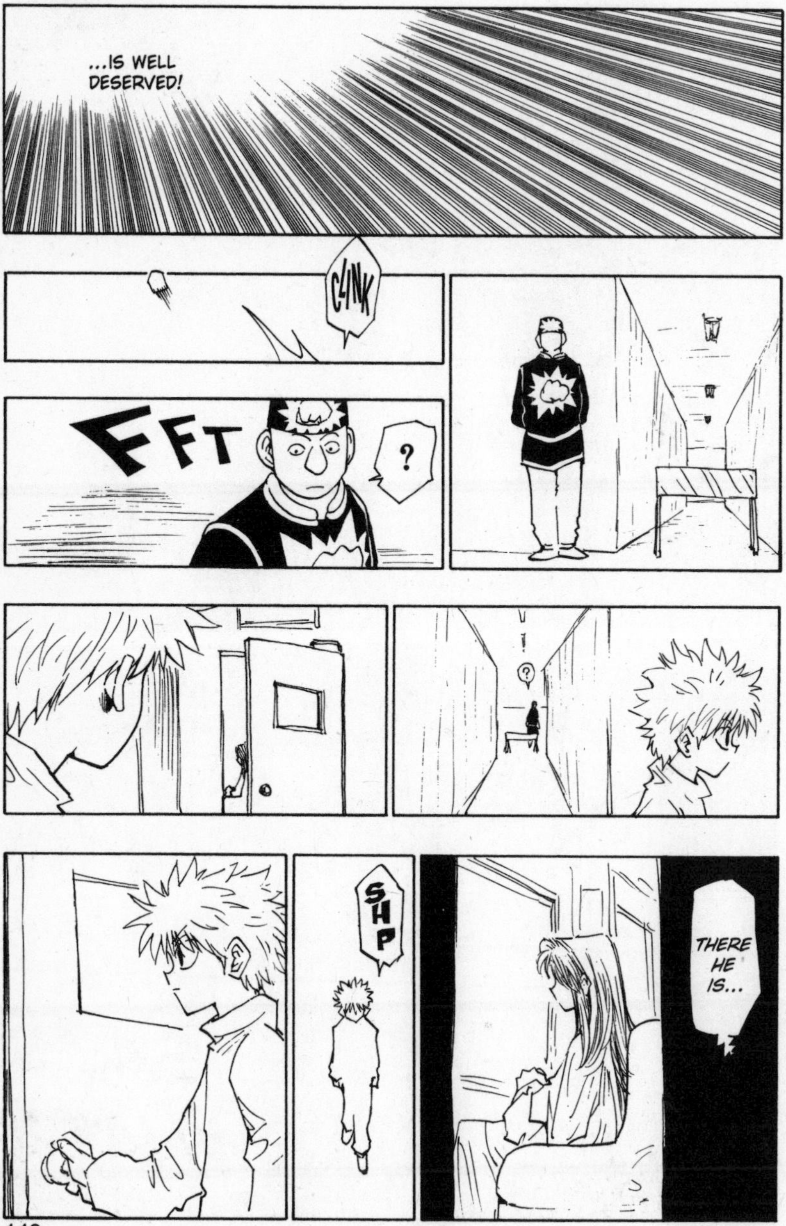

...IS WELL DESERVED!
CLINK
FFT
?
?
THERE HE IS...
SHP

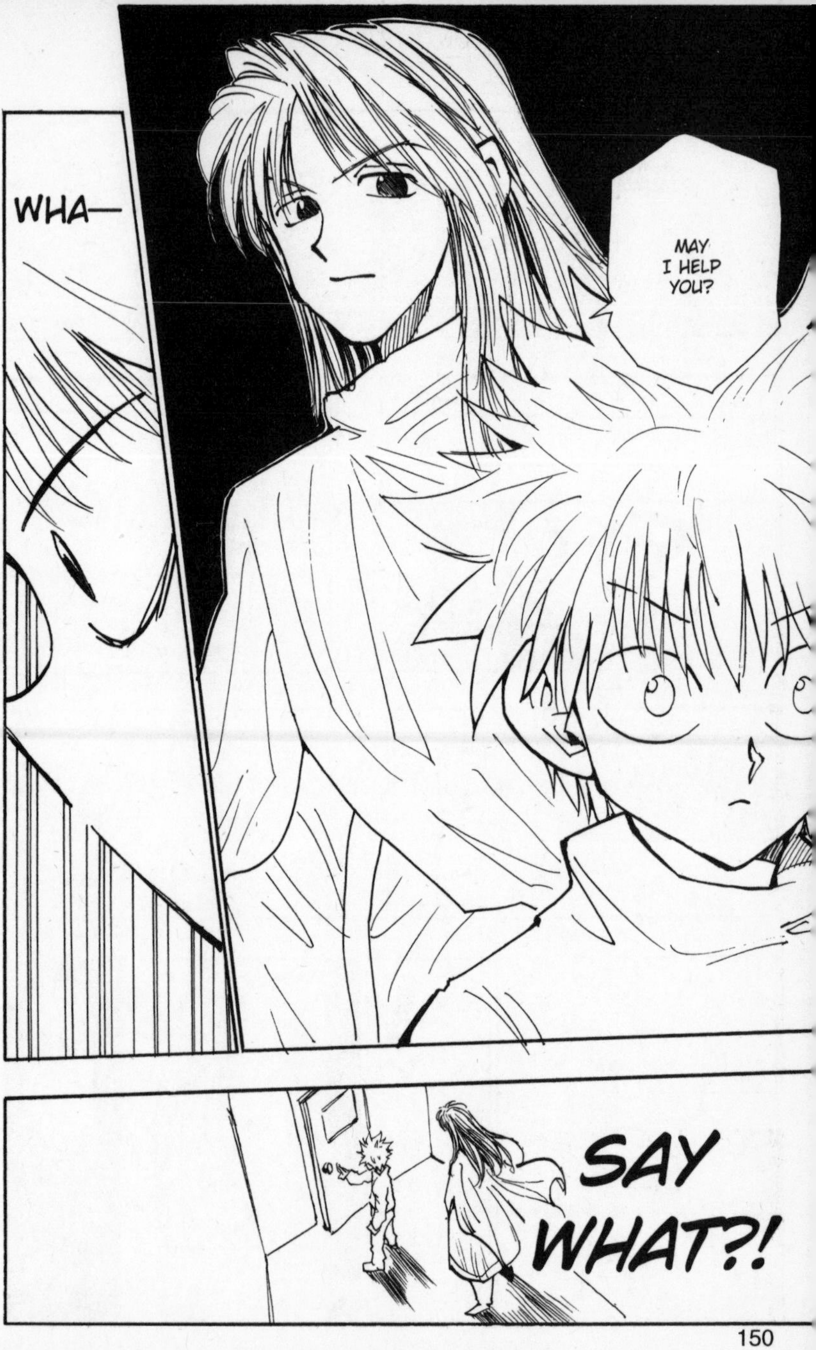
MAY I HELP YOU?
WHA—
SAY WHAT?!

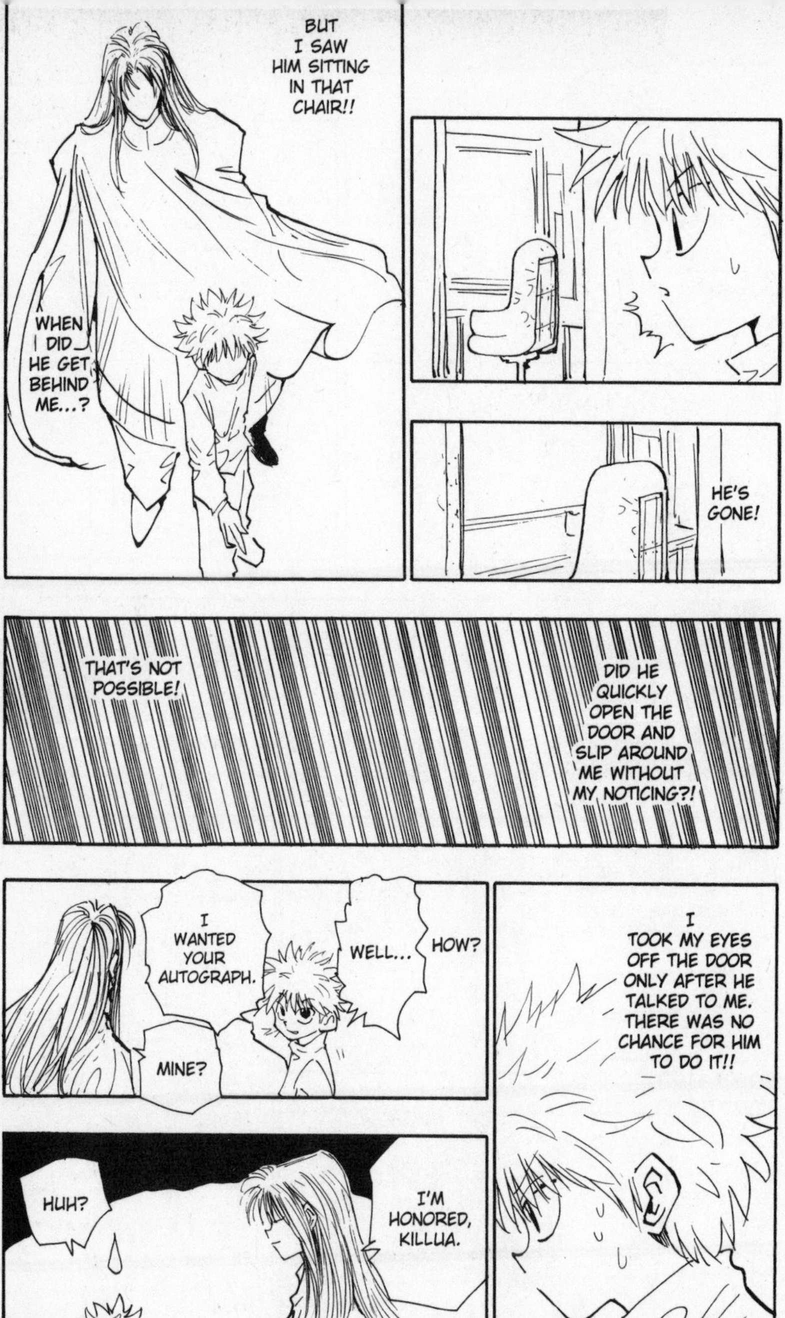
HE'S GONE!
BUT I SAW HIM SITTING IN THAT CHAIR!!
WHEN DID HE GET BEHIND ME...?
DID HE QUICKLY OPEN THE DOOR AND SLIP AROUND ME WITHOUT MY NOTICING?!
THAT'S NOT POSSIBLE!
I TOOK MY EYES OFF THE DOOR ONLY AFTER HE TALKED TO ME. THERE WAS NO CHANCE FOR HIM TO DO IT!!
HOW?
WELL...
I WANTED YOUR AUTOGRAPH.
MINE?
I'M HONORED, KILLUA.
HUH?

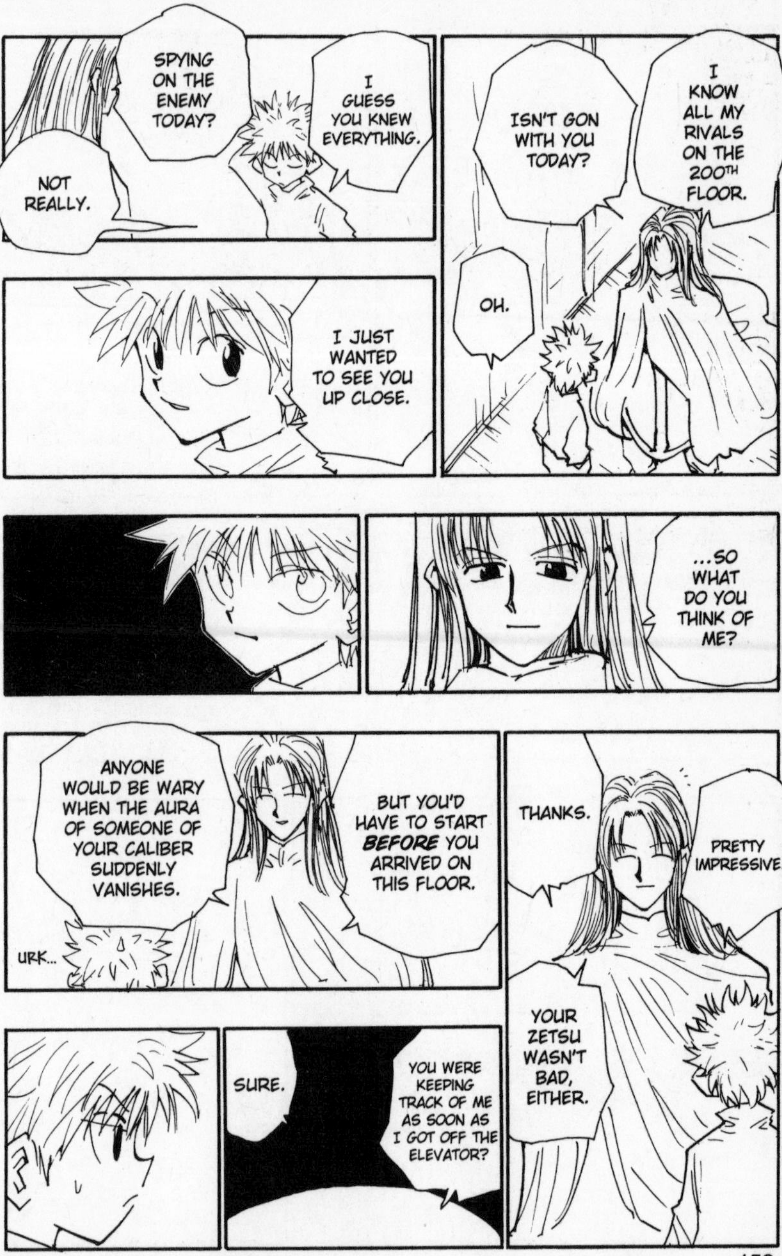
I KNOW ALL MY RIVALS ON THE 200TH FLOOR.
ISN'T GON WITH YOU TODAY?
OH.
I GUESS YOU KNEW EVERYTHING.
SPYING ON THE ENEMY TODAY?
NOT REALLY.
I JUST WANTED TO SEE YOU UP CLOSE.
...SO WHAT DO YOU THINK OF ME?
PRETTY IMPRESSIVE.
THANKS.
YOUR ZETSU WASN'T BAD, EITHER.
BUT YOU'D HAVE TO START *BEFORE* YOU ARRIVED ON THIS FLOOR.
ANYONE WOULD BE WARY WHEN THE AURA OF SOMEONE OF YOUR CALIBER SUDDENLY VANISHES.
URK...
YOU WERE KEEPING TRACK OF ME AS SOON AS I GOT OFF THE ELEVATOR?
SURE.

READ THIS WAY

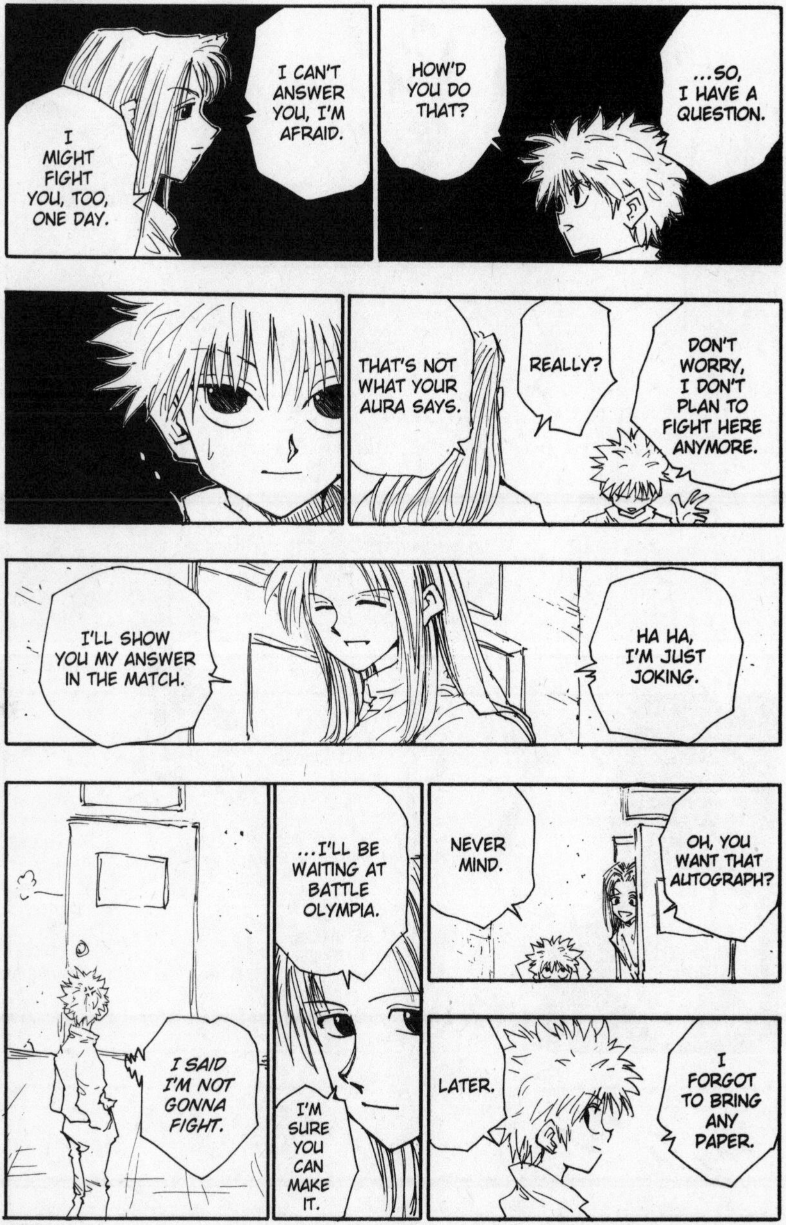
...SO, I HAVE A QUESTION.
HOW'D YOU DO THAT?
I CAN'T ANSWER YOU, I'M AFRAID.
I MIGHT FIGHT YOU, TOO, ONE DAY.
DON'T WORRY, I DON'T PLAN TO FIGHT HERE ANYMORE.
REALLY?
THAT'S NOT WHAT YOUR AURA SAYS.
HA HA, I'M JUST JOKING.
I'LL SHOW YOU MY ANSWER IN THE MATCH.
OH, YOU WANT THAT AUTOGRAPH?
NEVER MIND.
I FORGOT TO BRING ANY PAPER.
LATER.
...I'LL BE WAITING AT BATTLE OLYMPIA.
I'M SURE YOU CAN MAKE IT.
I SAID I'M NOT GONNA FIGHT.

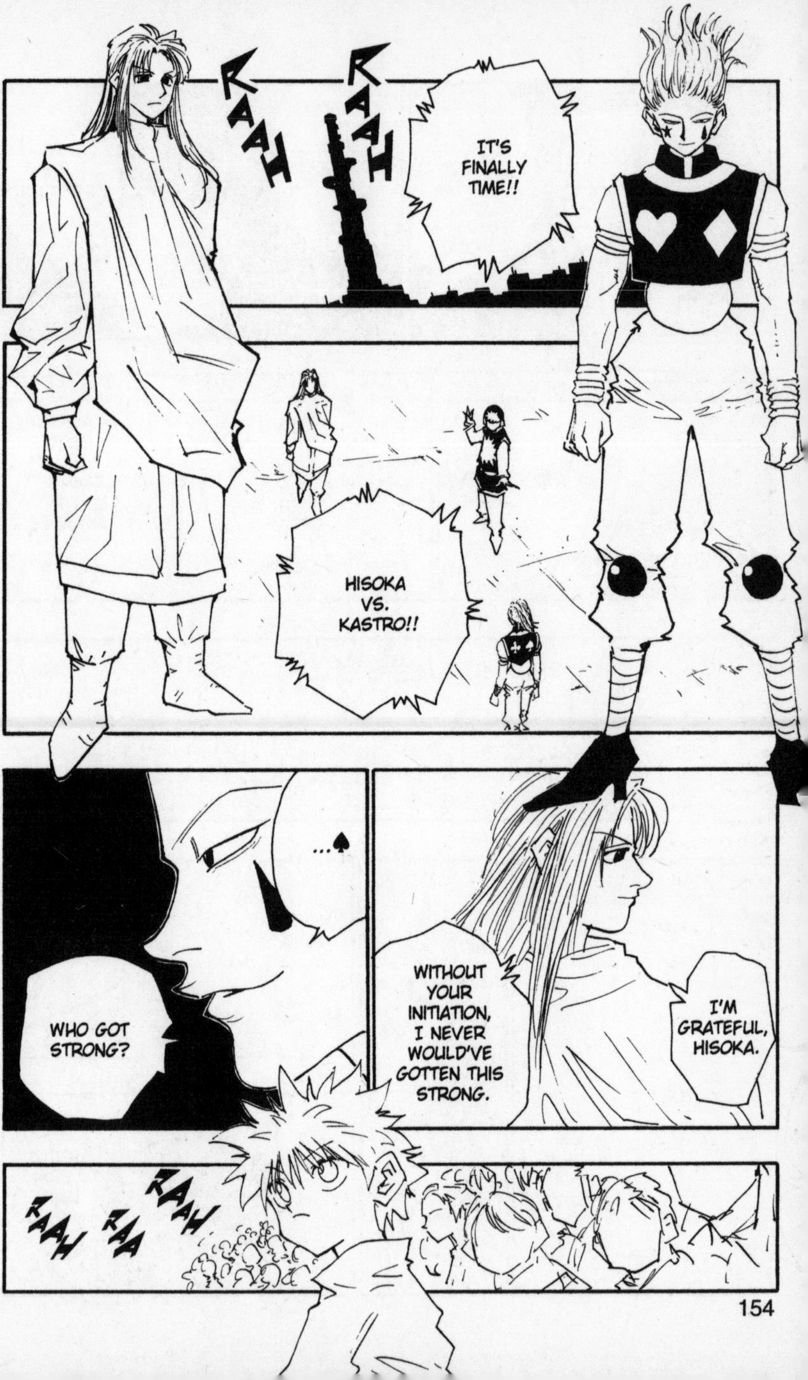
IT'S FINALLY TIME!!
RAAH
RAAH
HISOKA VS. KASTRO!!
I'M GRATEFUL, HISOKA.
WITHOUT YOUR INITIATION, I NEVER WOULD'VE GOTTEN THIS STRONG.
...♠
WHO GOT STRONG?
RAAH
RAA
RAAH

READ THIS WAY

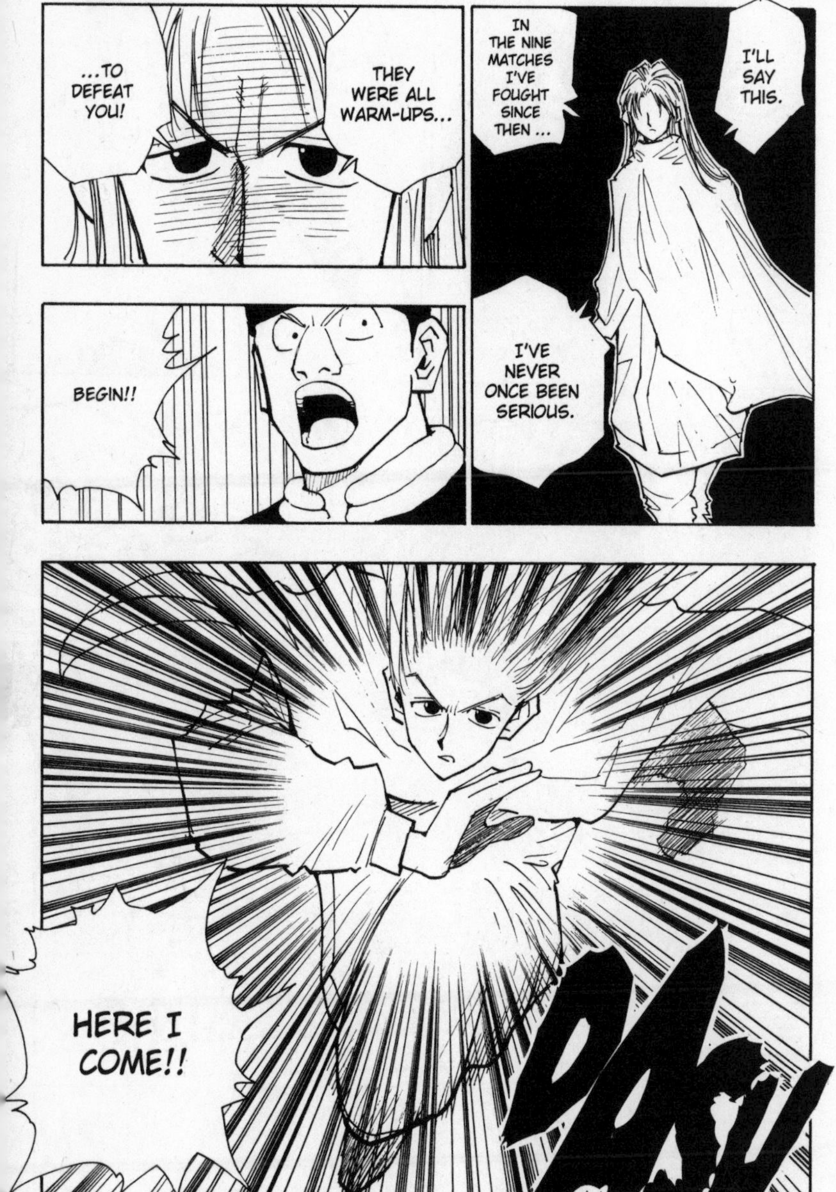
I'LL SAY THIS.
IN THE NINE MATCHES I'VE FOUGHT SINCE THEN ...
I'VE NEVER ONCE BEEN SERIOUS.
THEY WERE ALL WARM-UPS...
...TO DEFEAT YOU!
BEGIN!!
HERE I COME!!

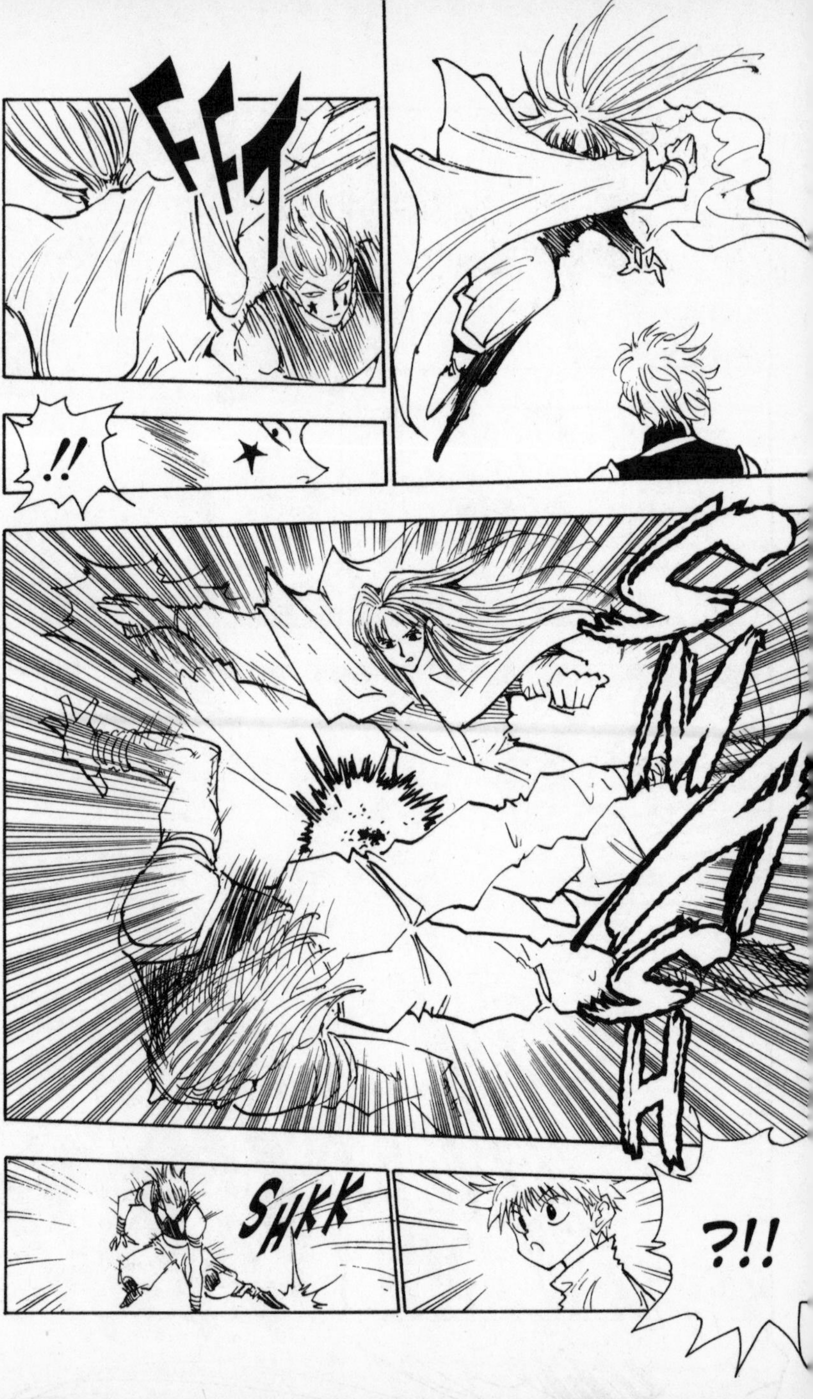
FFT
!!
SMASH
?!!
SHKK

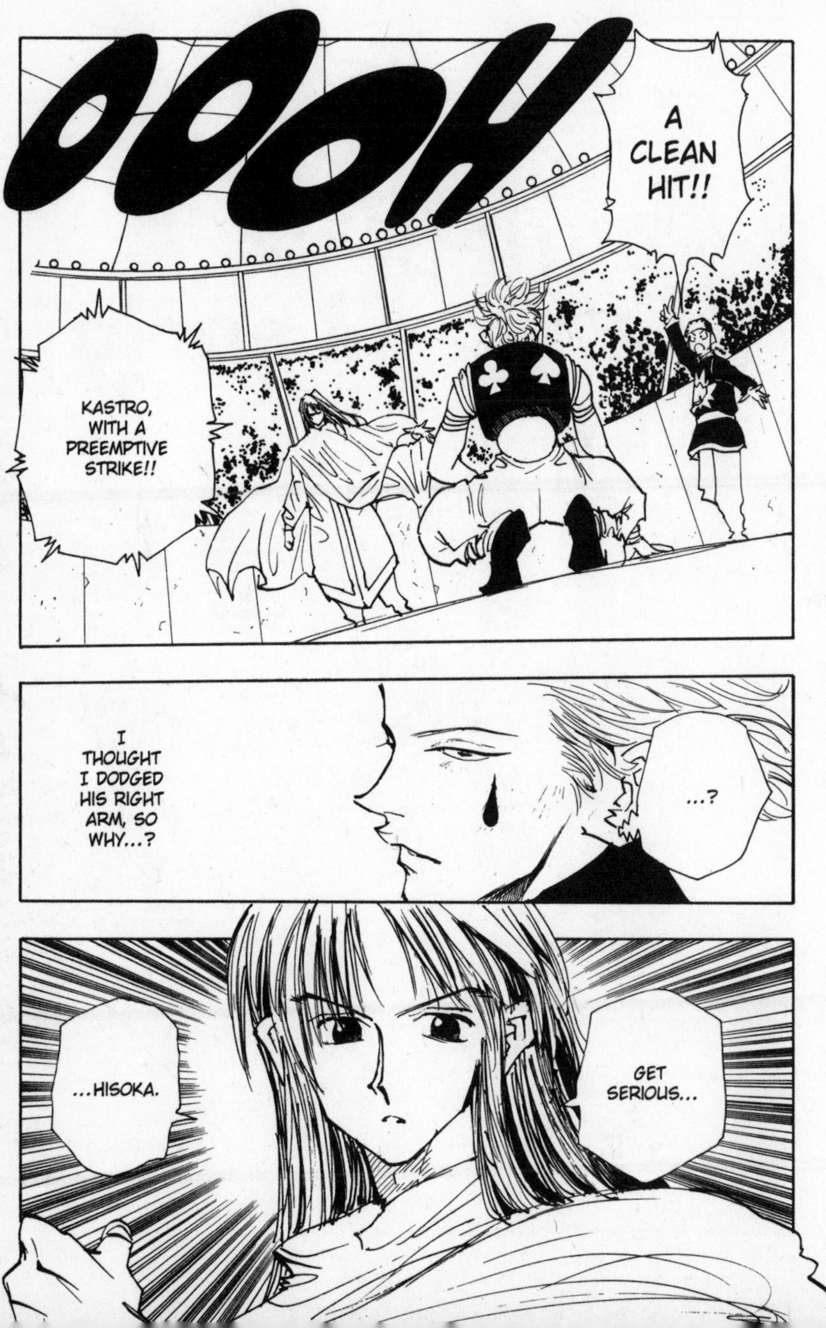
OOOH
A CLEAN HIT!!
KASTRO, WITH A PREEMPTIVE STRIKE!!
...?
I THOUGHT I DODGED HIS RIGHT ARM, SO WHY...?
GET SERIOUS...
...HISOKA.

Color-me-
Leorio

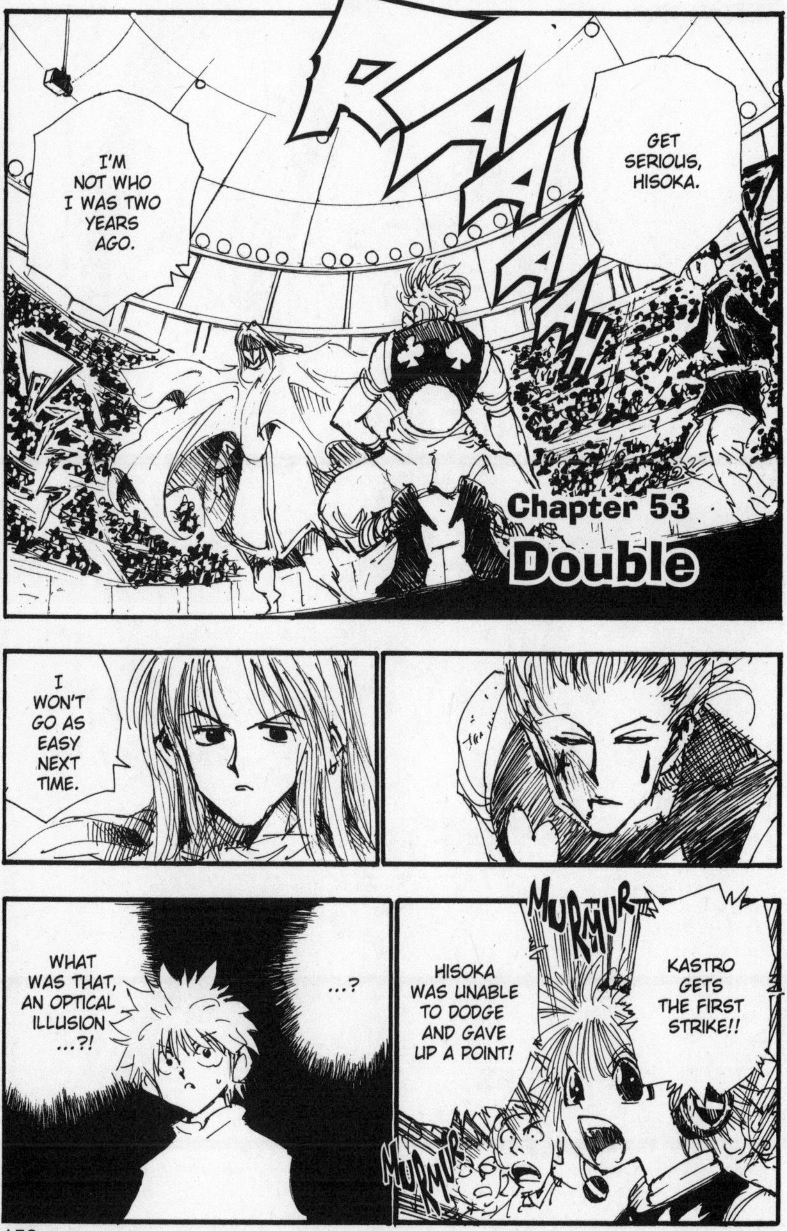
GET SERIOUS, HISOKA.
RAAAA
I'M NOT WHO I WAS TWO YEARS AGO.
Chapter 53
Double
I WON'T GO AS EASY NEXT TIME.
MURMUR
KASTRO GETS THE FIRST STRIKE!!
HISOKA WAS UNABLE TO DODGE AND GAVE UP A POINT!
MURMUR
...?
WHAT WAS THAT, AN OPTICAL ILLUSION ...?!

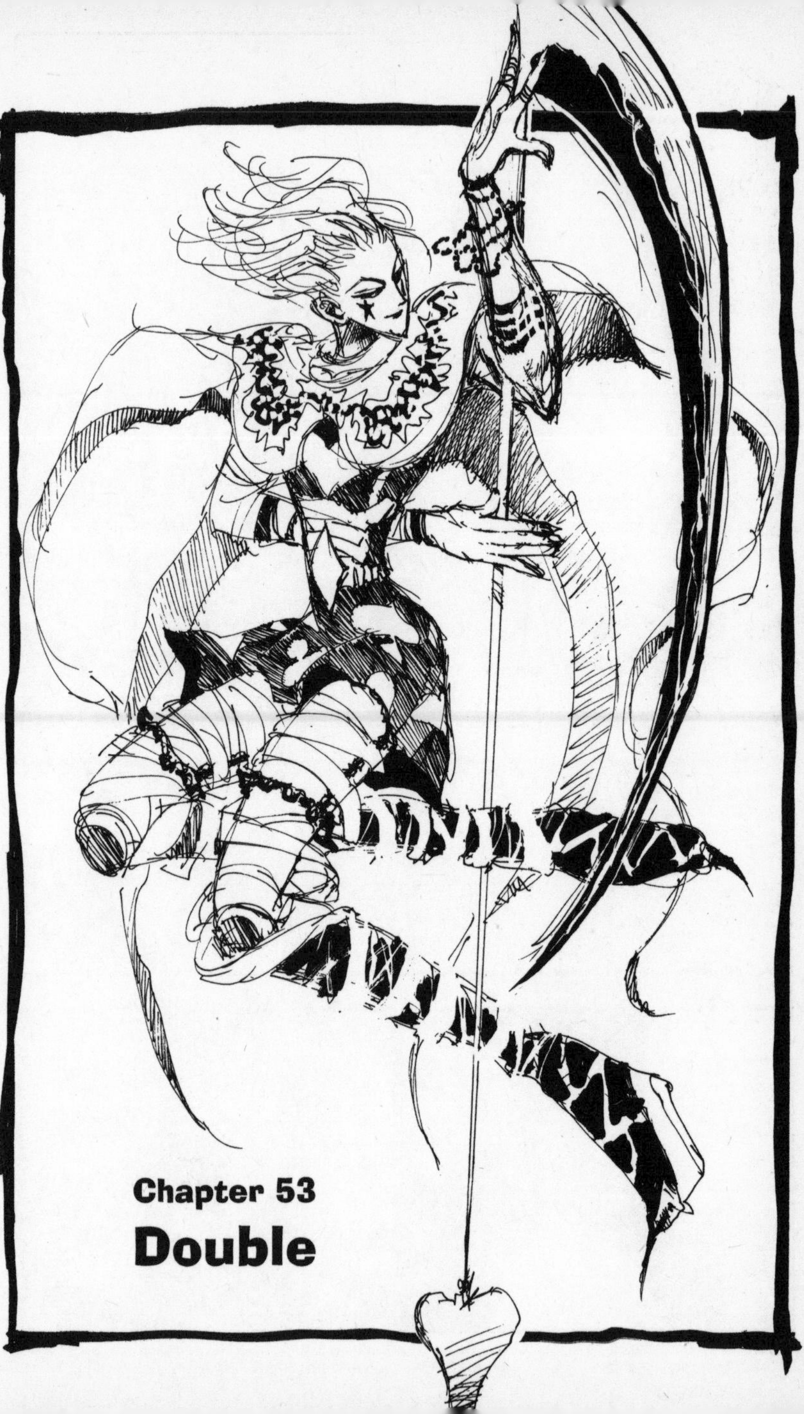

Chapter 53
Double

READ THIS WAY

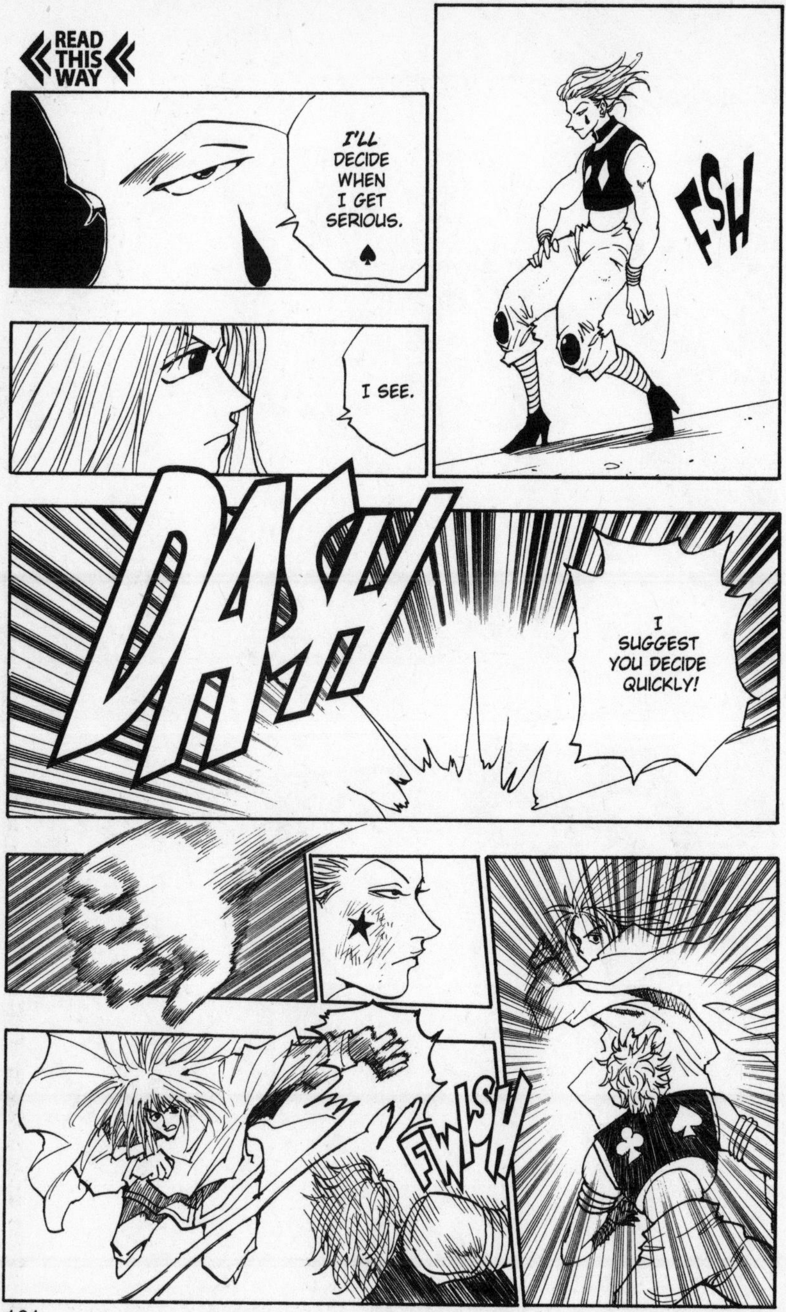
FSH
I'LL DECIDE WHEN I GET SERIOUS.
I SEE.
DASH
I SUGGEST YOU DECIDE QUICKLY!
FWISH

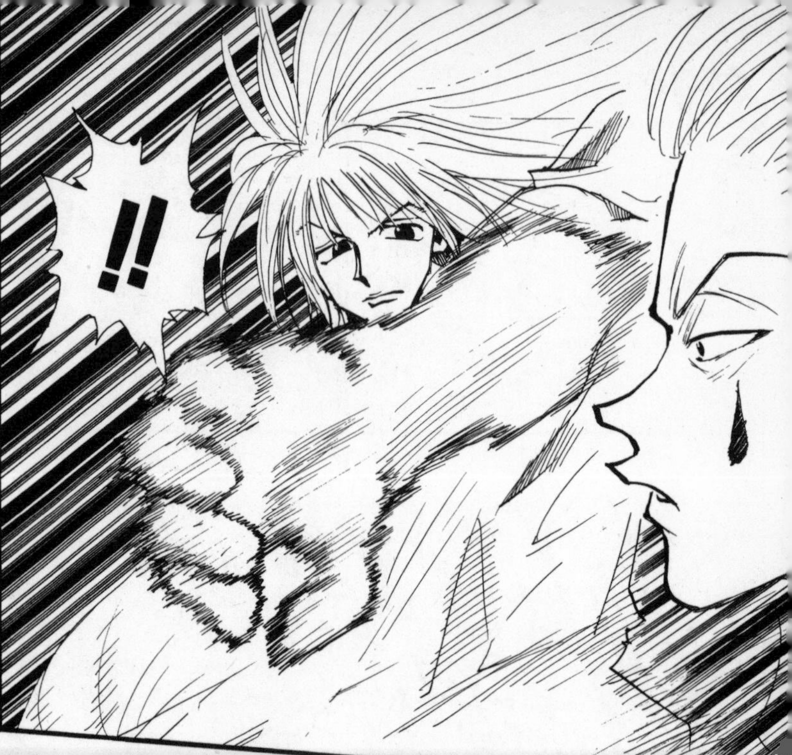
!!
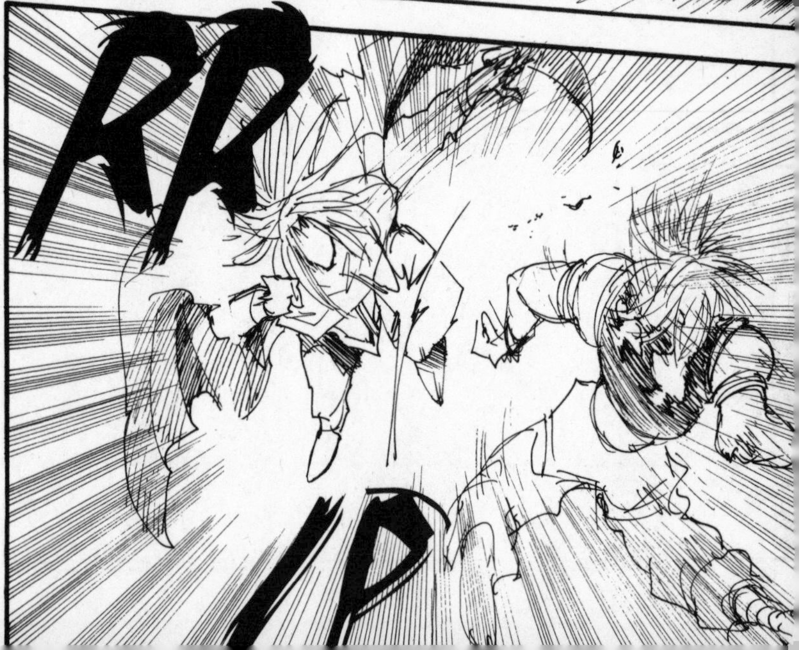
RRIP

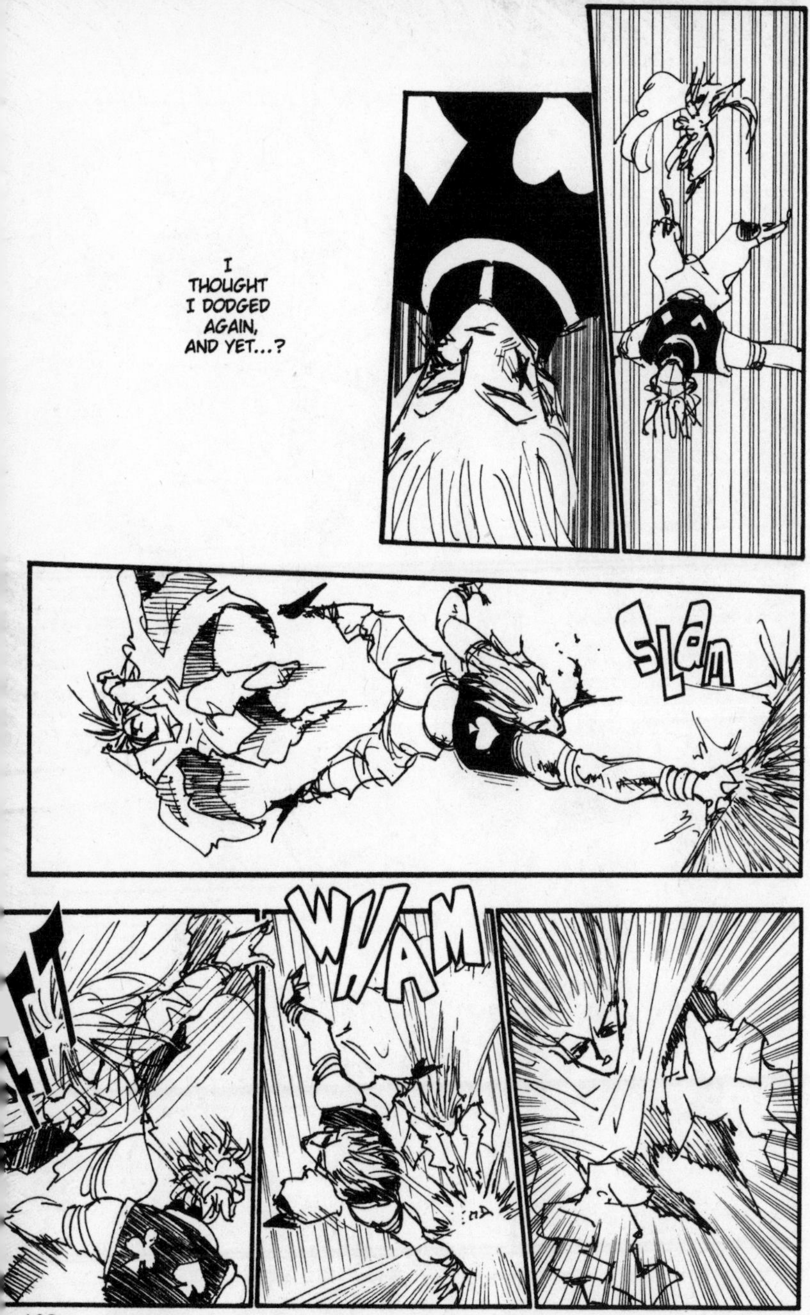
I THOUGHT I DODGED AGAIN, AND YET...?
SLAM
WHAM

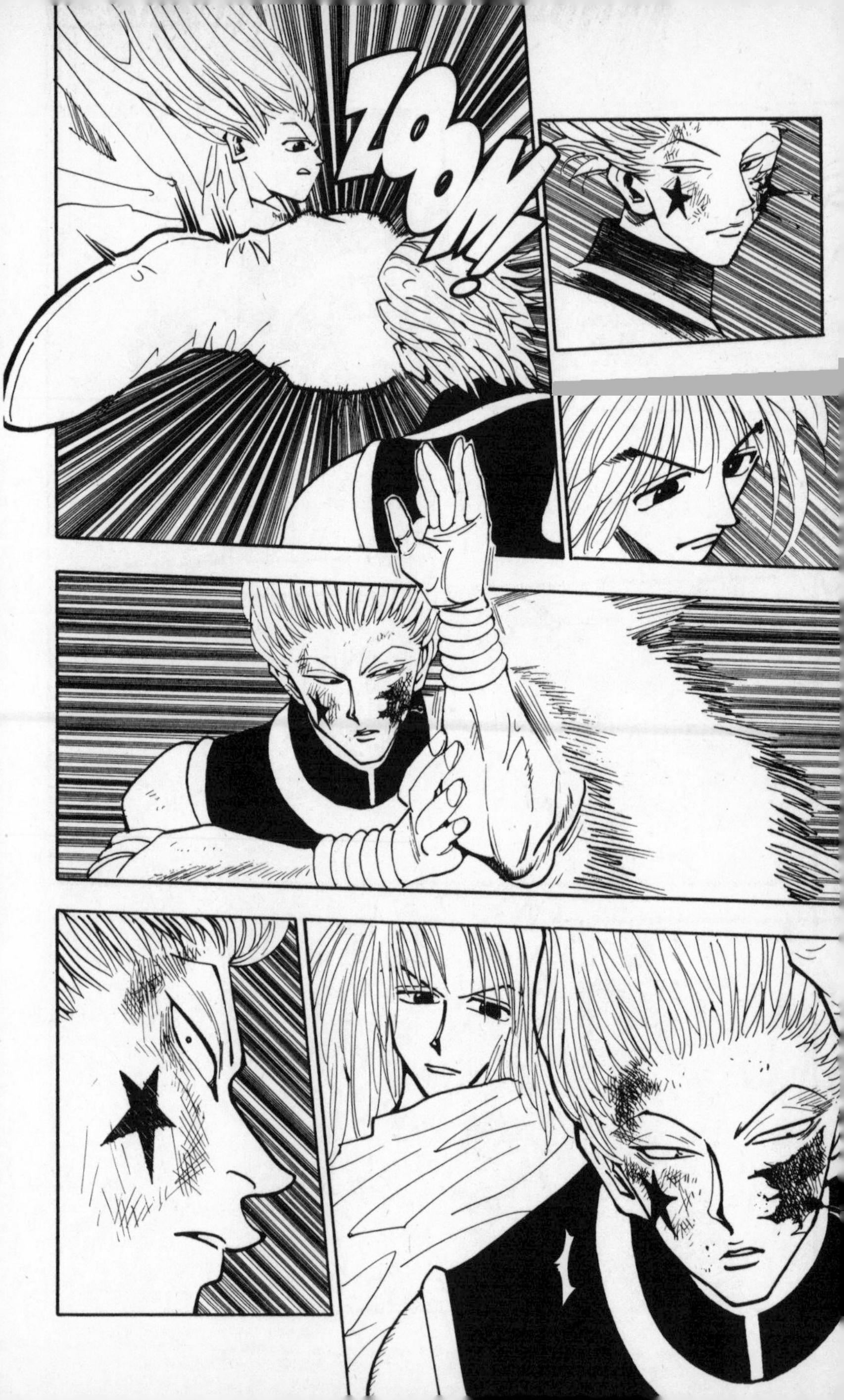
ZOOM!!

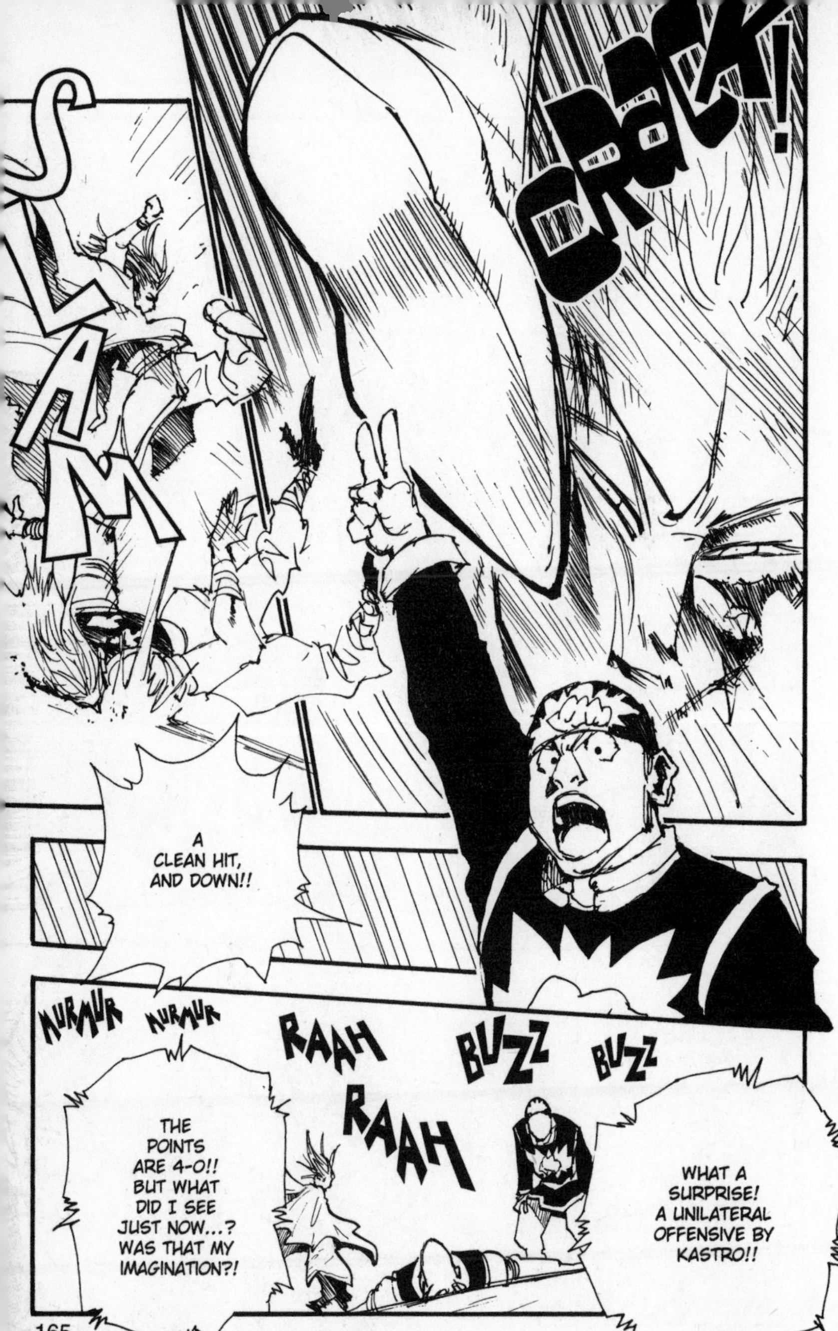
CRACK!
SLAM
A CLEAN HIT, AND DOWN!!
BUZZ BUZZ
RAAH RAAH
MURMUR MURMUR
WHAT A SURPRISE! A UNILATERAL OFFENSIVE BY KASTRO!!
THE POINTS ARE 4-0!! BUT WHAT DID I SEE JUST NOW...? WAS THAT MY IMAGINATION?!

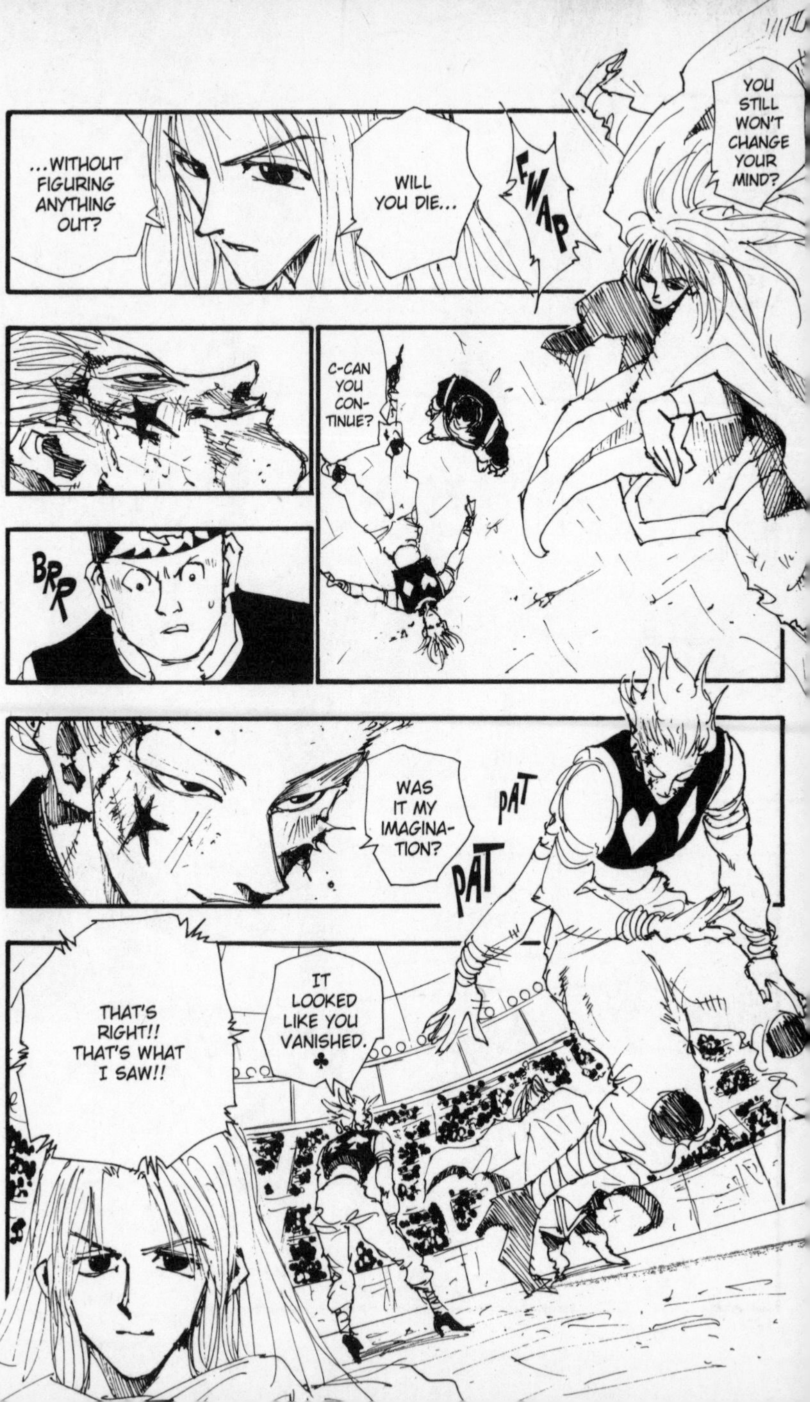
YOU STILL WON'T CHANGE YOUR MIND?
FWAP
WILL YOU DIE...
...WITHOUT FIGURING ANYTHING OUT?
C-CAN YOU CON-TINUE?
BRR
PAT
PAT
WAS IT MY IMAGINA-TION?
IT LOOKED LIKE YOU VANISHED. ♣
THAT'S RIGHT!! THAT'S WHAT I SAW!!

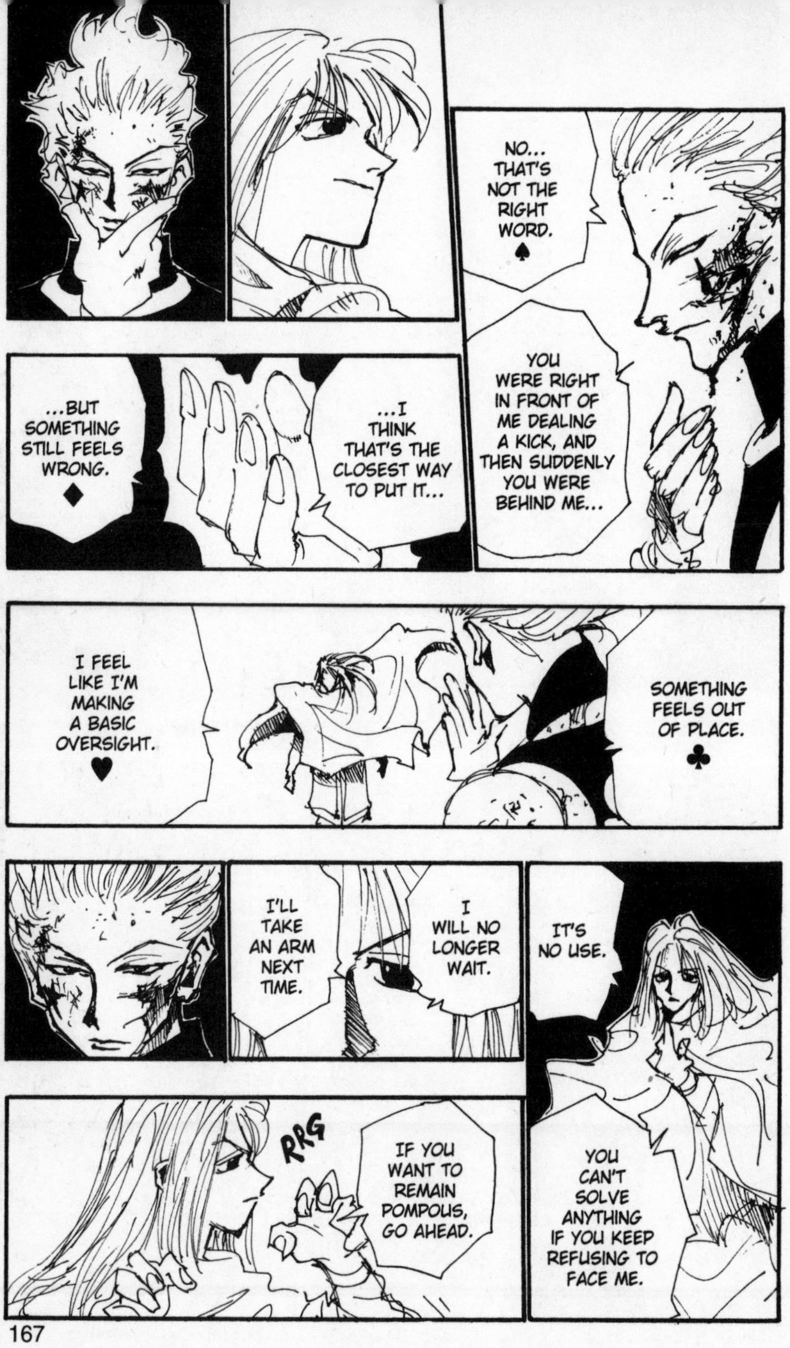
NO... THAT'S NOT THE RIGHT WORD. ♠
YOU WERE RIGHT IN FRONT OF ME DEALING A KICK, AND THEN SUDDENLY YOU WERE BEHIND ME...
...I THINK THAT'S THE CLOSEST WAY TO PUT IT...
...BUT SOMETHING STILL FEELS WRONG. ♦
SOMETHING FEELS OUT OF PLACE. ♣
I FEEL LIKE I'M MAKING A BASIC OVERSIGHT. ♥
IT'S NO USE.
YOU CAN'T SOLVE ANYTHING IF YOU KEEP REFUSING TO FACE ME.
I WILL NO LONGER WAIT.
I'LL TAKE AN ARM NEXT TIME.
IF YOU WANT TO REMAIN POMPOUS, GO AHEAD.
RRG

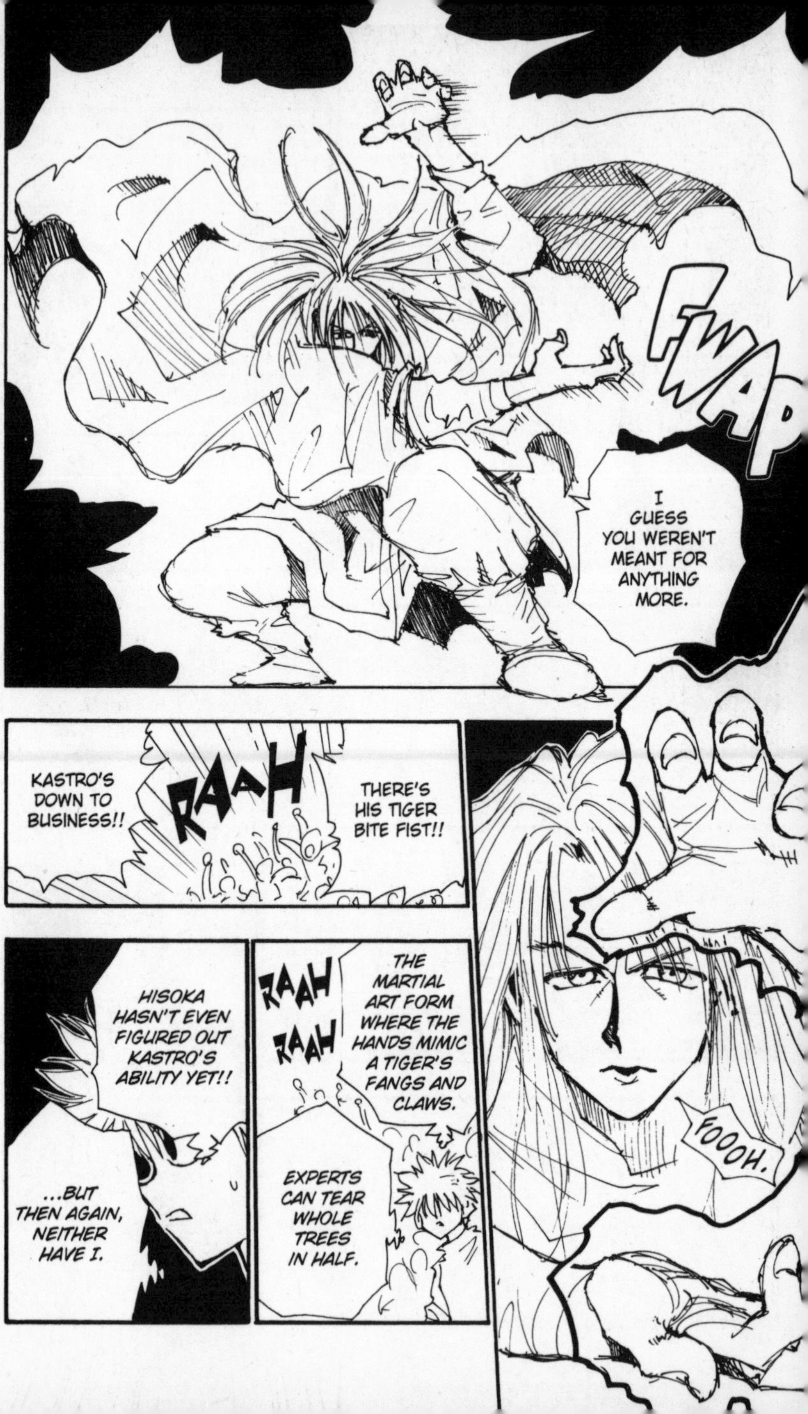
FWAP
I GUESS YOU WEREN'T MEANT FOR ANYTHING MORE.
FOOOH.
THERE'S HIS TIGER BITE FIST!!
RAAH
KASTRO'S DOWN TO BUSINESS!!
THE MARTIAL ART FORM WHERE THE HANDS MIMIC A TIGER'S FANGS AND CLAWS.
RAAH
RAAH
EXPERTS CAN TEAR WHOLE TREES IN HALF.
HISOKA HASN'T EVEN FIGURED OUT KASTRO'S ABILITY YET!!
...BUT THEN AGAIN, NEITHER HAVE I.

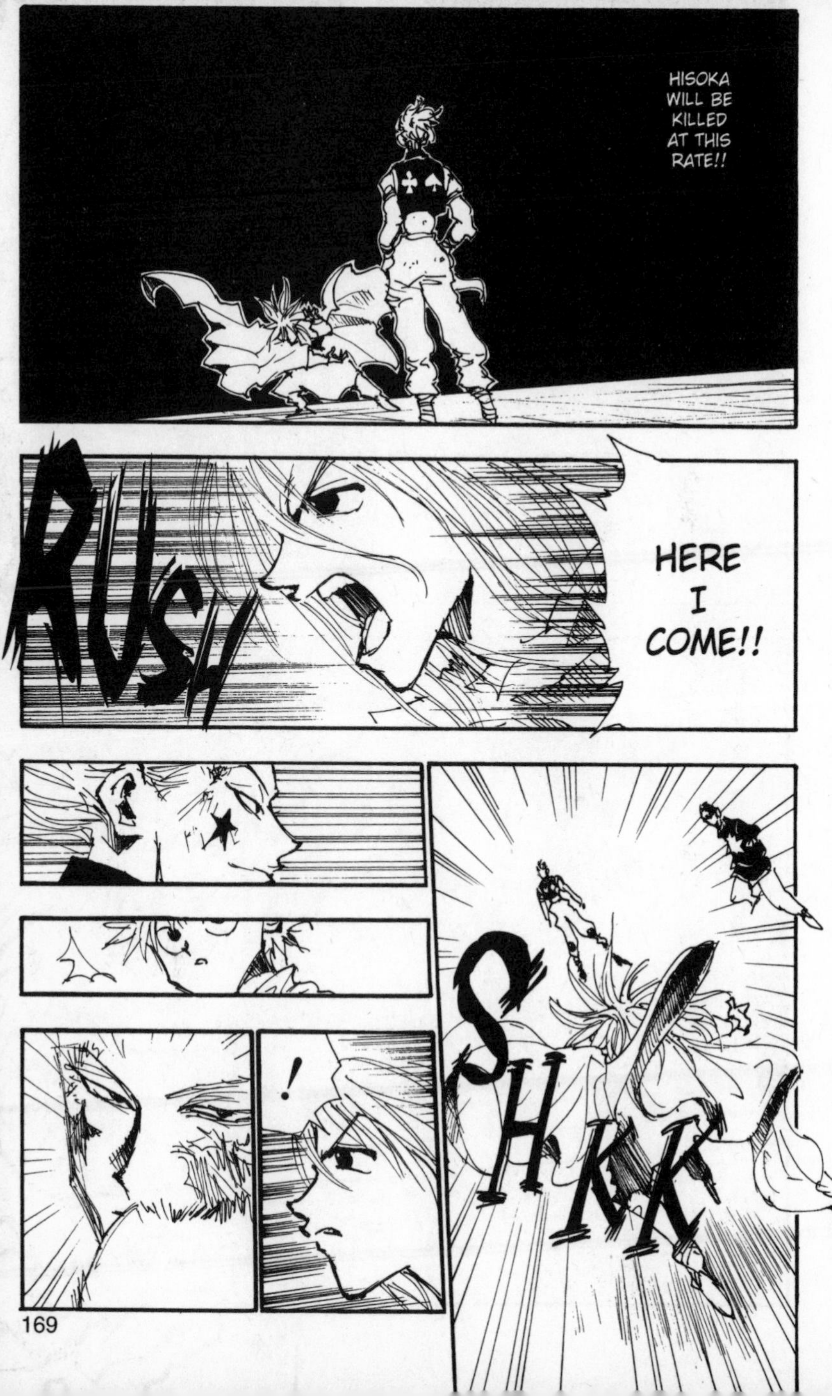
HISOKA WILL BE KILLED AT THIS RATE!!
HERE I COME!!
RUSH
SHKK
!

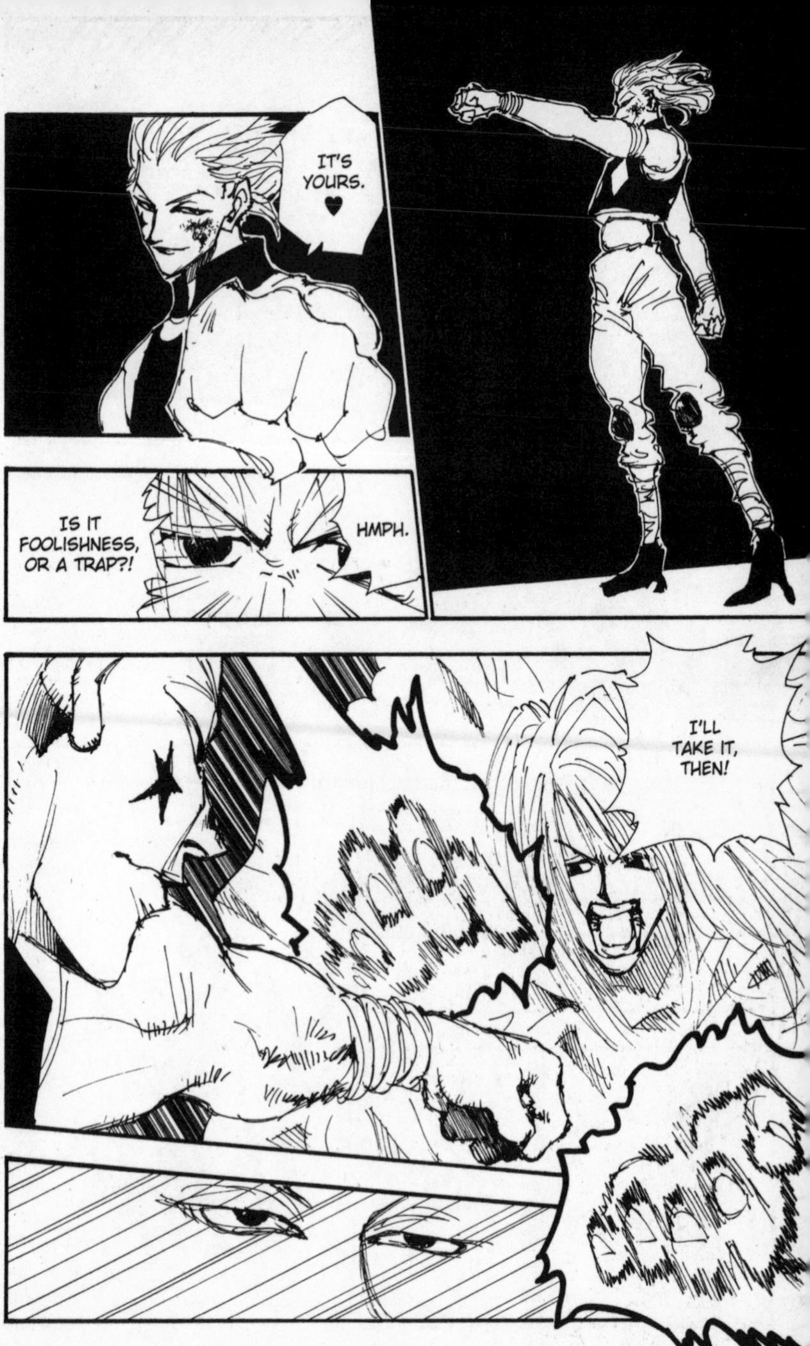
IT'S YOURS. ♥
HMPH.
IS IT FOOLISHNESS, OR A TRAP?!
I'LL TAKE IT, THEN!

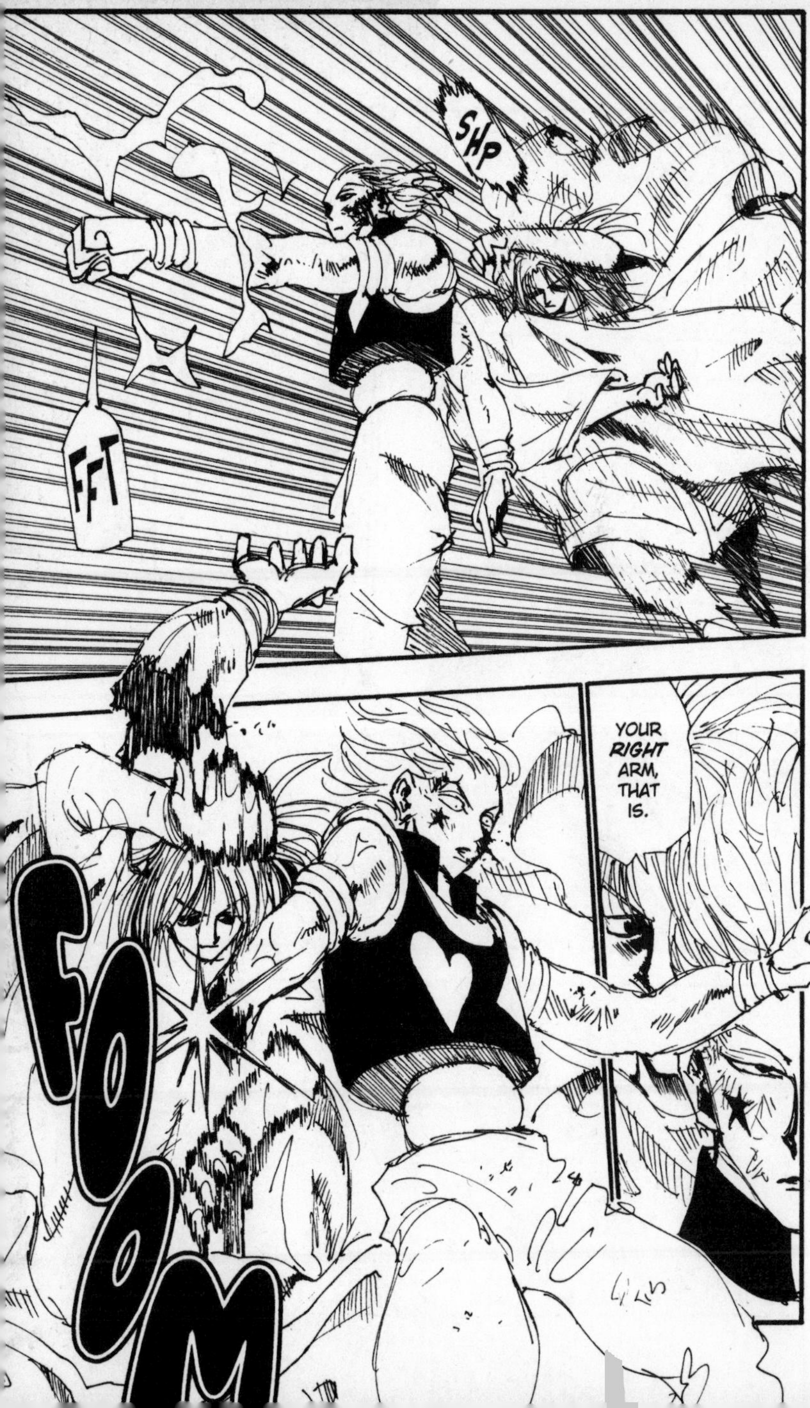
SHP
FFT
YOUR RIGHT ARM, THAT IS.
FOOM

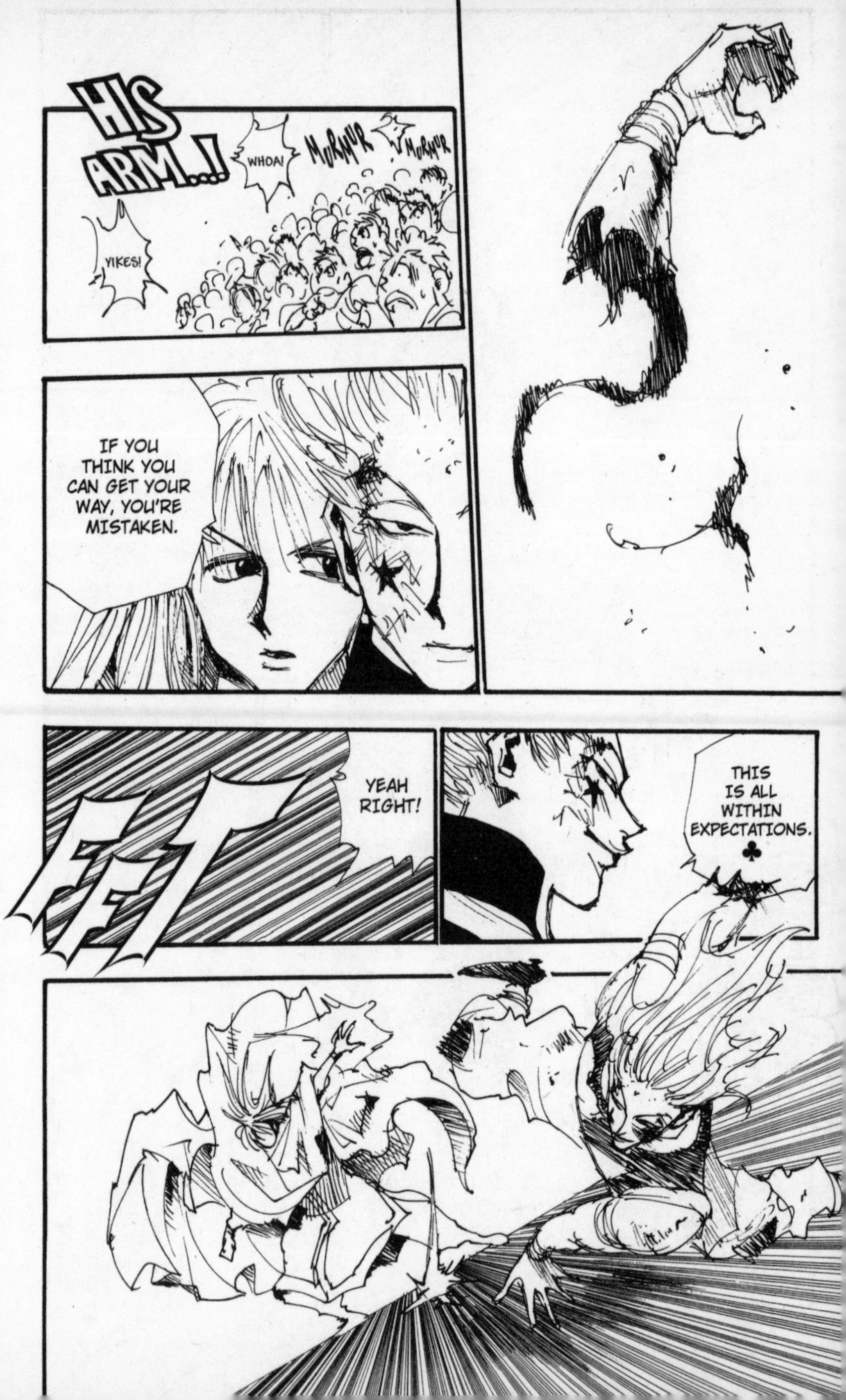
MURMUR
MURMUR
WHOA!
HIS ARM...!
YIKES!
IF YOU THINK YOU CAN GET YOUR WAY, YOU'RE MISTAKEN.
THIS IS ALL WITHIN EXPECTATIONS. ♣
YEAH RIGHT!

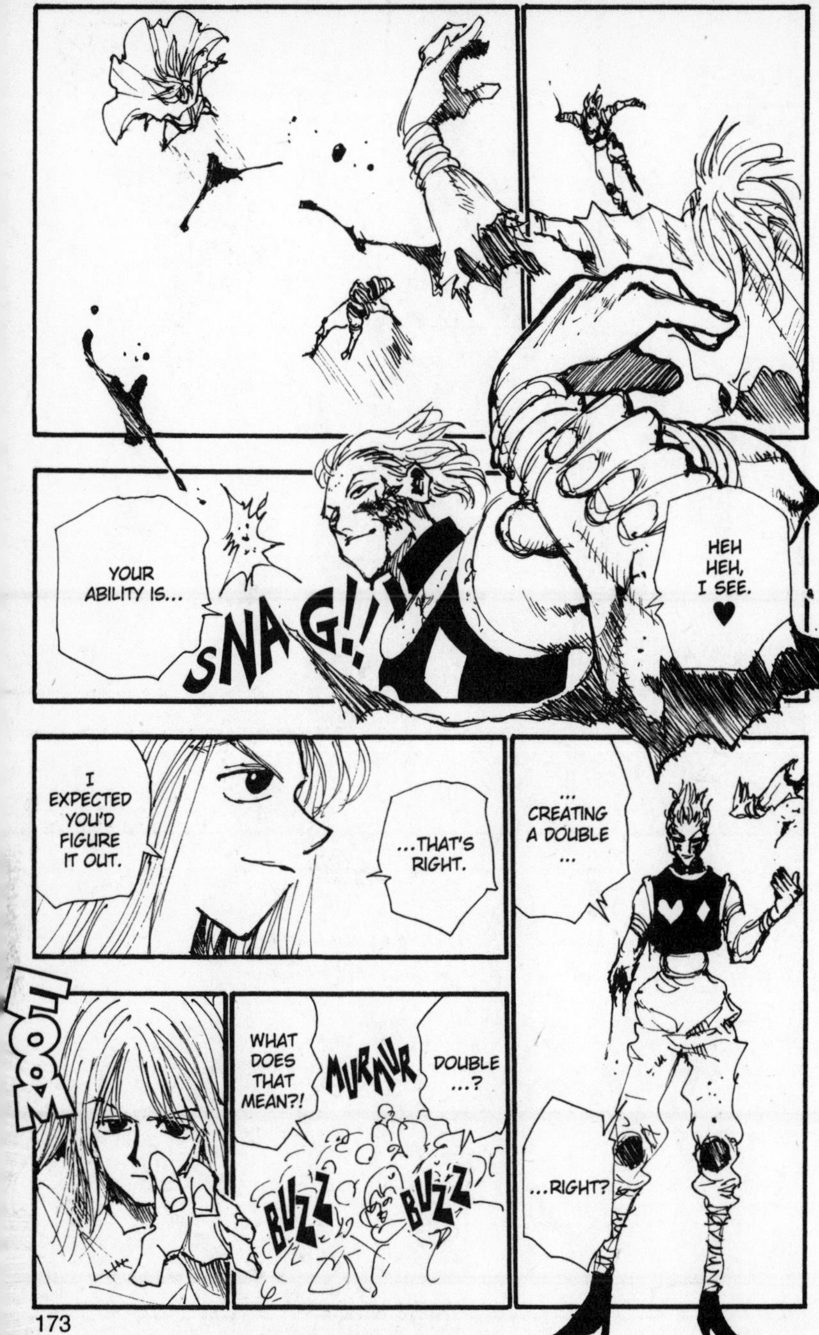
HEH HEH, I SEE. ♥
SNAG!!
YOUR ABILITY IS...
... CREATING A DOUBLE ...
...RIGHT?
...THAT'S RIGHT.
I EXPECTED YOU'D FIGURE IT OUT.
DOUBLE ...?
MURMUR
WHAT DOES THAT MEAN?!
BUZZ
BUZZ
LOOM

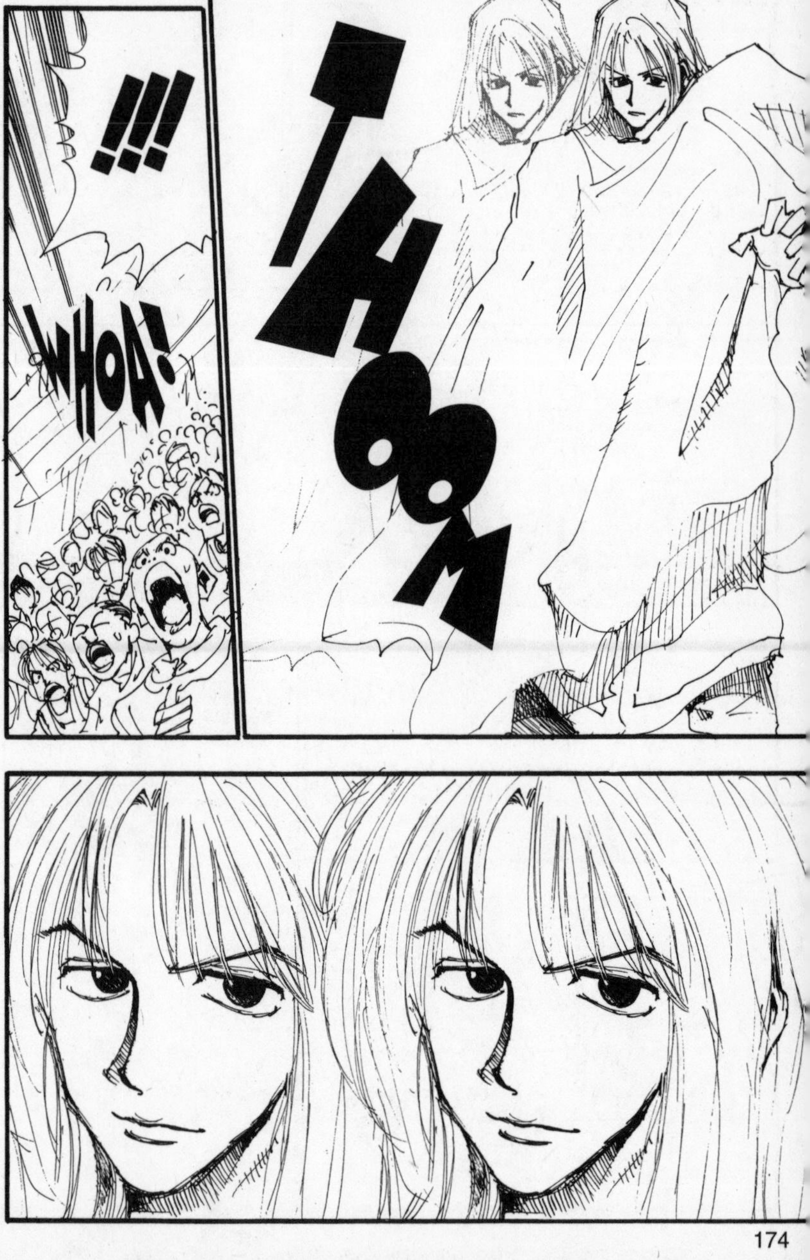
THOOM
!!!
WHOA!

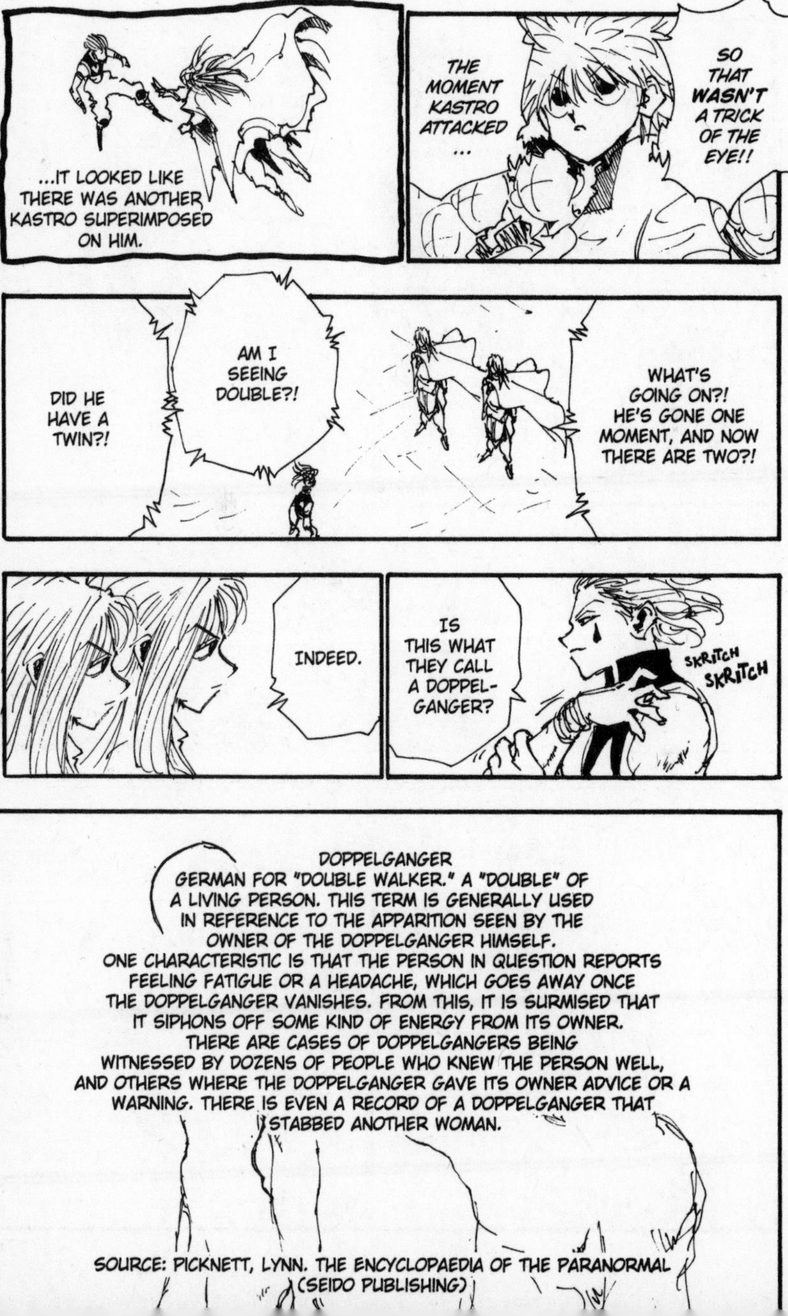

SO THAT WASN'T A TRICK OF THE EYE!!
THE MOMENT KASTRO ATTACKED...
...IT LOOKED LIKE THERE WAS ANOTHER KASTRO SUPERIMPOSED ON HIM.
WHAT'S GOING ON?! HE'S GONE ONE MOMENT, AND NOW THERE ARE TWO?!
AM I SEEING DOUBLE?!
DID HE HAVE A TWIN?!
SKRITCH SKRITCH
IS THIS WHAT THEY CALL A DOPPEL-GANGER?
INDEED.
DOPPELGANGER
GERMAN FOR "DOUBLE WALKER." A "DOUBLE" OF A LIVING PERSON. THIS TERM IS GENERALLY USED IN REFERENCE TO THE APPARITION SEEN BY THE OWNER OF THE DOPPELGANGER HIMSELF.
ONE CHARACTERISTIC IS THAT THE PERSON IN QUESTION REPORTS FEELING FATIGUE OR A HEADACHE, WHICH GOES AWAY ONCE THE DOPPELGANGER VANISHES. FROM THIS, IT IS SURMISED THAT IT SIPHONS OFF SOME KIND OF ENERGY FROM ITS OWNER.
THERE ARE CASES OF DOPPELGANGERS BEING WITNESSED BY DOZENS OF PEOPLE WHO KNEW THE PERSON WELL, AND OTHERS WHERE THE DOPPELGANGER GAVE ITS OWNER ADVICE OR A WARNING. THERE IS EVEN A RECORD OF A DOPPELGANGER THAT STABBED ANOTHER WOMAN.
SOURCE: PICKNETT, LYNN. THE ENCYCLOPAEDIA OF THE PARANORMAL (SEIDO PUBLISHING)

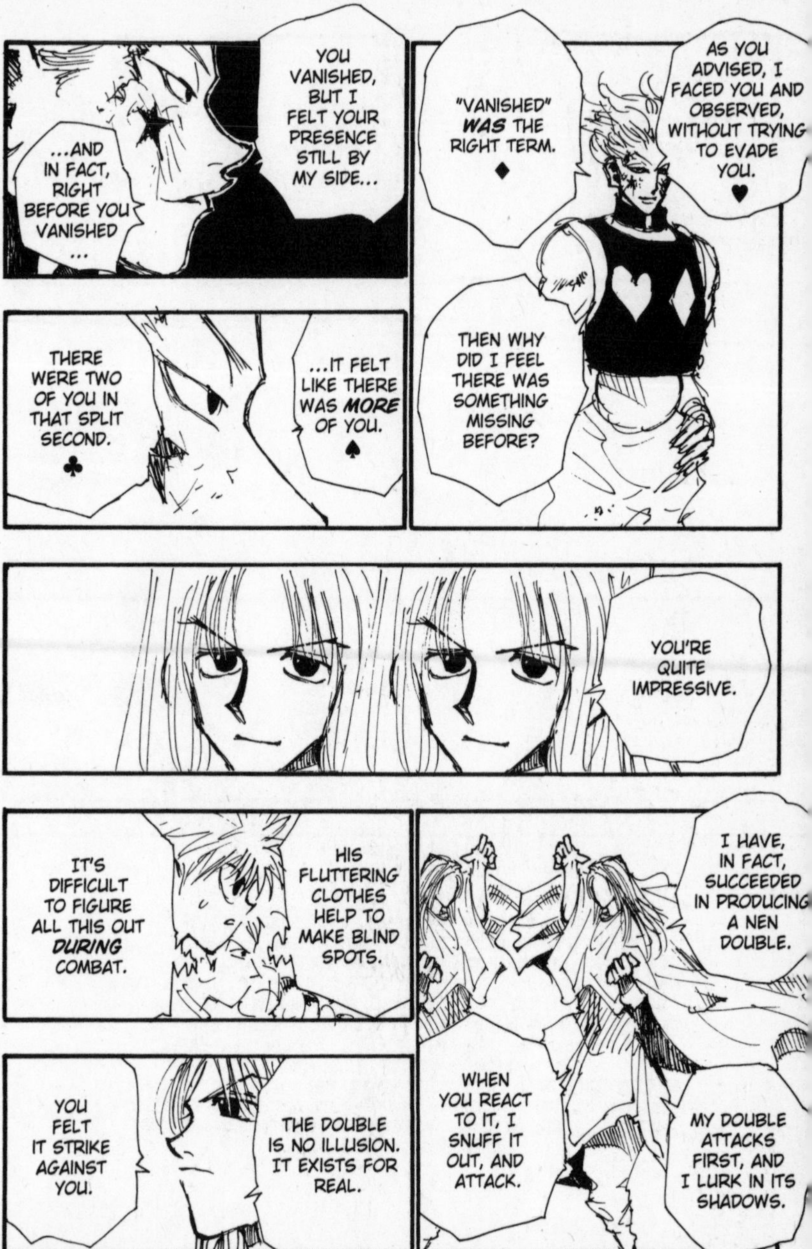
AS YOU ADVISED, I FACED YOU AND OBSERVED, WITHOUT TRYING TO EVADE YOU. ♥
"VANISHED" WAS THE RIGHT TERM. ♦
THEN WHY DID I FEEL THERE WAS SOMETHING MISSING BEFORE?
YOU VANISHED, BUT I FELT YOUR PRESENCE STILL BY MY SIDE...
...AND IN FACT, RIGHT BEFORE YOU VANISHED ...
...IT FELT LIKE THERE WAS MORE OF YOU. ♠
THERE WERE TWO OF YOU IN THAT SPLIT SECOND. ♣
YOU'RE QUITE IMPRESSIVE.
I HAVE, IN FACT, SUCCEEDED IN PRODUCING A NEN DOUBLE.
MY DOUBLE ATTACKS FIRST, AND I LURK IN ITS SHADOWS.
WHEN YOU REACT TO IT, I SNUFF IT OUT, AND ATTACK.
HIS FLUTTERING CLOTHES HELP TO MAKE BLIND SPOTS.
IT'S DIFFICULT TO FIGURE ALL THIS OUT DURING COMBAT.
THE DOUBLE IS NO ILLUSION. IT EXISTS FOR REAL.
YOU FELT IT STRIKE AGAINST YOU.

READ THIS WAY

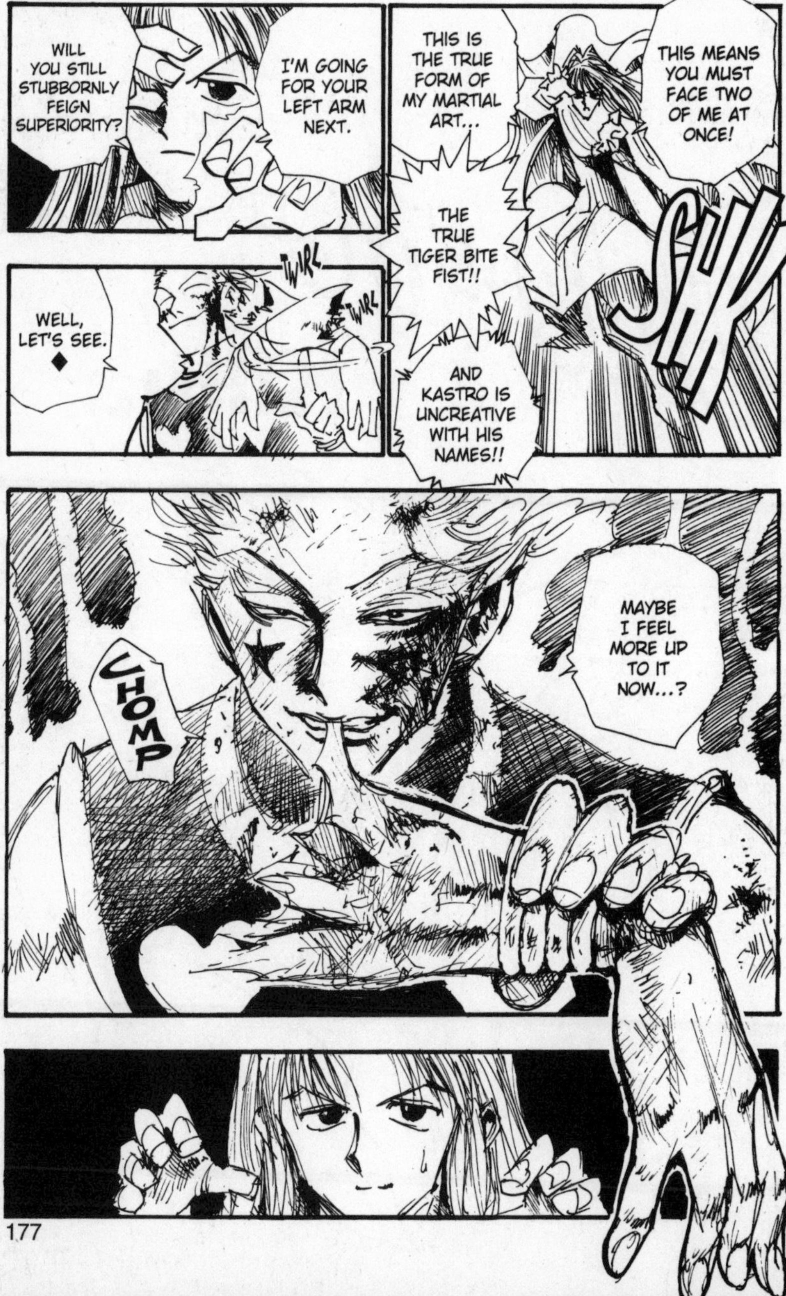
THIS IS THE TRUE FORM OF MY MARTIAL ART...
THIS MEANS YOU MUST FACE TWO OF ME AT ONCE!
SHK
THE TRUE TIGER BITE FIST!!
AND KASTRO IS UNCREATIVE WITH HIS NAMES!!
I'M GOING FOR YOUR LEFT ARM NEXT.
WILL YOU STILL STUBBORNLY FEIGN SUPERIORITY?
TWIRL
TWIRL
WELL, LET'S SEE. ◆
MAYBE I FEEL MORE UP TO IT NOW...?
CHOMP

Color-me-
Killua

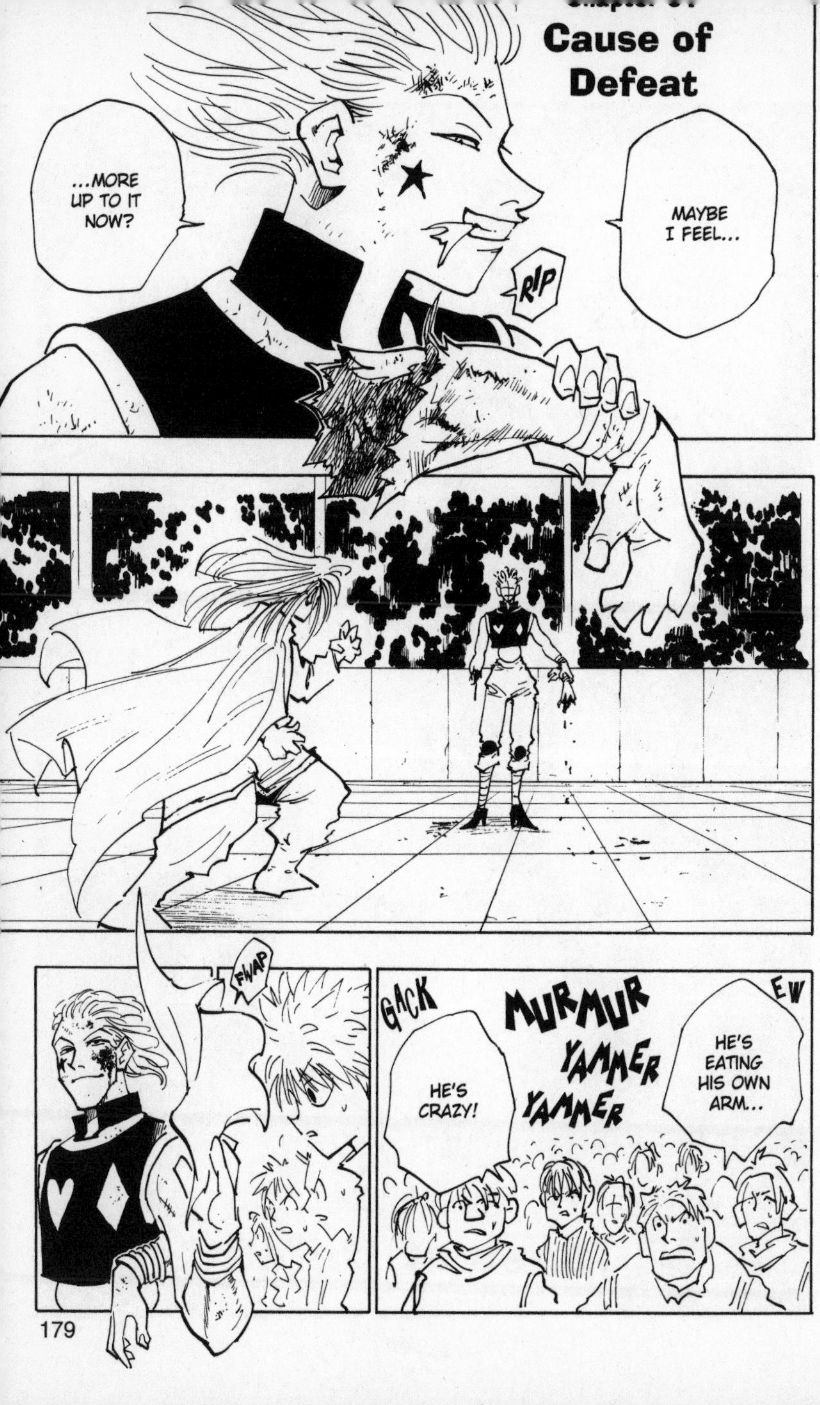
Cause of Defeat
MAYBE I FEEL...
RIP
...MORE UP TO IT NOW?
EW
HE'S EATING HIS OWN ARM...
YAMMER
YAMMER
MURMUR
HE'S CRAZY!
GACK
FWAP

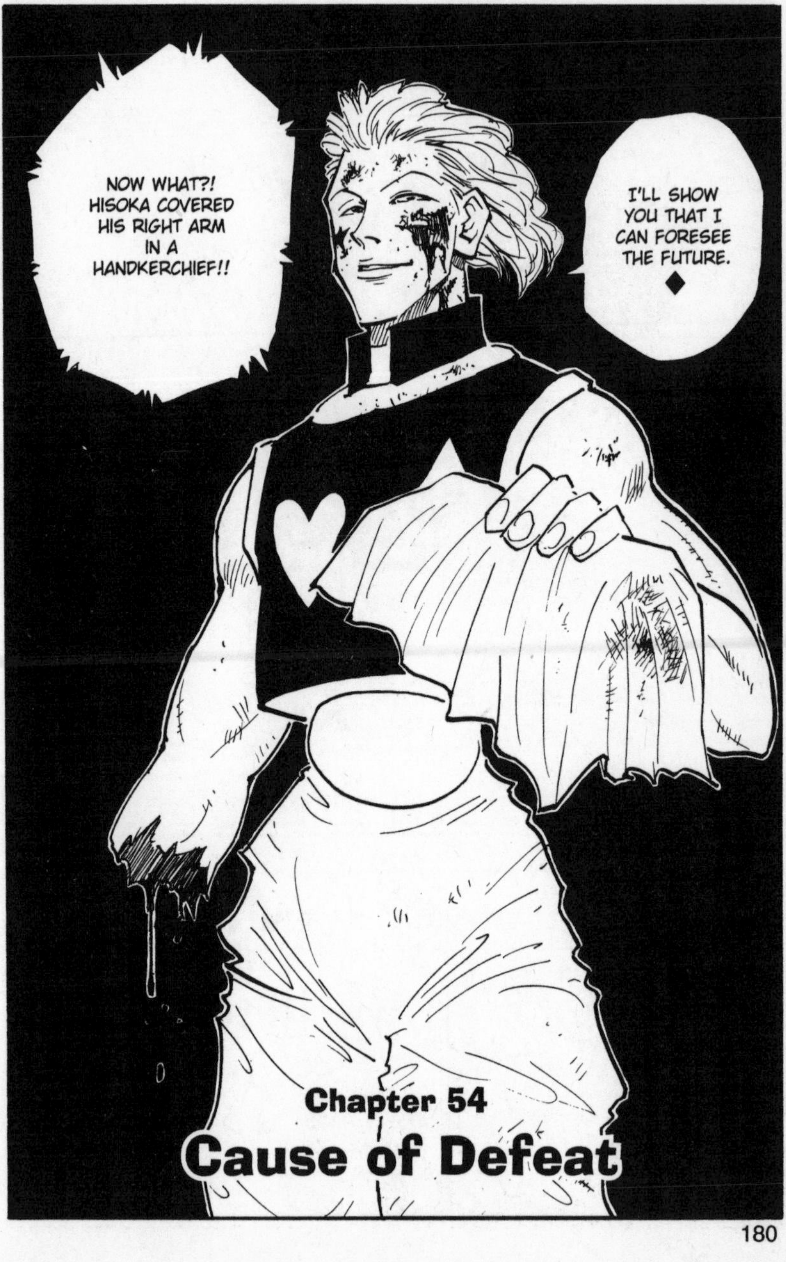
I'LL SHOW YOU THAT I CAN FORESEE THE FUTURE. ◆
NOW WHAT?! HISOKA COVERED HIS RIGHT ARM IN A HANDKERCHIEF!!

Chapter 54

Cause of Defeat

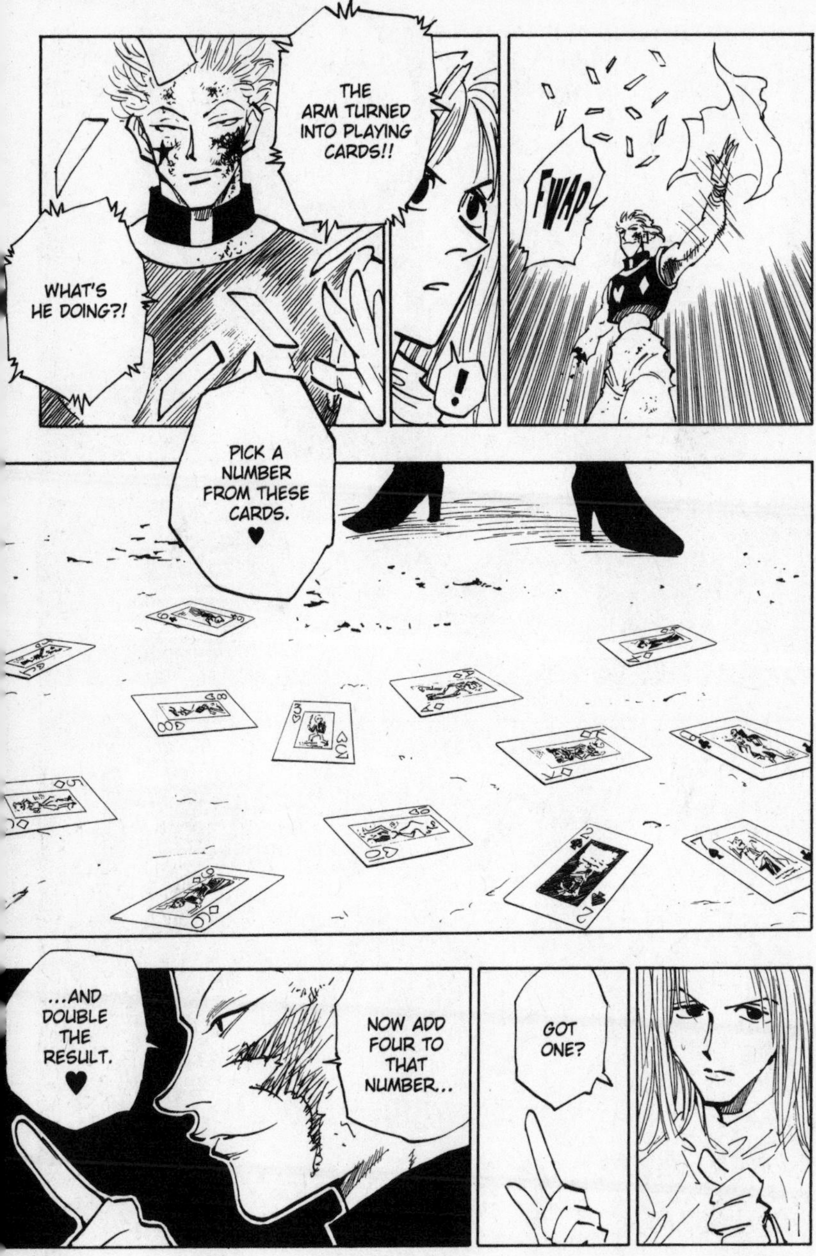
FWAP
THE ARM TURNED INTO PLAYING CARDS!!
!
WHAT'S HE DOING?!
PICK A NUMBER FROM THESE CARDS. ♥
GOT ONE?
NOW ADD FOUR TO THAT NUMBER...
...AND DOUBLE THE RESULT. ♥

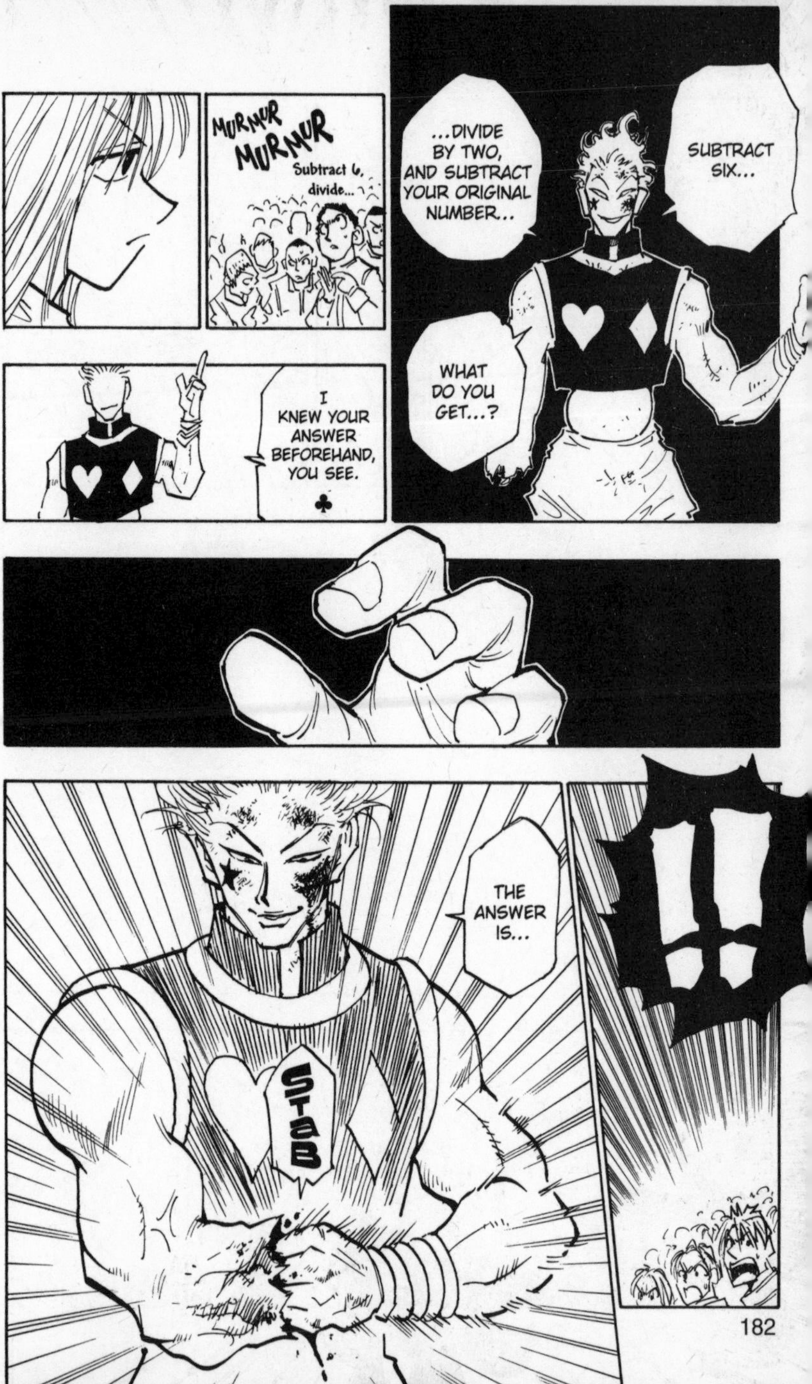
SUBTRACT SIX...
...DIVIDE BY TWO, AND SUBTRACT YOUR ORIGINAL NUMBER...
WHAT DO YOU GET...?
MURMUR MURMUR
Subtract 6, divide...
I KNEW YOUR ANSWER BEFOREHAND, YOU SEE. ♣
!!
THE ANSWER IS...
STAB

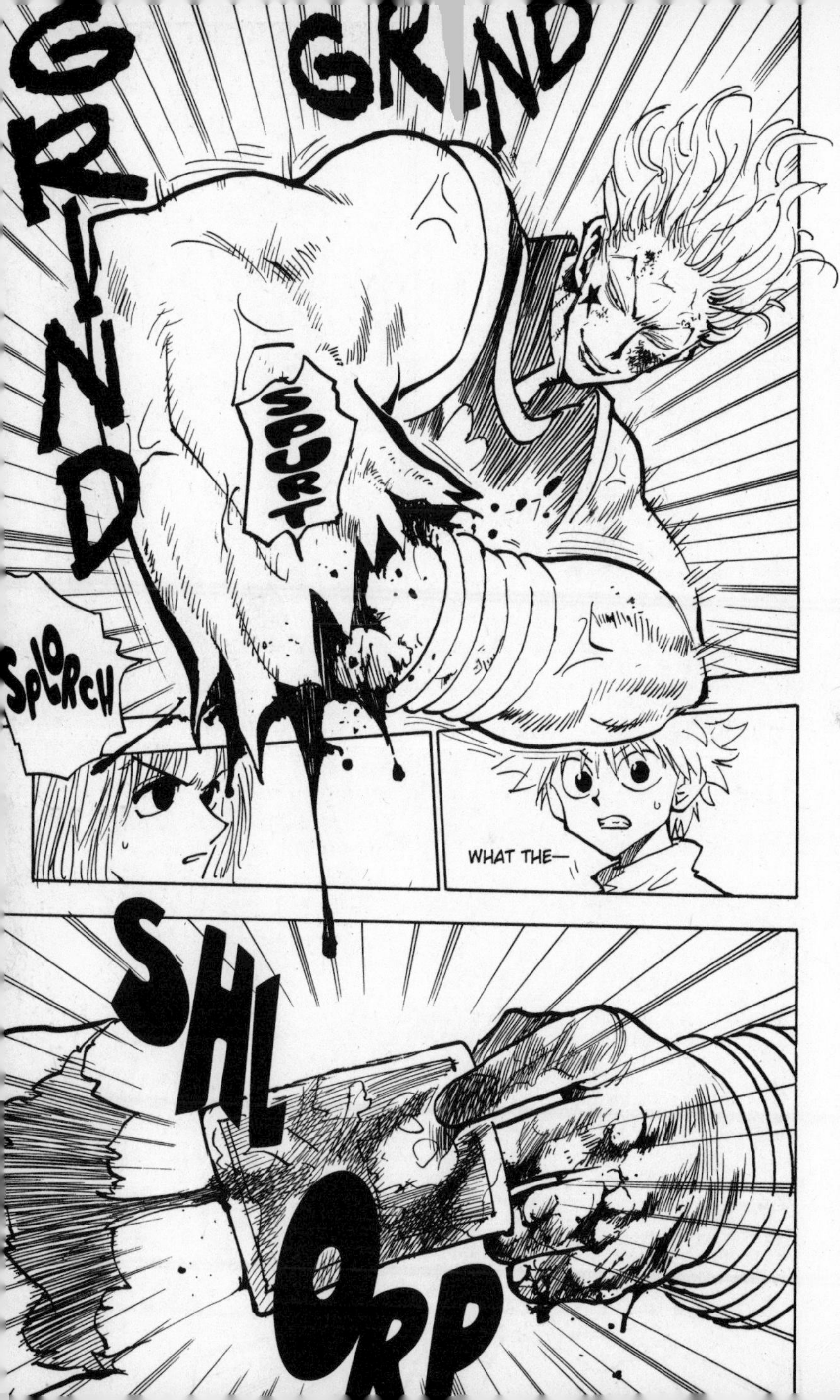
GRIND
GRIND
SPURT
SPLORCH
WHAT THE—
SHLORP

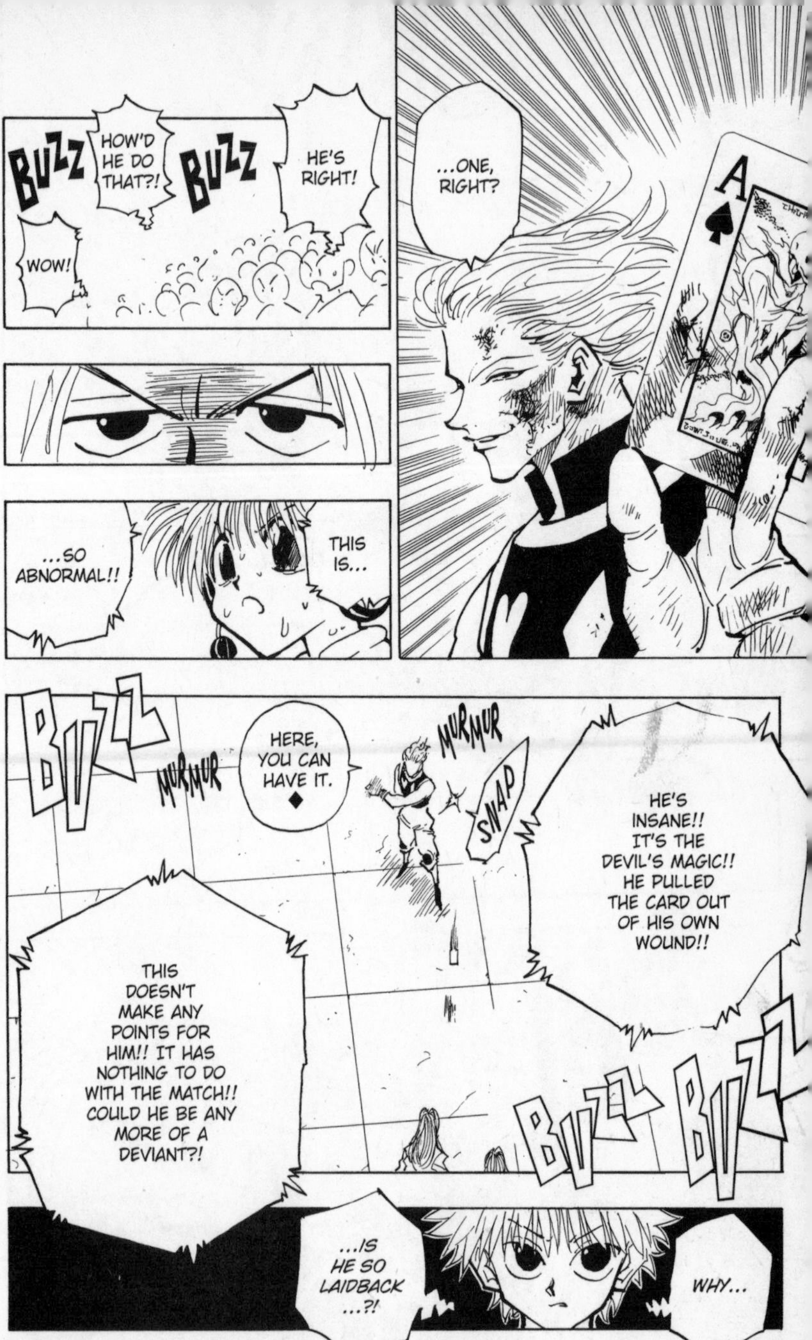
...ONE, RIGHT?
HE'S RIGHT!
BUZZ
HOW'D HE DO THAT?!
BUZZ
WOW!
THIS IS...
...SO ABNORMAL!!
HE'S INSANE!! IT'S THE DEVIL'S MAGIC!! HE PULLED THE CARD OUT OF HIS OWN WOUND!!
BUZZ BUZZ
SNAP
MURMUR
HERE, YOU CAN HAVE IT.
MURMUR
BUZZ
THIS DOESN'T MAKE ANY POINTS FOR HIM!! IT HAS NOTHING TO DO WITH THE MATCH!! COULD HE BE ANY MORE OF A DEVIANT?!
WHY...
...IS HE SO LAIDBACK ...?!

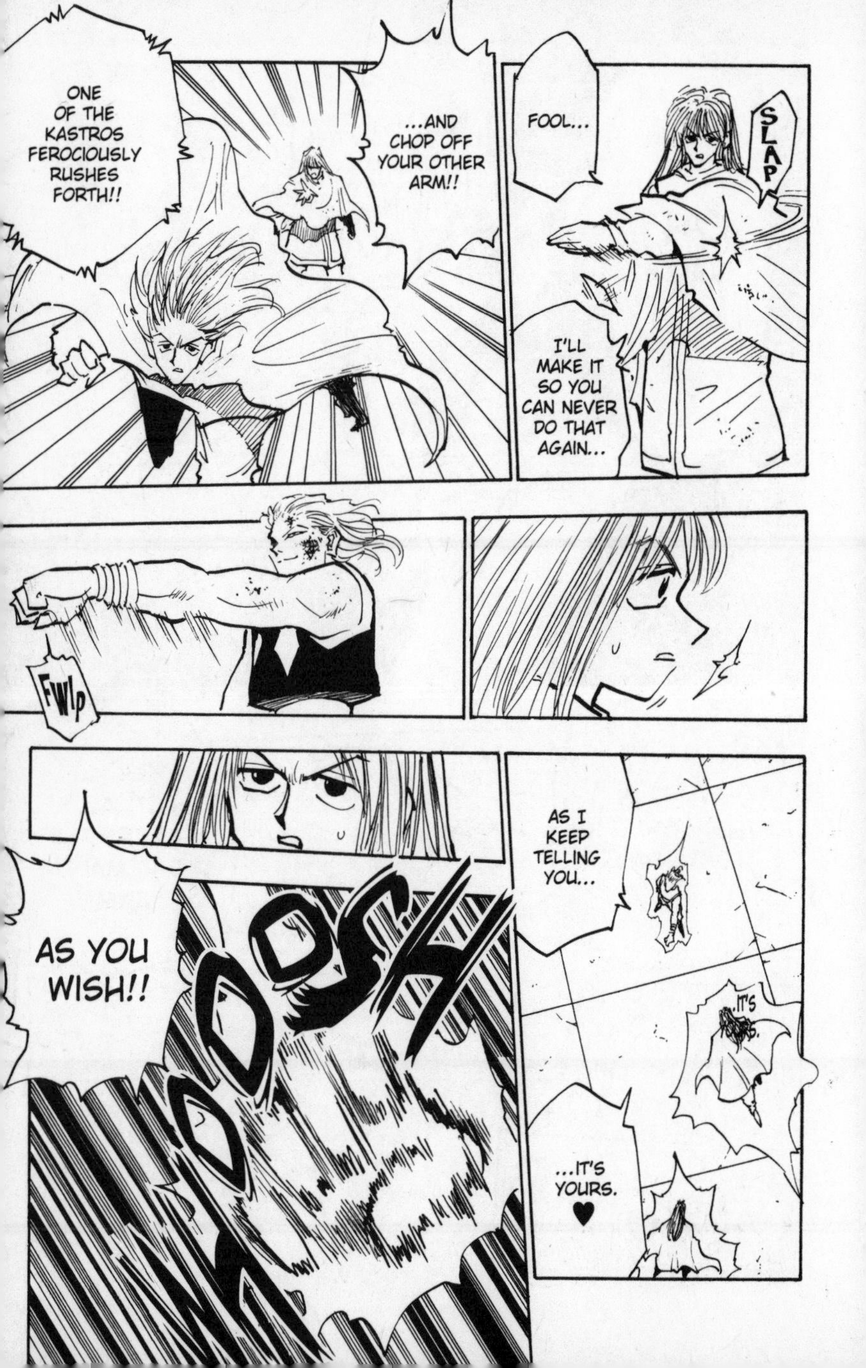
...AND CHOP OFF YOUR OTHER ARM!!
ONE OF THE KASTROS FEROCIOUSLY RUSHES FORTH!!
FOOL...
SLAP
I'LL MAKE IT SO YOU CAN NEVER DO THAT AGAIN...
FWIP
AS I KEEP TELLING YOU...
...IT'S YOURS.
...IT'S YOURS. ♥
AS YOU WISH!!

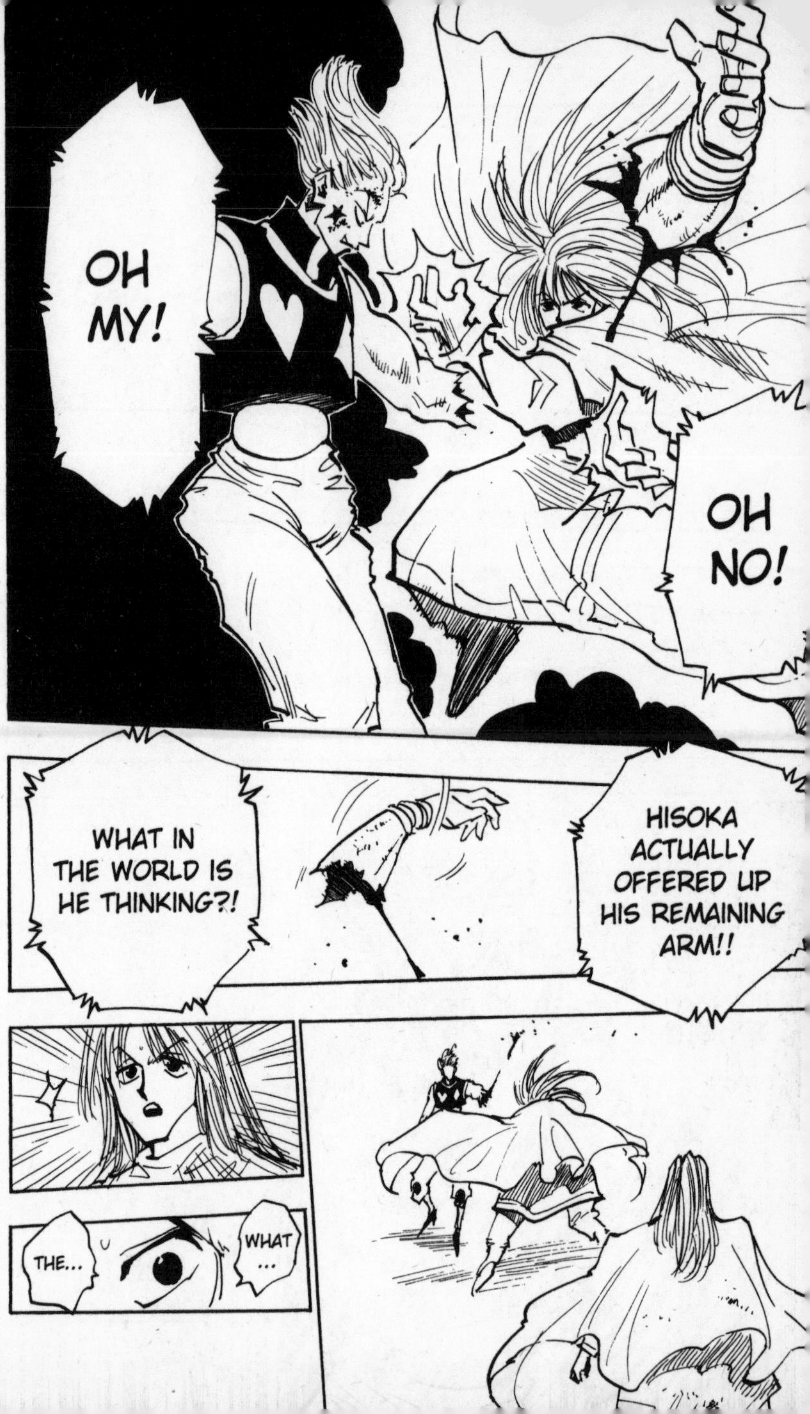
OH NO!
OH MY!
HISOKA ACTUALLY OFFERED UP HIS REMAINING ARM!!
WHAT IN THE WORLD IS HE THINKING?!
WHAT ...
THE...

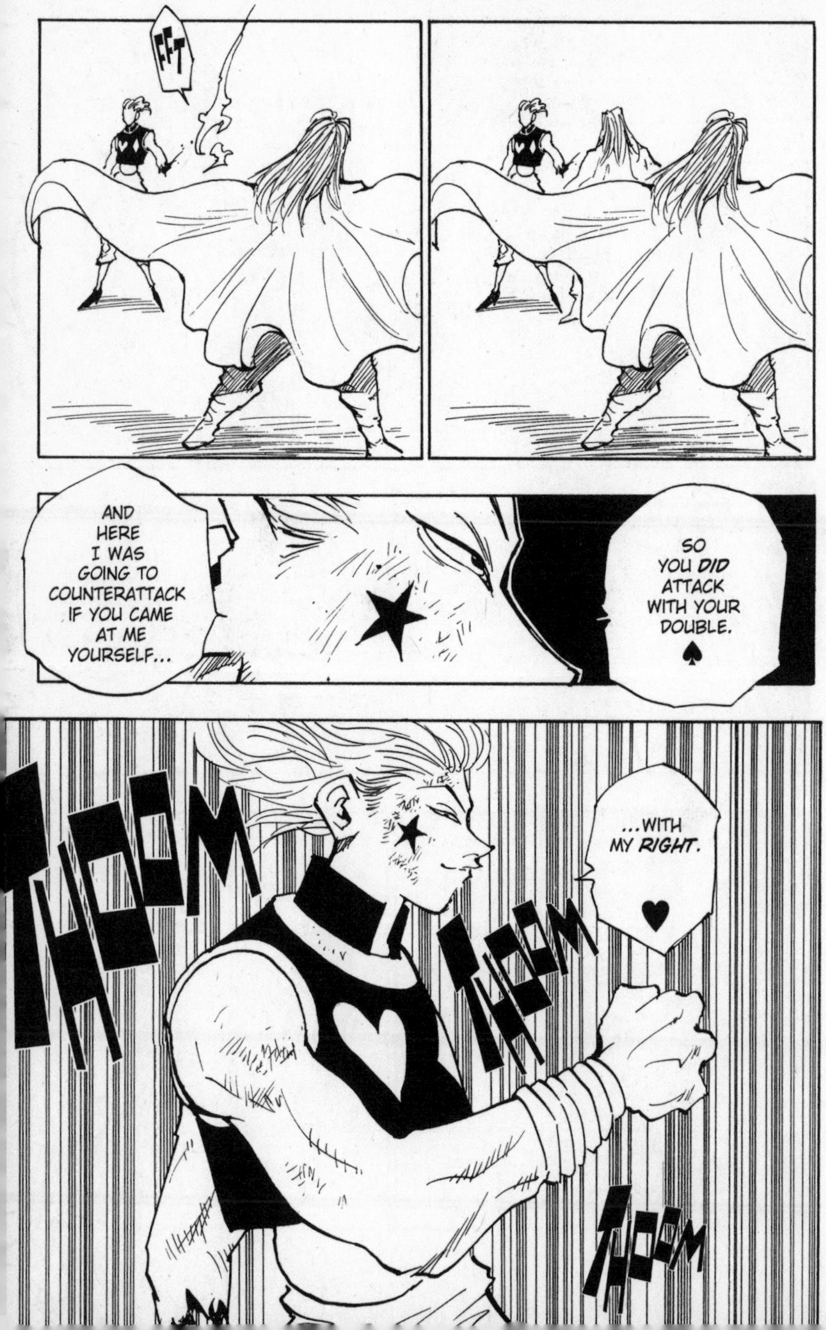
FFT
SO YOU DID ATTACK WITH YOUR DOUBLE. ♠
AND HERE I WAS GOING TO COUNTERATTACK IF YOU CAME AT ME YOURSELF...
...WITH MY RIGHT. ♥
THOOM
THOOM
THOOM

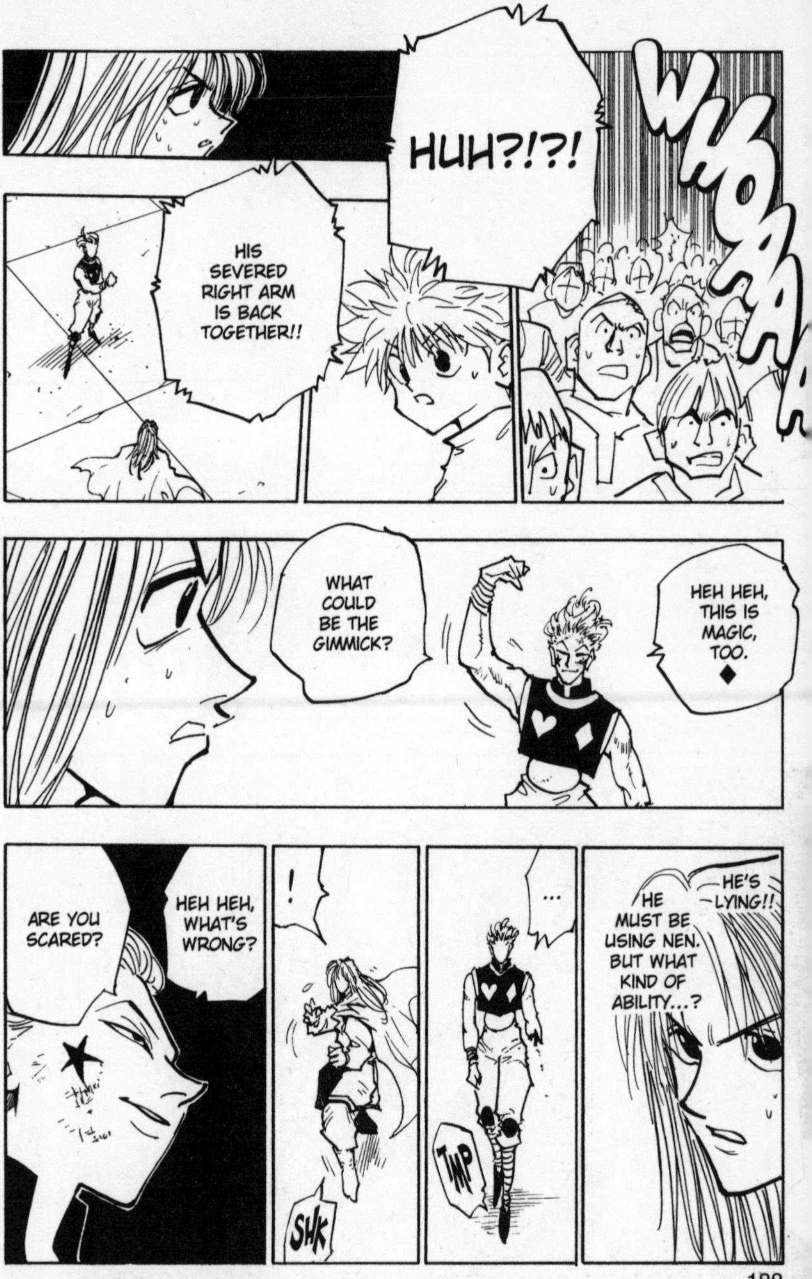

WHOAA!!
HUH?!?!
HIS SEVERED RIGHT ARM IS BACK TOGETHER!!
HEH HEH, THIS IS MAGIC, TOO. ◆
WHAT COULD BE THE GIMMICK?
HE'S LYING!!
HE MUST BE USING NEN. BUT WHAT KIND OF ABILITY...?
...
TMP
!
SHK
HEH HEH, WHAT'S WRONG?
ARE YOU SCARED?

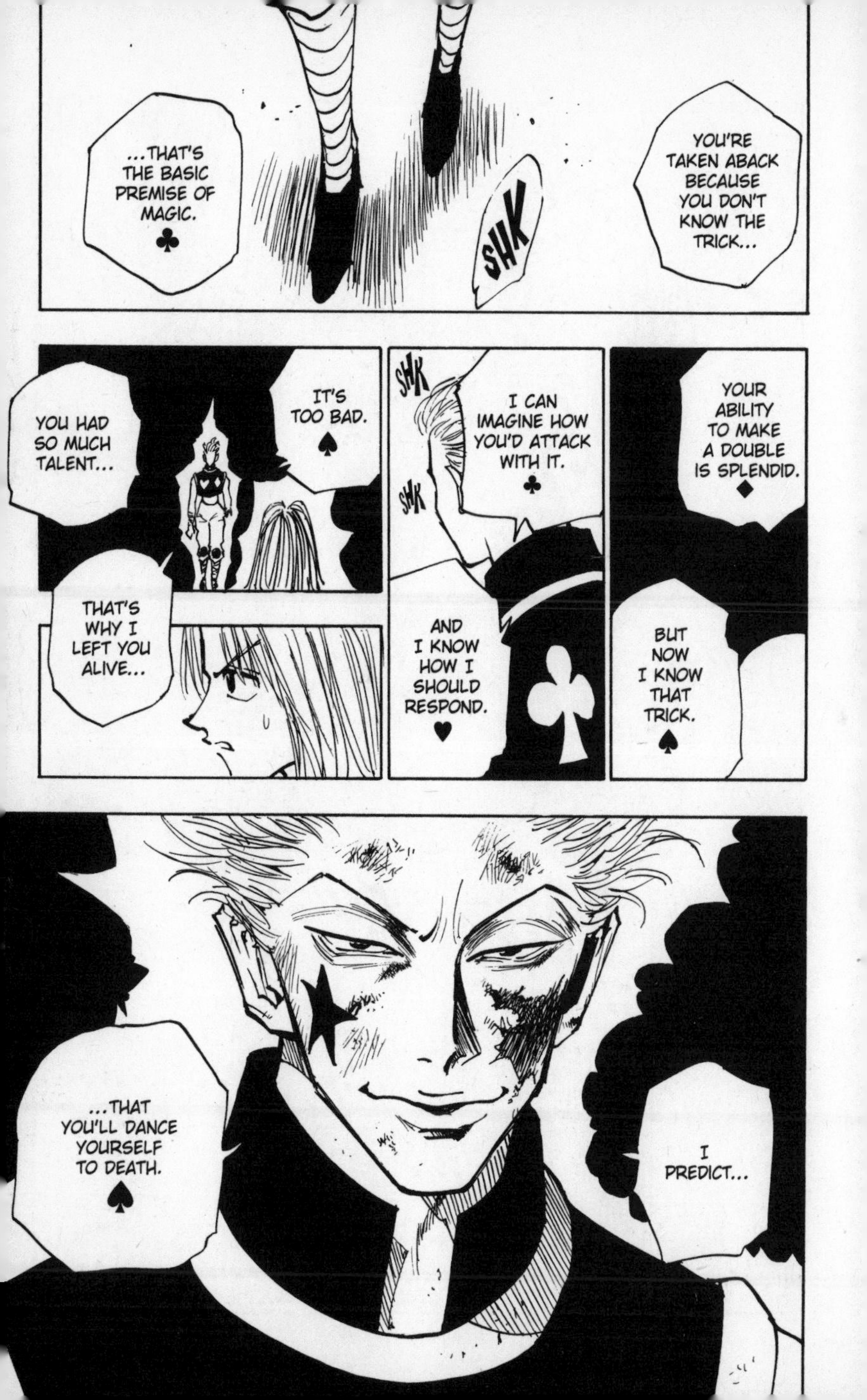
YOU'RE TAKEN ABACK BECAUSE YOU DON'T KNOW THE TRICK...
SHK
...THAT'S THE BASIC PREMISE OF MAGIC. ♣
YOUR ABILITY TO MAKE A DOUBLE IS SPLENDID. ♦
BUT NOW I KNOW THAT TRICK. ♠
SHK
SHK
I CAN IMAGINE HOW YOU'D ATTACK WITH IT. ♣
AND I KNOW HOW I SHOULD RESPOND. ♥
IT'S TOO BAD. ♠
YOU HAD SO MUCH TALENT...
THAT'S WHY I LEFT YOU ALIVE...
I PREDICT...
...THAT YOU'LL DANCE YOURSELF TO DEATH. ♠

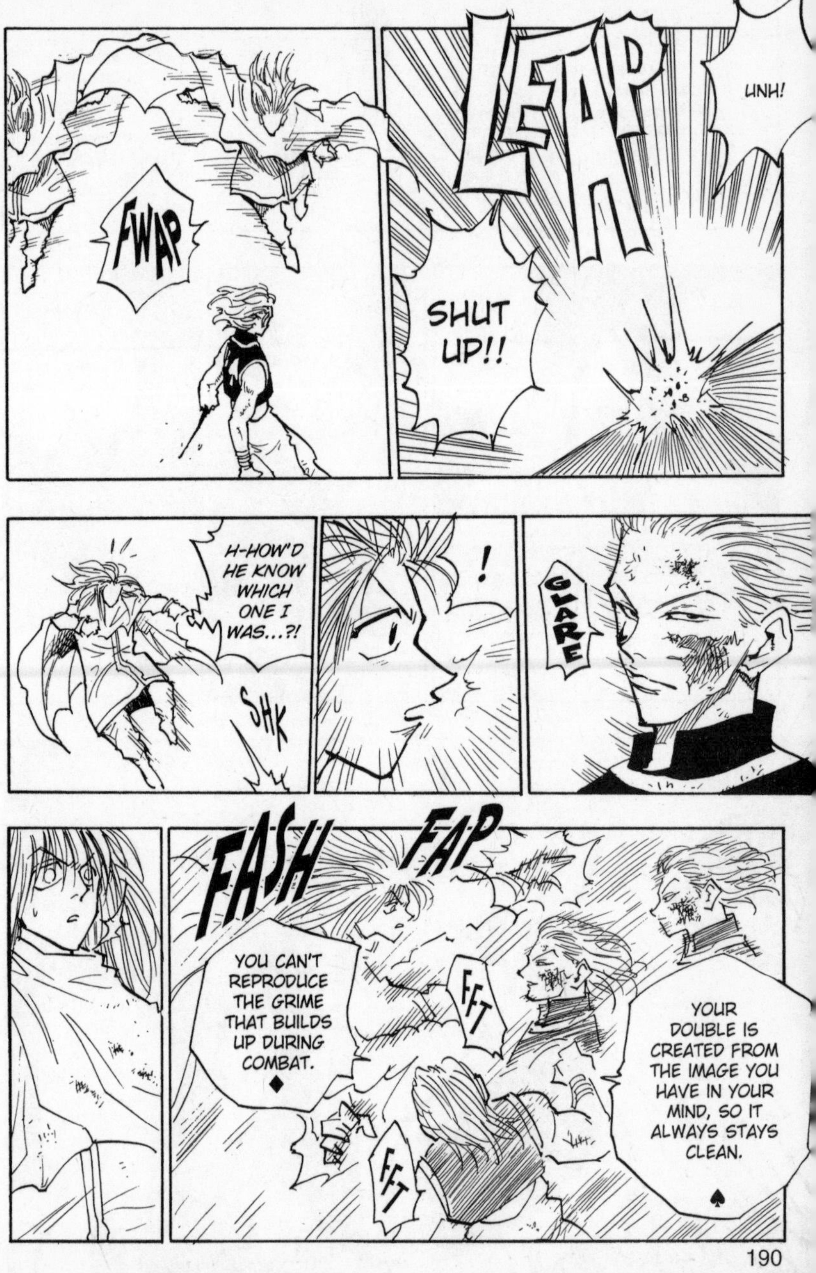
UNH!
LEAP
SHUT UP!!
FWAP
GLARE
!
H-HOW'D HE KNOW WHICH ONE I WAS...?!
SHK
FAP
FASH
YOUR DOUBLE IS CREATED FROM THE IMAGE YOU HAVE IN YOUR MIND, SO IT ALWAYS STAYS CLEAN.
FFT
YOU CAN'T REPRODUCE THE GRIME THAT BUILDS UP DURING COMBAT.
FFT

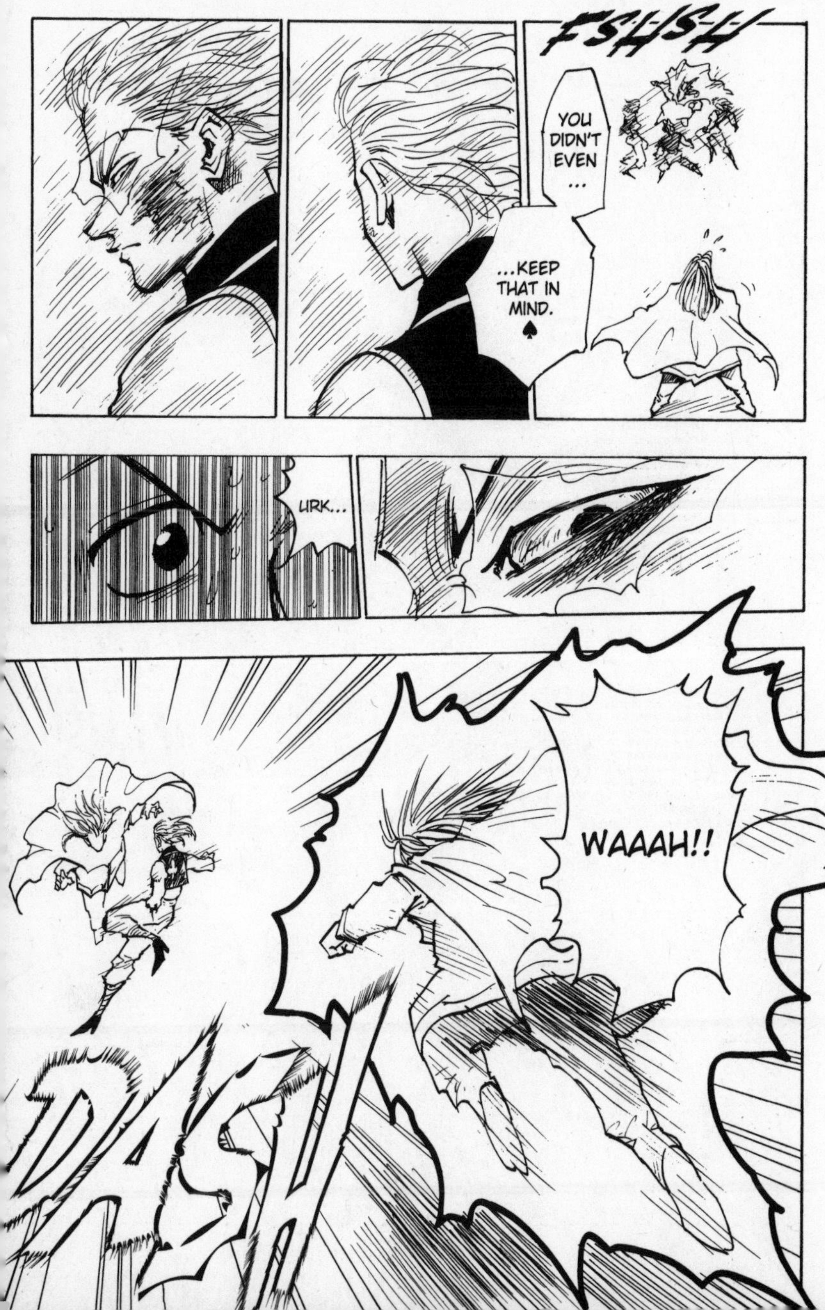
FSHSH
YOU DIDN'T EVEN ...
...KEEP THAT IN MIND. ♠
URK...
WAAAH!!
DASH

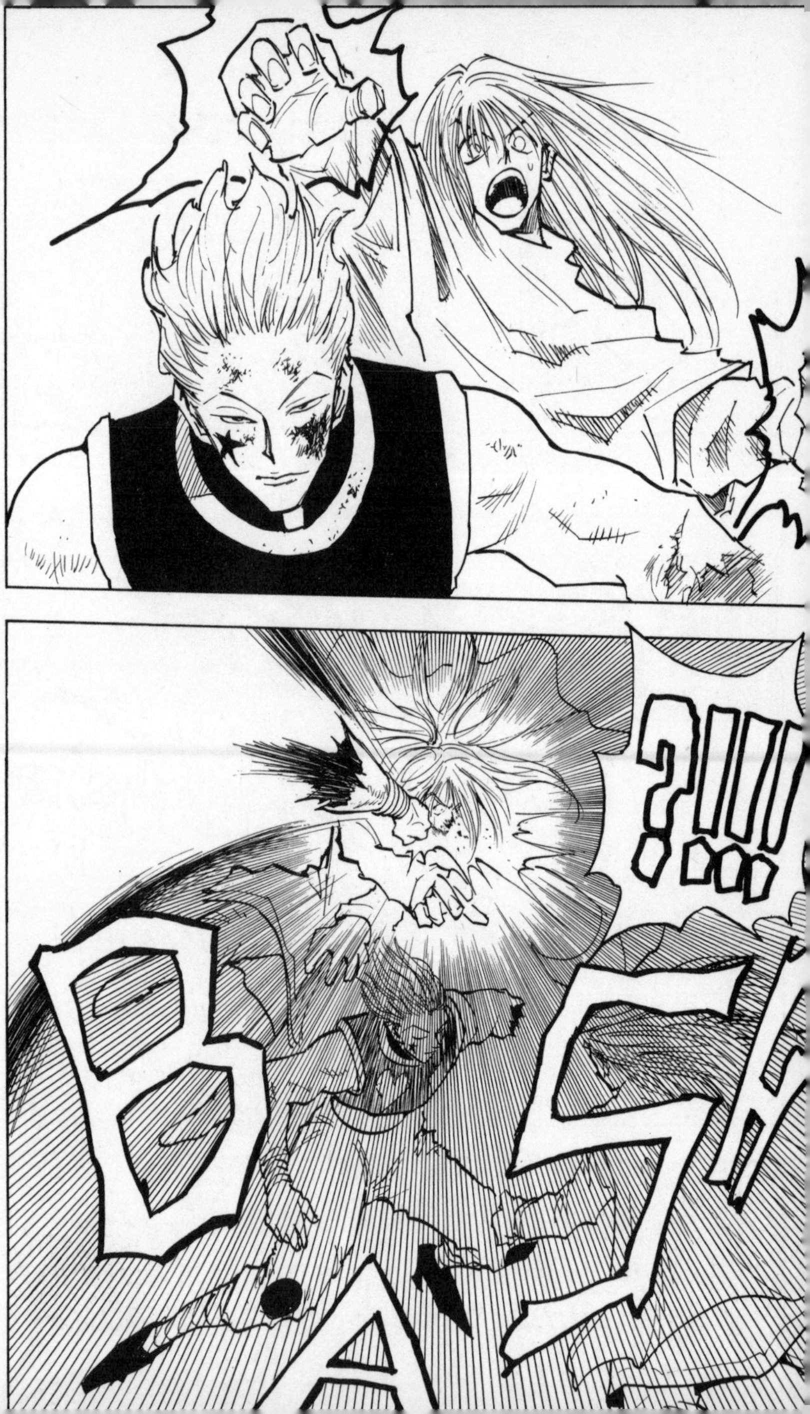
?!!!
BASH

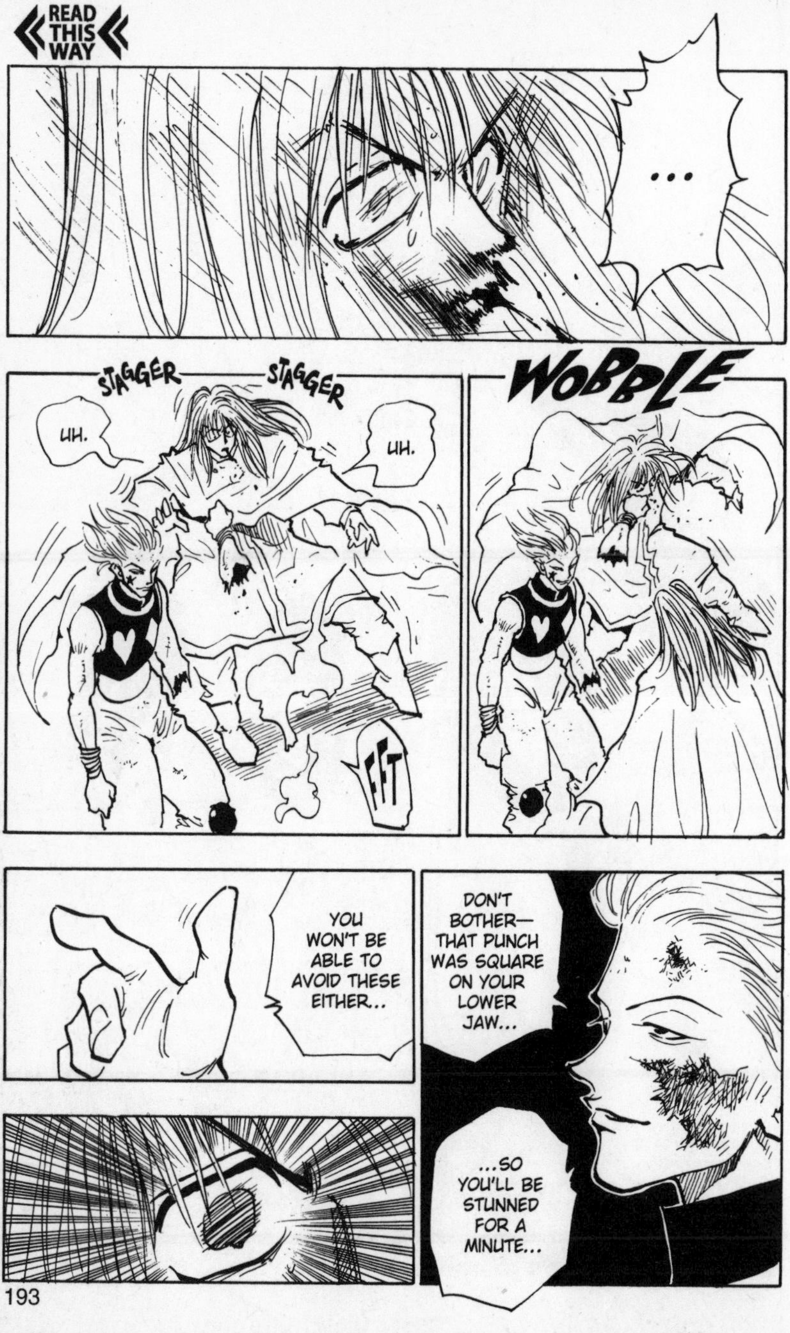
READ THIS WAY
...
WOBBLE
STAGGER
UH.
STAGGER
UH.
FFT
DON'T BOTHER—THAT PUNCH WAS SQUARE ON YOUR LOWER JAW...
...SO YOU'LL BE STUNNED FOR A MINUTE...
YOU WON'T BE ABLE TO AVOID THESE EITHER...

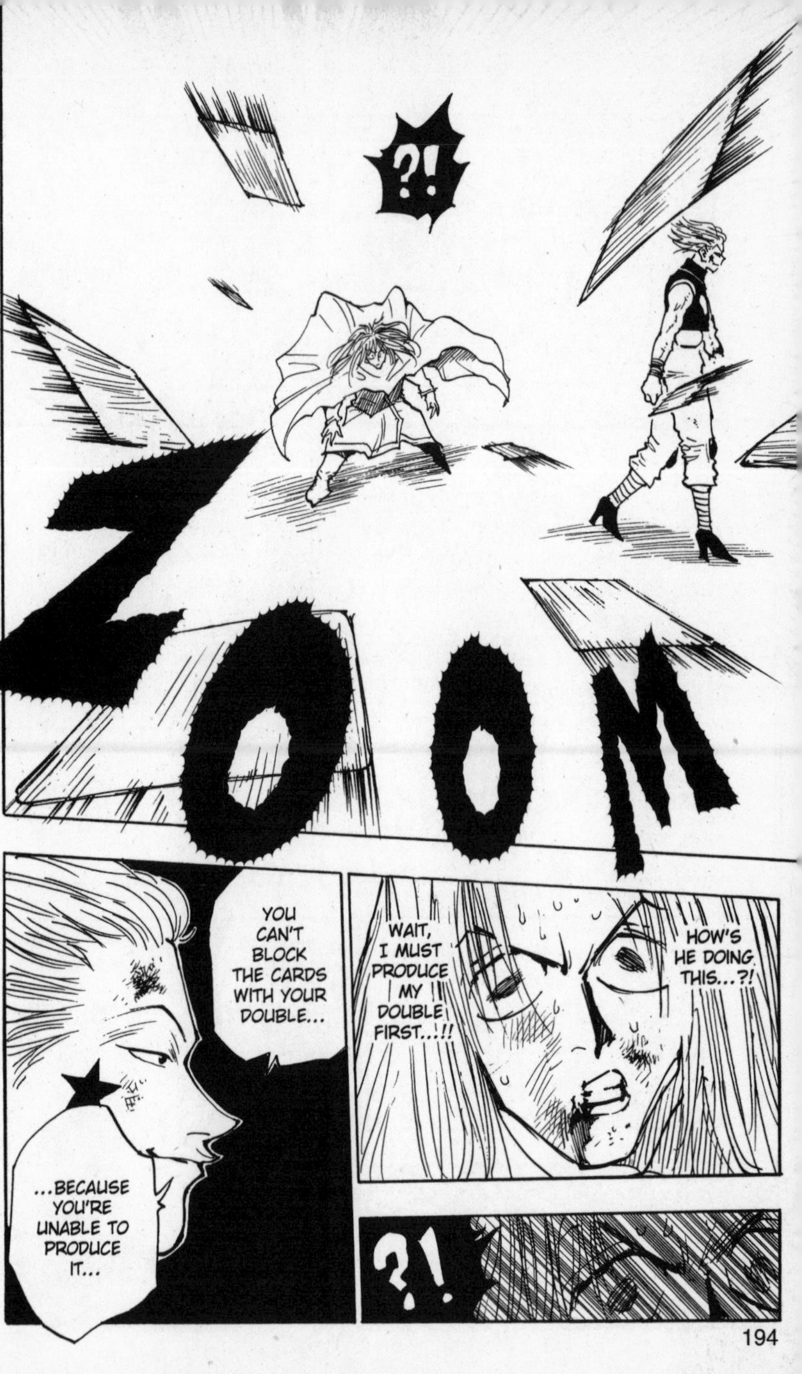
?!
ZOOM
HOW'S HE DOING THIS...?!
WAIT, I MUST PRODUCE MY DOUBLE FIRST...!!!
?!
YOU CAN'T BLOCK THE CARDS WITH YOUR DOUBLE...
...BECAUSE YOU'RE UNABLE TO PRODUCE IT...

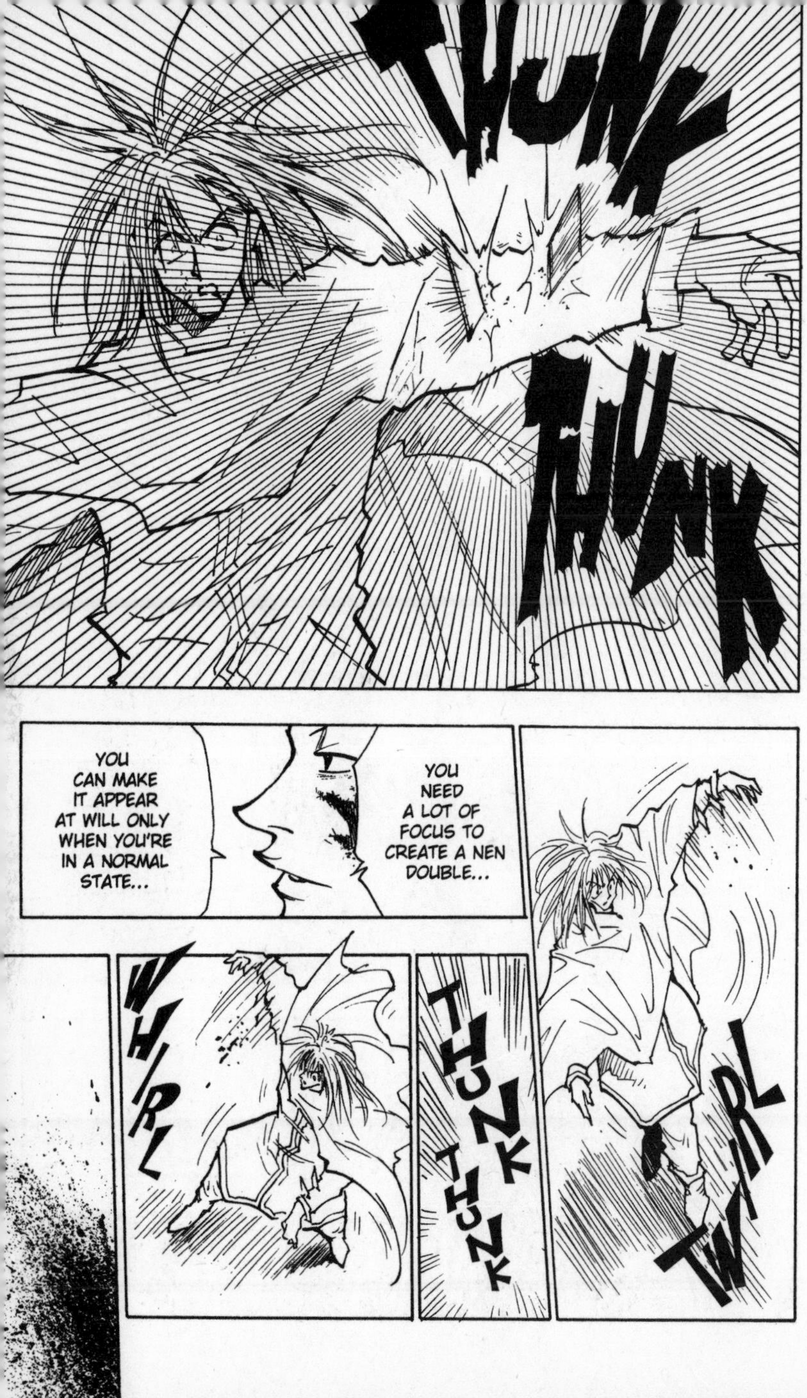
THUNK
THUNK
TWIRL
YOU NEED A LOT OF FOCUS TO CREATE A NEN DOUBLE...
YOU CAN MAKE IT APPEAR AT WILL ONLY WHEN YOU'RE IN A NORMAL STATE...
THUNK
THUNK
WHIRL

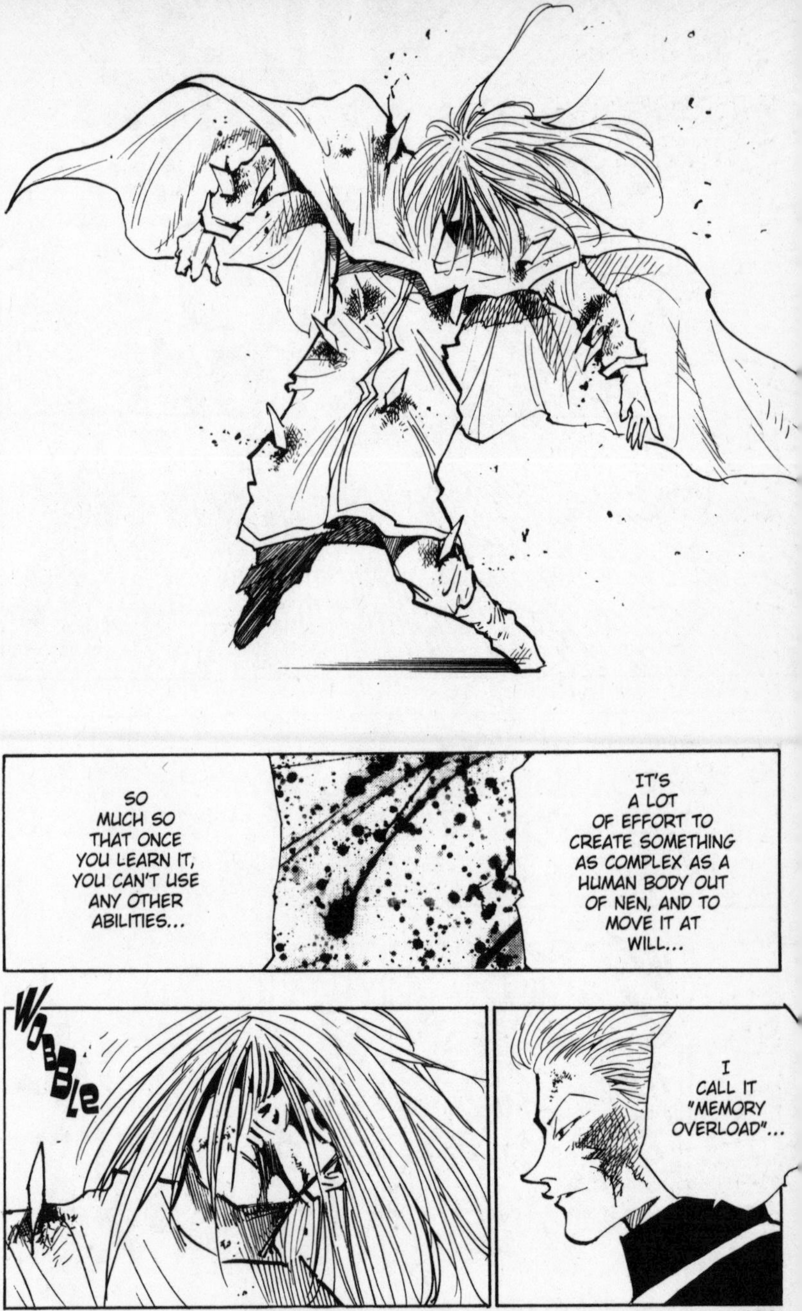
IT'S A LOT OF EFFORT TO CREATE SOMETHING AS COMPLEX AS A HUMAN BODY OUT OF NEN, AND TO MOVE IT AT WILL...
SO MUCH SO THAT ONCE YOU LEARN IT, YOU CAN'T USE ANY OTHER ABILITIES...
I CALL IT "MEMORY OVERLOAD"...
WOBBLE

READ THIS WAY

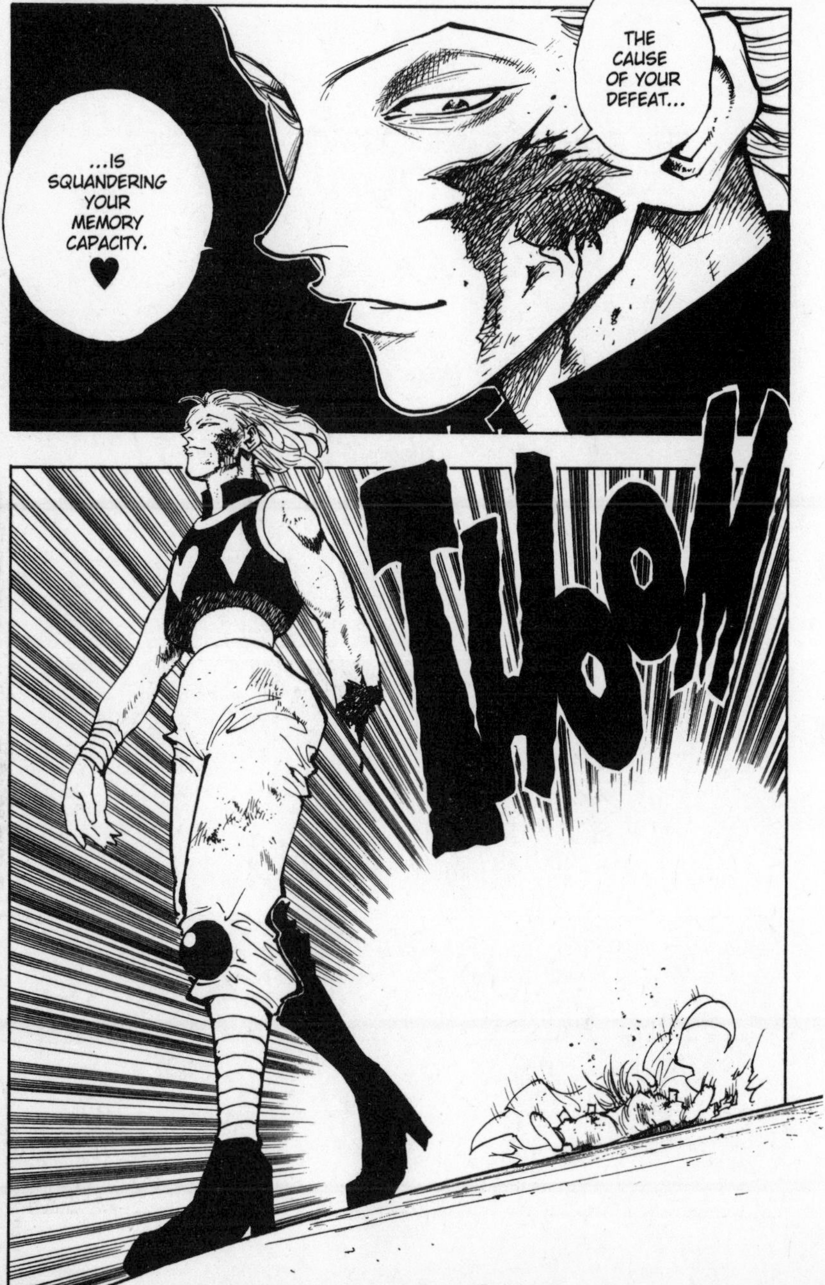
THE CAUSE OF YOUR DEFEAT...
...IS SQUANDERING YOUR MEMORY CAPACITY. ♥
THOOM

THE PICTURE I COULDN'T FIT ONTO THE COVER BECAUSE IT WAS TOO BIG.

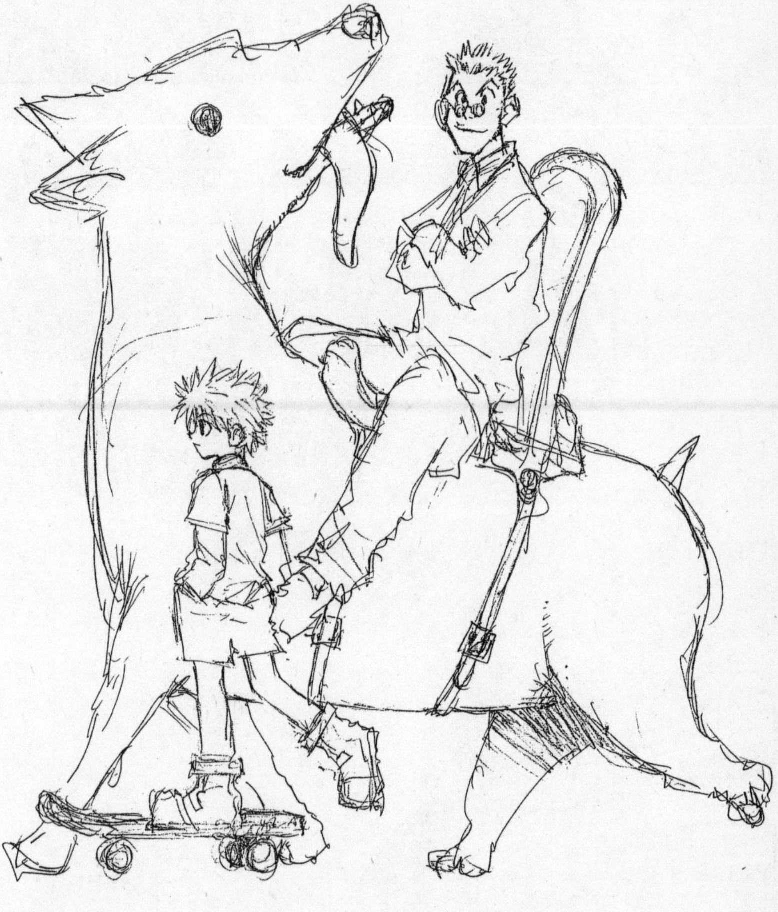

*THIS PAGE RAN IN JAPANESE SHONEN JUMP ISSUE 25, 1999 TO CELEBRATE THE 50TH EPISODE. (SOME DIALOGUE HAS BEEN ALTERED.)

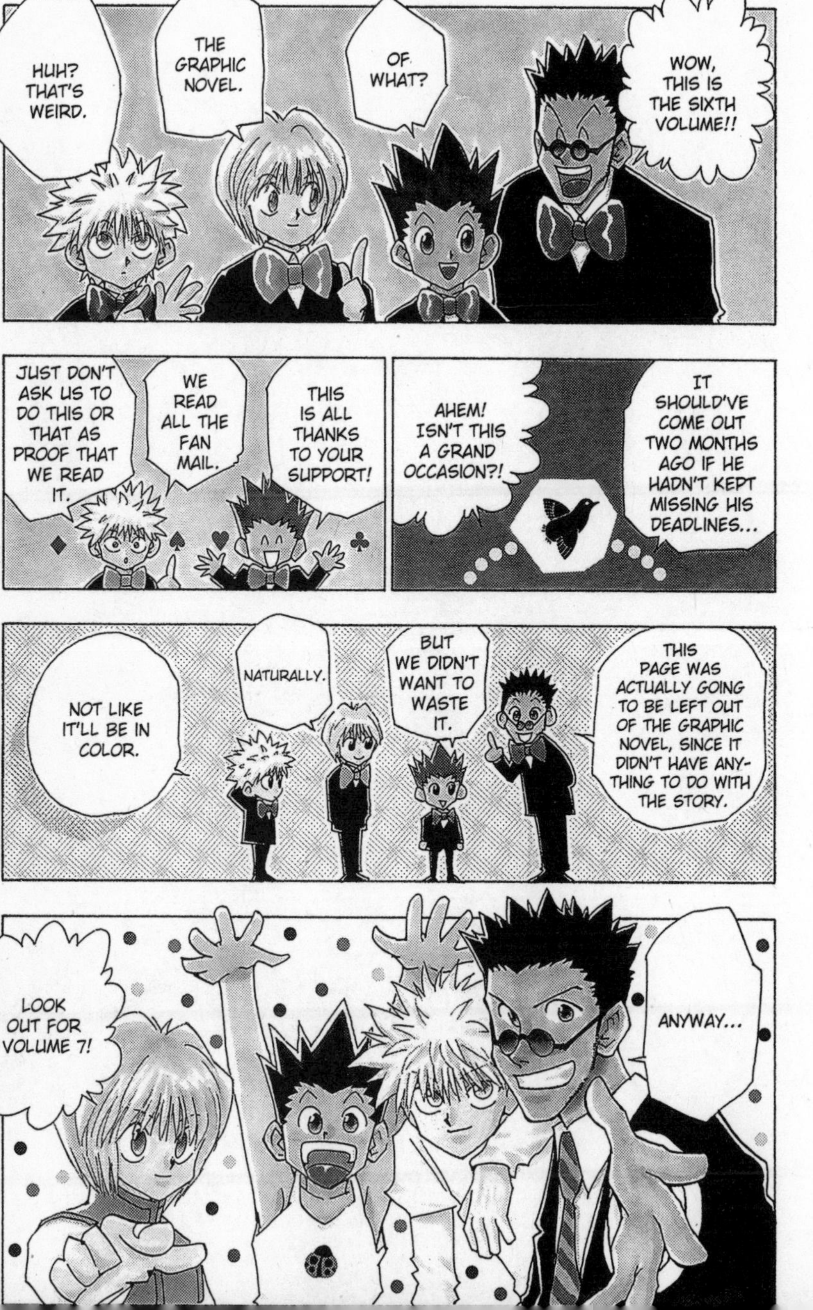
WOW, THIS IS THE SIXTH VOLUME!!
OF WHAT?
THE GRAPHIC NOVEL.
HUH? THAT'S WEIRD.
IT SHOULD'VE COME OUT TWO MONTHS AGO IF HE HADN'T KEPT MISSING HIS DEADLINES...
AHEM! ISN'T THIS A GRAND OCCASION?!
THIS IS ALL THANKS TO YOUR SUPPORT!
WE READ ALL THE FAN MAIL.
JUST DON'T ASK US TO DO THIS OR THAT AS PROOF THAT WE READ IT.
THIS PAGE WAS ACTUALLY GOING TO BE LEFT OUT OF THE GRAPHIC NOVEL, SINCE IT DIDN'T HAVE ANY-THING TO DO WITH THE STORY.
BUT WE DIDN'T WANT TO WASTE IT.
NATURALLY.
NOT LIKE IT'LL BE IN COLOR.
ANYWAY...
LOOK OUT FOR VOLUME 7!

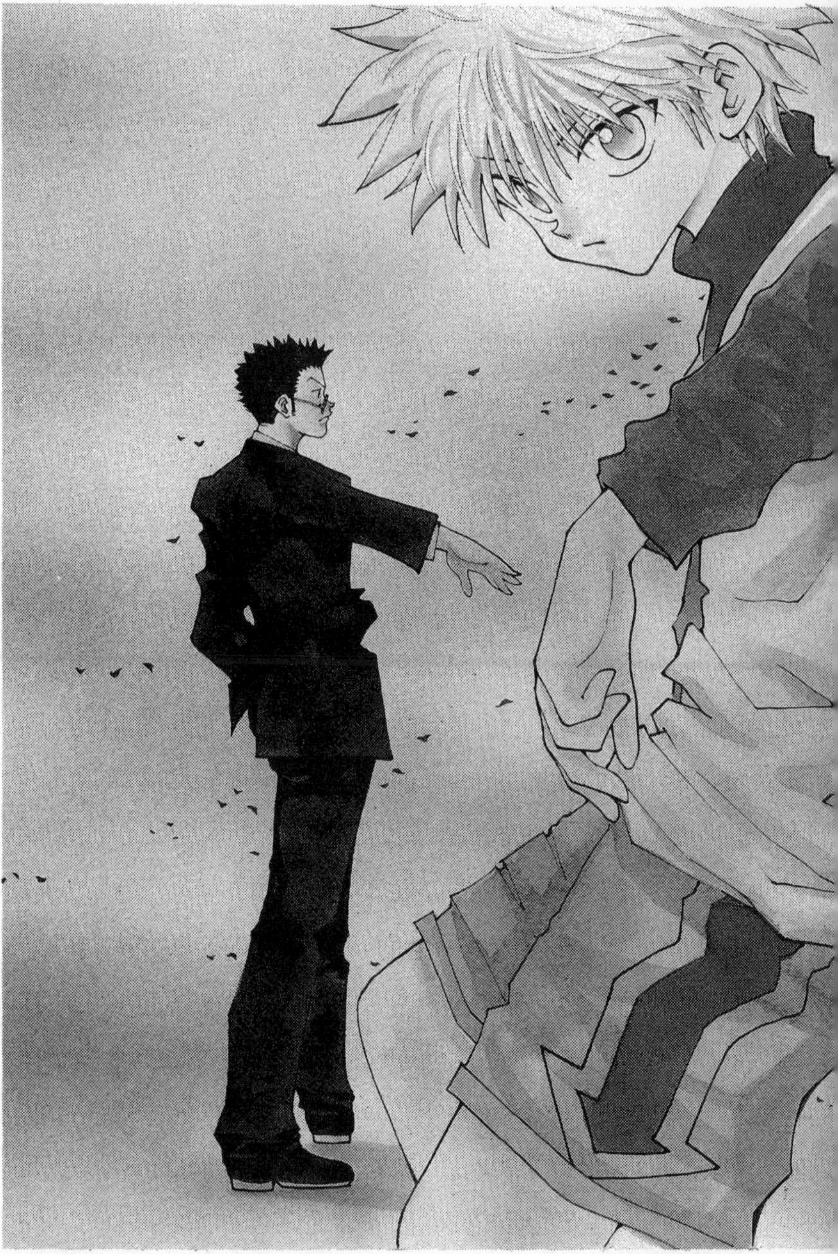

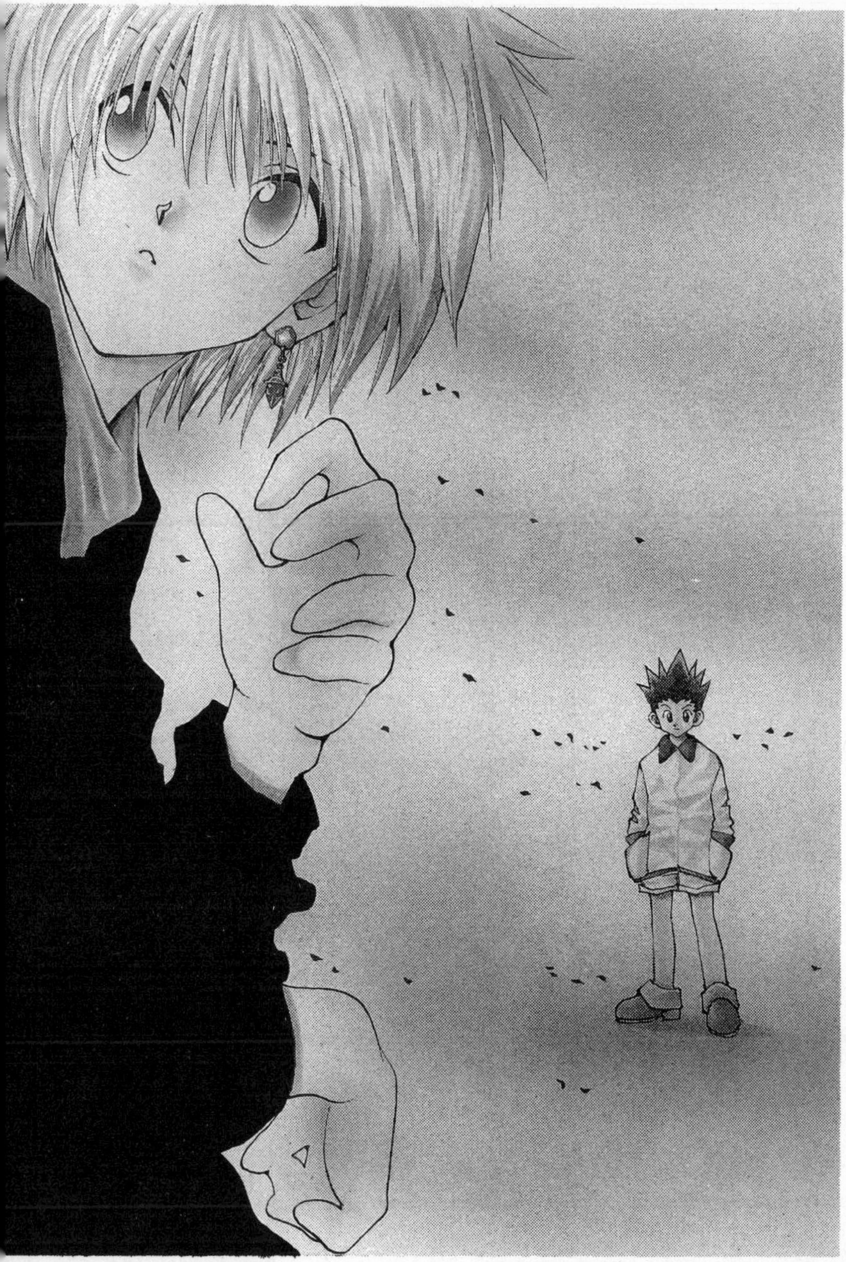

Coming Next Volume...

Gon and Killua continue their studies at the Heavens Arena, gaining skills in the hidden art of Nen—and passing the final secret test of the Hunter Exam. Now that he's a full-fledged Hunter, Gon feels ready to face Hisoka and pay him back for the favor on Zevil Island. But can he withstand the brunt of the mad magician's full attention?

Available Now!

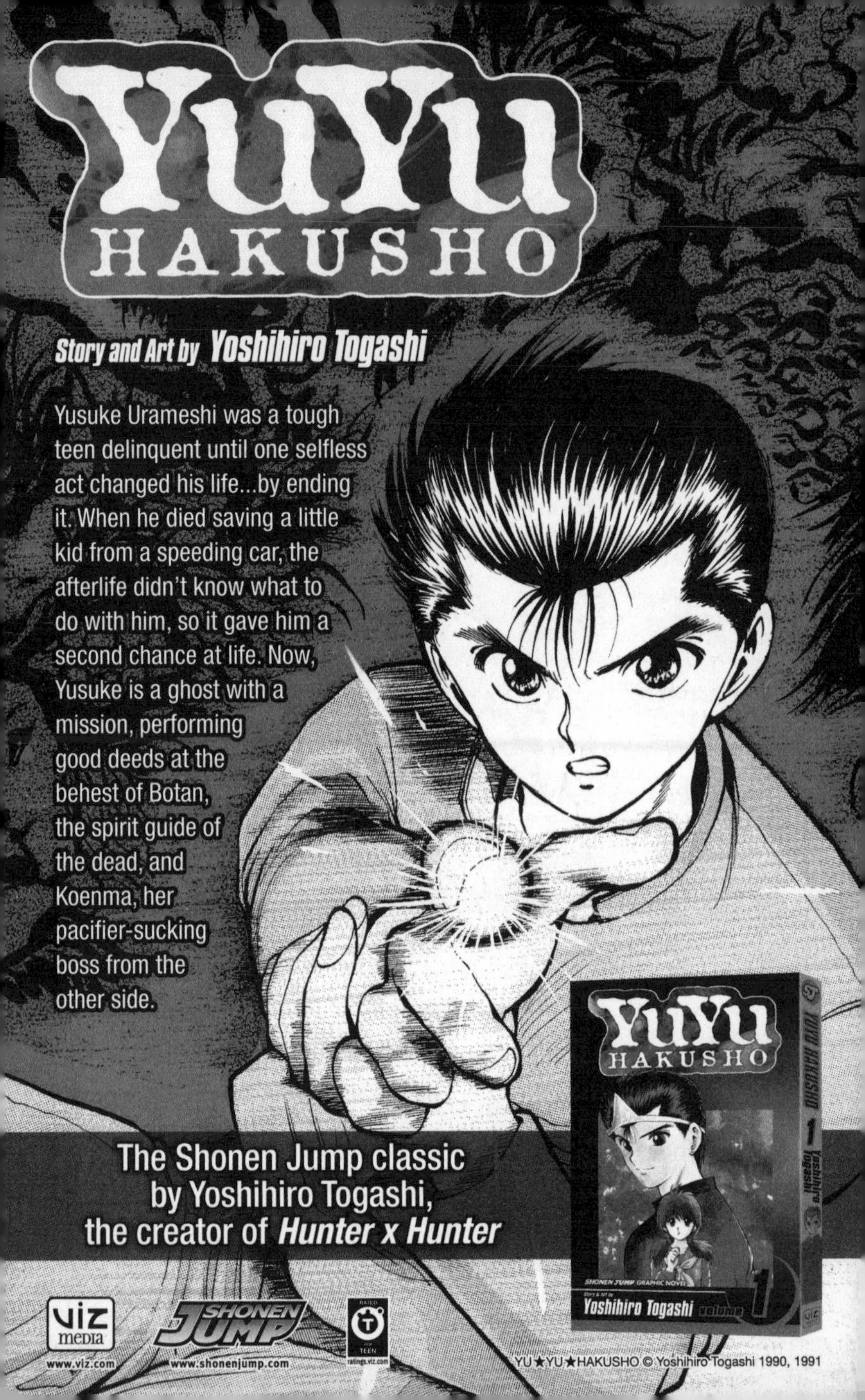
YuYu
HAKUSHO
Story and Art by Yoshihiro Togashi
Yusuke Urameshi was a tough teen delinquent until one selfless act changed his life...by ending it. When he died saving a little kid from a speeding car, the afterlife didn't know what to do with him, so it gave him a second chance at life. Now, Yusuke is a ghost with a mission, performing good deeds at the behest of Botan, the spirit guide of the dead, and Koenma, her pacifier-sucking boss from the other side.
YuYu
HAKUSHO
SHONEN JUMP GRAPHIC NOVEL
Yoshihiro Togashi
volume 1
The Shonen Jump classic by Yoshihiro Togashi, the creator of *Hunter x Hunter*
viz media
www.viz.com
SHONEN JUMP
www.shonenjump.com
RATED T TEEN
ratings.viz.com
YU★YU★HAKUSHO © Yoshihiro Togashi 1990, 1991

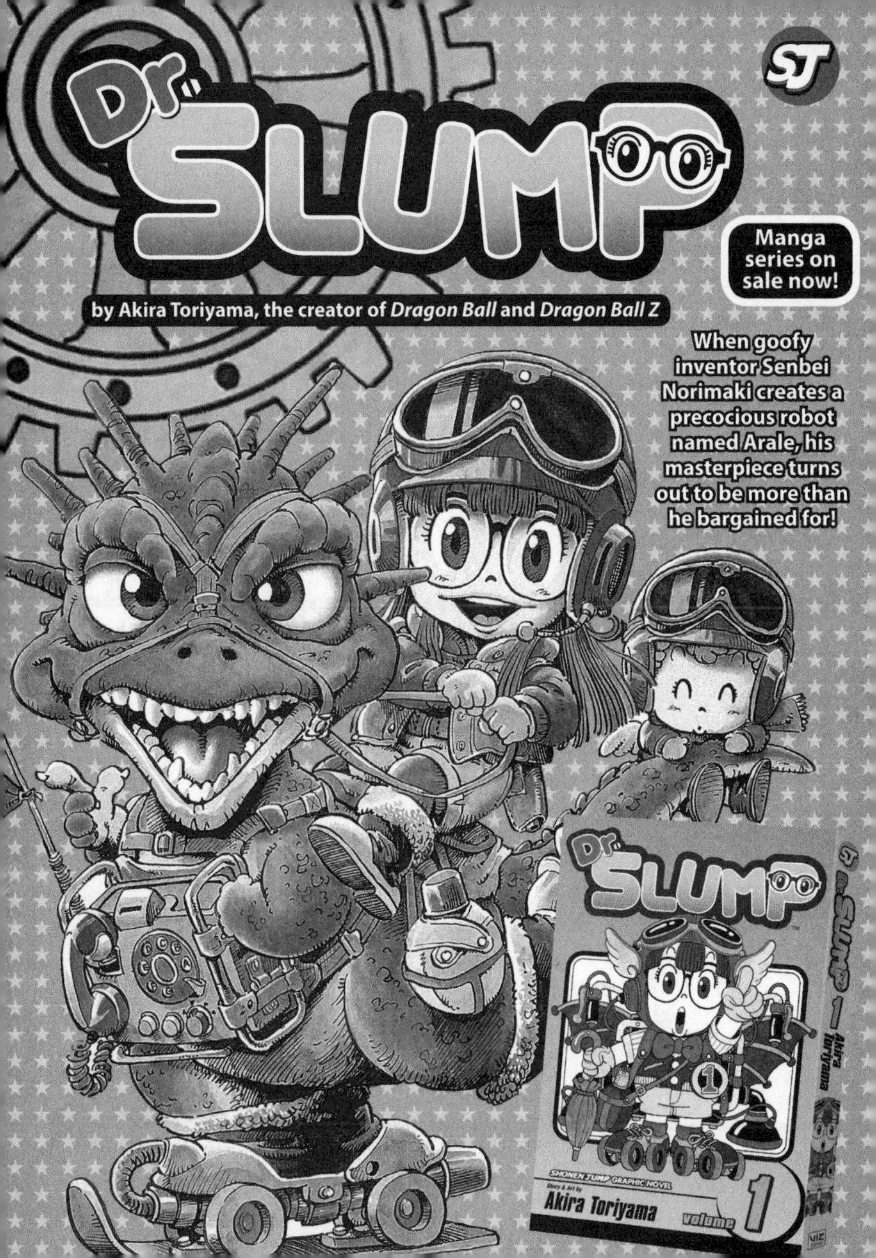
SJ
Dr. SLUMP
Manga series on sale now!
by Akira Toriyama, the creator of Dragon Ball and Dragon Ball Z
When goofy inventor Senbei Norimaki creates a precocious robot named Arale, his masterpiece turns out to be more than he bargained for!
Dr. SLUMP
SHONEN JUMP GRAPHIC NOVEL
Story & Art by
Akira Toriyama
volume 1

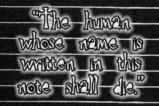

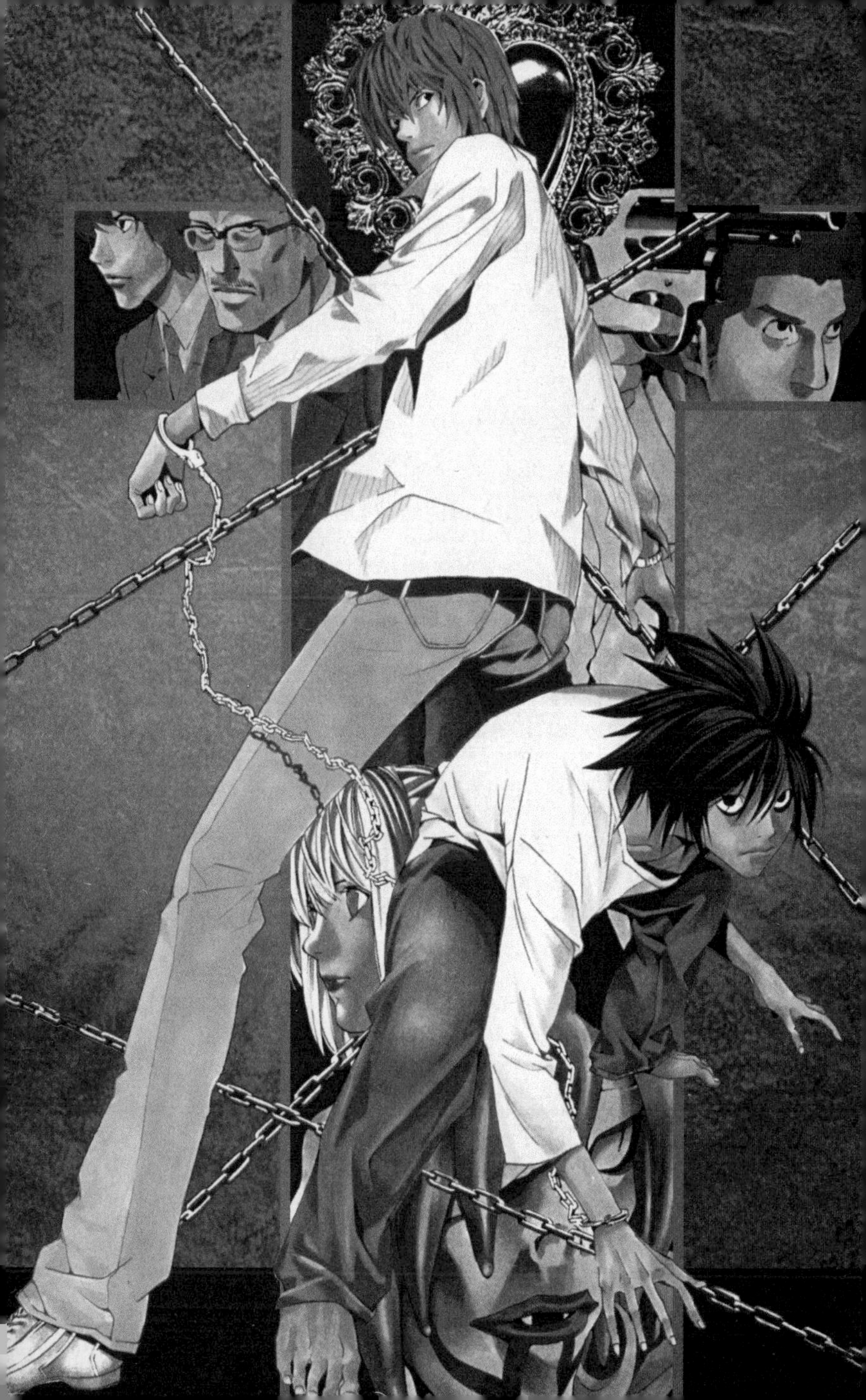

You're Reading in the Wrong Direction!!

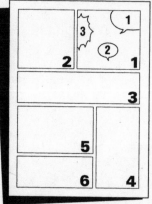

Whoops! Guess what? You're starting at the wrong end of the comic!

…It's true! In keeping with the original Japanese format, **Hunter x Hunter** is meant to be read from right to left, starting in the upper-right corner.

Unlike English, which is read from left to right, Japanese is read from right to left, meaning that action, sound effects and word-balloon order are completely reversed… something which can make readers unfamiliar with Japanese feel pretty backwards themselves. For this reason, manga or Japanese comics published in the U.S. in English have sometimes been published "flopped"—that is, printed in exact reverse order, as though seen from the other side of a mirror.

By flopping pages, U.S. publishers can avoid confusing readers, but the compromise is not without its downside. For one thing, a character in a flopped manga series who once wore in the original Japanese version a T-shirt emblazoned with "M A Y" (as in "the merry month of") now wears one which reads "Y A M"! Additionally, many manga creators in Japan are themselves unhappy with the process, as some feel the mirror-imaging of their art skews their original intentions.

We are proud to bring you Yoshihiro Togashi's **Hunter x Hunter** in the original unflopped format. For now, though, turn to the other side of the book and let the adventure begin…!

—Editor